Liberation for the Oppressed

Community *Healing* through *Activist* Transformation

A Call to *"CHAT"*

Gary L. Lemons, Ph.D., Editor

Paperback ISBN: 978-1-64719-994-4
Hardcover ISBN: 978-1-64719-995-1
Ebook ISBN: 978-1-64719-996-8

Published by BookLocker.com, Inc., Trenton, Georgia, U.S.A.

Printed on acid-free paper.

Library of Congress Cataloging in Publication Data
Lemons, Ph.D., Gary L.
Liberation for the Oppressed: Community Healing through Activist Transformation - A Call to "CHAT" / Gary L. Lemons, Ph.D., Editor
Library of Congress Control Number: 2021925303

BookLocker.com, Inc.
2022

Table of Contents

Dedication

bell hooks (1952-December 15, 2021)

I dedicate "CHAT" in *Liberation for the Oppressed* to bell. Her soulful, Black feminist vision of love for the oppressed embodies the legacy of Dr. Martin Luther King, Jr.'s enduring concept of a "beloved community." bell's commitment to it manifests itself throughout this book. It speaks to her activist legacy of Black survival and self-determination to end racism—as well as all forms of systemic and institutionalized oppression. In *Writing Beyond Race: Living Theory and Practice*, bell says, "To engage the practice of love is to oppose domination in all its forms." Her words live on.... In love with "education as the practice of freedom," she will always be my teacher.

Acknowledgments

First and foremost, I acknowledge that the University of South Florida Research Task Force Grant I received in 2020 for "Understanding and Addressing Blackness and Anti-Black Racism in our Local, National, and International Communities" enabled me to materialize my vision for *Community Healing through Activist Transformation, a Call to "CHAT" in Liberation for the Oppressed.* With the USF Grant my Co-Investigator, Black clinical therapist Risasi Milima and I conceptualized the "Emotional Freedom Train(ing) CHAT"—a community-based project for Black male survival and wellbeing. I remain beholden to him and those Black men who joined us on this journey, along with the professional African American activists (in and outside academia) with whom we collaborated. "Addressing Blackness and Anti-Black Racism," aligned with the scope and depth of the EFT-CHAT project, I invited USF students to come aboard the "Train". I especially thank the students who gave me permission to publish their writings based on bell hooks' groundbreaking book *Killing Rage: Ending Racism.* These students studied with me in the online version of the African American literature courses I taught in spring 2021. During the upsurge of the COVID-19 pandemic and the ongoing traumatic, life-threatening effects of racism in Black Indigenous People of Color (BIPOC) communities—these students deeply contemplated hooks' Black feminist anti-racist standpoint. Their writings in *Liberation for the Oppressed* represent the power of her intersectional approach to achieving critical consciousness toward "ending racism." Moreover, thanks to Lisa Melonçon, Interim Chair of the USF Department of English for her unwavering administrative support for my research agenda, which significantly underscored my aim to unite the EFT-CHAT program with my pedagogical vision of student anti-racist activism. Also, with much gratitude, I thank Debra Garcia (the English department's Academic Services Administrator) for her excellence in facilitating my grant-funding process.

Preface

Soul Work: My Calling for Community Healing through Activist Transformation
Gary L. Lemons

Hear my soul from the inside out
I have become a *Black* man with revolutionary thoughts for self-liberation it's true
How you see me on the outside shouldn't rely on a Eurocentric
racialized "other" view
My African ancestors were not born in just one color or hue
Their tribal interactions are yet another linguistic vocal counter-clue
Hear my soul from the inside out
When I look at myself
I see many creative Africentric images of liberation in my ONE whole-self
My Mind Body and Soul are composed of differences in what you may not see
But don't close your eyes—see all the Blackness in me that will always be
Hear soul from the inside out
Being Black for 500 years on this constitutionalized enslavement ground
has stood the test of time
Is white supremacy still an issue in this day and is it a crime?
What do you think? Through spoken words I play on my life-calling to give
The more I express myself the longer I live
Hear my soul from the inside out
For me spoken-word for freedom is a life-saving power
I have discovered it as my creative source for self-recovery hour after hour
Will I stop speaking out for liberation of the oppressed? My
answer will always be "No!"
Activism against racism performs as *soul work,* a live-stream
Black freedom talk show
Here my soul from the inside out
Let's begin to "chat" for Community Healing through Activist Transformation

In the *Oxford Languages Dictionary*, the word "chat" is defined in two grammatical forms through cyber-technology. As a verb it represents an "exchange [of] messages online in real time with one or more simultaneous users of a computer network," as in "I keep getting messages popping up on my screen from people wanting to chat." As a noun "chat" signifies "the online exchange of messages in real time with one or more simultaneous users of a computer network," as in "join Me for a live online chat Wednesday …" According to Merriam-webster.com, two definitions of "chat" are (a.) "to talk in an informal or familiar manner" and (b.) "to take part in an online discussion in a chat room." Long before "chat" became an integral, common word-choice/tech-tool for naming computerized everyday communication among folk, I thought of it as a strategic means to build community dialogue for activist engagement in support service for anyone in need of healing—in mind, body, and soul. For me, "chat" would become my *soul work* for enacting "community healing through activist transformation"—in and beyond academia.

"Hear My Soul from the Inside Out"

I open this "Preface" with my spoken-word poem "Here My Soul from the Inside Out." I not only employ it to introduce myself, but also to foreground my concept of *soul work* in struggle against anti-Black racism. Moreover, as a Black man contemplating his life-calling in "higher" education to liberate the oppressed, I call the writers in *Liberation for the Oppressed* to respond to it. I must admit that embracing my cultural identification with Blackness in an Africentric context has been a life-long personal struggle. Facing anti-Black racism in the U.S. from childhood to adulthood, I spent most of my life denying being Black—internalizing "whiteness" as the ideological foundation of the "American Dream". My dreaming to realize it meant that I had to be willing to erase my Blackness—to become invisible, ideologically assimilating into the benefits of being white.

Fully embracing my Blackness has been a long time coming. The price I paid for assimilating into whiteness left me emotionally broke from the inside out. However, I have come to a revolutionary homeplace of inner sanctity for Black love. This sacred residence for activist solidarity and alliance against anti-Black racism allows me openly and lovingly to embrace myself through the creative power of spoken-word. Through it, I possess an artistic tool for maintaining my soulful expression as a Black man of African descent in the U.S. Truthfully, as a symbolic and realized acronym,

"CHAT" represents my transgressive word-play demonstrating the critical need for activist dialogue in resistance to anti-Black racism.

In *Liberation for the Oppressed*, "CHAT" acts to break new ground for planting the seed of liberating hope—personified in the vision of a "beloved community," as imagined by Dr. Martin Luther King, Jr. In this deeply insightful context—considering the violent, deadly, and traumatizing effects of racism experienced by Black Indigenous People of Color (BIPOC) historically and in this contemporary moment in the U.S.—there remains a critical need for demonstrative, dialogical engagements that boldly promote the practice of anti-racism. In her "Prologue" to *Post-Traumatic Slave Syndrome: America's Legacy of Enduring Injury and Healing* (2005, 2017), Dr. Joy DeGruy speaks about the global history of the traumatizing effects of systemic oppression, specifically revealed in institutionalized human enslavement. She states:

> Throughout recorded history people have subjugated, enslaved, and at times even exterminated one another…. Furthermore, these crimes are perpetuated in a seemingly never-ending cycle…. Breaking this cycle and claiming our humanity will require much work from all of us. Those who have been the victims of years, decades, and centuries of oppression first must heal from injuries received first-hand, as well as those passed down through the ages. (iv)

In solidarity for social justice, people openly committed to calling out and acting in unity to end systemic and institutionalized racism perform the essential labor of love to realize freedom for the oppressed. First and foremost, as Dr. DeGruy professes throughout her book and commitment to anti-oppressive activism, anti-racist allies must expose the emotional effects of "Post Traumatic Slave Syndrome" (PTSS). Throughout my writings in *Liberation for the Oppressed*, addressing the emotional dehumanization of anti-Black racism, I employ the term "trauma" as a key signifier of its inner *and* outer life-threatening effects.

Not only are my spoken-words in "Here My Soul from the Inside Out" personal and political, they also embody my inspirited love for anti-racist dialogical activism. Moreover, I seek to link its conception integrally to the writers' works in *Liberation for the Oppressed* as well as my pedagogical practice of and for *soul work*. In the evolution of my scholarship devoted to teaching Black feminist-womanist theory and criticism—at the intersection of race, gender, class, sexuality, culture, and ability—I have continually contemplated and written about the self-liberating power students' voices can embody when unified in the ongoing struggle against the perpetuation of racism. I teach critical consciousness for ways to heal from PTSS. In my courses, I act to utilize "chat" as a crucial template for community building for well-being and self-recovery.

In 2020, the USF Research Task Force Grant "Understanding and Addressing Blackness and Anti-Black Racism in our Local, National, and International Communities" I received infused the realization of my vision for "CHAT". Promoting the practice anti-racist alliance-building in partnership with Black Clinical Therapist Risasi Milima (as my Co-Investigator), he and I created a research project we called "Black Men for CHAT and the Emotional Freedom Train(ing): Get on Board!" We conceptualized it as a 12-track online program for Black male well-being and self-recovery. Together, we conducted the program from October 2020-March 2021. However, at the time of its conception, I had no idea that Emotional Freedom Train(ing)—grounded in the seven principles of Kwanzaa (as conceived in the language of Swahili by Maulana Karenga, professor of African American studies in 1966[1])—would have such a profound impact on my vision of teaching in resistance to the trauma of anti-Black racism. As Karenga taught, the seven principles of Kwanzaa include: 1. Umoja (Unity), 2. Kujichagulia (Self-Determination), 3. Ujima (Collective Work and Responsibility), 4. Ujamaa (Cooperative economics), 5. Nia (Purpose), 6. Kuumba (Creativity), 7. Imani (Faith).

Strategically connecting these principles with my pedagogical approach to African American literature, I contemplated their inspirational agency through the lens of Black feminist-womanist thought. In each of the courses I taught during spring semester 2021 (one for undergrads, the other for graduate students), the Kwanzaa principles sustained and reinforced my dedication to teaching for Black liberation. Because of the COVID-19 pandemic USF mandated that all course be taught online. In line with it, the Emotional Freedom Train(ing)-CHAT project was also conducted in a virtual context.

Yet in this cyber-format, "chat" functioned as a critical source of inspiration in the USF grant project and my courses as well. The activist-centered dialogues I experienced with Milima and the Black male participants during the 12-track EFT program would act as a catalyst for me to compel my students to engage in online soulful "chat(s)" in resistance to anti-Black racism. During that spring 2021 literally life-challenging semester, in both my African American literature courses, students and I confronted the life-threatening pandemic of racism. Together my students and I crossed the social programmatical "tracks" of race, gender, class, sexuality, and ability to confront the ill-induced trauma of systemic and institutionalized anti-Black racism. Once again, according to Dr. DeGruy:

> Since the time the first enslaved Africans arrived in the Americas, in the early 1500s, to the present day, Europeans and their descendants have gone to great lengths to justify the 500 hundred years of trauma and dehumanization they and their institutions produced. The effects of this trauma and dehumanization are observable today, and can be explained by the theory of Post Traumatic Slave Syndrome. (52)

In line with the theory of Post Traumatic Slave Syndrome and its dehumanizing implications over the course of 500 years, in *The Mark of Slavery: Disability, Race, and Gender in Antebellum America* (2021), Jennifer L. Barclay researches the history of anti-Black racism and its connection to disability. Considering this, Barclay pointedly notes that until this contemporary moment scholarship focused on the subject of slavery rarely engaged its intersectional relation to the physical and emotional trauma of the history of enslaved Africans in the U.S.—

> Parallel to the relative lack of attention that historians of slavery paid to disability until recently, few disability historians explicitly address slavery and the relationship between racism and ableism that was so integral to the institution's material and ideological underpinnings.... This binary approach ignores the deep imprint of chattel slavery on the long sweep of American history.... A disability history of slavery lays a necessary foundation for more thorough, critical examination of how race and disability shaped [B]lack life in the post-emancipation decades. At the same time, it lends a new angle on the intellectual history of race. (4-5)

Very clear in the trailblazing scholarship of DeGruy and Barclay is the fact that anti-Black racism, contextualized in the history of slavery in the U.S., continues to be physically, emotionally, and psychologically dehumanizing. Therefore, its traumatizing effects in the lives of African Americans must be viewed from an intersectional standpoint not only connected to gender, class, and sexuality, but also critically addressed in studies of Black experience(s) of disability. Barclay asserts: "Given the tremendous, far-reaching significance of slavery in the nation's history, it is essential to reckon with how disability—as lived human experience and social and cultural metaphor—intersected with the [U.S. foundational 'Constitution' of the chattel enslavement of Africans]" (4).

A Calling in the Spirit of Love: Confessing the When, Where, and How My Soul Work Began

In the production of my scholarship over the course of time, as a Black male professor supporting Black feminist-womanist theory and criticism, I would comprehend the complexity of African American identity through the lens of "intersectionality" as Kimberlé Crenshaw termed it in *Critical Race Theory: The Key Writings that Formed the Movement* (1995). Thus, being critically conscious of the complexity of systemic and institutionalized oppression, I must continually link my critique of anti-Black racism with its interconnection to issues of patriarchy, sexism, classism, homophobia, *and* ableism.

While I have not formally studied or researched the subject of disability related to the effects of Post Traumatic Slave Syndrome (PTSS), I can attest to the experience of disability imposed upon me as a disheartening form of ableism. Early on in childhood, I faced certain academic challenges related to my intellectual ability. It began when I was

> … a six-year-old child entering first grade at the all [B]lack student Catholic school (in my hometown of Hot Springs, Arkansas) run by a white diocese … I was cast as outside the norm by the white nun who taught my class. I was left-handed. As such, clearly in front of my classmates, I was continually tapped on that hand with a wooden ruler the teacher held to prompt me to write with my right hand. While she persisted in this strategy, it never worked. Eventually, she reported my 'disability' to the head-sister (who was also white) in charge of the school. At the end of the school year, she called my parents to meet with her. Present at the meeting with them, I (as well as they) had no idea what I had done to be the subject of this meeting. I (and they) listened carefully as the sister told them that the school did not have the resources to work with me due to what she characterized as my severe learning deficiency.
>
> In fact, the head-sister told my parents that given the situation, I could no longer attend the school. She recommended that I be placed in a school that offered 'special education.' My parents … listened quietly without contesting what they heard and were told to do. The head-sister's declaration that day marked

the beginning of my identification as a special education student. Both having grown up in Arkansas, nationally known for its segregated schooling through the late 1950s, my parents the next year enrolled me in the all [B]lack elementary school near our home. While I had no idea that I was a slow learner, the [B]lack female teachers I had from second to sixth grade made me feel like I fit in with the regular kids at the school. They did not make special education a designation of marginalization and abnormality. (*Caught Up in the Spirit! Teaching for Womanist Liberation* xv-xvi)

In the process of releasing the internalization of ableism in my educational development, I also remember growing up in a Black church setting that also compelled me to contemplate inner-healing as a ministerial calling for *soul work*.[2] I grew up listening to "grown" Black church folk telling their inspirational stories of survival, especially recounting their struggles against racism. They called them "testimonies." All of them had gripping stories to tell. Sharing them was an integral part of every church service.

However, experiencing racially integrated education in high school, I would unknowingly assimilate into the idealization of "whiteness" as the path to professional success, equated with the aim of desegregated schooling. In deed and action, I had internalized the notion that *higher* education in a PWI truly represented my way up the "ivory" tower to success. Moreover, I was the only Black student in *all* my English courses, as an undergraduate through my graduate school training. Also, in this context, the courses (focused exclusively on white "British and American" literature, written mainly by white male authors) were taught by white professors—most of whom were women.

As I have written in *Black Male Outsider, a Memoir: Teaching as a Pro-Feminist Man* (2008), only in one literature course I took during my graduate studies at New York University as a doctoral student did the white woman professor require students to read a text by Black author. That author was bell hooks: her book *Feminist Theory: From Margin to Center* (1984). Before the end of the semester, the professor (who had been a graduate student of hooks when she was a professor at Yale University) invited hooks to give a talk on campus. I attended the talk. At the end of it, I approached hooks and asked her to sign my copy of her book. She did. In retrospect, as I have written, reading *Feminist Theory: From Margin to Center* changed my life. In the book's closing chapter, "Feminist Revolution: Development Through

Struggle," she says, "Our emphasis must be on cultural transformation: destroying dualism, eradicating systems of domination. Our struggle will be gradual and protracted. Any effort to make feminist revolution here can be aided by the example of liberation struggles led by oppressed peoples globally who resist formidable powers" (163).

In hindsight, in that course on "Contemporary Feminist Literature," I learned exactly what hooks promotes in this passage not only for "feminist revolution," but for how it "can be aided by the example of liberation struggles led by oppressed peoples globally who resist formidable powers." For those of us committed to activist resistance against the perpetuation of racism, we have documented proof—from the Civil Rights movement in the 1950s through the Black Power movement in the 1960s to the Black Lives Matter movement in this day and time—that the struggle must continue. For the *liberation for the oppressed*, we must join together in action to end systemic and institutionalized oppression all over the world.

Through her vision of Black feminist liberation, bell hooks compelled me to move "from the margin to the center" as a Black man who would eventually accept his calling to practice a revolutionary vision of *higher* education. Two years after I received my doctorate in English at New York University in 1992 (while residing in South Orange, New Jersey), I would travel to Hot Springs, Arkansas to be officially ordained as a minister on December 5, 1994.[3] When I began as professor teaching at Eugene Lang College (the undergraduate division of the New School University) in 1994, I also served as a clergy member of a Black church in Newark, New Jersey. During my time there, I collaborated with JoAnn Oliver, a "sista" in the church who had founded a ministry aimed to help anyone in need of self-recovery (whether related to drug addiction, sexual and/or domestic abuse, low self-esteem, ableism, poverty, among other forms of self-deprecation). To complement this community-based project, I planned to establish a "Center for Healing And Transformation." Yet, for many complicated reasons, this "CHAT" never materialized. However, in 2007 having accepted a professorship in the English department at the University of South Florida, I remained focused on teaching African American literature at the intersection of Black feminist and womanist studies.

Reclaiming the Power of Revolutionary Black Theology

In reality, I put my commitment to Black theological activism on hold. It would not be until 2014, when the Chair of the English Department asked me to teach a literary studies course titled "The Bible as Literature." Teaching it prompted me to reconnect my ministerial activism to Black liberation struggles—not only confronting issues of racism, but also those interrelated to sexism, classism, homophobia, and ableism. Having come to critical consciousness about the intersectional relationship between racist injustice and other forms of systemic oppression, at the same time, I would also comprehend the complexity of biblical literary studies through Black liberation theology. The activist-oriented writings of Dr. Martin Luther King, Jr, and the radical works of James H. Cone would significantly impact my pedagogical practice.[4] In particular, as a revolutionary professor of liberatory theology, Cone taught and wrote about having to "reconcile" King's non-violent approach to racism with Malcolm X's "by any means necessary" standpoint. He addresses this conflict in the 1989 "Preface" of the reissued edition of *Black Theology and Black Power* stating:

> Since I was, like many African-American ministers, a devout follower of Martin King, I tried initially to ignore Malcolm's cogent *cultural* critique of the Christianity as it was taught and practice in black and white churches. I did not want him to disturb the theological certainties that I had learned in graduate school. But with the urban unrest in the cites and the rise of Black Power during the James Meredith March in Mississippi (June 1966), I could no longer ignore Malcolm's devastating criticisms of Christianity, particularly as they were being expressed in the articulate and passionate voices of Stokely Carmichael, Ron Karenga, the Black Panthers, and other young African-American activists. For me, the burning theological question was, how can I reconcile Christianity and Black Power, Martin Luther King Jr.'s idea of nonviolence and Malcolm X's 'by any means necessary' philosophy? The writing of *Black Theology and Black Power* was the beginning of my search for a resolution of that dilemma. (xxvi)

Even more compelling for me—beyond reconciling political, ideological differences between King and Malcolm X—is Cone's self-reflective journey is his unabashed willingness to call out sexism in the Black Power Movement, as well as in his own thinking. Reflecting about his use of sexist language in the revised published version of *Black Theology and Black Power* in 1989, Cone remarks:

The publication of the twentieth-anniversary edition tempted me to rid *Black Theology and Black Power* of its sexist language (as I did in the revised edition of *A Black Theology of Liberation* [Orbis, 1986) and also insert some references to [B]lack women. But I decided to let the language remain unchanged as a reminder of how sexist I once was and also that I might be encouraged never to forget it. It is easy to change the language of oppression without changing the sociopolitical situation of its victims. I know existentially what this means from the vantage point of racism…. The same kind of problem is beginning to emerge in regard to sexism. With the recent development of womanist theology as expressed in the articulate and challenging voices of Delores Williams, Jackie Grant, Katie Cannon, Renita Weems, Cheri Gilkes, Kelly Brown, and others, even African-American male ministers and theologians are learning how to talk less offensively about women's liberation. Many seem to have forgotten that they once used exclusive language. (xxviii-xxix)

I would be impressed by Cone's willful expression of his inner thoughts and feelings in *Black Theology and Black Power* concerning his theological stance to Black liberation. At the same time, his standpoint reinforced my critical consciousness of the ways sexism erased the activist contribution of womanist theology conceptualized by Black women. Cone's outspoken words of self-reflection that reinforced his radical perspective as an anti-sexist Black male teacher, minister, and theological scholar transformed my sense of community healing—wholistically in mind, body, and spirit. I learned from him that anti-racist theology involves struggle to end all forms of oppression. He enabled me to realize my ministerial calling in and outside academia. Moreover, noted Black theologian and professor Cornel West in his Introduction to the "50th anniversary edition" of Cone's book (2018), significantly underscores the life-transformative power of his writings:

We need more intellectual work like this: work that comes from the heart and the soul and mind, the type of intellectual work that the academy does not know what to do with it … [I]n this text, Cone is dealing with not just the death of Martin [Luther King, Jr.], nor the death of so many freedom fighters of all colors, though disproportionately black. He is also dealing with the death of something in him; it is the death of the 'Negro' and the birth of 'blackness.' It is the death of a certain kind of deferential disposition to white supremacy in the hearts and minds and souls of black people themselves and the birth of a certain kind of self-assertiveness—a courage to be. (xi; xiii)

Once again, reading Cone's writing radically transformed my intellectual and theological standpoint, especially related to how I would teach courses in biblical studies, as well as African American literature. Truthfully, in the words of Cornel West, personally I "need[ed] more intellectual work like this: work that comes from the heart and the soul and mind...." Teaching anti-racism at the intersection of "the heart and the soul and mind," enabled me to resist the ideology of racial assimilationism in a PWI (Predominately White Institution). As Cone states, "... to ask blacks to act as if color does not exist, to be integrated into white society, is asking them to ignore both the history of white America and present realities.... Instead, in order for the oppressed black to regain their identity, they must affirm the very characteristic which the oppressor ridicules—*blackness* (*Black Theology and Black Power,* 20). What exactly is *"blackness"* related to Black identity? According to M. Keith Claybrook, Jr. in "Black Identity and the Power of Self-Naming" (September 10, 2021),[5] "Black identity is the most political social identity used to identify people of African descent in the United States." Aligned with Cone's interpretive view of Black identity politics, Claybrook further states:

> Black activists in the 1960s and 70s redefined and recreated what it meant to be Black in the United States. Their efforts demanded dignity and human respect for people of African descent. Being Black was about the right to be self-naming, self-defining, self-determining, and exercising individual and collective agency.[6]

Ultimately, I would come to realize in studying James H. Cone's writings and those of Black feminist and womanist writers, like those of bell hooks among others, is that story-telling has and continues to function as an act of Black survival. In the Introduction to his book *My Soul Looks Back*, Cone writes, "Through the act of storytelling, the story teller receives a 'little extra strength' to 'keep on keeping on' even though the odds might be against him or her. Testimony is a spiritually liberating experience ...." (11). Cornel West, having shared his story in March 2021 about being denied tenure at Harvard University as a professor in its Divinity School and the Department of African American Studies (returning to teach at Union Theological Seminary)[7] views Cone's activism in *Black Theology and Black Power* as "fascinating." West is particularly drawn to Cone's willingness to share his own inner, emotional struggle for self-survival—especially after the death of Dr. King. West cites Cone's words: "This is a word to the oppressor, ... not in hope that he will listen (after King's death who can hope?) but in the expectation that my own existence will be clarified." West's response—

That is powerful, to me. It is existential crisis, self-examination, self-interrogation, self-clarification and, most importantly, self-justification. And I believe that it is a question all of us, including young people today, ought to ask a number of times in our lives. It is not just questioning one's self in terms of what one is doing; not just examining one's self in terms of trying to connect one's profession or vocation to a cause; a set of principles bigger than all of us. Rather, it is one's self-justification. Why is one doing what one is doing in the face of such unjustified suffering, unnecessary social misery, and unmerited pain in the world? How do you respond to that question? (xiv-xv)

As discussed in the Introduction to *Breaking Bread: Insurgent Black Intellectual Life* (from the beginning to the end of this book), bell hooks and Cornel West enact a serious "intellectual" dialogue confronting anti-Black racism. hooks states, the critical need for a "subject-to-subject recognition that is an act of resistance" … toward a "decolonizing, anti-racist process" (5):

> **bh [bell hooks]** … we must first be able to dialogue with one another, to give one another that subject-to-subject recognition that is an act of resistance that is part of the decolonizing, anti-racist process. So to some extent, we invite all readers then to rejoice with us that this subject-to-subject encounter can be possible within a White supremacist, capitalist, patriarchal context that would, in fact, have us not be capable of talking to one another. (5)

West's response clearly aligns with her standpoint, as he states—

> **CW [Cornel West]** This does not mean that we subscribe to an exclusive Afro-centricity, though we are centered on the African American situation. Nor does it mean that we valorize, that we promote a Euro-centric perspective, though we recognize that so much of the academy remains under the sway of a very narrow Euro-centrism. Instead we recognize Black humanity and attempt to promote the love, affirmation, and critique of Black humanity, and in that sense, we attempt to escape the prevailing mode of intellectual bondage that has held captive so many Black intellectuals of the past. (5-6)

Contemplating this as soul work, I have realized my calling for justice "in the face of such unjustified suffering, unnecessary social misery, and unmerited pain in the world."

Notes

[1] Karenga originated the term "Kwanzaa" in the Swahili phrase *matunda ya kwanza*, meaning "first fruits of the harvest."

[2] I first used this phrase in the title of the anthology I edited titled *Hooked on the Art of Love: bell hooks and My Calling for Soul Work*, BookLocker, 2019.

[3] The ordination took place at Angel Gabriel COGIC (Church Of God In Christ), the church named by my father, Rev. Frederick Gabriel Lemons who served as its Pastor.

[4] On the back cover of *Black Theology and Black Power*, the biographical statement reads: "James H. Cone, who died in 2018, was Bill and Judith Moyers Distinguished Profess or Systematic Theology at Union Theological Seminary. His many books included *A Black Theology of Liberation, Martin & Malcolm & America, Said I Wasn't Gonna Tell Nobody,* and *The Cross and the Lynching Tree,* winner of the 2018 Grawemeyer Award in Religion. He was elected to the American Academy of Arts and Sciences."

[5] I first read this article when one of my colleagues Dr. Cynthia Patterson shared it with me in an email on the day of its publication.

[6] aaihs.org/black-identity-and-the-power-of-self-naming/

[7] www.the crimson.com, "Harvard Reversed Course and Offered Cornel West Consideration for Tenure After Public Outcry, He Ways," Meera S. Nair and Andy Z. Wang, *Crimson* Staff Writers, March 11. 2021.

Works Cited

Barclay, Jennifer L. *The Mark of Slavery: Disability, Race, and Gender in Antebellum American*, University of Illinois Press, 2021.

Claybrook, Jr., M. Keith. "Black Identity and the Power of Self-Naming." aaihs.org/black-identity-and-the-power-of-self-naming/ (September 10, 2021.)

Cone, James H. *Black Theology and Black Power.* 50th ed., Introduction, Cornel West. Orbis Books, 2018 (original edition 1969, Harper & Row).

--- *My Soul Looks Back.* Orbis Books, 1986.

Crenshaw, Kimberlé, Neil Gotanda, Gary Peller, Kendall Thomas, editors, *Critical Race Theory: The Key Writings that Formed the Movement,* The New Press, 1995.

DeGruy, Joy. *Post Trauma Slave Syndrome: America's Legacy of Enduring Injury and Healing.* Joy DeGruy Publications, Inc., 2017.

hooks, bell. *Feminist Theory: From Margin to Center.* South End Press, 1984,

hooks, bell and Cornel West. *Breaking Bread: Insurgent Black Intellectual Life,* South End Press, 1991.

Lemons, Gary. Scott Neumeister, and Susie Hoeller. *Let Love Lead on a Course to Freedom.* BookLocker.com, Inc., 2019.

Lemons, Gary. *Hooked on the Art of Love: bell hooks and My Calling for Soul Work,* BookLocker,com, Inc., 2019.

Walker, Alice. *In Search of Our Mothers' Gardens: Womanist Prose,* Harcourt Brace & Co., 1983.

Introduction
Voices for the (R)evolutionary Value of "CHAT"
Confronting Anti-Black Racism
Gary L. Lemons

The time to speak a counter hegemonic race talk that is filled with the passion of remembrance and resistance is now. All our words are needed. To move past the pain, to feel the power of change, transformation, revolution, we have to speak now—acknowledge our pain now, claim each other and our voices now.

bell hooks, *Killing Rage: Ending Racism*

Grammatical Transgression

The Capitalization of "Black" and "Blackness" for Anti-Racist Consciousness

Initially, when I began the editing process for this anthology, I called for each contributor to capitalize any reference to "Black" and/or "Blackness"—specifically related to African American identity. As shared in the "Preface," I situated this request interconnected to my own journey in struggle to identify with Black identity and Blackness. Thus, the editorial progress toward the completion of *Liberation for the Oppressed* would be clearly linked to the years of my evolution to critical race, Black self-consciousness. Moreover, as I look back over the course of my education as an "English" major enrolled in PWIs (Predominately White Institutions) context—from undergraduate through graduate school—sadly I never considered the colonized, racial self-denial I internalized. More than ever, today I fully comprehend the life-threatening implications grounded in the erasure of my racial identity, both personally and politically. In truth, even in my dissertation "Black Men in Feminism: Race, Gender, and Representation in the Writings of Frederick Douglass and W.E.B. Du Bois" (332 pages, March 1992), through most of my published writings up to 2019— I never capitalized any references to "Black" or "Blackness" related to African American identity. In Actuality, I never considered *Black* as racially important to emphasize. Having read many African American writers before and after the 1960s Black Power movement who did or did not focus on a transgressive politic of capitalization, I never felt the need to align my scholarly production with a *pro*-Black grammatical agenda.

However, now publicly professing my inner need to demonstrate my allegiance to the Black Lives Matter movement, I intentionally in my scholarship capitalize on the liberatory agency of grammatical transgression in resistance to anti-Black racism. More than anything, I have come to reject ideas of what it means to be grammatically "correct"—particularly as it pertains to my Black identity. For all of my academic career, as a Black male student trained in canonical, white-male dominated British and American literature, I realize that my education was rooted in my being colonized to believe that academic excellence was/is about conforming to the correctness of whiteness. My academic training was never about my racial identity connected to being Black or possessing a love for Blackness. In truth, caught up in academic credibility and acceptance in PWIs, I had simply become the "invisible [*black*] man".

In this contemporary moment when anti-Black racism has taken an even more deadly turn for the worst, my having arrived at a self-liberating place of Black critical race consciousness has been life-saving. In "Black Identity and the Power of Self-Naming," M. Keith Claybrook, Jr. clearly points this out:

> Contemporary scholars and writers have continued to engage the question of identity and terminology. Yaba Blay's, *(1)ne Drop: Shifting the Lens on Race,* continues this discourse she states that, 'capitalization is a matter of reality and respect—respect not only for other people but for myself.' In regards to being Black, she argues, 'My identity is important, and therefore I capitalize it.' In 2014, Lori Tharps, 'The Case for Black with a Capital B' argues, 'Black should always be written with a capital B. We are indeed a people, a race, a tribe. It's only correct.' Ultimately, being Black was not about color alone, but also self-definition self-determination, and an affinity towards Black people's racialized socio-cultural group denoting their peoplehood. Designating Black not simply as an adjective but a pronoun bestows people of African descent human respect and dignity.[1]

The more and more I read writings by African American authors from the Black Power movement and in this contemporary moment, the more I have become critically aware of the anti-racist imperative for the capitalization of Black racial referentiality.

Considering the necessity for progressive, anti-racist conversations to be had between individuals—across differences of race, gender, class, sexuality, and ability—now is the time for "CHAT". *Liberation for the Oppressed* represents a calling for critically conscious folks to join together for the enactment of strategies devoted to the eradication of racism—at the intersection of all forms of systemic and institutionalized oppression. Specifically, in this context, advocating life survival for Black Indigenous People of Color in the U.S. must be actively engaged. Considering the emotional and physical trauma BIPOC communities have experienced in the past and continue to deal with in their everyday lives to this day, there must be a renewed call for liberating, anti-racist dialogues leading to activist self-transformation for social justice.

The Struggle for Racial Justice Must Continue, even as "We Wear the Mask"

> We wear the mask that grins and lies,
> It hides our cheeks and shades our eyes,—
> This debt we pay to human guile;
> With torn and bleeding hearts we smile,
> And mouth with myriad subtleties.

> "We Wear the Mask," Paul Laurence Dunbar

Considering the life-threatening implications of the COVID-19 pandemic, the lives of all people in the U.S. and globally have been challenged not only physically, but emotionally and mentally. The potentially deadly effects of the virus adversely impacted and traumatically affected people's everyday lives in ways that will never be forgotten. From a personal and pedagogical standpoint, as a Black male college professor teaching African American literature in the wake of the pandemic and the murder of George Floyd, among many other Black folks, I have kept on my mask not only to survive, but also to hide the heart-breaking depth of my emotional trauma. Masking my inner pain didn't just start with the deadly variants of COVID, it began when I was born as a *Black* American in a land founded constitutionally upon the institutionalization of white supremacy. In my life journey to survive it, I put on a (white) mask to assimilate into the life-saving privileges of *whiteness*—even if it made me "grin and lie". I wore the mask to survive. The first time I read Paul Laurence Dunbar's poem, "We Wear the Mask" was in a course on African American literature I taught in 2009 in the English department at USF. During the surge of the COVID pandemic, I purposely purchased a mask in the color "black". I have continued to wear it wherever I go—in and outside my home. While no one has ever asked me about the color of my mask, even as I have seen whites, Blacks, and other people of color wearing a "black" mask, I always think about it in the context of Dunbar's poem.

With "We Wear the Mask" in my thoughts every time I put on my "black" colored mask, I wear it not only to save my life from the deadly effects of COVID, I wear my "black" mask as a metaphorical representation of my heart-filled desire to own my *Blackness*—inside out. I no longer hide my feelings regarding my struggle to survive as a Black man in the U.S. In my study of and teaching African American literature, it has meant literally un-masking the history of my racialized colonization, having internalized the belief as a Black boy growing up in the South that "white was right". Ridding myself of my white mask and replacing it with a "[B]lack" one changed the course of my personal life and my pedagogical practice—rooted in activist struggles in love for ending systemic and institutionalized oppression.

Liberating Citations: "… creating a new culture, a place for the *beloved community*"

I maintain that the call to end racism must be grounded in enlivened dialogues created by a unified, collective body of people committed in love for the liberation of *all* the oppressed. In this day and time, anti-racist solidarity means that these individuals must take on challenging conversations about ways systemic and institutionalized racism continues to be perpetuated. In *Killing Rage: Ending Racism* (1994), bell hooks writes:

> Some days it is just hard to accept that racism can still be such a powerful dominating force in all our lives. When I remember all that black and white folks together have sacrificed to challenge and change white supremacy, when I remember the individuals who gave their lives to the cause of racial justice, my heart is deeply saddened that we have not fulfilled their shared dream of ending racism, of creating a new culture, a place for the *beloved community* (263).

For two decades, I have written about and taught writings by bell hooks. As I first wrote in *Black Male Outsider, Teaching as a Pro-Feminist Man, a Memoir* (2008). In this book, I begin by acknowledging the transformative impact of her presence in my life as a doctoral student and professor:

> I will always be indebted to bell hooks, who coadvised my dissertation on the pro-woman(ist) writings of Frederick Douglass and W.E.B. Du Bois. Since then her writings on [B]lack masculinity, feminist memoir writing, and progressive education have immeasurably contributed to the foundation of the feminist antiracism I practice in the classroom (ix).

In 2019, I edited an anthology titled *Hooked on the Art of Love: bell hooks and My Calling for Soul Work.* Composed of writings and visual art by contributors— across differences of race, gender, class, sexuality, age, ability, and culture—I conceptualized this work inspired by hooks' book *Art on My Mind: Visual Politics* (1995). As the Preface to *Hooked on the Art of Love*, I speak out directly to bell. I say—

Over the course of three decades—as I have continued to read, study, write about, and teach your writings—they would lead me on a course to self-liberation. As a self-defined, [B]lack feminist activist—you have taught me to put my life on the line (in the college classroom [and] in books I have written … I have learned from you to express my-*self* personally, politically, pedagogically, *and* spiritually. In these ways, I interpret your writings as *soul-work*—centered on the love for human rights and social justice…. I have learned from you that *soul-work* is an essential form of self-activism. It's 'all about love' (2).

Moreover, in *All about Love: New Visions* (2000), hooks claims the redemptive power of love for social justice "even in the face of great odds"—

Redeemed and restored, love returns us to the promise of everlasting life. When we love we can let our hearts speak…. On my kitchen wall hang four snapshots of graffiti I first saw on construction walls as I walked to my teaching job at Yale University years ago. The declaration, 'The search for love continues even in the face of great odds,' was paint in bright colors (xi; xv).

Her experiential vision of a beloved community follows that envisioned by Dr. Martin Luther King, Jr. during the Civil Rights movement. I, too, profess the life-saving power of this visionary community founded upon activist commitment to love for social justice. I have envisioned *Liberation for the Oppressed* as yet another liberating, dialogical text for the love of soul work.

In my pedagogical scholarship and its activist-oriented practice, I contend that confronting anti-Black racism is *all about love* for social justice. In "Beloved Community: A World without Racism," the final chapter of *Killing Rage: Ending Racism* (1995)—hooks writes:

Some days it is just hard to accept that racism can still be such a powerful dominating force in all our lives. When I remember all that black and white folks together have sacrificed to challenge and change white supremacy, when I remember the individuals who gave their lives to the cause of racial justice, my heart is deeply saddened that we have not fulfilled their shared dream of ending racism, of creating a new culture, a place for the *beloved community* (263).

Additionally, in *Writing Beyond Race: Living Theory and Practice* (2013), hooks consistently talks back to "imperialist white supremacist capitalist patriarchy." She says: "This phrase is useful precisely because it does not prioritize one system over another but rather offers us a way to think about the interlocking systems that work together to uphold and maintain cultures of domination" (4). With this in my mind and heart, throughout *Liberation for the Oppressed,* I "chat" about it as a strategic means to bring folks together—in and outside academia—committed to anti-racist alliance.

Each of the four Parts of *Liberation for the Oppressed* composes writings by individuals across differences of race, gender, class, sexuality, generation, and ability. Collectively, these folks represent the life-transforming power of my *Call to "CHAT."* Advocating the practice of love for community alliance toward ending anti-Black racism, also many of the contributors strategically align their voices with struggles to end sexism, capitalism, homophobia, and ableism.

Part I: Black Men Breathing Together on the Emotional Freedom Train(ing): A 12-Track Journey for Black Male Self-Recovery

As I note in the Preface to *Liberation for the Oppressed*, the acronym "CHAT" stands for "Community Healing through Activist Transformation." I strategically employ it as the critical foundation for the University of South Florida Task Force 2020 Grant I received—"Understanding and Addressing Blackness and Anti-Black Racism in Local, National, and International Communities." Conceptually, it enabled me and Black, Clinical Therapist Risasi Milima to create a six-month, 12-track, online, cyber-space journey for Black male well-being. From October 2020-March 2021, co-leading a community-based collaborative project, we titled it "Black Men for CHAT and the Emotional Freedom Train(ing): Get on Board!" We met with the participants two times each month during a one-and-a-half-hour online session over the course of the training process. In the context of the global traumatizing impact of the COVID-19 pandemic and the racialized trauma related to the murder of George Floyd, Briana Taylor, and Ahmaud Arbery, among others—we and the participants challenged each other to dialogue about our feelings of racial trauma.

Moreover, with the participants, Risasi Milima and I were compelled to examine ways issues of systemic and institutionalized oppression were self-disheartening on multiple levels for the grant participants, as well as members of their families. Ultimately, during the Black men for CHAT, a 12-track EFT journey, the project aimed to promote meaningful conversations for self-recovery between the participants and those prompted by activist speakers included in the project (invited clinical therapists, professionals, consultants, and anti-racist allies) known for their liberating community-building service. Overall, there were 20 Black males who consistently participated in the monthly online sessions. During this self-emancipating EFT passage—Milima, the invited professional speakers, and I prompted the participants to produce self-reflective writings in response to subject matter and questions generated throughout the course of the sessions. Part I of *Liberation for the Oppressed* not only includes written responses by the Black male grant participants, as they dialogue about questions posed to them, it also composes written versions of presentations offered by the professional speakers who join us during the EFT12 tracks.

Connecting the EFT Tracks with My Vision for "CHAT"

Considering the "Local, National, and International Communities" conceptual outreach of the USF Research Task Force Grant in 2020, I conceptualize *Liberation for the Oppressed,* as my activist demonstration of it. I purposely aimed to connect the Emotional Freedom Train(ing) 12-track project with the longstanding anti-Black racist stance I continue to practice in the college classroom. Collectively, in Part I-IV of this anthology, the contributors and I literally put our lives on the line as we write about what it means to talk about systemic racism. Also, having become critically aware of the self-deadening trauma of its internalization, we map the course of our critical anti-racist consciousness for self-recovery and community healing. In line with this strategic process of writing from the inside out as my vision of *soul work*, I hope our words will compel potential readers of this book to contemplate self-liberating ways to confront the emotional challenges that the subject of race and racism can provoke. Additionally, I hope that our writings will prompt readers to think about the life-saving power of unity for anti-racist allyship.

In this visionary configuration, liberatory alliance for racial justice stands to show that now is the time to end the trauma and dehumanizing effects of anti-Black racism. I contend with longstanding Black feminist scholar, cultural critic, and professor bell hooks that silence about the traumatization of racism is complicated. In *Killing Rage: Ending Racism* (1995), hooks says that "to 'talk race'"—in and of itself—is personally painful for her:

> … I find myself reluctant to 'talk race' because it hurts. It is painful to think long and hard about race and racism in the United States. Confronting the great resurgence of white supremacist organizations and seeing the rhetoric and beliefs of these groups surface as part of accepted discourse in every aspect of daily life in the United States startles, frightens, and is enough to throw one back into silence (1;3).

At the same time, it is clear for hooks that silence is not the solution to the hurtful experience of racism. However, not only does it raise the issue of one's "right"/choice not to talk about racial injustice, but it also exposes systemic and institutionalized ways many people—across racial differences—have been colonized to believe that racism is no longer a problem today. It only existed in the past. To be real, choosing not to talk about the harmful effects of racism simply perpetuates the history of its real, life-threatening outcomes.

Overall, as documented many of the writings in *Liberation for the Oppressed* personify hooks' groundbreaking path to community healing in resistance to anti-Black racism. Many of the book's contributors have learned ways to enhance the struggle for anti-racist self-recovery. Many of their writings align with my teaching strategies confronting the intersectional, deadly effects of systemic and institutionalized oppression. Many of the writers' works function as life-saving evidence of unwavering dedication to freedom for *all* oppressed people. hooks also speaks about preeminent importance of self-decolonization for freedom from systemized oppression in *Outlaw Culture: Resisting Representations* (1994). She states, "When I look at my life, searching it for a blueprint that aided me in the process of decolonization, of personal and political self-recovery, I know that it was learning to look both inward and outward with a critical eye. Awareness is central to the process of life as the practice of freedom" (248). Writings not only by African Americans in Part I, but all those by contributors in Parts II-IV represent critical self-awareness for building community alliance against anti-Black racism within *and* beyond an academic context—across differences of race, gender, class, sexuality, and ability. More specifically, Parts II and III include writings by USF students who studied with me in a graduate course I taught spring 2021 focused on books by bell hooks. One of them included *Killing Rage: Ending Race*.

Parts II and III Teaching While Black "Online": Once in a Life-Time

Before the COVID-19 pandemic, having taught in-person, face-to-face college courses for more than two decades, I never had a desire to teach any of my courses online. Yet, I will always remember the deeply emotional experience of not returning to on-campus classrooms after spring break in March 2021 (to the end of the semester). During that spring semester, I taught two courses in African American literature—one for graduate students (as noted above, the other for undergraduate students). I titled the graduate course "bell hooks and Autocritography." I describe it as follows:

> This course centers on the writings of radical, Black feminist author bell hooks—beginning with her first book *Ain't I a Woman: Black Women and Feminism* (1981) which she wrote at age 19. In this course, we will map hooks' trajectory as a longstanding Black feminist-womanist cultural critic/theorist, scholar, and professor. As one of today's most activist voices in the struggle to eradicate all forms of systemic and institutionalized oppression—particularly related to representations of Blackness and African American identities—hooks positions the critical importance of intersectionality in her writings. Considering the effects of race, gender, class, sexuality, culture, ability, and generational lineage—in her life (her)stories, she strategically merges autobiography with social critique.

The undergraduate course focused on writings by a number of Black authors from the Harlem Renaissance to the present. Yet my intersectional approach to it (similar to the graduate course on hooks) sought "to foreground and to capture the complexities of Black identity and culture—across differences of gender, class, sexuality, abilities, and generational foundations. In these ways, [students would become critically conscious of] the multi-dimensionality of African American life and the cultural foundations of what it means to be 'Black'-identified in the United States." In this course, the students also read *Killing Rage: Ending Racism*. However, in line with USF's safety protocols in spring 2021, calling for a fully computer-generated version of the classroom environment in response to the pandemic, I strategically reconceptualize the syllabus for each course. Yet, in both courses, students still read this revolutionary text.

Teaching both my undergrad and graduate courses in this new cyber-space classroom in my home office caused me to spend much time during the remaining semester reflecting on the theory and practice of my anti-racist pedagogy. No longer did I experience what I now consider the "privilege" of face-to-face contact with my students. In the cyber-classroom, life for me and my students had to take a new *course* of action. In the meta-reality of this computer-generated, cybernetic environment— we had to rethink ways of being *real* with each other. As I've stated, in all the years of my teaching career, I never imagined or desired teaching online. However, having to teach online—considering the life-threatening effects of the COVID pandemic—I would come to realize how deeply I had taken for granted my privilege of teaching in-person. Yet, at the same time, I had no choice but to take on the challenge. had been about literally engaging the face-to-face complex realties of being a Black male professor teaching African American literature in predominately white classrooms in a PWI context.

Teaching in an online classroom for the first time not only required that I had to revise my syllabi, it also challenged me personally to re-envision my approach to teaching and practicing anti-racism. However, in the new virtual space one technical aspect of it really resonated with me. During our online class discussions, students could either unmute their microphone and speak out in what I called "discussion starter participation." On the other hand, if they preferred, they could write their comments in "chat". More than in the face-to-face class meetings we had experience before the pandemic, in the online format students in both courses were much more willing to be openly honest in expressing and sharing their thoughts and feelings— especially related issues of racism. I, too, responded back in "chat" with comments. Openly conversing with my students via "chat" enlivened my hope that we could work through the trauma of the pandemic, even as we confronted the emotional trauma of white supremacy represented in bell hooks' writings and those by other Black authors we studied in the undergrad African American literature course. While students were not required in either course to show their faces visually via the camera setting, it no longer became important to me that our conversations had to be visually documented in face-to-face screen imagery. However, during each of the on-line class sessions we met in both the undergrad and grad courses, I asked three to four students to lead class discussions. I did, however, request that they control their camera setting to allow everyone in class to see their faces. What I came to realize in this virtual classroom was that while seeing each of the students' faces was visually engaging, it became much more important to interact with them related to what they communicated in their "discussion starter" presentations and comments in "chat".

Talking race with students who willingly promoted social justice actually became more important than seeing their faces. The power of voices supporting freedom for the oppressed became the *face* what it means to be anti-racist. Black/students of color and white students in both courses boldly spoke out and wrote in resistance to anti-Black racist ideology, mythology and stereotypes—perpetrated historically and in this contemporary moment. Considering that each of the courses concentrated on a critique of anti-Black racism, as stated. I had students in both of them read and write responses to bell hooks' book *Killing Rage: Ending Racism.* I assigned this book for both courses because it clearly supports my vision of activist solidarity for anti-racist "CHAT" (community healing through activist transformation). In the last chapter of the book, "Beloved Community: A World Without Racism," hooks says,

> To live in anti-racist society we must collectively renew our commitment to a democratic vision of racial justice and equality. Pursuing that vision we create a culture where *beloved community* flourishes and is sustained. Those of us who know the joy of being with folks from all walks of life, all, races, who are fundamentally anti-racist in their habits, need to give public testimony. We need to share not only what we have experienced but the conditions of change that make such an experience possible. The interracial circle of love that I know can happen because each individual present in it has made his or her [or their] own commitment to living an antiracist life and to furthering the struggle to end white supremacy will become a reality for everyone only if those of us who have created these communities share how they emerge in our lives and the strategies we use to sustain them (271-272).

Autocritography: Where the Personal and Professional Intersect

> [Autocritography] is a self-reflexive, self-consciously academic act that foregrounds aspects of the genre typically dissolved into authors' always strategic self-portraits. Autocritography, in other words, is an account of individual, social, and institutional conditions that help to produce a scholar and, hence, his or her professional concerns. Although the intensity of investigation of any of these

conditions may vary widely, their self-consciously interactive presence distinguishes autocritography from other forms of autobiographical recall (7).

Michael Awkward, *Scenes of Instruction, a Memoir* (1999)

In the evolution of my pedagogical practice and activist-oriented scholarship in African American literary and cultural studies, I have sought to demonstrate critical connections between the personal and the professional. Over the course of time, while I have written about my personal experiences confronting racism, I have strategically linked them to my scholarly research and analysis of ways it also impacted the history of my professional career as a Black male student and professor in PWIs. At the same time, I would become committed to studying and teaching Black feminist and womanist critique of systemic and institutionalized oppression. Thus, in this academic context, I write and teach about ways anti-Black racism is interconnected to sexism, classism, homophobia, ableism, as well as other forms of systemized domination. Linking autobiographical narrative with my activist scholarly and pedagogical focus—in the words of Michael Awkward—my writing represents "an account of individual, social, and institutional conditions that help[ed] to produce [me as] a scholar and, hence, [my] professional concerns." In fact, in *Caught Up in the Spirit! Teaching for Womanist Liberation* (2017), I write about Awkward's conceptualization of autocritography and its impact on my approach to teaching for "CHAT" in African American literature:

> Rather than lecture to my students as a 'professorial expert' in the field of [B]lack literary studies, I practice a way of teaching centered on critical dialogue between me and my students. Their written responses act as the framework for us to 'talk-back' to works by [B]lack authors we study. Together our voices interaction to create a conversational environment in the classroom that is rich and multi-layered. The key term in the written and verbal interaction I promote in this space is *collaboration* (59).

As I have shared, in spring semester 2021, the graduate course I taught focused on writings by bell hooks. The course was composed of 13 students, the majority of them white. Only three of the students identified as BIPOC. We began the semester studying *Ain't I a Woman: Black Women and Feminism* (1981) hooks' first published book. She wrote it at the age of 19. During the semester, while reading other writings by her, we mapped hooks' trajectory as a longstanding Black feminist-womanist cultural critic/theorist, scholar, and professor. As one of today's most activist voices in the struggle to eradicate all forms of systemic and institutionalized oppression—particularly related to representations of Blackness and African American identities—hooks positions the critical importance of intersectionality in her writings. Considering the effects of race, gender, class, sexuality, culture, ability, and generational lineage—in her life (her)stories, she strategically merges autobiography with social critique. In *Teaching to Transgress: Education as the Practice of Freedom* (1995), bell hooks states:

> Teaching is a performative act. And it is that aspect of our work that offers the space for change, invention, spontaneous shifts, that can serve as a catalyst ... that calls everyone to become more and more engaged, to become active participants in learning ... bearing witness to education as the practice of freedom (11).

Exploring how bell hooks employs autocritography as a pedagogical "performative act" in her writing style allowed us to engage it a strategic form of personal and professional learning style "bearing witness to education as the practice of freedom." I also specified that students utilize Awkward's rhetorical concept in the writings each of them produced in the course. I suggested that it would enable them to comprehend the range, depth, and scope of the revolutionary vision of feminism hooks advances in her writings.

Strategically, I conceptualized this graduate course as a means to advance the groundbreaking dimensions of the liberatory standpoint that hooks so boldly advocates as the foundation for critical personal reflection for self-recovery, healing, social, and political agency. In the course—as readers, writers, and teachers engaged in the study of writings by hooks—we applied autocritography as a critical, life-transformative genre to grapple with ways our own varying, complex identities influence our textual analyses of hooks' works. First and foremost, through the study of hooks' writings, we would comprehend her struggle in support of the eradication of historical and prevailing myths, stereotypes, and (mis)representations of Black identities in a culture of white supremacy, patriarchy, classism, and (hetero)sexism, and ableism. Secondly, our analysis of her writings would help us to understand more fully the discursive strategy she employs in (her)stories of what it means to be a Black feminist writer, professor and activist. In sum—as a Black feminist, theory-rich course grounded in the emancipatory literary, cultural, critical, and scholarly production of bell hooks—I envisioned it as forging a self-liberating path for student commitment and investment in the preeminent legacy of hooks' intellectual and activist revolutionary *herstory*.

As my published writings document the transformative impact of hooks' works in my life, autocritography represents my longstanding commitment to the liberating power of Black feminist and womanist thought—in and outside the college classroom. I learned from hooks that the classroom can be a strategic location for the demonstration of teacher/student activism. As noted in *Black Male Outsider* I write about hooks challenging my one-dimensional, masculinist and (hetero)sexist ideas of Black manhood. Overall, many of her writings would become the groundwork for my personal, professional, and pedagogical practice actively supporting struggles to end all forms of systemized oppression.

Putting One's Life on the Line: Confronting Systemic, Racist Injustice

In *Liberation for the Oppressed*, many of its contributors literally put their lives on the line in resistance to systemic and institutionalized racial oppression. In particular, many of them write openly about traumatic experiences they have or would face in what it means to "talk race" in opposition to racism at the intersection of other traumatizing forms of oppression and domination. Having become critically aware of the self-deadening effects of internalized racism, many of them map the course of their journey toward the practice of love for the oppressed. Having become critically conscious of their possible complicity with racism by not speaking out about its hurtful traumatizing effects—much like hooks, many of them employ personal narrative to speak out for the necessity of racist decolonization. Many of them support the need for alliance-building dialogue for social justice, as they address strategic ways to end racism interconnected to other forms of systemic domination. Overall, in Parts II and III, the contributors write in unity not only to address the painful, emotional challenges that the subject *and* experiences of racism can provoke in oneself, but also to envision paths to self-recovery—contemplating and acting for community healing.

Part IV: Mission Accomplished—Hope for a "Beloved Community"

Like all *beloved communities* we affirm our differences. It is this generous spirit of affirmation that gives us the courage to challenge one another, to work through misunderstandings, especially those that have to do with race and racism. In a *beloved community* solidarity and trust are grounded in profound commitment to a shared vision. Those of us who are always anti-racist long for a world in which everyone can form a *beloved community* where borders can be crossed and cultural hybridity celebrated. Anyone can begin to make such a community by truly seeking to live in an anti-racist world. If that longing guides our vision and our actions, the new culture will be born and anti-racist communities of resistance will emerge everywhere. This is where we must go from here.

bell hooks, *Killing Rage: Ending Racism*

In communal solidarity with bell hooks' vision of what must guide us on a liberating path for "anti-racist communities of resistance" [to] emerge everywhere," indeed, the contributors in Part IV collectively voice their personal, political, and professional standpoints with individuals in Parts I-III promoting "a *beloved community* where borders can be crossed and cultural hybridity celebrated." Part IV also comprises writings about *Killing Rage: Ending Racism* by students who studied with me in my spring 2021 online, undergraduate African American literature course. Also, two essays in Part IV are written by individuals for whom I served as "major professor" for the completion of their doctoral work in literary studies.[2]

Further underscoring the critical need for ongoing anti-racist "CHAT" (as illustrated in the Conclusion to *Liberation for the Oppressed*) once again I create an imaginary "chat" with bell hooks as my longstanding Black feminist-womanist mentor. In this imagined dialogue, over the course of time, I share that she taught me *(r)evolutionary* ways to interrogate racism through the lens of intersectionality. Aligning it with ways to advocate struggles for liberating the oppressed across differences of identity, hooks radically opened my eyes to the complex, intersectional dynamics of systemic and institutionalized domination. Inspired by her representation of Dr. Martin Luther King, Jr.'s vision of a "beloved community," I called out to the contributors of *Liberation for the Oppressed* to illustrate "CHAT" as a soulful testament of the inner-healing power of anti-racist activism. Overall, as the Editor of this anthology during its production process, I witnessed holistically the revolutionary agency of the contributors' *movement* to write for "community healing through activist transformation." Ultimately, I believe the writings by Black Indigenous People of Color and those by white allies that compose this book will enable its readers to experience the liberating intervention of the Emotional Freedom Train(ing) for self-recovery, as conceptualized by Risasi Milima.

As a Black male professor committed to teaching against systemic and institutionalized oppression grounded in an anti-racist, intersectional standpoint—assigning students to read and write about *Killing Rage: Ending Racism* in my African American literature courses in spring semester 2021—I believe it challenged both me and my students willfully to confront the trauma of anti-Black racism. Collectively, our writings in *Liberation for the Oppressed* act as a motivational testament to the power of what hooks references as "engaged pedagogy"—

> [It] necessarily values student expression…. When education is the practice of freedom, students are not the only ones who are asked to share, to confess. Engaged pedagogy does not seek simply to empower students. Any classroom that employs a holistic model of learning will also be a place where teachers grow, and are empowered by the process. That empowerment cannot happen if we refuse to be vulnerable while encouraging students to take risks…. Professor who embrace the challenge of self-actualization will be better able to create pedagogical practices that engage students, providing them with ways of knowing that enhance their capacity to live fully and deeply. (*Teaching to Transgress: Education as the Practice of Freedom* 20-22)

Hopefully, my interpretation and practice of "engaged pedagogy," in complement with writings by my students in *Liberation for the Oppressed*, will inspire readers of it to contemplate the liberating power of anti-racist allyship—across differences of race, gender, class, sexuality, and ability. For me and *all* the writers in this book, it represents a hope-filled journey to a path of "self-actualization" as we long to find a "beloved community." Once again, I assert that "CHAT" as the conceptual template for this book symbolizes the life-saving freedom of *soul work.*

Notes

[1] Claybrook, Jr., M. Keith. "Black Identity and the Power of Self-Naming." aaihs.org/black-identity-and-the-power-of-self-naming/ (September 10, 2021.)

[2] Scott Neumeister and Maggie Romigh each received a PhD. in literary studies in the Department of English at the University of South Florida.

Works Cited

Awkward, Michael. *Scenes of Instruction, A Memoir.* Duke University Press, 1999.

Dunbar, Paul Lawrence. "We Wear the Mask." *The Norton Anthology of African American Literature*, edited by Henry Louis Gates Jr. and Nellie Y. McKay, W.W. Norton and Co., 2004, p. 918.

hooks, bell and Cornel West. *Breaking Bread: Insurgent Black Intellectual Life.* South End Press, 1991.

--- *Killing Rage: Ending Racism.* Henry Holt and Co., 1995.

--- *Teaching to Transgress: Education as the Practice of Freedom.* Routledge, 1994.

--- *Art on My Mind: Visual Politics.* Henry Holt and Co., 1995.

--- *All about Love: New Visions.* William Morrow and Co., Inc., 2000.

--- *Writing Beyond Race: Living Theory and Practice.* Routledge, 2012.

--- *Outlaw Culture: Resisting Representations.* Routledge, 1994.

--- *Ain't I a Woman: Black Women and Feminism.* South End Press, 1981.

--- *Teaching Community: A Pedagogy of Hope.* Routledge, 2003.

Lemons, Gary. *Black Male Outsider, a Memoir: Teaching as a Feminist Man.* State University of New York Press, 2008.

--- *Hooked on the Art of Love: bell hooks and My Calling for Soul Work.* BookLocker.com, Inc., 2019.

--- *Caught Up in the Spirit! Teaching for Womanist Liberation.* Nova Science Publishers, 2017.

"A Poem for Those Who Dare"
Thandabantu Iverson

Black males daring to be fathers

Black mothers who must be both

breathe in the love and honor of your people

you teach us to stand and walk into this world

you show us how to resist and make it thru

you nurture even when you lack

you heal our wounds with your own scarred hands

you show us that remembering is thinking and feeling across lives

measuring our deaths in the times it took to fight

with whatever we had

you are the seeds of SPIRIT

planted so we

will grow to be new citizens of light and love

who will dare to be human ending injustice

making the earth anew

Part I
Black Men Breathing Together
On the Emotional Freedom Train(ing)
A 12-Track Journey for Black Male Self-Recovery

As acknowledged and discussed in the Preface to *Liberation for the Oppressed*, in 2020, I received a University of South Florida Research Task Force Grant focused on "Understanding and Addressing Blackness and Anti-Black Racism in Our Local, National, and International Communities." It allowed me to collaborate with Black, Clinical Therapist Risasi Milima (aka Larry G. English) to create a program for Black male self-recovery. Calling together Black males for critical dialogue about the complexities of Black identity and community building for anti-racist activism, we titled the program "Black Men for CHAT (Community Healing through Activist Transformation) and the Emotional Freedom Train(ing): Get on Board!" We structured it as a 6-month, 12-track therapeutic journey. Considering the health-risking conditions related to the COVID-19 pandemic from the beginning of the program in October 2020 through March 2021, we conducted our meetings online.

During two Saturdays each month we met in sessions not only to promote consciousness-raising work enhancing Black male wellbeing, but we also boarded the train(ing) to build ongoing survival strategies in Black communities. In this self-emancipating meeting space we created, participants learned strategic ways to end the traumatic and deadening effects of institutionalized forms of racist oppression—as well as other forms of social injustice interconnected to it. During the 12-track "emotional freedom" journey, we also reached out to professional activist speakers (known for their liberating community-building service) to join us. These motivational speakers included David, Ikard (author of *Lovable Racists, Magical Negroes, and White Messiahs*, 2017), Adrian Miller (author of *Soul Food: The Surprising Story of an American Cuisine, One Plate at a Time*, 2013), Katurah Jenkins-Hall (noted Black psychologist), Vincent Adejumo (professor of African American political studies), Gabriel Green-Lemons (pharmacist and economic consultant), and Kristofer Newsome (2018-2021 President of the USF Black Faculty and Staff Association). Some of their presentations are documented in Part I of *Liberation for the Oppressed*. Overall, their visionary voices deeply enlivened our ongoing CHAT with the EFT Black male participants.

What follows is the outline of the program (from October 2020-March 2021). It opened with the participants' registration, orientation, and intake process:

Track 1 (Oct. 10) "CHAT" and "EFT": What Do They Mean? Preparing for the Journey, Gathering Artifacts

—"Black Men Preparation for CHAT at the EFT Station House: Get on Board!

—"Educating for Critical Self-Consciousness: The Value of Black Self-Reflection and Expression"

Track 2 (Oct. 24) Unpacking *Negro* Luggage and *Colored* Luggage Baggage: Examining Internalized Racism and Alliance Building

—"Holistically Restoring African Cultural Values in Mind, Body, and Soul: An Overview"

—"Participant Rest-Stop: Building Community for Inclusion: Bridging Differences"

Specifically, this session will focus on discussion of strategies for bringing individuals together—across differences of race, gender, class, sexuality, ability, transnationality, and generations—for promoting anti-racist consciousness and support for social justice.

November 2020-March 2021: Tracking the Principles of Kwanzaa

From November 2020 through March 2021—the EFT tracks and CHAT aligned with the seven principles of "Kwanzaa."[1] Conceptualized in 1966 by Maulana Karenga (born Ronald McKinley Everett), a primary member of the Black Power movement and noted scholar, professor, and Chair of Africana studies at California State University. The seven principles of Kwanzaa are celebrated from December 26 to January 1. In order, they include (1) "Umoja" (unity), (2) "Kujichagulia" (self-determination), (3) "Ujima" (collective work and responsibility), (4) "Ujamaa" (cooperative economics), (5) "Nia" (purpose), (6) "Kuumba" (creativity), and (7) "Imani" (faith). These seven principles will function as the core tracks to reinforce the mission of "Black Men for CHAT on the Emotional Freedom Train(ing)."

Month 2: November 2020 "Introduction to Kwanzaa Principles"

Through November we continued the orientation and intake process. By the end of November, the cohort-participant membership closed.

- **Track 3 (Nov. 7)** "Unifying body, mind, and soul in Black Male Communities".

- **Track 4 (Nov. 21)** "Self-determination: Telling my (His-)Stories, I'm Black *Male* and Proud"

Month 3: December 2020

- **Track 5 (Dec. 5)** "Black Men Working Together and Being Responsible for Our Own Survival"

- **Track 6 (Dec. 19)** "The Price of Black Male: Economic Assessment"

Month 4: January 2021

- **Track 7 (Jan. 9)** "Black Male Life Purpose(s): What I/We have Been Called to Do"; Session 2 "Discovering Black Men's Creative Power"

- **Track 8 (Jan. 23)** "Keep the Faith: Black Men and the Spirit of Love"

Month 5: February 2021

- **Track 9 (Feb. 6)** "One Community for Social Justice in the Spirit of Love"

- **Track 10 (Feb. 20)** "Self-Assessment: Writing Back: Remembering Our Legacy for Black Liberation—I/We Have Arrived: Where Do I/We go from Here? —Breathe!"

Month 6: March 2021

- **Track 11 (Mar. 6)** "Speaking Our Words: Hear Our Voices"

  Participants share writings they have produced focused on their experiences of CHAT and the "Emotional Freedom Train(ing)."

- **Track 12 (Mar. 20)** "Life-Travelers: Carrying on Your Emotional Emancipation" (overall reflection on the outcomes of the CHAT and EFT program).

As Risasi Milima and I reviewed the program at the close of 12-track training journey, we created a series of questions requesting responses from the participants. These questions related to subject matter that grounded each of the two monthly online meetings. Aimed to determine the program's success, we linked our questions with those presented by Kristofer Newsome in his track 5 presentation "Black Men Working Together and Being Responsible for Our Own Survival." Our concept of Black male emotional and mental wellbeing functioned as the core foundation for the written responses we received from participants. First, we offered a list of questions specifically related to "chats" conducted during the EFT journey:

> What inner emotional luggage do you need to unpack? What have you discovered about yourself as a Black man on the Emotional Freedom Train? What is your plan for the future? Why did you decide to start your own business related to the Black community? What do you love most about Black culture? What have been some of the psychological effects of racism you have had to confront? How does it feel to be a Black man in the U.S.? What do you know about your African ancestry?

Secondly, we asked participants to respond in writing to questions Kristofer Newsome posed to those participants who attended his session:

> At which level can a Black male teacher have a larger impact on the students that they work with—high school age or college age? With society seeming to be getting worse, as the head of your household, do you have a gun in your home to protect you/your family? At what age did you learn how to be financially literate? Who were your examples that influenced you on how you show and receive love to your significant other? When was the last time that you cried? When was the last time that you asked for help? What is the legacy that you want to leave/you are creating? What is the book that you would recommend for a Black male to read? What is something new that you learned about Black history since the murder of George Floyd?[2]

Notes

[1] As I note in the Preface to *Liberation for the Oppressed*, Karenga conceptualized the term "Kwanzaa" in the Swahili phrase *matunda ya kwanza*, meaning "first fruits of the harvest."

[2] The written responses of Black males who responded to both Kristofer Newsome's questions and those that Risasi Milima and I created appear in Part I.

1
Words in Action: Liberatory Voices
Speaking Out for Self-Recovery
Gary L. Lemons

We are rooted in language, wedded, have our being in words. Language is also a place of struggle. The oppressed struggle in language to recover ourselves—to rewrite, to reconcile, to renew. Our words are not without meaning. They are an action—a resistance. Language is also a place of struggle … The most import of our work—the work of liberation—demands of us that we make a new language, that we create the oppositional discourse, the liberatory voice. Fundamentally, the oppressed person who has moved from object to subject speaks to us in a new way. This speech, this liberatory voice, emerges only when the oppressed experience self-recovery.

> bell hooks, *Talking Back: Thinking Feminist, Thinking Black* (1989)

I'd like somebody to mention that day that Matin Luther King, Jr., tried to give his life serving others. / I'd like for somebody to say that day that Martin Luther King, Jr., tried to love somebody. / I want you to say that day that I tried to be right on the war question. / I want you to be able to say that day that I did try to feed the hungry. / I want you to be able to say that day that I did try in my life to clothe those who were naked. / I want you to say on that day that I did try in my life to visit those who were in prison. / I want you to say that I tried to love and serve humanity. / Yes, if you want to say that I was a drum major, say that I was a drum major for justice. Say that I was a drum major for peace.

> Dr. Martin Luther King, Jr., *A Gift of Love: Sermons from Strength to Love and Other Preachings* (1963)

Longing for the Words and Labor for Life

In this essay, I employ the self-emancipating words bell hooks articulated in *Talking Back: Thinking Feminist, Thinking Black* and that which Dr. Martin Luther King, Jr. documented in *A Gift of Love: Sermons from Strength to Love and Other Preachings*. Their inspirited discourse reaffirms my practice as a Black male activist teacher, scholar, and ordained minister. Over time, as I represent in the discussion that follows, most of the scholarship I have produced concentrates on my pedagogical practice surrounding the liberating agency of self-recovery in resistance to anti-Black racism. For me, in *Talking Back* and *A Gift of Love* writings, bell hooks and Dr. King both speak words that demonstrate the power of love committed to ongoing struggles against racism.

However, as I have written and continue to teach, bell hooks directly speaks out against the interconnection between institutionalized oppression and domination—particularly rooted in "imperialist white supremacist capitalist patriarchy." In *Writing Beyond Race, Living Theory and Practice* (2013), she states:

> When I first began to use the phrase *imperialist white supremacist capitalist patriarchy* to characterize the interlocking systems that shape the dominator culture we live within, individuals would often tell me that they thought it was just too harsh a phrase. In the past ten years, when I've used the phrase at lectures, more often than not audiences respond with laughter was an expression of discomfort, that the true nature of our nation's politics were being exposed. But as the laughter followed me from talk to talk I began to see it as a way to deflect attention away from the seriousness of the this time. (36)

More than ever, as I would come to know and teach, anti-Black racism is bound up in the historical, literally deadening ideology of white supremacy—as both writings by hooks and Dr. King maintain. However, in my pedagogical experiences talking with students about the dehumanizing implications of white supremacy—at the intersection of gender, class, sexuality, and ability—in courses I teach has never invoked laughter as a way to avoid dealing with it. Discussions with my students about the life-threatening effects of white supremacy in the lives of Black Indigenous People of Color in the U.S. has been challenging. My insisting that they speak out about the perpetuation of anti-Black racism, in addition to writing about it is especially difficult. Yet, considering trauma of racism many BIPOC are experiencing in this contemporary moment, in the classroom I openly share with students my need to take a deep breath when beginning discussions aimed to confront the traumatizing effects of white supremacy. In all honestly, engaging in anti-racist dialogue in and outside academia continually enables me to recover myself and embrace my *Black* identity. As my "gift of love," it gives inspirited meaning to who I am and my will to live free from the shackles of white supremacy. I write, teach, and act out words of freedom for my own survival.

Deep in my soul, I long for words of restoration, for reconciliation, for communal relationship with people standing against racism. I take hold of the "demand" to write for my life and the lives of all the oppressed—across differences of race, gender, class, sexuality, and ability. I have longed to be a member of a community of people acting to move those trod upon from "object to subject". I tell my students that we must begin to speak to each other in "new way[s]." In and outside the college classroom, I employ anti-oppressive language to challenge everyone with whom I "chat" about the ill and deadly effects of white supremacy to envision a world without racism—a place where our hearts open up to the soulful agency of self-recovery for racial equality. Like bell hooks and Dr. King, I too long for a "beloved community" where individuals across borders of difference can be whole in mind, body, and soul. In this visionary community, we can live creatively, freely, and joyfully in love and labor for freedom of the dispossessed.

As a teacher and scholar of the visionary writings of bell hooks, I would come to realize the impact Dr. King's labor as an activist for racial justice would have upon her as a Black feminist theorist, cultural critic, and professor. Over time, having contemplated the interconnection between the anti-racist standpoints of hooks and Dr. King, I have often imagined the two of them talking to each other about the meaning of a "beloved community." As Dr. King conceptualized it, hooks has referenced this phrase many times in her writings, especially in her book *Killing Rage: Ending Racism.* It embodies King's commitment to education for social justice, therefore, constituting an unwavering call for the enactment of critical anti-racist pedagogy.

In teaching the radical activism of hooks and Dr. King dedicated to racial equality and equal rights for the oppressed, I create a "chat" between the two them (based on their written and spoken words, across historical time-lines). In an imaginary interview, I link together their belief that racism will not end until the active practice of love to end systemic and institutionalized oppression begins. As hooks proclaims in *Writing Beyond Race: Living Theory and Practice* (2013), Dr. King's words still radiate with hope in love with education for critical consciousness aimed to support community alliances in resistance to the injustice of racism.

A "Chat" with bell hooks and Dr. Martin Luther King, Jr.[1]

For Community Healing through Activist Transformation

Gary: Thank you bell and Dr. King for joining me in this conversation focused on the subject of education for critical anti-racist consciousness. To begin, bell one of the most compelling chapters in your book *Killing Rage: Ending Racism*, you title "Black Intellectuals: Choosing Sides" (226-39). Please share your intention for writing it.

bell: "Throughout much of our history in the United States, African Americans have been taught to value education—to believe that it is necessary for racial uplift, one of the means by which we can redress wrongs engendered by institutionalized racism. The belief that education was a way to intervene in white supremacist assumptions that black folks were intellectually inferior, more body than mind, was challenged when unprecedented numbers of black students entered colleges and universities, graduated with degrees, yet found that racist assumptions remained intact" (226).

Gary: So, the achievement of Black earning degrees in institutions of higher education has not been as successful in resistance to racism as many of us think?

bell: "It was challenged by the reality of racial assimilation—the creation of a cultural context wherein those educated black folks who had 'made it' often internalized white supremacist thinking about blackness. Rather than intervening in the status quo, assimilated educated black folks often became the gatekeepers, mediating between the racist white power structure and that larger mass of black folks who were continually assaulted, exploited, and/or oppressed. Nowhere was this trend more evident than in colleges and universities" (226).

Gary: Many times, I have written about the traumatic negativity of Black internalized, racial assimilationist thinking ("better white than black"). Honestly, for all the years of my academic training in PWIs (Predominately White Institutions), I never fully realized the dept of the "degrees" to which I had internalized white supremacy—until I began to study your writings (in the late 1980s as a doctoral student).

bell: "When militant black resistance to white supremacy erupted in the sixties with the call for black power, the value of education was questioned. The ways in which many educated black folks acted in complicity with the existing racist structure were called out. Even though some black academics and/or intellectuals responded to the demand for progress education that would not reflect white supremacist biases, the vast majority continued to promote conservative and liberal notions of assimilation" (227).

Gary: Remembering the course of my assimilationist "success" experienced in PWIs as a Black student (as I have written) has been about self-recovery. In the majority white universities I attended, it was mostly about disconnecting myself from anything to do with "Black power." I was taught ways that complemented "liberal notions of [racial] assimilation" founded upon ideas of white privilege(s). From this standpoint, I successfully climbed up the ladder of the "ivory" tower. This was my goal for *higher* education.

Recognizing the Goal of "True Education"

Gary: Dr. King, as bell has shared her critique of Black assimilation into white supremacist ideas of educational success, what do you think should be the goal of education?

Dr. King: "The function of education is to teach one to think intensively and to think critically. Intelligence plus character—that is the goal of true education."

Gary: Dr. King, I believe you and bell are saying the same thing about the need for teaching critical consciousness—especially about "think[ing] critically" related to issues of race and one's "character." bell in your book *Teaching to Transgress: Education as the Practice of Freedom* (1994), you address the need for teachers to be risk-takers—openly sharing challenges they face in their personal experiences.

bell: "In my classrooms, I do not expect students to take any risks that I would not take, to share in any way that I would not share. When professors bring narratives of their experiences into classroom discussions it eliminates the possibility that we can function as all-knowing, silent interrogators" (21).

"I made my commitment to intellectual life in the segregated [B]lack world of my childhood" (*Killing Rage: Ending Racism,* 227).

Being Vulnerable in the Classroom: Restoring our Mind, Body, and Spirit

Gary: Please say more about the need for professors/teachers to be vulnerable with regard to sharing their life experiences with students in the classroom.

bell: "It is often productive if professors take the first risk, linking confessional narratives to academic discourses so as to show how experience can illuminate and enhance our understanding of academic material. But most professors must practice being vulnerable in the classroom, being wholly present in mind, body, and spirit.

Progressive professors working to transform the curriculum so that it does not reflect biases or reinforce systems of domination are most often the individuals willing to take the risks that engaged pedagogy requires and to make their teach practices a site of resistance" (my emphasis, *Teaching to Transgress*, 21).

Gary: Dr. King, you and bell link together the idea of self-reflection as a life-saving "function of education [that teaches all students] to think intensively and to think critically." What I hear you both telling us is that "true education" for liberation is about challenging students *and* teachers to stand against all forms of oppression, in and outside the classroom, with the power to be free.

bell: "Black intellectuals who choose to do work that addresses the needs and concerns of black liberation struggle, of black folks seeking to decolonize their minds and imaginations, will find no separation has to exist between themselves and other black people from various class backgrounds…. The desire to share knowledge with diverse audiences while centralizing black folks and our struggle for self-determination, without excluding non-black audiences requires different strategies from those intellectuals normally to deploy disseminate work" (*Killing Rage: Ending Racism,* 234-5).

Gary: You both are saying that students and teachers need to become critically conscious of the dehumanizing effects of oppression across differences of systemic and institutionalized domination. bell, you, and Dr. King clearly point out that Black "struggle for self-determination" must include "CHAT" with "non-Black [activist] audiences." Thus, teaching the need to address issues of social injustices rooted in racism must be linked to critical knowledge of classism as well—in and outside Black communities.

Teaching Against Systemic Oppression: "Now is Not the Time for Silence"[2]

Dr. King: "Nothing in all the world is more dangerous than sincere ignorance and conscientious stupidity … Darkness cannot drive out darkness; only light can do that. Hate cannot drive out hate; only love can do that."

Gary: Dr. King, you and bell are telling us that we are all in the darkness of this day experiencing the trauma of COVID-19 and the systemic virus of racism at the intersection of other forms of oppression. We need to teach the light of the liberating power of anti-oppression. Dr. King you are right, "Hate cannot drive out hate; only love can do that." But when hatred is normalized in a racist, anti-Black Indigenous People of Color ideological context—the absence of love leads us all into the deadly darkness of white supremacist assimilationist thinking.

Dr. King: "In the End, we will remember not the words of our enemies, but the silence of our friends … The time is always right to do what is right … Faith is taking the first step even when you don't see the whole staircase."

Gary: bell, as you have stated, many Blacks and People of Color in PWIs continue to struggle for inclusion, equity, and voice—as our presence and intellectual power may be dismissed. In liberal institutional settings, "Diversity" has become more like a "window-dressing" strategy. Many of us in higher education have put on what Black poet Paul Laurence Dunbar historically called the "*mask* that grins and lies"[3] to cover over our pain, sadness, and despair. However, as you write about your personal experience of racism in *Killing Rage: Ending Racism*, you pointedly express that Blacks should not hide "rage" against white supremacy—as it gives way to "dangerous apathy and hard-heartedness … promot[ing] passive acceptance of victimization" (17).

bell: "Confronting my rage, witnessing the way it moved me to grow and change, I understood intimately that it had the potential not only to destroy but also to construct. Then and now I understand rage to be a necessary aspect of resistance struggle. Rage can act as a catalyst inspiring courageous action…. Racial hatred is real. And it is humanizing to be able to resist it with militant rage.

Forgetfulness and denial enable masses of privileged black people to live the 'good life' without ever coming to terms with black rage. Addictions of all sorts, cutting across class, enable black folks to forget, take the pain and the rage away, replacing it with dangerous apathy and hard-heartedness. Addictions promote passive acceptance of victimization" (my emphasis, 16-17).

Gary: bell you reinforce this point in the chapter "Refusing to Be a Victim" in *Killing Rage: Ending Racism.* Considering Black struggle against racism continues in this day and time, please say more about the need for Black folk to end "passive acceptance of [our] victimization."

bell: "White folks who want all black Americans to repudiate a victim-focused identity must be prepared to engage in a subject-to-subject encounter with [B]lack folks who are self-determining. To embrace this shift would be to open up to the very vision of full racial equality which [Dr.] King [you] found so many white Americans could not imagine. Those white Americans who are eager to live in a society that promotes and rewards racial equality must be willing to surrender outmoded perceptions of black neediness that socialize them to feel comfortable with us only when they are in a superior, caretaking role. Until masses of white Americans confront their obsessive need for a black victim who lacks the agency to call for an accounting that would really demand a shift in the structure of this society, the rhetoric of victimization will continue to flourish" (59).

Be a "Transformed Nonconformist" for Social Justice: The End of Victimhood

Gary: Well, Dr. King, in chapter 2 of your book *A Gift of Love*, you teach and preach about the power of being a "Transformed Nonconformist."

Dr. King: "Even [as] certain of our intellectual disciplines persuade us of the need to conform … Success, recognition, and conformity are the bywords of the modern world where everyone seems to crave the anesthetizing security of being identified with the majority … In spite of this prevailing tendency to conform, we [as lovers of the Divine Creator] have a mandate to be nonconformists … *The hope of a secure and livable world lies with disciplined nonconformists who are dedicated to justice, peace, and brotherhood [and sisterhood]. The trailblazers in human, academic, scientific, and religious freedom have always been nonconformists. In any cause that concerns the progress of [human]kind, put your faith in the nonconformist!*" (my emphasis, 11; 17)

Gary: Rather than conform to racial standards of a society promoting white privilege(s)—we as Black Indigenous People of Color *and* committed, antiracist white people must reclaim our nonconformance to embrace liberatory ideas of "true education" for true self-transformation. Dr. King, in your vision of nonconformist education, where students and teachers embark upon a journey for the freedom of self-wholeness—in mind, body, and soul—will this path lead us to a new Civil Rights movement for the love of social justice education?

Dr. King: "Love is the only force capable of transforming an enemy into a friend … Life's most persistent and urgent question is, 'What are you doing for others?'… The ultimate measure of a man [or woman] is not where he [or she] stands in moments of comfort and convenience, but where he [or she] stands at times of challenge and controversy…. The call for intelligence is a call for openmindedness, sound judgment, and love for truth."

Gary: I agree. This is not a time just for folk to sit in "comfort and convenience." All of us should move and act out our stand for social justice and human rights for all oppressed Black Indigenous People of Color. bell, you, address this point in your book *Writing Beyond Race: Living Theory and Practice.*

bell: "Just as I turned to [your] writing [Dr. King] in my early twenties to renew my spirit, more than twenty years later I returned to this work as I experience renewed spiritual awakening, an ever-growing awareness of the transformative power of love. Like [you], I had been undergoing a conversion, not in the conventional sense of a defining moment of change, but rather conversion as a process, an ongoing project. As I studied and wrote about ending domination in all its forms it became clearer and clearer that politics rooted in a love ethic could produce lasting meaningful social change. When I traveled the nation asking folk what enabled them to be courageous in struggling for freedom—whether working to end domination of race, gender, sexuality, class, or religion—the response was love. (97)

Gary: Dr. King as you and bell affirm the hope-filled promise of "nonconformist" education for social justice, you are clearly telling us that this is not a time just for us to sit in classroom spaces of "comfort and convenience." In these "times of challenge and controversy," we must move, speak out, and stand together for the *love* of social justice.

"Infinite Hope [for] the Human Race": In Spite of …

Gary: Dr. King you spoke these words on Aug. 28, 1963, in your famous "I Have a Dream" speech from the steps of the Lincoln Memorial in Washington, D.C. Please repeat them here.

Dr. King: "We must accept finite disappointment, but never lose infinite hope…. I have a dream that one day [as you all may recall in] the state of Alabama, whose governor's lips [were] dripping with the words of interposition and nullification, [that the time you are living in] will be transformed into a situation where little black boys and black girls [and children of all colors] will be able to join hands with little white boys and white girls and walk together as sisters and brothers.... I say to you today, my friends, that in spite of the difficulties and frustrations of the moment, I still have a dream."

Gary: Dr. King and bell, as we continue this conversation, what else would either of you like to say to us?

Dr. King: "Together we can and should unite our strength for the wise preservation, not of races in general, but of the one race we all constitute—the human race."[4]

bell: "The time to remember is now. The time to speak a counter hegemonic race talk that is filled with the passion of remembrance and resistance is now. All our words are needed. To move past the pain, to feel the power of change, transformation, revolution, we have to speak now—acknowledge our pain now, claim each other and our voices now.... In counter hegemonic race talk, I testify in this writing—bear witness to the reality that our many cultures can be remade, that this nation can be transformed, that we can resist racism and in the act of resistance recover ourselves and be renewed" (*Killing Rage: Ending Racism,* "Introduction," 6-7).

"Beloved Community: A World Without Racism"

Gary: bell in the last chapter of your book *Killing Rage: Ending Racism,* you express your feelings about the continued struggle to end racism, as you remember Dr. King's vision of a "beloved community." On page 263, you state: "Some days it is just hard to accept that racism can still be such a powerful dominating force in all our lives."

At the same time, you remember the liberating power of the Civil Rights movement as it brought radical African Americans and whites together who believed in racial justice for Blacks in the U.S.

bell: "When I remember all that black and white folks together have sacrificed to challenge and change white supremacy, when I remember the individuals who gave their lives to the cause of racial justice, my heart is deeply saddened that we have not fulfilled their shared dream of ending racism, of creating a new culture, a place for the *beloved community*" (*Killing Rage: Ending Racism,* 263).

Gary: bell, I must say that in remembering Dr. King's vision of hope for the creation of a beloved community—you really inspire your readers to believe that one day for those of us longing for an anti-racist society in the U.S. can be realized.

bell: "Many citizens of these United States still long to live in a society where *beloved community* can be formed—where loving ties of care and knowing bind us together in our differences. We cannot surrender that longing—if we do we will never see an end to racism … Those of us … who still cherish the vision of *beloved community* sustain our conviction that we need such bonding not because we cling to utopian fantasies but because we have struggled all our lives to create this community. I have struggled together with white comrades in the segregated South. Sharing that struggle we came to know deeply, intimately, with all our minds and hearts that we can all divest of racism and white supremacy if we so desire" (*Killing Rage: Ending Racism,* 263-4).

Gary: Clearly bell, you speak words of hope that you, Dr. King, envisioned. The both of you call us to remember the importance of action to center love for racial justice in longing for a *beloved community.* I will always remember the two of you envisioning this community where love must be the foundation for change.

bell: "… only by realizing that love in concrete political actions that might invoke sacrifice, even the surrender of one's life, would white supremacy be fundamentally challenged. We [will realize] the sweetness of *beloved community*" (*Killing Rage: Ending Racism,* 265).

"[Dr. King, your] vision of living out lives based on a love ethic is the philosophy of being and becoming that could heal our world today. A prophetic witness for peace, an apostle of love, [you have] given us the map. [Your] spirit lights the way, leading to the truth that love in action is the spiritual path liberates" (*Writing Beyond Race: Living Theory and Practice,* 97).

Gary: Honestly, bell and Dr. King what I have heard *and* witnessed in this "chat" is your unwavering devotion to activist "love" for freedom to end racism. For me in this conversation, together your voices have been self-liberating. In your activist, inspirited calling, you both clearly insist that racism will end only when there is a "subject-to-subject encounter" resistance to it. Without doubt, you tell us that we *and* our anti-racist allies must confront the racial injustice Black Indigenous People of Color in the U.S. continue to experience—triggered by the trauma of white supremacy. As this dialogue comes to a close, I sincerely thank each of you for the life-saving words you both have given in your sacrificial offering of communal solidarity. Education for critical anti-racist consciousness must continue.

Higher Education for Critical Anti-Racist Consciousness: In *and* Beyond Academia

As cited in my "Introduction" to *Liberation for the Oppressed*, I strategically link written responses by Black males who participated in the University of South Florida "Understanding and Addressing Blackness and Anti-Black Racism" research grant I received in 2020 with writings composed by students in my African American literature undergraduate and graduate courses I taught in spring 2021. This collaborative endeavor offered me yet another opportunity to form community alliances with individuals across differences of race, gender, class, sexuality, culture, generation, and ability. Conceptually connecting their writings to Dr. King's vision of a "beloved community" and bell hooks' ongoing commitment to it, I particularly envision my *Call to "CHAT"* as a continued, activist-oriented demonstration of resistance to the perpetuation of white supremacy.

Notes

[1] In this imaginary "chat", I include quotes by Dr. King as noted below in the Works Cited, as well as particular passages he wrote in his book *A Gift of Love: Sermons from Strength to Love and Other Preachings.*

[2] This phrase is the title of an essay by professor Fanni V. Green in *Building Womanist Coalitions: Writing and Teaching in the Spirit of Love* (2019).

[3] The title of Paul Laurence Dunbar's poem is "We Wear the Mask" (1895).

[4] Dr. King delivered these words on May 5, 1966, upon accepting the Planned Parenthood Federation of America's Margaret Sanger Award.

Works Cited

Dunbar, Paul Laurence, "We Wear the Mask." *The Norton Anthology of African American Literature,* edited by Henry Louis Gates Jr. and Nellie Y. McKay, W.W. Norton & Co., 2004, p. 918.

hooks, bell. *Teaching to Transgress: Education as the Practice of Freedom.* Routledge, 1994.

--- *Killing Rage: Ending Racism.* Henry Holt and Co., 1995.

---*Writing Beyond Race: Living Theory and Practice.* Routledge, 2013.

King, Jr., Martin Luther. *A Gift of Love: Sermons from Strength to Love and Other Preachings.* Beacon Press, 1963.

https://www.usatoday.com/story/news/nation/2019/01/21/martin-luther-king-jr-quotes-10-most-popular/2636024002/

2
One Black Man's Journey on the Emotional
Freedom Train(ing) Path
Risasi Milima

"It doesn't matter how many awards I receive, never forget you are not white, Be Black and proud." This is what my mother said to me in December 1995, four months before her death. This was a realization, that despite the accolades that I would go on to receive, and my other so-called move to internalize the power of "whiteness", at that point in my life, I had become too assimilated in white culture.

Today, I recognize this white culture assimilation as internalized racism. Internalized racism is insidious and self-nefarious. In 1995 I began to examine just how much I had bought into the illusion of inclusion into white culture. I began to read a selection of Black authors first suggested to me by Felecia Wintons, owner of Books For Thoughts, a Black owned book store. Sadly, Felecia is deceased today, but remains for me a pleasant memory of a sister that shared with me many inspirational literary moments. Felecia suggested that I read a book titled *The Celebration of Kwanzaa*, by Dr. Maulana Karenga, and this suggestion began the path for my own emotional and physical journey along the African cultural identity road. I began that year to celebrate Kwanzaa, and by the next year, I ended all formal recognition of any European orientated holidays. I began to host a dinner and an end of Kwanzaa party on Jan 1, 1996.

By 2001 I began to identify as a Black Nationalist in recovery from the disease of Internalized Racism Disorder (IRD). Although not technically a clinical term in the DSM 5, Diagnostic and Statistical Manual, acculturation and other disorders such disassociation fugue and other conditions don't accurately grasp the damage of 500 years of racist indoctrination in the U.S. This indoctrination has been compared to Stockholm Syndrome, a condition where the captive becomes enthralled almost romanticized by their captor. Let's face it, some Black people are in love with the white "massa", and will do anything to protect, identify and defend their racial captivity and allegiance to whiteness as meaningful. Internalized Racism Disorder causes many Blacks to deny ourselves, our strengths, our beauty and our own humanity. For example, looking back over my life, examining my mental and emotional proximity to whiteness, I denied myself healing for early signs of depression I experienced related to the death of my mother. Additionally, I denied

41

and ignored my mother's depression and grief as well. My mother lost her best friend of 40 years two months prior to her own death in 1995. I was unaware of the depth of grief and depression that this caused my mother, as I was used to seeing and believing this strong Black woman was invincible and could weather any storm. I'm not sure why I ignored all the signs of her lost interest in life, reduced eating, no calls for her usual dip of snuff or anything like herself. Two months later that year, my mother died after a week of hospice care at the home of my only known first cousin. I listened to all the stories of others of how I needed to remain strong for the family. How showing my sadness in the hospital emergency room a week prior to death was not a good thing. I wish that I had fought that toxic masculinity propaganda that was rooted in a slavery mentality of the Black man as incapable of pain and grief. This behavior appearing strong, denying pain and grief denies the reality that expressing emotions and releasing tears and stress is healthy for us all.

I have been in recovery for over 25 years from the disease IRD which has insidious symptoms. The symptoms include suffering from false historical lessons, cultural misappropriation, and deprivation of cultural knowledge. Recovery can begin in many ways. The Emotional Freedom Train workshop is one among others that may explore the syndrome and symptoms I've described. I believe one has to be intentional about recovery, because there many things that look like consciousness and awareness, but often are little more than diversity agendas and other similar treatments that appear helpful to African-Americans. I have found that unless one deals directly with the issues that 500 years of racist infection have inflicted, diversity and for that matter multiculturalism only scratch the surface and don't deal with the issues of racial trauma head on.

Overt External Racial Trauma and Internalized Racism are very real. When measuring the stress, life expectancies, quality of life and overall wellbeing of People of African Descent, the hard facts are clear. These vast health disparities take a deeper toll on all of us. The leading cause of stress and poor mental health, particularly related to African-American men is racism. African-Americans need access to affordable, culturally relevant clinicians and resources to begin the long-term recovery that is critically needed. That was one of the desires I expressed in creating the original workshops through my first organization I conceptualized called The Alpha Step Training for Human Development. Although I created some workshop experiences that explored cultural appreciation in 1996, these workshops did not take on the deeper task of starting training for emotional freedom and self-support. Those workshops would come into being later after I read the works of authors such as Asa G. Hilliard III, Kobi K.K. Kambon, and others.

My History

I was born and raised spending my early years in Brooklyn, NY, at a time when the world was coming alive with Black Pride. James Brown and James Baldwin were just two of the great talents and visionaries of the day. Their self-discovery and willingness to display in their creative works as empowering Afro-centric themes had a great impact on the USA as a whole and nearly all of us as young Black men and women. African-Americans boldly displayed Afro-centric clothing, conducting name changes e.g., Muhammad Ali and started the early days of celebrating Kwanzaa and so much more. I was caught up in this new theme of Black revolutionary consciousness, although I would not claim it overtly as a self-transformative consciousness, but more as an imitation of what I saw. In this respect, it was about my personal need for more direct exposure to African-American studies. I might have continued with this consciousness awakening to Blackness had I attended an HBCU, but I did not.

In fact, by 14 years old I was living in rural North Carolina, in a little "French-Italian" town called Valdese. Valdese was a town of contradictions, clearly divided by race and income in the various neighborhoods. Many of the residents of Valdese (the name which roughly means "Men of the Valley") were children, grand and great-grand-children of the original settlers that had arrived in the United States during the European migration of the late 19 and early 20th century. A local European descent American male resident of the town had written a play about the early settlers of Valdese, which depicted the discrimination and hatred that the new settlers experienced by the White people who were in the area before the earliest French-Italians arrived. These Waldensians (a religious cultural designation) were once descendants of the early French protestants of the 18th century, were depicted in the play as a religious and cultural ethnic group that experienced immense prejudice in the United States. This background is important to my evolving mindset because I was fully indoctrinated into their story. I was an extra in the play and served as stage manager for many seasons in the events organized surrounding their story. during the eighties many African Americans began to wonder where and when their story was to be told in similar dramas. In the early seventies *Roots* by Alex Haley had made its debut, and this television series really drove the need for me to learn more of the authentic story of Africans that had descended, survived and the many ways they broke through the two thousand years of African colonization, and enslavement first by the Romans, and later by Europe and white Americans.

The Inspiration

In 2011 I attended the inaugural of an event in Washington, DC called "Out on the Hill". This event was hosted by the National Black Justice Coalition (NBJC). The NBJC is a national organization that fights for the civil rights of Same Gender Loving men and women. The NBJC/OOTH conference occurred simultaneously with the Congressional Black Caucus (CBC) and offered trainings on how to advocate and influence legislation on important racial justice and social issues.

As I was walking through the convention hall where vendors and organizations that help to sponsor such events, I stopped at one particular table to discuss the organization's mission. In fact, what had attracted me to the booth area was the t-shirt the GLBTIQ2-S advocate was wearing. On it were the words: "I can't even think straight," a clever play on the words to highlight the cause. I immediately got the message and thought about the phrase the entire weekend.

The information and inspiring actions of the activists from the OOTH event, and my previous exposure to the great works of Dr. Joy DeGruy motivated me to create formally the initial start of the Emotional Freedom Workshop. I had realized that during my clinical training the power of thinking and beliefs. All change begins with thoughts—not only believing that the change is needed, but the actual thoughts on why the change is needed, what needs to be changed, and what the new thoughts must be to sustain the change. As I began to explore my thinking systems, I reflected on how much I operated and lived my life based on the Eurocentric indoctrination of the ideology of whiteness that all peoples of the United States undergo. I posit that a large percentage of People of African Descent are so indoctrinated into the racialized white thinking system e.g., Canace Owens, Clarence Thomas, among others that they are slaves to it. Many Blacks are afraid to abandon the beliefs and values of Eurocentric white supremacy.

The Journey

Emotional Freedom Training (EFT) explores African culture, values and beliefs and for many individuals who participate in it, they are for the first time introduced to the terms of Cultural Identification, Black Joy, Black Empowerment and more. The greatest feedback comes from individuals who discover much about themselves as they explore themes such as Spirituality and being Christian X, a term used by many to decrease the influence of European "religious doctrine" that proposes Christianity is a White construct. A key learning objective is to increase cultural knowledge and ways to implement it into the everyday life as a resiliency to historical and contemporary racial trauma.

Considering the outcomes of my most recent installment of EFT, as demonstrated in the USF "Understanding and Addressing Blackness and Anti-Black Racism" research grant, I clearly experienced ways it added as a significant component to Gary Lemons' concept of Community Healing through Activist Transformation (CHAT) in *Liberation for the Oppressed*. The 12-track EFT process allowed for the coming together of men of African Descent to "chat" about ways they continue to live, surviving the traumatic history of racism and white supremacy in the United States. For me personally, the experience with the brothers on the Emotional Freedom Train(ing) journey was breathtaking. To note, the Swahili word for "brothers" is "Ka ka". For me and Gary, ~~and~~ these men quickly became just that African connected brothers for the love of Black liberation. During the 6-month EFT journey, most of the participants shared their stories of triumph thriving through the regular, ongoing pitfalls of life. The men continually shared what it means to live and be whole as Black males in these United States and, indeed, most of the world in areas stolen and imprisoned by Europeans.

EFT-CHAT left me with a sense of community and connection to the greater whole and that is the nature of what I call the GIFT. I discovered some key strategies that will aid ~~my~~ me in further anti-racist activist work, such as distinguishing between pseudo and passive anti-racism actions and intentional anti-racism actions. I hope that EFT-CHAT encourages Ka Kas to unite for emotional, physical, and spiritual wellbeing in their individual communities. I hope they continue to write down glorious stories of self-survival and share them with others especially other men. To recognize the gift of the great Universe Energy is to embrace, celebrate, and uplift the fullness of Humanness created truly in the Creator's light which by my account is Black. The universe is all Black!

3

CHAT with Black Men on the Emotional Freedom Train
We Have Arrived, Remembering Our Legacy—
Jerod Allen, Andrew Walker, Vincent Adejumo, Kristofer
Newsome, Darren L. Gambrell, and Troy Legette

Based on the University of South Florida's Research Task Force Grant award "Understanding and Addressing Blackness and Anti-Black Racism in our Local, National, and International Communities" that Gary L. Lemons received in 2020, he and Risasi Milima (a well-known Black clinical therapist in the Tampa Bay area) conceptualized a 12-Track Emotional Freedom Train(ing) CHAT project for Black males that began in October 2020 through March 2021. The project centered on emotional wellbeing sessions for its participants. Not only did the 12 tracks specifically focus on this subject matter, but they also engaged questions dealing with Black male survival and self-recovery. While Milima and Lemons acted as "conductors" for the train(ing), they also invited activist speakers to join with them. The professional community activists who boarded the train(ing), also conceptualized questions to enhance the program's dialogical structure. One of the speakers— Kristofer Newsome (the 2018-2021 President of the USF Black Faculty and Staff Association, BFSA)—joined the project not only as a participant, but also as a presenter for one of the training sessions titled "Black Men Working Together and Being Responsible for Our Own Survival." During his presentation, Newsome asked the participants to respond to a series of questions about what it meant for them to be Black and male-identified, particularly in the struggle and survival against systemic racial oppression. The questions Newsome posed during his presentation significantly underscored those Milima and Lemons had conceptualized as the groundwork for the 12-track EFT-CHAT. What follows are documented responses by those of the project's participants who gave the conductors permission to publish them. Collectively, these responses represent the liberating power of dialogue for emotional, Black male self-recovery. This "chat" presents an uncensored, personal conversation challenging its readers to become more critically aware of the complex dynamics of Black male identity in this contemporary moment.

At which level can a Black male teacher have a larger impact on the students that they work with—high school age or college age?

Jerod: In a perfect educational system, Black students would have consistent access to Black male teachers through the entirety of their educational journey. But I'm sure if you are a Black person who has experienced attending school in America since 1865, that you know for a fact that our educational system is far from perfect. Students, especially Black students need to Black male figures who can be reference points to success. Currently if students are exposed to Black teachers at all it is after the fourth grade. Which to most doesn't seem odd, but in "Countering the Conspiracy to Destroy Black Boys," Dr. Jawanza Kunjufu explains that Black male students endure what he calls the "Fourth Grade Failure Syndrome," which basically states that by the time a student of color (mainly boys) reach the 4th grade, they are no longer motivated nor enthusiastic about reaching high levels of success in their educational lives. And the lack of Black male teachers is listed as one of the main contributing factors to the development of this syndrome.

Unfortunately, the educational programing we submit our children to endure is not concerned with equipping our non-white children with the tools, know-how and opportunities to develop strong, self-sustaining communities. And as in all other realms of socio-economics, the Black male is especially undervalued, under-paid and under-utilized. Simply stated the Black male teacher has little to no value in our current educational system, unless they have fully "sold-out" or directing athletic or musical programs.

Furthermore, the lack of Black male involvement in early childhood education has an astounding effect on the Black child psychic. During these formative years, children begin to formulate their self and group identity and also begin to construct their value formations that direct them in the exploration of their inherit purposes. Not having access to Black males during this time further perpetuates the white supremacy culture's mandate to devalue Black male influence.

Therefore, if the concern is positive impact for students, we must provide alternative access points to Black males for students. Children at any age of their schooling should have access to at least three successful males outside of their homes. It is essential that Black males make themselves more visible, consistent and intentional in the lives of the school age children in our communities.

Andrew: A Black male teacher can have a larger impact on high school age students because there is most likely more opportunity to spend time impacting the students. There may be time that is of greater quality.

Vincent: A Black male teacher can have a larger impact on the students that he works with in high school since it is still in the developmental age range.

Kristofer: I believe that a Black male teacher can have a larger impact on students at the high school level because of the increased opportunity for engagement in high school. At the high school level, students and teachers have a good chance to engage with one another throughout the four years the students are there. Also, if the teacher helps with extracurriculars, they have even greater opportunity to impact the students.

However, I feel that at the high school level, we feel like we know everything and do not need a mentor or listen to anyone older than us at that time. When I was in college, I was seeking out mentors that looked like me and could help me navigate my next steps on my path to graduation, especially when I decided to change my major. I was fortunate that my supervisors for my job on campus we Black males and females that were willing to share their wisdom with me so that I could pursue the career that I have now. I know that an impact can be made at both levels but if a high school student is willing to listen, learn and value the knowledge of their elders, they have the chance to have a lasting impact for the rest of their lives. As a sidenote, I want to make sure that we acknowledge the impact that the staff members also have on students at both levels. That cafeteria worker, bus driver, assistant coach or whatever staff role a person has, they might see the students more than the teachers do. That bus driver that waits an extra two minutes for the student that is running late, the cafeteria work that gives that extra dessert or food item to the student that is either hungry, cannot afford lunch or both, or the coach that goes the extra mile to help the student-athlete and possibly their family. This group of people should also be recognized for the impact that they have on students.

Troy: I think that a Black male teacher would have a larger impact on students in college because the amount of exposure available increases because of surrounding resources. There are subject matters with high concentration areas that go deeper into specific facts and experiences. Sometimes students come from areas that have close relationships to issues or problems that will allow others to hear from that person's mouth versus an assumption. Lastly—with the various groups, cultures, and levels of intellect—discussions would fulfill the many inquisitive minds matching the level of certain expectations.

With society seeming to be getting worse, as the head of your household, do you have a gun in your home to protect you/your family?

Jerod: With everything going on in the world right now it is not intelligent to be of lawful age to own a firearm and not exercise that right to not only own a firearm, but to also receive regular training on how to use the firearm for home and self-protection. In fact, every household should have the following in their homes:

1. .22 caliber rifle: Bolt action or semi-automatic

2. Semi-automatic handgun

3. Revolver style handgun

4. Shotgun

5. AR platform rifle

Each one of these firearms address specific survival and home defense needs. For example, every home should own or have unrestricted access to a .22 LR firearm. The .22 LR is the most produced, stockpiled and accessible ammunition in the United States. Because of this, the majority of all firearms in the U.S. have models manufactured to the specifications of .22 LR shell.

Andrew: Yes, there is a gun the house.

Vincent: Yes.

Kristofer: No, I do not feel comfortable around guns and I do not believe that in my heart that I have the ability to pull the trigger. I rather try to fight it out with my hands and hope that no one has to die from the altercation. I understand why people have a gun(s) but it is just not for me and my immediate family.

Darren: Although purchasing a gun has crossed my mind and my wife and I have spoken about it many times, we still have not purchased a handgun. In one sense, I feel like a weapon is not needed due to living in a gated community. However, I also know living in such a community is a false sense of security. The biggest factor to consider is the kids. We do not want to unnecessarily expose them to potential danger.

Troy: No, I do not have a gun in my home at the present. However, who knows what decisions and choices are necessarily based on the evolution of the world. I'm thankful to live in an environment where the craziness of life isn't knocking at our door. My family chose to educate ourselves, grow, save up earnings, and relocate to areas less in need of armed protection.

At what age did you learn how to be financially literate?

Jerod: I believe that financial literacy continually evolves as individuals evolve financially. Money consciousness on the other hand means becoming a person who is aware of the financial implications inherent in their daily activities. Now I did not become money conscious until I was 32. The only reason I became money conscious then is because I started working for a banking and credit card company. Even though I studied economics as my major in college, I did not have a full understanding on how money can work for and why credit worthiness is important in the construction and implementation of the life you want to achieve as a consumer.

We all receive financial education as we grow up, but that education is not always optimal or even good for that matter. For instance, I grew up in a household where you did not talk to bill collectors and if need be, lie to get them from continually making contact attempts. This taught me to only make purchases when able to pay in full and to not negotiate terms for the repayment of debts. As sad as this may seem, this is the reality for many. Most people live their entire lives not knowing that money should be used as a vehicle and not the primary need of survival.

Andrew: I stated my journey toward financial literacy in my late twenties using a reference such as the Cheapskate Quarterly and the Green Pages.

Vincent: I learned how to be financially literate at the age of 12.

Kristofer: I learned about the value of money in the sixth grade when I worked for my uncle over the summer. I opened a bank account and learned how to save money. I also enjoyed being able to buy the video games that I wanted to without having to ask for money from my mother or grandparents! However, I became financially literate when I went to college and had to work multiple jobs to pay for school, rent and any other items that I want to engage in, while having to send my mother money randomly. So, this would be around the age of 20 or 21 years old. It was interesting to think about the conversations that I had with my father about credit and how it works prior to college but not realizing the importance of those conversations until I had messed up my credit score. Fortunately, I have become wiser with my money, improved my credit score and now feel better about talking about my finances.

Darren: I was well in my thirties when I started learning and the learning continues. Like many college students, I made the mistake of getting credit cards and using them not to my benefit.

Troy: I honestly have to say that I became financially literate during my introduction to college. I was able to work at Macy's and was a driver for the airport. It was then I applied for my first store credit card and began using credit. The year was back in the Mid 90s. I think that my preparation with understanding how to build credit and manage debt would have been a better experience. I didn't mess my credit up but I could have made better choices of how to use it. Bottom line I had no game plan or strategy for myself. As an accountant, I am finally implementing a game plan to build credit and minimize debt. There is no finger to blame, but in the future, it may help to ensure it's a high school class subject needed to be discussed.

Who were your examples that influenced you on how you show and receive love to your significant other?

Jerod: A major part of the formation of our inherit purposes is relational. Meaning that during our rearing years, we begin to assign roles, responsibilities, preferences, attractions and tastes that dictate the type of relationships we will invest ourselves in going forward. I personally formulated my relational views, biases and initial operation procedures from those individuals I grew up watching their relational interactions. My parents, grandparents, aunts, uncles and the others direct investors as my references on how to behave relationally.

As I got older, it became evident that the learnings, values and operating procedures toward those I chose to love were not optimal. I had begun to live out what the Christian church would refer to as generational curses. If in confrontation with a woman and if I became fearful, insecure or felt as if I was being disrespected- I saw nothing wrong with talking to a woman aggressively as long as i didn't call them out of their name. Because this was how my father operated when I was growing up. I also learned how to love hard and be loyal to a fault.

After many failed romantic and platonic relationships, I began to recognize that it was time for me to change that way in which I went about building intimacy in relationships. In order to do so I needed to find new working examples on how to serve those in relation to me and also my direct environment. This around the same time that I began to pay more attention to and be more intentional on the development of my spiritual man. And as I got deeper into the bible and spent more time growing the intimacy between God and myself, that relationship became my reference point for all my other relationships.

My relationship with God has now become my go to in how to deal and operate within all my other relationships. This standard lets me know how I should always treat and serve those in relation to me and also provides me with a set of operating procedures to use when actions or situations occur that have the power to negatively impact the stated goals of a relationship.

Andrew: My parents influenced me on how to show love. However, culture, society and later my faith community showed me how to demonstrate love.

Vincent: The mother and father of friends are examples that influenced me in how I show love to my wife?

Kristofer: For good or bad, my father's parents were my most significant role models that influenced how I show love and receive it. My grandparents had been together for more than 60 years. They both always should be so much love. As I reflect on how they showed their love to one another, I can see how I show my love to my significant other. They both were hard workers and made sure that their children did not want for anything. My grandfather was a provider and made sure to take care of any maintenance around the house.

My grandmother was an amazing cook that made sure that dinner was ready when everyone was ready to eat. As they grew older, my grandmother enjoyed traveling, exercising, going to church and wearing fancy clothes. While my grandfather enjoyed taking care of the yard, going grocery shopping, watching sports and falling asleep in his recliner downstairs in the basement as the television watched him. So, what I took from my grandparents was that it was important to for me to be a provider and make sure that my significant other does not want for anything. The problem with that for me was that I would sometimes work too much and would miss out on giving my significant other the quality time that could strengthen our relationship together because I was so worried with taking care of all the bills. I figured that if I was a good provider, I would be considered a good mate but I have learned that it takes more than being a good provider to be a good mate.

Troy: My parents and family are the greatest influences I have in my life. To compliment what they have reflected, external sources tickled my curiosity encouraging me to sample a few mimicking experiences with wonderful ladies of the opposite gender.

When was the last time that you cried?

Jerod: Not exactly sure when the last time I cried. But I do know that my reasoning for crying has changed over the past few years. As a child and young man much of my crying was the product of being hurt or experiencing some type of emotion that I could not either communicate or explain. Early in the morning on December 13, 1994, I found my grandmother had transitioned in her sleep holding my two-year-old brother. I didn't cry on that day or the next. Like most black 80's babies, my grandmother was my world. Gloria Allen tried her hardest to fill every possible void I could have in order to fill me with love, education and faith. I must have repressed the memories of the day of her funeral, because the only thing I can remember is seeing her lying there in her casket and tears just running down my face. I wanted to wail, but I couldn't. I was the eldest male child and all I can remember is telling myself that I had to hold it together for my mother, aunts and cousins.

After that day crying became severely scarce. My life was changing, my thoughts were changing, my environment was changing, so I changed. I went from being a care free, curious boy to a strategic, strong willed militant young man and crying had no value to me. My eyes were baron until I experienced my first heartbreak. For the first time at the age of 18, I had to deal with the emotional products of lost love and betrayal. The young lady that I thought would be my young bride was caught in a compromising position with someone I regarded as a brother. This event galvanized a generational curse of subduing emotional hurt with self-medication of alcohol, sex and unfocused use of time. From this a cycle formed that bonded me for the next 15 years.

It wasn't until the morning of July 8, 2007, when my daughter was born that I ever cried due to the emotion of joy. Well, some of it was joy. There was also a lot of fear involved, but crying out of fear was normal. It wasn't until about six years ago that the process and act of crying changed for me. At the time I was emotionally bound and my emotional intelligence was non-existent. Then due to yet another failed relationship I was forced to spend time alone and that's when I realized we are truly never alone. God made his presence felt in a big way. For the first time I could openly access the freedom of crying in praise, which is my now essence of joy.

I am no longer held to the prison of only expressing emotion by tears out of negative experiences. I am free enough to cry from seeing the beauty and truth in God by seeing a rainbow after a midday Central Florida thunderstorm. As the intimacy between God and me grows, the meaning of my tears evolved. It is true that there are times that my tears are still a product of hurt, loss and misunderstanding, but most of the time my tears are reserved to the expression of how marvelous God is and has always been.

Andrew: It has been several years since I had a really good cry.

Vincent: The last time I cried was in 2015.

Kristofer: I cried at my father's funeral three years ago. In my life, I have mainly cried at funerals of my family members. The only other time that I can remember crying that hard was when I my significant other at the time broke up with me. I knew that I wanted to marry her and I knew how I was going to propose but after being a relationship for almost three years, she decided that I was no longer the person she wanted to be with. I cried for four days straight and I had no clue that I had so many tears in my body nor did I know that a heartbreak could hurt so much.

Darren: It was 2010 at my family reunion as we were recognizing those who passed away. Although my first son was born in January 2009, my father never had an opportunity to meet him before passing in December 2009.

Troy: The last time I cried was first when my grandmother passed away years ago, and then recently when my father reached the end of his stretch April 30th, 2021.

When was the last time that you asked for help?

Jerod: I ask for help all the time. My kingdom purpose is provisioned by the help of others. And in order for this to come to pass, I am tasked with asking for help.

Andrew: It has been about two years since I was in a time when or in a space where I needed emotional support.

Vincent: The last time I asked for help was in 2019.

Kristofer: As I sit here, the most recent time that I asked for help was asking a multiple people to serve on search committee related to a new job vacancy. I guess that I have also asked for help when I have conversations with friends, family, colleagues, and sometimes random strangers to gain words of wisdom on various topics. Overall, I try not to ask for help. I do my best to not ask for help because I do not want to be a burden to anyone else nor do I want to owe someone for their assistance.

Darren: I ask for help often professionally with different tasks. Personally, I only ask for help from my wife and that isn't very often. We are very fortunate!

Troy: My involvement daily requires me to ask for help at any given moment. I'm just thankful that my pride and ego are not ashamed to open up those doors that will allow me to receive.

What is the legacy that you want to leave/you are creating?

Jerod: The legacy that I am now creating is directly connected with my Kingdom Purpose. As I mature in my relationship with God and accept who he has designed me to be, the legacy I am preparing becomes more vivid. Strong community, education, business and land ownership are the foundation of the legacy I am preparing for the next three generations. This legacy will not be a lifestyle, but rather a set of proven strategies, methodologies and precepts that will allow those connected to stay tapped in their creative vein by staying focused on God's Kingdom Purpose for their lives.

Recently my desire to help facilitate the education of the Black community has transitioned into an intense desire to assist in the building of highly functional and economically independent Black communities. We as black people have to revert to the sense of community of days past. Segregation is a major key to social, economic and political power. We have attempted the desegregation route and it is not working. I am tasked with assisting in the creation of universal models of building self-sustaining Black communities.

In my heart of hearts, I believe that the first step to developing strong self-sustaining communities is changing the way we as Black individuals, families and groups are educated and effectively and efficiently govern how our children are educated, who educates our children and build an emphasis on being producers instead of consumers. As stated in question one, our education system was not built with the intent to build or maintain strong Black communities. Knowing this and not doing anything and everything to change this is foolish. We no longer can wait for the system to change itself. Part of my legacy is disrupting the current education system and providing an optimal learning experience for the entire Black family, not just children.

A key component in the development of self-sustaining Black communities is providing the learning, tools and opportunities needed to shift the collective mindset to one focused on providing goods and services to the community. Business ownership and land ownership and development are essential to the task of reaching socio-economic normalcy. Like many other cultural and ethnic groups, Blacks have to develop areas that are conveniently accessible, populated and attractive for our Black dollars to circulate and grow.

Andrew: A life of being helpful, showing love through being generous.

Vincent: The legacy I want to leave are connected to assets for family and an upstanding reputation.

Kristofer: I want those that come behind me to have a better and easier life than I had. I want them to be able not to live in fear of anything. I want them to understand that it is cool to be smart and there is nothing wrong with being a good person. Lastly, I want whoever comes behind me to know the real history (positive and negative) of what actions has brought us to the place that they are at and hopefully they understand and appreciate the sacrifices others have made to help make their life better.

Darren: I hope to leave a legacy where my kids do not have to start from ground zero. It is our desire for our kids to graduate with ZERO debt. We also plan to leave them with a home in Florida that they can live in or it could be an investment property. Finally, I would love for both of my sons to join my fraternity.

Troy: Great question! The legacy I want to leave is a good, strong, and powerful name along with a contribution to my family, culture, and world. Whatever it may be, if it comes from me, it can be replicated, used, and be valued by someone.

What is the book that you would recommend for a Black male to read?

Jerod: I have a list of books that I believe every Black person should read, but if I had to only choose one—my answer would be the bible. But to answer this question, I would recommend *Think and Grow Rich* by Napoleon Hill. This book is what I like to call the "faithing manual." The author of this book studied, interviewed and analyzed some of the richest men in history and developed a 13-step process for manifesting the life you want to live by developing the understanding that "your thoughts are things."

As a Black man in America, it can be hard to believe that we can live the lives we want without having to sacrifice who we are and who we have been called to be. To put this simply, as a Black man in America it can be hard to develop the power of faith. Hill provides a model that addresses men holistically. Managing your thoughts, actions, networks and sexual expression are all areas in which Black males need guidance and development.

Andrew: The first book that comes to mind is *Jesus and the Disinherited* by Howard Thurman.

Vincent: The *Autobiography of Malcolm X*

Kristofer: *The Conversation* by Hill Harper

Troy: A book that I would recommend for a Black male to read is *The Mis-Education of the Negro* by Carter G. Woodson published in 1933.

What is something new that you learned about Black history since the murder of George Floyd?

Jerod: Unfortunately, I have not learned anything about black history since the transition of George Floyd. The past year has only solidified the learnings that I already knew. I know that the value of my life even in 2021 is not worth a damn to the white supremacy culture of the world. I know that the time for real change has to be now. I know that my people are getting tired and fed up. I know that the youth in my community are not concerned with peacefully coming to terms with the white supremacy culture. I know that if Blacks don't take drastic measures in ensuring the development of strong Black communities, we will forever be second class citizens.

Andrew: I learned about ways and origins of soul food that cornmeal was used to make corn cakes, hot water bread and hush puppies. Also, I now know that original Red drink is made from hibiscus and is also called Bissop.

Vincent: I learned since the murder of George Floyd that there were "Black" civilizations in the Western hemisphere before Columbus.

Kristofer: I learned about the African American Policy Forum and the Say Her Name movement. Check out their website at https://www.aapf.org/

What inner emotional luggage do you need to unpack?

Vincent: The inner emotional luggage that I need to unpack is my obsession with perfection.

Kristofer: I think that I have to unpack my inner emotional luggage related to trying to be a better husband. I feel that there are times that I am not doing enough to be a good husband. I know that I can be hard on myself but I believe that I could do more to be a better provider, protector, friend, help mate and head of our household. I am still learning how to be a good husband as I did not grow up with a role model in my immediate household.

Darren: I have some emotional luggage to unpack related to the relationship I have with my mother. However, she hasn't shown she is ready to move forward because that would take some going back and owning up to the truth. She likes to rewrite history as a way of protecting her ego.

Andrew: I still have unprocessed anger. I resent having my integrity questioned by an old white woman grab her purse when I come her way, when it appears like I could afford to buy anything she needs.

Troy: Something new that I learned about Black History since the murder of George Floyd is that people are becoming more aware of what is happening in our communities. People are becoming more knowledgeable about the legal and justice system. Lastly, more people are becoming educated in the mind about the need for anti-racism to allow us to act mature and professional in terms of seeking favorable results for justice.

What have you discovered about yourself as a Black man on the Emotional Freedom Train?

Vincent: I have discovered the art of patience.

Kristofer: That I am not the only person to feel the way I have been feeling on various topics. While we all might not have had the same life experiences, we have had some shared emotions and we all realize that this type of space for Black men is needed for us to grow, support and encourage one another.

Darren: What I have discovered about myself as a Black man on the Emotional Freedom Train is that I need healing!

Andrew: I still have emotional baggage that needs unpacking ... especially negative self-talk.

Troy: I discovered that there is still a lot to learn when sharing awareness, open to discuss whatever, the fight for various types of freedom is needed, the struggle for being Black is still alive, and people are willing to come together making an effort to bring forth the greater good of success in *change*.

What is your plan for the future?

Vincent: My plan for the future is to expanded my family and become a business/job creator. Kristofer: I am not sure. I am in flux about possibly becoming a middle school and/or high school teacher. I know that I have helped the various students that I have met during my time working at the college level. However, I have been serving as an assistant coach for a local high school girls flag football team and I have enjoyed sharing my excitement for the game, along with life lessons. I really believe that I could have a greater impact on the students at an earlier age.

Kristofer: I am not sure. I am in flux about possibly becoming a middle school and/or high school teacher. I know that I have helped the various students that I have met during my time working at the college level. However, I have been serving as an assistant coach for a local high school girls flag football team and I have enjoyed sharing my excitement for the game, along with life lessons. I really believe that I could have a greater impact on the students at an earlier age.

Darren: I now live for my sons! Most of what I do relates to ensuring they have the tools needed to be successful and ensuring future generations will be in a better place than where they were.

Andrew: My plan is to read, work, connect and write ...

Troy: My plan for the future is to focus on becoming a better version of myself. Loving myself. Respecting myself. All of which so I can do so with others for the greatness of African Americans and overall humanity.

Why did you decide to start your own business related to the Black community?

Vincent: Black business correlates to Black power in this system.

Kristofer: I have not started my own business yet. If I were to start a business, it would be a mentorship program that would focus on life experiences, help with academics, learn about the importance of finances and a basic knowledge of the law.

Andrew: I have not started a business yet.

Troy: I decided to start my own business so that I can change the habits acquired throughout our culture toward continuing to embrace ourselves and to accept each other. My sick and tired of being tired literally became intolerable and desperately needed a change.

What do you love most about Black culture?

Vincent: I most love the innovativeness of Black culture.

Kristofer: I love everything about Black culture because I would not be who I am without the Black culture being in existence! Our style, our food, our jokes, our willingness to stand up for what is right, our intelligence and beauty! We are amazing!

Darren: I love our women!

Andrew: I love the creative power that is demonstrated by all the expressive arts especially dance, music, foodways, and inventions.

Troy: I love the Black culture because it endures the elemental fact of starting from the bottom and now, we are here. Appreciating the opportunity to regain a greater good of sense, civilized mentalities, conscious awareness, education, applications of natural talent, and leaving imprints of a powerful identity.

What have been some of the psychological effects of racism you have had to confront?

Vincent: One of the psychological effects of racism I have had to confront is being fearful to live in my own skin

Kristofer: The stress of worrying about what might happen to me, my family, and friends just because we are Black. The fear that my 6-year-old nephew will be harassed for just wanting to have fun, like any other kid his age would want to. The fear that because my brother-in-law is tall and in good shape is considered a threat because he is Black. The fear that my wife will be mistreated and disrespected in the workplace, on top of not receiving the credit she deserves for all the great things that she does for the department.

Andrew: I have had to deal with self-esteem, self-doubt, false comparisons.

Troy: Some psychological effects of racism I had to confront involved a 'biased opinion' of a serious legal matter which haunts me today.

How does it feel to be a Black man in the U.S.?

Vincent: For me, it feels anxiousness to be a Black man in the U.S.

Kristofer: Depending on the day, it feels great. On other days, I am nervous about going outside. Multiple times in the last month, I have seen Pro-Trump supporters outside on the corner, one block away from where I live. Every time I see them, I get nervous about driving pass the group. At the end of the day, no one is going to stop me from being proud of my heritage and of being Black!

Darren: It is difficulty! I feel like I am always walking on eggshells and having to make others feel comfortable around me. As Darren Gambrell, I feel as if I can't be my true self—especially at work. I often feel like I am damned if I do and damned if I don't. Getting ahead is not an option.

Andrew: I feel vulnerable while still needing to let myself love all of myself …

Troy: As a Black man in the U.S., I honestly feel I have a chance to do and be whatever I want. I know some have faced head-on unnecessary limitations and were confronted by roadblocks of unfairness in our very own way of experience. I think walking a straight path of opportunity allows us to pursue what it is we want—especially when we establish somewhat of a game plan or strategy. However, if we stray from it and choose various shortcuts, that is when everything gets tougher—tougher in the sense of making every stereotype a 'truth'.

What do you know about your African ancestry?

Vincent: Just enough to understand my purpose in this society.

Kristofer: I do not know much about it. I still have more to learn about my African ancestry.

I am proud to say my father's side of the family has done an amazing job of educating the family on our ancestry. With the exception of last year and this year, we have had a family reunion each year since the 70's and can trace our roots back to 1835 to the slave blocks in Charleston South Carolina. Roughly three years ago, I completed a DNA test and learned even more.

Andrew: I know my dad has significant amount of gene pool from Nigeria, Ghana, Cameron, and Mali....

Troy: All I will say is that I have a great grandfather that I met who grew up and experienced hard times that any African American in the U.S. would not have been at ease with. As I mature, I continue to understand the importance of living the life he and other families during that time *wished* for.

In Retrospect: Reflecting on the (His)Stories of Black Men in the U.S.

While reflecting on the deeply moving responses of Black male participants to the questions posed to them during the 12-track EFT-CHAT program, I thought about their connection to the written (his)stories of Black men I have read in *Brotherman: The Odyssey of Black Men in America—An Anthology* (1995), edited by Herb Boyd and Robert L. Allen. The writings of "brothers" in this book represent self-determined ways to survive the historical trauma of anti-Black racism in the U.S. Holistically, they express narrative freedom in the six Parts of the book—across differences of time, family, community alliance, creative expression in the arts, economic status, sexualities, African rootedness, generation, and revolutionary activism. About the employment of the term "brotherman" as the book's main title, in the "Introduction" the Editors state:

'Brotherman!' is a special greeting among Black men. With that single world a bloodline is invoked, a gender proclaimed. It is a verbal handshake, a shared mantra that expresses much more than a mere hello. This greeting was first heard in the euphoric Sixties. But it still resonates today, carrying a number of meanings for Black men no matter who they are—whether they work in offices in three-piece suits or hop down the street in shredded pants with their caps turned backward. Their coded exchange of 'brotherman' signals immediate recognition and rapport. It conveys a message that is at once an affirmation, an affectionate embrace, and a battle cry. It proclaims: *Our blood lines and soulforce are the same and we have a common fate—what happens to one happens to all.* (xxi)

Of the more than 150 well-known African American Black males in this groundbreaking anthology, I include a short list of them to reaffirm their revolutionary journey of survival for Emotional Freedom and "self-determination"—

Frederick Douglass, *W.E.B. Du Bois*, Marcus Garvey, Howard Thurman, George C. Fraser, Richard Wright, *Langston Hughes*, Claude McKay, *Paul Laurence Dunbar*, John Henrik Clarke, *Jean Toomer*, *Wallace Thurman*, Countee Cullen, *Malcolm X*, *Martin Luther King, Jr.*, *James Baldwin*, Amiri Baraka, Yusef Salaam, *Calvin C. Hernton*, *Clarence Major*, *Ralph Ellison*, Kalamu Ya Salaam, Ishmael Reed, *E. Lynn Harris*, Melvin Dixon, Ernest J. Gaines, Essex Hemphill, Derrick K. Bell, Arthur Ashe, Arnold Rampersad, *John Edgar Wideman*, *Spike Lee*, Jackie Robinson, Cassius Clay (Muhammad Ali), Kareem Abdul-Jabhar, Satchel Paige, Duke Ellington, Miles Davis, Quincy Jones, Alex Haley, Ice T, Earvin "Magic" Johnson, Manning Marable, Louis Farrakhan, *Maulana Karenga*, Molefi Kete Asante, *Kevin Powell*, *Richard Perry*, *Henry Louis Gates, Jr.*, *Michael Eric Dyson*, *Cornel West*, *John A. Williams* (my emphasis).

About the liberating power of their narrative authority, Boyd and Allen assert:

These voices now echo from *Brotherman*. Some of them are as old and commanding as the Black men whose blood became the ink of powerful slave narratives. Some are recent as that gaggle of postmodern writers stepping out beyond hip-hop, New Jack, and neo-retro effusions. *Brotherman* is both a literal and metaphorical map of the Black man's quest for self-determination reflected through the multifaceted prism of his fiction and nonfiction writings. (xxi)

At the same time, toward the production of the anthology, the Editors clearly note the editorial allyship of women in its "Acknowledgements": "It is rather ironic that a book almost exclusively about Black men is in reality the product of a team of gifted women.... And there are other women who made extraordinary sacrifices and lent a helping hand and heart..." (xix). Certainly, as I have written time and time again, without bell hooks' longstanding commitment to *ending racism*, I would not be the Black male scholar and professor I am whose work is grounded in Black feminist-womanist critiques of systemic and institutionalized oppression.

Yet there has been a number of Black men who have enable my inner-healing and self-recovery from the experiential trauma of racism. Among the *Brothers* I have chosen to list above, those whose names are italicized have profoundly influenced my personal and professional evolution as a professor of African American studies. I have either taught their writings in my courses and/or included them in the production of my scholarship.

During the course of my life as graduate student at New York University in the department of English, I remember it never offering a graduate course on Black writers. Moreover, during my study there, I remember it also not having a Black faculty member in literary studies. However, before finishing the department's (canonical) "English" requirements to obtain my doctorate, I would come to know the soulful power of African American literature—without having been "formally" taught it. Through life-changing interactions with highly esteemed Black writers—bell hooks, Calvin C. Hernton, *and* John A. Williams—I would become a *Black* scholar and teacher. As my dissertation focused on hooks' Black feminist theory and criticism, I interpreted her standpoint through the lens of Hernton's radical critique of Black male sexism and patriarchy in African American literature and my study of the revolutionary, pro-womanist writings of Frederick Douglass and W.E.B. Du Bois.

John A. Williams and the Soulful "Price" of Critical Race Consciousness

In light of my *pro*-Black academic path to critical self-consciousness, I will never forget the impact well-noted and esteemed novelist John A. Williams had in this life-transforming journey. Indeed, coming to know him while I was a student at NYU, would also be personally and professionally life-saving. In hindsight, I experienced the "price" Williams paid toward the beginning course of my soulful reclamation of Blackness, with hooks and Hernton. In *Black Male Outsider, a Memoir: Teaching as a Pro-Feminist Man*, I write about this moment—

I met the [B]lack novelist John A. Williams in 1987, three years after first meeting bell hooks. Williams was a visiting professor during the spring term. I did not actually meet Calvin Hernton until years after I had finished doctoral work in the English department, but I came to know Hernton's writing as a "self-proclaimed" feminist literary critic. Not only did writings by these three individuals have a profound impact on my views of American literary study, but as intellectual mentors, they helped to shape my professional identity as an African Americanist. Indeed, having since experienced the joy of fostering mentoring relationships with students of color and white students, I know the influence a faculty member of color, can have in the life of a student of color, especially at a majority white institution.

John A. Williams opened my mind to the joy of reading the [B]lack literary text. He came to the English department for one semester as a visiting professor in the creative [writing] program. Apparently, having gotten my name through the department chair, he contacted me about covering several sessions for him in an undergraduate African American literature class he was teaching. I agreed, while (as stated) possessing no formal knowledge of [B]lack literature. Both excited and afraid, I met with the students during the week he had to be away. The class was small and majority [B]lack. While I have no recollection of the texts professor Williams assigned for me to teach, I recall the students' enthusiastic response to the reading assignments during class discussion. I made no mention of my ignorance of the selected writers they read or the field of [B]lack literature in general. [The point was to sound like I knew what I was talking about. The students bought it.]

Upon professor Williams' return, he thanked me taking over for him, told me that the students liked me, and presented me with a check for $350. I was completely caught off guard; he had not given any indication that my services would be compensated. What would I spend the money for, what did I need? Like the suddenness of a revelation, it occurred to me that I had no books by [B]lack authors, except for hooks' *Feminist Theory [from Margin to Center]*. I decided to begin my own library of [B]lack books with Professor Williams' check. I began with his novel *The Man Who Cried I Am*, Richard Wright's *Native Son*, Paula Giddings' *When and Where I Enter*, Angela Davis' *Race, Women and Class*, Ann Petry's *The Street*, Ralph Ellison's *Invisible Man*, Zora Neale Hurston's *Their Eyes Were Watching God*, *Selected Poems of Langston* Hughes, Alice Walker's *The Color Purple*, Ntozake Shange's *For Colored Girls,* and Calvin C. Hernton's *The Sexual Mountain and Black Women Writers,* among others.

I keep in the top drawer of my writing desk at home a letter Professor Williams wrote to me in April 1991. It came toward the end of the first semester of my first full-time college teaching job in New York City. I had seen him briefly one evening at a production of a show on Broadway called *Black Eagles*, and he writes 'Dear Gary … It was good to see you and bask once again in your enthusiasm for [Black] literature." We had corresponded a couple of times previously about a paper I had written on [B]lacks in Shakespeare and a piece on William Blake's antislavery poem, "The Little Black Boy." For an author of his stature, I was amazed that he maintained a writing connection to me. I marveled at his enthusiasm, interest, and considerable knowledge in the subjects I was writing about in graduate school. Never telling him how the check he had given me was spent, I simply noted in the inside cover of each: 'Purchased with funds from John A. Williams.' Little did he know in 1987, $350 went a long way toward not only establishing a library of noteworthy [B]lack writers, it would represent the establishment of my place in the tradition of African American literature as a student and professor of it. As brief as my association with John A. Williams was, during the one semester he taught at NYU, it was enough time to ignite in me a passionate love of [B]lack literature I possess to this day.

One of the books I purchased with professor Williams' check was Hernton's *The Sexual Mountain and Black Women Writers*. At the time, having read little pro-feminist criticism by [B]lack men beyond that of Arnold Rampersad, Henry Louis Gates, Jr. and Houston Baker (among a few other lesser-known names), this slender volume further opened my eyes to the possibilities of [B]lack male feminism. Its title essay appeared as a separate essay in 1984. The essay provided me an initial historical reference counterpoint to masculinist versions of the [B]lack literary tradition. I also credit the essay for helping me create the list of [B]lack female-authored books I initially purchased. Moreover, Hernton's ardent, pro-feminist defense of [B]lack women writers in the essay so inspired me that I changed my dissertation topic from art and politics in William Blake's poetry to an exploration of the impact of feminism on [B]lack female and male writers. In the process, having [begun] a historical search for other [B]lack male proponents of feminism, I discovered the pro-feminist writings of Frederick Douglass and W.E.B. Du Bois, among others. Reflecting on the racial implications of the literary education I received in majority white English departments (from undergraduate through graduate school), it was clear to me the white (male) writer and critic had functioned to reify whiteness in my literary imagination. However, because of the literary mentorship of bell hooks, *John A. Williams*, and Hernton, before I left NYU, I had begun to *re*imagine my racial and gender identity through the experience of [B]lack literature. (my emphasis, 115-17)

Together hooks, Williams, and Hernton would inspire me to write *Black Male Outsider, a Memoir: Teaching as a Pro-Feminist Man* (2008). Continuing to focus on research about the history of radical Black male resistance not only to racism but sexism as well, I would be led to write *Womanist Forefathers: Frederick Douglass and W.E.B. Du Bois* (2012). Moreover, mapping my "self-taught" Black coursework on writings by African American authors, I document it in *Caught Up in the Spirit! Teaching for Womanist Liberation* (2017).

Works Cited

Boyd, Herb and Robert L. Allen. Editors, *Brotherman: The Odyssey of Black Men in America—An Anthology,* Ballantine Books, 1995.

Lemons, Gary L. *Black Male Outsider, a Memoir: Teaching as a Pro-Feminist Man,* State University of New York Press, 2008.

--- *Womanist Forefathers: Frederick Douglass and W.E.B. Du Bois,* State University of New York Press, 2012.

--- *Caught Up in the Spirit! Teaching for Womanist Liberation*, Nova Science Publishers, 2017.

4

The Price of Being a Black Male
And the Power of Economic Assessment
Gabriel Green-Lemons

To begin, I am a Black male who graduated from Rutgers University in New Brunswick, New Jersey in 2007 with a degree in biological sciences. I then went on to earn a Pharm.D. from Touro College of Pharmacy in New York City in 2012. I started my career as a pharmacist the same year, but had an underlying feeling that something was missing. I did not get clarity on what that something was until 2014 when I read *Rich Dad Poor Dad* by Robert Kiyosaki. The book introduced the concept of financial freedom to me. Financial freedom occurs when passive income becomes greater than the expenses needed to maintain my quality of life.

In 2014, I also married my beautiful wife, Claudine. In 2015, I partnered with some friends and attempted to fix and flip seven houses in New Jersey and lost a lot of money not knowing what I was doing. In 2016, my first daughter Aria was born. In 2017, my wife and I finished climbing out of the debt I had taken on in the attempt to flip the houses. In 2018, we bought, renovated, rented, and refinanced (BRRR'd) our first rental property. In 2018, my second daughter Zuri was born. In 2019, we BRRR'd our second and third rental property. In 2020, my wife and I joined a community of seasoned real estate investors interested in buying apartment buildings. In 2020, the COVID-19 pandemic rocked the world.

During the pandemic, I joined The Gold Society, a book club and safe space for intelligent Black men dedicated to deep analysis of the history of race relations and wealth in America. We have read the following books thus far:

- *The Half Has Never Been Told: Slavery and the Making of American Capitalism* by Edward Baptist

- *Stony the Road: Reconstruction, White Supremacy, and the Rise of Jim Crow* by Henry Gates

- *The Color of Law: A Forgotten History of How Our Government Segregated America* by Richard Rothstein

- *The New Jim Crow: Mass Incarceration in the Age of Colorblindness* by Michelle Alexander

- *A Short History of Reconstruction* by Eric Foner

- *The Bitcoin Standard* by Saifedean Ammous

This brings me to the price of being Black and male in America. First let's get some historical context Black men. Specifically, American Descendants of Slaves (ADOS) are currently dealing with the consequences of slavery, Jim Crow segregation, redlining, and mass incarceration. American slavery was the total subjugation of the Black male for the purpose of building white wealth. Jim Crow segregation was a system of second-class treatment in public and private spaces, galvanized into legislation by propaganda focused on portraying the Black male as an animalistic rapist of white women. Redlining, which still occurs unofficially today, consisted of housing segregation policies implemented on a national scale to prevent Black people from moving to the suburbs with whites to buy homes. Mass incarceration is total subjugation of the Black male through use of the legislative and penal system. What do these four have in common? They attempted to perpetuate the destruction of Black wealth creation.

What is wealth? One of the first definitions that appears when doing a google search of "wealth" is "An abundance of valuable possessions or money." An anonymous IG financial guru has called it "assets minus liabilities". Another perspective, which I heard on a financial education podcast, defined wealth as the "amount" of days one can go without having to sell his or her time for money. I agree with this viewpoint.

Let's get some context through statistical data. Black men consistently earn less than white men regardless of if they are raised poor or rich. However, no such income gap exists between Black and white women raised in similar households. The sons of Black families from the top 1% of household income had about the same chance of being incarcerated on a given day as the sons of white families earning $36,000. The marriage rate of Black Americans with parents in the top 1% of household income is about the same as white Americans from household with parents making $18,000 per year (less than the 20th percentile of household income). In 2016, the median net worth of a white household was just under $180,000. The median net worth of a Black household was less than $20,000. The average white high school dropout has a higher net worth than the average Black college graduate.

Now that we have some context, here are my proposed solutions that contribute to Black male economic success—

1. Marry the right partner.

2. Stay faithful and do what you can to stay married.

3. Have all of your children with the same partner.

4. Continuously buy/create income-producing assets.

5. Do not save your money in a currency that is continuously losing value due to inflation. Consider saving in Bitcoin.

6. Set SMART goals.

7. Raise your children to be productive members of society that buy income-producing assets.

8. Consider purchasing a life insurance policy.

Finally, consider reading these books:

- *The Half Has Never Been Told: Slavery and the Making of American Capitalism* by Edward Baptist

- *A Short History of Reconstruction* by Eric Foner

- *The Color of Law: A Forgotten History of How Our Government Segregated America* by Richard Rothstein

- *Black Labor White Wealth* by Claud Anderson, Ed.D.

- *The Bitcoin Standard* by Saifedean Ammous

5

My Statement about the Recent Acts of Racism
and Injustice
Kristofer Newsome

To those that will take the time to read this letter, 6/4/2020—

I have had the honor and privilege to serve as the President of the University of South Florida's Black Faculty and Staff Association, from 2018-2021. I am a Black man, a son, a grandson, a husband, a nephew, a cousin, an uncle and friend to many people. I am emotionally and mentally drained from seeing the news on almost any day but especially now. This past Saturday evening going into Sunday morning, I have been additionally saddened, frustrated, disheartened, worried, angered and tired. I do not have the heart to watch the 8-9 minutes video of George Floyd being murdered. I have become fatigued and wounded from being in meetings this week, in which I saw and heard my colleagues and students crying as they shared their feelings about the injustices that have occurred. There is a saying that when negative things happen in the United States of America, the negative item impact Black people at least twice as hard. When positive things happen in the United States of America, the positive effects are received at half the rate for Black people.

- Which one of these statuses make me a threat when I walk down any street in a hoodie with a bag of skittles and a can of iced tea?
  - Trayvon Martin—2012

- Which one of these make me guilty until proven innocent and permit law enforcement (or permit a white person to serve as a proxy for the police) to serve as the judge, jury and executioner without having the opportunity to have a fair trial through the judicial system?
  - Amadou Diallo—1999, Rekia Boyd—2012, Shelly Frey—2012, Michael Brown, Jr.— 2014, Bettie Jones—2015, Mya Hall—2015, and many others.

- Which one of these statuses give me the chance to have longer mandatory legal sentences and to be looked at as an adult for a crime that I am convicted for even though I am 18 years old or younger?

- Which one of these titles stops me from being allowed to breathe?
  o George Floyd—2020, Eric Garner—2014 and Tanisha Anderson—2014

- Which one of these items gives inherit permission for lesser pay for the same work as my white counterparts?

- Which one of these titles does not allow me to feel safe to play in the park or at a community pool party as a teenager?
  o Tamir Rice—2014 and Dajerria Becton—2015

- Which one says that I am a suspect in my own home when someone else mistakenly enters my home and believe that they are in their home?
  o Botham Jean—2018

- Which one of these statuses increase the likelihood that I will be pulled over by the police and possibly not make it home alive?
  o TyRon Lewis—1996, Walter Scott—2015, Sandra Bland—2015, and Philando Castile— 2016

- Which one of these items says it is alright for someone to shoot me because they do not like my choice of music or the volume of the music?
  o Jordan Davis—2012 and Elijah Al-Amin—2017

- Which one of these statuses adds to my intersectionality and reduces the chance that my murder case will go unsolved/not treated as a priority because I am either a woman or member of the LGBTQ+ community?
  o Tamla Horsford, Athena Cadence, Celine Walker, Antash'a English, and Cathalina James—All in 2018, Tony McDade and Nina Pop—2020

There is one answer that is common to all of the aforementioned questions. It is being Black. I have another question to ask: Why does history continue to repeat itself within this country, state and city? The simple answer is because of the privileges afforded to white people in this country via the systemic racism within the legal system, governmental policies related to housing, education, access to healthcare, unequal pay and unemployment rates. There are many more subjects that could be added to this list but I encourage you to do some research and learn more about this history. The reason this is racism and not prejudice is because racism is the belief that a particular race/group of people are superior to another, based on various prejudice beliefs and have created governmental policies and laws to ensure that one race/group maintains power over the other races/groups. You can watch a video in which a group of white people are asked if they would switch lives with the richest, most famous and any other positives social statuses you can think of instead of possibly being an economically challenged white person. None of the white people were willing to make that trade of race.

As I compose this message, I do not have the emotional energy to watch the eight to nine minutes video of George Floyd (age at time of death—46 years old) being murdered by law enforcement in Minneapolis over possibly using a counterfeit twenty-dollar bill. I do not have the strength to watch the video of Ahmaud Arbery (26 years old) attempting to engage in healthy physical activity in Brunswick, Georgia but instead is followed, chased, and murdered by white men that want to be a proxy for the police and the court system. My heart aches knowing that Breonna Taylor (26 years old) was shot eight times while in her home in Louisville, Kentucky by law enforcement while attempting to serve a search warrant, to the wrong house and that had already been served. All three of these tragedies have happened this year between February and May. I have to make sure that I share my excitement and pride in knowing that USF faculty and staff members walked along side of USF students as they all peacefully protested for change! Others have found different ways to show their support through social media posts, making donations to bail bonds funds and other related causes, and/or by just checking on how one another is feeling. How does history repeat itself you may ask?

Every day my spouse is concerned that I might not make it home safely, especially during this time of COVID-19 because I am encouraged to wear a mask on my face to limit the chance of spreading/catching the virus. That mask adds to white people's fear that I am a threat to them. However, if I do not wear a mask, I am still a threat to white people. My wife's, my family's, and my friends' concern for me is reciprocal because we all know that no matter our age, education, income, or influence—we are Black! We are seen as less than. We are seen as the suspect. And then we are not seen at all! We are not seen by white people. Injustices are ignored because they only happen to Black people. This has to stop because Black people want to live and not merely exist in this world. We want and demand to be treated fairly and equally to any other person on this planet, in this country, in this state of Florida, in the Tampa Bay area, on the USF campuses! Why is it so hard for Black people to be respected and to be treated as equals by people that are not Black? At what age did your parents have a conversation about racism with you? At what age did your parents have a conversation about how to act when confronted by the police? At what age do you have to have these conversations with your children, nieces and nephews, or younger cousins? If these conversations have not or do not happen in your family, speak with any Black person to learn more about these conversations. Please understand that is difficult to breathe and live free as a Black person because we have so many fears and anxieties that white people and others that have privilege do not have to be concerned about.

Here are three more times that similar tragedies occurred:

2014—Eric Garner (46 years old) is confronted by New York City police because of possibly selling loose cigarettes in front of a store. Eric Garner and George Floyd both told the police officers that were applying the deadly choke holds on them—"I can't breathe!" Shamefully, both Eric Garner and George Floyd were correct and died from the choke holds that were applied to restrain them.

2012—Trayvon Martin (17 years old) was shot by George Zimmerman because George Zimmerman felt threatened by Trayvon Martin walking down the street in Sanford, Florida while wearing a grey hoodie, holding a bag of candy and a can of iced tea. George Zimmerman was arrested and later found not guilty of the fatal shooting by a jury.

2018—In September, Botham Jean (26 years old) was shot in his home in Dallas, Texas by Amber Guyger when she mistakenly entered Botham Jean's home, believing it was hers. Amber Guyger believed that Botham Jean was a burglar within Guyger's home and shot Jean in the chest.

Additionally, there have been protests in Tampa and St. Petersburg before this past weekend. In June 1967, Martin Chambers (19 years old) was shot by police officer James Calvert. There were three days of protest and riots along Central Avenue. In 1987, the deaths of Otis Miller (35 years old) and Melvin Hair (23 years old) by white Tampa police officers led to protests and riots again. In 1996, there were protest and riots in St. Petersburg following the shooting death of TyRon Lewis (18 years old) by police following a traffic stop. While the protest and riots that are taking place now do not focus on the death of local residents, the refrain is the same, a Black man or woman has lost their life by either white police officers or people going beyond reasonable force to enforce the law on their own.

Everyone, not just Black people or minority groups, has the charge to engage in meaningful conversations that causes lasting and positive changes in policies/laws at all levels. Without the conversations, things will either stay the same or the voices of the disenfranchised will not be heard. When the voices of the disenfranchised and downtrodden people are not heard or acknowledged, there are limits to the positive changes that can be made. The people in power do not want significant changes that could lead to a reduction in their power. Due to the lack of more impactful changes to governmental policies and laws, we will continue to repeat the past.

How do the Black faculty and staff within the USF system feel currently? The following are comments from many of the USF Black faculty and staff members, along with allies, about their feelings and emotions:

- USF leadership cannot only "pause to think about racism" but we must actively engage one another to combat racism daily. I am sick of white faculty perpetuating the notion that racism is Black people's concern.
- The USF President's statement was mostly invisible until Tuesday, June 2, 2020 when [now retired] President Steven Currall's message was made readily and easily accessible on the front page of the USF home page. When the president's statement was first released on Saturday, May 30, 2020—it was nowhere to be found on the front page of the USF website. It took multiple clicks and/or a search to find the statement.
- We must hold people at USF accountable, including leadership.
- Black faculty and staff members are having to find ways to have difficult conversations about racism with their children (as young as 4 years old) and how to represent themselves appropriately so they can come home safe (hopefully) related to any interactions they might have with police, even before the recent murder of George Floyd. Black faculty and staff members have to express our love for our children, re-affirm our children to let them know that they should be proud to be Black and how to handle the racist events that we face. As Black people, we too, want to create a better life for our children so they do not have to face the same hardships that we did growing up. We want our Black children to have hope that brighter days are to come. We want our Black children to be able to run around freely and play with children of all backgrounds without fear of harm and bias against our children.
- Black faculty, staff and students are exhausted! Black people and our allies have been telling our stories for decades. While there have been some positive changes,

we still have more changes to make to create meaningful, lasting positive impacts that will uplift Black people and the entire United States of America.

- The Black faculty and staff are finding ways to survive instead of being able to enjoy the fruits of our labor. We are struggling to find the energy to stay positive and maintain hope. However, the Black people understand that we must strive to find and share positive outlets to replenish our energy, to keep fighting and support one another.

- When I contemplate that Dylan Roof murdered six people as they welcomed him to worship with them in their church, and he was arrested peacefully, and afforded his due process. George Floyd was suspected of forgery and was beaten and killed.

    The recent events which propelled us to this renewed stand for the fundamental human right to breathe and to live can threaten to overwhelm us. I draw from the strength of our mothers during slavery times who watched their sons brutalized, maimed, and murdered and who sometimes had to smother their own babies in order to silence them and keep themselves and others safe. We WILL emerge from this horror stronger ... and still we rise.

- The difficult conversations that everyone is taking part in now are heartbreaking and soul crushing. However, Black people have always had to have these conversations. Right now, we hope that white people and any allies that are protesting for positive change are finally listening and willing to make the necessary changes.

- It is extremely challenging to avoid all forms of media as Black people. We want to start our healing processes through forgiving those that trespass against us. It is hard to do when we all can read and see the continual killing of Black people, the lack of justice for those lives lost and the absence of concern for Black people overall.

- I think we need to express how saddened we were to not see a message from leadership, how there's been no space provided for Black faculty and staff to get together to process how we are feeling before we jump into supporting students, there needs to be systemic change and a commitment to this as much as we saw communication about COVID-19 and us being number 1 in the state for Performance based metrics.

- I really feel that USF perpetuates racism by not holding faculty and staff accountable when a person (Black or another minority group) is treated in a negative way because the white faculty or staff member knows that they have white privilege and will not get in trouble for using it.

The awareness is troublesome for me because I know that my white counterparts do not see me as equal in their eyes, but only as a servant to get their job completed. Keeping silent means you agree with what happens on the USF campus and are not willing to change the status quo. I feel like I come to work under a group of buddy, buddy systems when we have staff meetings - whites on one side and Black people on the other. When we have outings, the same thing happens, even when I have tried to change my spots. The white employees will come into the meeting and just move to the other side. They show you, you are not important and they are not afraid to do so.

- My thoughts are that the message in response to this, not just national but global situation, from the university president, is very difficult to locate unless you're really hunting for it on the USF website (prior to Tuesday, June 2, 2020). It is a good, strong message but it is buried in the website. I would like to see this statement made more prominent on the USF homepage, or at the very least on the USF News homepage because it is happening right now, it is news, and it impacts all of our students, faculty, staff, administrators, and everyone on this campus. If we truly care, we will be open, prominent, and transparent in such messaging.

That's part 1 for what we need to do at a bare minimum. We should follow this up, again at a minimum, with a statement from a university official on camera (as the university did for our campus with COVID-19 updates) expressing the thoughts of the university on this in that same space where it can be easily found.

Action items: Please refer to the unified message from a coalition of Black Faculty and Staff leadership from around the USF System titled "Call to Action—USF Black Employees 2020." The unified message contains the action items that have been shared with the USF administration to create lasting, positive and impactful changes.

In closing, I encourage you to review the various statements that have been shared by the members of USF leadership, especially the one from Dr. Charles "Charly" Lockwood—Senior Vice President, USF Health and Dean for USF Health Morsani College of Medicine. We cannot be afraid to say the word "Black". We cannot act as if by ignoring what is going on, you will not be affected. We must not allow our fear to consume us and prevents us from supporting/fighting for justice and positive changes. The [retired] USF President, Steven Currall's message states: "I believe we must support and care for each other during times like these and not forget that each of us is empowered to stand up to injustice whenever and wherever it occurs." We must also remember that we have to continuously fight against injustice every day because we cannot simply wait for another horrible video of a Black person suffering to feel motivation for action! While the Black community is asked to forgive another miscarriage of justice, we should not have to suffer any more man-made atrocities. We cannot walk alone in creating positive and lasting systemic changes!

Stay safe, remain in good health, find ways to remain positive and support each other.

6

One Community for Social Justice in the Spirit of Love
Vincent Adejumo

Historically Patrolled

It was once said that there is no "Community" without "Unity". As it pertains to African Americans, this statement is not only gospel, but it also has been essential for their survival in America. It was only through unity that enslaved Africans in America were able to not only survive, but thrive in the immediate aftermath of the civil war despite entrenched obstacles. Obstacles they faced were traumatic terrorism in the form of the Klu Klux Klan, grandfather voting clauses, share cropping, menial education centers, and Jim Crow Laws.

The ability of the formally enslaved Africans to overcome those obstacles in the aftermath of the civil war is nothing short of astonishing since the basic function for which Africans were transported to America was for the sole purpose to serve as a footstool for white supremacy. Within this context, the formally enslaved did not have any agency of their own and were not only treated as property, but also were defined as such within the U.S. constitution and in state and local ordinances. With such forceful factors at the forefront of the now newly minted African Americans, the idea of unity over the years has proven to become elusive.

The basis of elusiveness begins with the idea of former enslavers utilizing the criminal justice system to assert their dominance over African Americans. The power base of using the criminal justice system as a force of dominance has its foundations in the "slave patrols" that were started in South Carolina in the early 1700's and subsequently became prevalent in slave-holding states. The patrols were constructed of all white male volunteers with an agenda to use vigilante tactics to enforce slave codes and black codes. The slave patrols became more prominent in every region of America when the Fugitive Slave laws of 1793 and 1850 were passed which allowed them to hunt the enslaved who had escaped. Once captured, they were either returned to their master and/or sold back into slavery.

The spirit of these patrols set the tone for African Americans in future generations to constantly be under surveillance by the state and plant the seeds for discord within the community. The seeds of discord would further be defined in negative stereotypical depictions of African Americans by politicians, producers of news media, and producers of popular culture that reinforced the idea that they are inferior. Depictions such as the Jezebel, Brute, Mammy, Uncle Tom, Pickaninny and Sambo continue to be perpetrated. These stereotypical depictions not only reinforced the white supremacist ideals of African Americans to whites, but also to African Americans themselves in the form of internalized racism.

Revolutions within the community over several decades such as "Respectability politics", "Back to Africa", "Civil Rights", and "Black Power" have served to expose internalized racism and rejuvenate cultural pride and unity. However, as it stands in this contemporary era, "Black Culture" is not a readily defined subculture as it was when Black cultural revolutions were taking place in their respective time periods. The non-definition of "Black Culture" in this current era has thus allowed there to be no unity in the community. Gone are the days of asking your neighbor for a cup of sugar. Gone are the days of asking your neighbor to feed the dog while you are on vacation. Gone are days in which you could trust public school officials to effectively discipline your children. Gone are the days in which the process for constructing a wholistic family included dating, then marriage, then children.

What is termed as "traditional values" in this era is looked upon by a large contingent in the African American community as being "toxic" or "privileged". Alas, the African American community is further divided along antiquated lines such as gender, sexuality, class, and nationality. These antiquated lines most often are glaring on social media platforms in which each subgroup within the community express their personal experiences. Experiences that are born out of bearing the weight of white supremacy but manifest itself into a constant barrage of unproductive banter that further drives a stake in the antiquated lines. From Black men and Black women pontificating about love and respect to first- and second-generation Blacks from foreign countries bantering with native born African Americans about limited political and social capital, the divisiveness has widened each year with the advancement of social media.

Divisions Remain

While the divisions remain, the system of white supremacy continues to force its will on the African American community. This enforcement is manifested by a widening economic gap between African Americans and whites. The widening economic gap not only stems from the vestiges of enslavement, it is also spurred on by a society that does not value diversity, inclusion, or belonging but instead values the same old status quo. Specifically, the status quo of white males as the ultimate enforcer, whether it be in the corporate boardrooms, the university meeting rooms, or the political backrooms. With the advent of constant surveillance by law enforcement, discrimination from equal pay, and burgeoning divisions within the community, it is no wonder that various factions emerged pertaining to social justice work that is specific for African Americans.

These divisions began to rear its head, first with the killing of Trayvon Martin in 2012 by George Zimmerman. The murder of Martin and the subsequent acquittal of George Zimmerman in part due to the Stand your Ground Laws of Florida provided the spark for two main social justice groups to become the prominent face of social justice for Blacks in America: Dream Defenders and Black Lives Matter. In its initial iteration, Dream Defenders fashioned itself as a Civil Rights group that was interested not only in addressing police brutality, but also focusing on larger issues that affect African Americans such as the school to prison pipeline system, public housing, and Stand Your Ground Laws primarily in the state of Florida.

Dream Defenders also views itself as having a socialist political ideology that is against capitalism and especially "Black capitalism". Dream Defenders is also an advocate for Black feminist ideals and international resistance to issues of oppression, for example, in Palestine and Mexico. Throughout 2012 and 2013, Dream Defenders gained international attention due to protesting the Stand Your ground laws at the capitol steps of Florida and proposed policies to end them.

Black Lives Matter, on the other hand, started off as a #Hashtag on social media. The hashtag was created by Opal Tometti, Alicia Garza, Patrisse Cullors to garner attention to George Zimmerman's acquittal after killing Trayvon Martin. After Mike Brown's death in 2014, the three women organized to form the #Hashtag movement into an organization. Much like Dream Defenders, the Black Lives Matter movement also concerned itself with Stand Your Ground laws and the promotion of Black feminism. What propelled Black Lives Matter to international prominence was their ability to organize protests not only all over the United States, but also in places such as the United Kingdom and France.

The Black Lives Matter Network also was a major factor politically in that the organized protest and constant advocacy of police departments across the country resulted in them incorporating body cameras into their budget. Election seasons of

2014, 2016, 2018, and 2020 forced candidates for local positions up to the presidency of the United States to contend with the idea that "Black Lives Matter" and address how to communicate to their political bases whether they were for or against the idea of "Black lives mattering".

To that end, Black Lives Matter and Dream Defenders were both instrumental in spotlighting the disparities in the prison population between whites and Blacks. As of 2021, although African Americans make up 13% of the United States overall population, they accounted for nearly 40% of the inmate prison population. Both movements have also addressed the now 35+ billion-dollar spending on the so called "War on Drugs" legislation that has also played a role in the increase incarceration of African Americans today compared to the 1980's. Both groups addressing the War on Drugs spending and Stand Your Ground laws are a direct challenge to the system of white supremacy. A system that capitalizes on the displacement of African Americans and specifically of African American men which in turn results in the destabilization of the community. While there is a long history of African American males being targeted for violence in the United States by vigilantes and state sponsored law enforcement, the narrative within the Black Lives Matter network and to an extent Dream Defenders has been reversed.

Reversed from highlighting the vulnerability of unarmed Black males in the presence of the police to one that over exaggerates "Black male patriarchy" and more specifically intimate partner violence. For example, Dream Defenders on their official website states that "Today, the leading cause of death for Black women ages 18-34 is death at the hands of her partner. 1 in 3 women are raped. On top of this, Black women are the fastest growing prison population. Women face violence not only at the hands of the state but also in our communities."[1]

Unfortunately, each statement within this paragraph can be disputed with studies and research from official government outlets. For example, according to the Center for Disease and Control, the top three leading causes of death for Black women were unintentional injuries, cancer, and heart disease.[2] The Center for Disease and Control also states that 1 in 5 Black women or 22% have experienced rape at some point in their lifetime.[3] And according to the Bureau of Justice Statistics and Buchholz, the

---

[1] https://dreamdefenders.org/ideology/
[2] https://www.cdc.gov/women/lcod/2017/nonhispanic-black/index.htm
[3] https://www.cdc.gov/violenceprevention/pdf/nisvs_executive_summary-a.pdf

incarceration rate of Black women in state and federal prison has decreased from the mid-1990s to 2020.[4]

So, while the notion that Black women face violence at the hands of the state and within the community is true to an extent, it is vastly overstated when taking a closer look at official studies. Characterizing intimate partner violence propagated by Black men against Black women as an epidemic by Dream Defenders is Black misandry and plays into a long-standing white supremacist narrative that Black men are "super predators" that need to be tarred, feathered, and imprisoned.

Black Lives Matter also uses misandry in their rhetoric as it pertains to the structure of the Black family. On their "Who We Are" page of their official website, Black Lives Matter proclaimed "We disrupt the Western-prescribed nuclear family structure requirement by supporting each other as extended families and 'villages' that collectively care for one another, especially our children, to the degree that mothers, parents, and children are comfortable."[5]

The reason why this statement can also be classified as misandry is because it does not specifically define fathers within the family structure as it does mothers. It also reinforces another long held false characterization that Black fathers are not active in the lives of their children. Organizations and individuals who promote this idea of Black fathers being absent in their children's lives most often conflate marital rate statistics to absentee fathers. The lack of marriage in the African American community compared to other communities can have adverse effect in certain aspects of day-to-day life, most prominently in wealth building. However, a person that is not present in the household does not mean they are not active in their child's life.

To support this point, a study by the Center for Disease and Control found that "Black fathers (70%) were most likely to have bathed, dressed, diapered, or helped their children use the toilet every day compared with white (60%) and Hispanic fathers (45%)."[6] The CDC also found in the same study that "[a] higher percentage of Black fathers aged 15–44 (27%) took their children to or from activities every day compared with white fathers (20%)." These statistics exemplify the importance that

---

[4] https://www.statista.com/chart/18376/us-incarceration-rates-by-sex-and-race-ethnic-origin/

[5] https://www.aol.com/news/black-lives-matter-removes-language-185621063.html

[6] https://www.fatherhood.gov/dadtalk-blog/responsible-fatherhood-its-more-common-you-might-think

Black fathers play in the lives of their children. Black Lives Matter as an organization gaining recognition in part due to unarmed Black men getting killed by police and vigilantes while simultaneously devaluing the lives of Black men by not including them in their conception of family structure is hypocritical and dishonest.

Family Love in Justice

In America, family and familial ties are the basis for the most important aspects of life. Education, wealth generation, ethics, and social wellbeing all have ties in one way or another to the stability of family. For social justice as it pertains to the African Americans to truly be effective, universal agape love must be the center of all interaction and understanding in each sub-culture and intersection of the Black community. The pitting of one sub-group against another within the community is counterproductive and, in the end, serves to benefit the white supremacist enemy that has been present since the founding of this country. Fighting for social justice on behalf of African Americans must be streamlined into clear goals for the group as other minorities in this country have done.

For example, Asian Americans were able to advocate for social justice of their group by masterfully organizing each sub-culture in their community and by building partnerships with allies that had their best interest at heart pertaining to anti-Asian hate initiatives in the wake of the Coronavirus pandemic. In May of 2021, President Joe Biden signed a federal anti-Asian hate bill into law which allows the Department of Justice to expedite investigations of hate crimes directed towards Asian-Americans and provides financial resources in the form of grants to prevent and respond to hate crimes. Asian Americans were able to utilize their social capital to mobilize their community and force President Biden to sign the legislation into law.

Within the context of social justice, the African American community must look beyond pegging social justice simply as a criminal justice issue. The goal of social justice as it pertains to African Americans should be equity, not equality. Equity is defined as being fair and impartial. The struggle that African Americans have faced post slavery in America has consistently been for fair access to resources and to be judged impartially in every aspect of society.

Those who advocate for social justice either as an African American or on behalf of African Americans as an ally must ground their advocacy in equitable results. Love and culture as the foundation of social justice that stresses equity is the most effective solution moving forward for African Americans. Social justice advocates should take great care in ensuring that this ideology is implemented effectively and minimize as much as possible the antagonizing of sub-groups within the Black community. Failing to do so will manifest in disunity in the community and, thus, render the move towards tangible solutions that result in equitable results lost for generations.

Works Cited

Bernstein, Brittany. (2020, September 21). *Black Lives Matter Removes Language about Disrupting the Nuclear Family from Website*. Click here to refresh. https://www.aol.com/news/black-lives-matter-removes-language-185621063.html.

Buchholz, K., & Richter, F. (2021, February 19). *Infographic: Black Incarceration Rates Are Dropping in the U.S.* Statista Infographics. https://www.statista.com/chart/18376/us-incarceration-rates-by-sex-and-race-ethnic-origin/.

Black, M.C., Basile, K.C., Breiding, M.J., Smith, S.G., Walters, M.L., Merrick, M.T., Chen, J., & Stevens, M.R. (2011). The National Intimate Partner and Sexual Violence Survey (NISVS): 2010 Summary Report. Atlanta, GA: National Center for Injury Prevention and Control, Centers for Disease Control and Prevention. https://www.cdc.gov/violenceprevention/pdf/nisvs_executive_summary-a.pdf

Centers for Disease Control and Prevention. (2019, November 20). *Leading Causes of Death-Non-Hispanic black Females - United States, 2017*. Centers for Disease Control and Prevention. https://www.cdc.gov/women/lcod/2017/nonhispanic-black/index.htm.

Ideology. Dream Defenders. (n.d.). https://dreamdefenders.org/ideology/.

National Responsible Fatherhood Clearinghouse. (n.d.). *Responsible Fatherhood. It's more common than you might think*. Fatherhood.gov. https://www.fatherhood.gov/dadtalk-blog/responsible-fatherhood-its-more-common-you-might-think.

7
Keep the Faith: Black Men and the Spirit of Love
Katurah Jenkins-Hall, Ph.D.

Introduction

What an honor it is to be allowed to share in *any* healing space to which I am invited. I am a Healer. What a special honor it is to be invited to an affinity space of all Black men, for which my brothers and colleagues trust me completely to be a source of healing even as they and others present themselves vulnerable. And so, I enter the virtual sacred space of the Emotional Freedom Train(ing) and Community Healing through Activist Transformation … and also into this writing space prayerfully, as one who knows her Creator, assertively but gently, as one who heals with words, nondefensively as one who listens to learn, and respectfully, as the mother, sister, lover, friend, human being who champions the survival of Black men as they/we negotiate the dreadfully poisonous spaces of stereotypes, negative expectations, fractured relationships, abuse, neglect, stress, unemployment, targeted violence, discrimination, racism, white supremacy domination, and gender bias. List your poisons. My brothers, I have an idea of the skin you are in, though your body and minds were created and socialized differently than mine. And because our thinking and being have been socially constructed, our experiences and perspectives are different. Yet, pain is genderless, colorless, and does not discriminate. And, though we wear it differently, sometimes glaringly, oft times subtly—I see your pain. And, when I don't, your own body keeps the score.

Yet, you welcome me like a beautiful African Queen and I feel safe in the cocoon of your affirmations. I have faith in your ability to survive, and enough faith to love you into health and wellness. With my words, I breathe a life of faith and hope, and the spirit of love. For it is by faith and love that we find our greatest healing.

Keep the Faith

Faith is the 7th Principle of Kwanzaa. A common definition of faith is confidence or trust in a person or thing. According to Kwanzaa principles, Faith means to believe with all our hearts in our people, our parents, our teachers, our leaders, and the righteousness and victory of our struggle.

For those who value the sacred text found in the book of Hebrews Chapter 11, faith is the assumption of things hoped for and the evidence of things not yet seen. If you can see it, it is not faith. We cannot yet see the victory of our struggle, and it is painful when we lose heart as victory seems like an elusive concept within the perpetual struggles for respect, basic human rights, and equity for Black men. However, if you know it and see it in your spirit, and you understand it is not for now, but for a future time; if you are able to believe forthrightly, and walk righteously in what you know is coming, then you are walking and living by faith. Whether your faith is in the wisdom of the ancestors, the prayers of your fore- parents, or the God who created you, faith is a powerful manifestation of our future hopes and dreams. So, I implore you to keep the faith!

Perhaps more important than faith, which necessarily looks towards future hope, is love, which is now and for eternity. After heaven and earth have passed away, three things will remain (1 Corinthians 13): Faith, Hope, and Love. And the greatest of these is love. There are many ways of defining love.

- The love of God (Creator or Spirit), described in Greek as Agape, often described as unconditional love, the highest form of love that is patient, kind, unselfish, enduring.

- The love of Self, not in the extremes of thinking more highly of yourself than you should, but in understanding that you are fearfully and wonderfully made by the Creator as one of his special masterpieces.

- The love of Community—Ubuntu—in African philosophy that we cannot love deeply or completely without understanding our relationship with and interdependence in relationship with others in community—I am because you are.

- Love of Brother—Philia, a Greek description of love between brothers or friends in which your attention is on common goals, common interests, common gifts, common heritage, such that you minimize the differences that divide you.

- Love of Partner—Eros, a Greek description that describes romantic/sexual attraction where your entire focus is on the object of the one you love. It is passionate love that comes from physical affection.

- Love of Progeny—Storge, a Greek description of liking someone through the fondness of familiarity for example, family love.

- Ma'at—an ancient Kemetic (Egyptian) concept, comprised on principals of truth, justice, harmony, reciprocity, balance, which results in ultimate peace in the afterlife.

Do you have the courage to Love? For God has not given us the Spirit of fear, but of power, love and a sound mind. In fact, wisdom teaches us that "Perfect" love casts out fear. Conversely, we also know that we hate what we fear. Could fear be the underlying reason for the hate that is so easily bestowed upon Black people, and particularly, Black men?

I submit to you that the answer to some of our healing is the right spirit of love between human beings who fear each other. Perhaps one of our greatest areas of historical challenge and pain is the relationship between Black men and women. We don't love each other unconditionally. Instead, we judge each other's way of being by standards we have learned within the context of white supremacy. In such an atmosphere, we compete with each other; we invalidate each other; we find no common goals or fondness for each other; and there is little truth, justice, harmony, reciprocity or balance between us. In fact, we adhere to the notions of Eros (erotic love) based on physical attraction based on Eurocentric ideals and materialism, based on the ability to simulate wealth.

In the African tradition of Ma'at (according to the book, *Complementarity: Thoughts for African Warrior Couples* by M. Baruti), African-centered relationships are better served by practicing what Baruti refers to as "Complementarity." Complementarity is a core principle of Ma'at in which two differently qualified, yet intimately interacting individuals work towards a wholistic balance.

According to Baruti, complementarity is central to all African relationships. The choice of mates boils down to who will stand beside you as you both go about the business of helping to build a new powerful African world reality. Those with fierce intent as change agents must have what he refers to as a "warrior spirit." A warrior spirit must be matched with a complementary warrior spirit, otherwise neither spirit will be satisfied. Warriors settling for mates who choose not to be "African" (African-centered) become easier targets for seduction out of their African-centered vision for a more equitable world.

Purpose must rule over passion if we are to be satisfied in sustaining relationships. Therefore, if you are passionately about the business of doing your work, your study, your community involvement, your communicating; and attending to the needs of our people as a nation, your complement will be there doing the same things.

Although Baruti's work is about heterosexual relationships among Black people any relationship grounded in the Western conceptions love do not work for "warriors" who join forces as complements. In fact, According to Baruti, sex should be considered as only a secondary ingredient in any solid dynamic African-centered complementary relationship between emotionally mature partners.

Western relationships are marked with aggression, violence, betrayal, and division. All illusions of peaceful, loving, complementarity brought on by romance is short-lived. What we know as powerful romance provides a moment of peace within which individuals can safely sexually ravage each other. Slow courtship is preferred to speedy romance in complementarity relationships. Love is built overtime. ***Shared vision (not the feeling of love) keeps complementary relationships on track.***

Complementarity also means that acts of sex are not abusive, selfish, or quantitative. They are not destructive, domineering, or submissive. African sexuality does not condone promiscuity or infidelity. It does not cater to insatiable sexual appetites. Sex is not the most important thing in a marriage between complements. When sex occurs it is in fact, a spiritual act.

Notice my language shifted to "African" from "Black."

The year 2019 marked 400 years since the first enslaved Africans arrived on U.S. shores in British ships. In commemoration, there was a movement/pilgrimage all last year of Black Americans towards West African shores. It was called, "The year of the great return ..." God blessed me and a group of friends from all over the U.S. to return with a purpose in mind. As we visited the Cape Coast "Slave Castle" in Ghana, Africa, we witnessed firsthand the underground dungeons, a space of intentional terror, death, and darkness to hold enslaved Africans against their will. This imposing fortress was often the last memory enslaved Africans had of their homeland before being shipped off across the Atlantic, as this signified the beginning of their journey to America and other unknown shores. This was but a prelude to the imposing fortresses of white supremacy domination that would be faced within the context of the middle passage, the peculiar institution of slavery, the Jim Crow laws, the mass incarceration of Black men, and the blatant death threats of living while African in America.

As we visited these so-called "slave-castles," our intent was to pay homage and express gratitude to our ancestors, so we wore white to symbolize our reverence and their righteousness, and the undeniable eternality of our bonds. Walking through the Door of No Return, I whispered to my great, great-grandmother Dietta Sheffield, who was sold on an auction block in Virginia around 1865 "we've returned grandmama! We represent African families from all across America, who exited these doors ... And, on your behalf, and because you could not ... we returned!"

We, all over the world, are a brilliant, beautiful, warm, compassionate, hardworking, creative, emotionally expressive, passionate, spirit-filled people and We are all here! Men and women, standing with love and faith until we are recognized as a people of strength.

Black men, we are more than just a color, we are African people of incredible power to survive, unshakable faith to believe and endure, and extravagant love to love our Creator, ourselves, our partners, our families, and our communities with purpose and on purpose. Our freedom cannot be taken by shackles, prison bars, whips, chains, dogs, or water hoses. Freedom is a state of mind!!

We've come this far by faith! I wish you the Spirit of Love for the days ahead!!

Part II
Killing Rage: Ending Racism
Long Time Struggle for Freedom

In counter-hegemonic race talk I testify in this writing—bear witness to the reality that our many cultures can be remade, that this nation can be transformed, that we can resist racism and in the act of resistance recover ourselves and be renewed.

bell hooks, *Killing Rage: Ending Racism* (1995)

The circumstances which I am about to narrate, and which gave rise to this fearful tempest of passion, are not singular nor isolated in slave life, but are common in every slaveholding community in which I have lived. They are incidental to the relation of master and slave, and exist in all sections of slaveholding countries.

Frederick Douglass, *My Bondage and My Freedom* (1855)

… I am not tragically colored. There is no great sorrow damned up in my soul, nor lurking behind my eyes. I do not mind at all. I do not belong to the sobbing school of Negrohood….

Zora Neale Hurston, "How It Feels to Be Colored Me" (1926)

8
Surviving the Trauma of Racism: Teaching and Writing for Self-Recovery
Gary L. Lemons

For those of us who write, it is necessary to scrutinize not only the truth of what we speak, but the truth of that language by which we speak. For others, it is to share and spread also those words that are meaningful to us. But primarily, it is necessary to teach by living and speaking those truths which we believe and know beyond understanding. Because in this way alone we can survive, by taking part in a process of life that is creative and continuing, that is growth.

Audre Lorde, *Sister Outsider* (1984)

Even if black men do not agree with the whole of black feminists' analysis of sexism in the black community, we are still obligated to listen sensitively to black feminists if we expect to hold the community together in the struggle for freedom. There will be no freedom for any one of us until all of us are free.

James H. Cone, *My Soul Looks Back* (1986)

Living to Write, Speak, and Teach the Truth

It has taken years for me to comprehend that writing while Black must be about strategically connecting myself with *Blackness* in an African American circumstantial framework. Writing about what it *means* to be Black in the U.S. is about having to confront the dehumanizing history of the constitutionalized representation of white supremacy. Unequivocally, I have come to realize that writing about Blackness in struggle against the inhumanity of white supremacy means that my words for liberation of the oppressed must be transgressive. Writing to transgress boundaries of racist separatism, I have found the words of Audre Lorde critically insightful when she says, "[I]t is necessary to scrutinize not only the truth of what we speak, but the truth of that language by which we speak" (*Sister Outsider*, 43). For me, these words have been self-liberating in my personal and professional life.

As a young Black boy growing up in the South during the Black Power movement in the 1960s, in the "light" of integrated schooling with white teachers and students, however, I was never taught anything about social justice reforms and the histories of

Black liberation in struggle against white supremacy. As segregated schooling ended in my hometown of Hot Springs, Arkansas in 1968—as Black kids we were then educated and normalized to believe integrated schooling was an anti-racist high goal achievement. Yet, at the same time during this experience, I never had one class taught by a Black teacher in high school.

As I have written in the past, even in my college experiences as an "English" major (from undergraduate through graduate school in a PWI context), I never had a course taught by a BIPOC professor. From my time in undergraduate school through my labor as a doctoral student trained as an English major in all PWIs (Predominately White Institutions), in all my literature courses (taught by white male and female professors), I spoke and wrote papers in ways that intentionally affirmed my assimilationist thinking passing as white. Trained to speak and write in "proper" English, I consistently crossed every "t" and dotted every "i". I continually checked my voice and papers, over and over again, to make sure they adhered to correct, historically white standards of grammar and sentence structure. I was trained always to speak and write in "complete sentences". In hindsight, speaking and writing this way meant hiding any *Black*-identifiable self-expression. Hiding it signified my having passed the white test of intellectual power. Having been colonized to believe that whiteness was the path to my success as student and potential scholar, I accepted my Black self-erasure. For me, assimilation into white academia via entrance into "English" departments was only about studying the history of British and American literature by white *male* writers. As I have written many times, I was the only Black/student of color in my English courses I took during the mid-1970s to the early 1990s. In truth, as dark as my skin is, I was actually the *invisible* Black male student.

In hindsight, in a traditional PWI context I felt no need to question my willingness to erase my racial identity. I passed all of my English classes with at least a "B" grade or higher. Yet today, even as I marvel at my unwavering tenacity to speak, write, and teach in resistance to anti-Black racism, I remember the lyrics from the Black gospel song "How I Got Over" (originally recorded by Clara Ward in 1951). In truth, even to this day I say to myself, "You know that my soul looks back and wonders, how I got over?" Fundamentally, the answer to this question is much larger than my personal experience. In the longstanding Black struggle against racism in the U.S., the answer has to do with the historical truth of Black survival in the face of white supremacy. Even in the supposed "progress" associated with racially integrated schooling in the U.S., Black history remains a controversial subject related to teaching anti-racist consciousness and activism. In 2021, the governor of Florida acted to ban the teaching of "critical race theory" in state supported schools.

In my progress toward self-recovery—coming to own my identity as a pro-womanist Black male writer, scholar, and professor of African American literature and biblical studies—I comprehend the profound, soulful implications of looking back over my life experiences and addressing the dehumanizing, traumatic effects of anti-Black racism in spoken-word:

"Captured, Bought, and Sold Out"

I am the aftermath of slavery, the product of racism.

Why did it take me so long to realize this "ism"?

It was in me even before I was born.

Nobody told me my history; I would have been a scorn?

"Is this a complaint?"

If it is will you put in a constraint?

I am just tired of being sad because I don't know who I am.

I am the aftermath of slavery, the product of racism.

Why did it take me so long to realize this "ism"?

It was in me even before I was born.

Nobody told me my history; I would have been a scorn?

"Is this a complaint?"

If it is will you put in a constraint?

I am just tired of being sad because I don't know who I am.

What you mean? Don't you know your name is Sam?

Sam—the one who "step and fetch it."

That's what I thought. There's no problem, I knew I had been bought.

I was always known as "black" chattel to be purchased by the highest bidder.

You better try to pass the test, just like the rest.

They know how to get over.

Man, you ain't nothin' but a push-over.

Give it up. Give up what?

You know what I'm talking about—just take the cut.

Why you still complainin'? Don't you see how much it's rainin'?

You know you a "black" fool. Gone ahead and get in the pool.

You drownin' with all this here clownin'.

Man, you need to act the part to play the part.

What part you talkin' 'bout? The part that put you out.

Outside the norm that's where you belong.

I know man—ain't got a pot to piss in.

That's what they all said back then.

 But back "then" is now. I feel like we come to the en'.

You ain't got know mo' hope? Man, I just need some dope.

That's how you keep makin' it through the pain?

I just told you I can't take no mo' rain.

This is hell! Welcome Man, you just fell.

I always been down. You just figured out, you still on the groun'?

The game ain't over yet; you still got to take my bet.

How I'm gonna win when I'm all wet.

Man, you just keep cryin'. Why don't you start tryin'?

What you mean? Keep tryin' to get free?

I have no idea who I want to be. They took my name from me.

You can come up with another name of your own that ain't "Sam."

You telling the truth? You need to build a dam.

That will keep the rain of the pain out.

Brother, you givin' me the idea that I don't have to pout?

That's right! Get up and begin the fight to live right.

I thought you wus tellin' me to get up and fight them. No Man, you must fight for Him.

Who "Him?" Brother I talkin' 'bout the ONE who made you long time ago.

The One who made you before you start callin' yourself a "Negro".

You mean to tell me that I matter to Him. Yeah, you never heard that hymn?

Oh, you mean the one "How I Got Over?"

That's the one I'm talking 'bout without a doubt.

That means I got to look back from the beginning to know who He is.

That's exactly right. From that point, you can begin yo' fight.

He didn't make you to take you out in that chain.

He made you to come from behind to take up the gain.

You mean I get to make a lot of money? You really think money is the honey?

Let's get it straight; He wants to take you to the land of milk and honey—not money.

There's a new land, and it ain't in the North. You ran there to get away from them.

But guess what. What? They in the South and in the North too.

Man, all this land was created by Him for all of you.

Who "you?" You always asking questions, but you not listen' to my directions.

I told you to look back to the beginnin'. There you will find that He made everybody equal.

It ain't got nothin' to do with how much money you can make; all that shit is fake.

He's the ONE who loved you so much that He died for all of us called "human beings".

You know what, it's time for you to put on the rings.

What rings you talkin' 'bout? Put on the rings of freedom.

They will be the symbol of the end of slavery. Recover all that wus lost—your mind, body, and soul. The day is comin' when the rain will come to purify, so that we can begin to glorify.

They can put "In God We Trust" on every bill they create to get a mate.

But be sure of one thing—it won't do away with the hate.

I put on one ring, but it's kinda tight and it sting.

It won't fit until you lose the weight. Help them get rid of all their hate.

But I thought "white" was always right—bein' "black" mean get back. Man, you need to take a flight.

Go where our people see the freedom light.

There they don't plant and pick cotton.

We know its rotten.

Right brother, we don't like cotton in the 'hood.

Now, I startin' to understand what I should.

Yeah, you really need to begin to erase that brand. I know I been branded, but I'm beginnin' to see my "Blackness". Yeah Man, it's all about its exactness. Now live to be FREE! Amen

And the Truth Shall Set Us Free

bell hooks and Alice Walker underscore Dr. King's idea that the soul and life of a community created in love begins with the inner power of survival for self-recovery. In "Saving the Life that is Your Own: The Importance of Models in the Artist's Life," Walker writes—

It is, in the end, the saving of lives that we writers are about. Whether we are 'minority' writers or 'majority.' It is simply in our power to do this.

We do it because we care…. We care because we know this: the *life we save is our own* (*In Search of Our Mothers' Gardens*, 14).

In the opening chapter of my pedagogical monograph *Caught Up in the Spirit! Teaching for Womanist Liberation* (2017), I write the following in a section titled "Writing to Free Myself to Teach"—

… as a [B]lack male having grown up in the South under the oppressive regimes of white supremacy and patriarchy—in coming to know the healing and self-transforming power of feminism envisioned by bell hooks and Alice Walker—I have become the womanist man I am today. In the process, I began a lifetime journey toward comprehending *and* accepting Alice Walker's definition of what it means to be a "womanist". For me, embracing her has moved me not only to accept my [B]lack identity, but also the complex identities of all persons— "*Regardless.*" While differences of race, gender, class, and sexuality have made a difference in how I see and relate to individuals I encounter in my personal and public life—being a womanist has taught me that I must speak and stand in alliance will all 'Folk(s)' who have been marginalized and/or treated inhumanely because of their difference(s). Having grown up as a [B]lack boy in a small town in the South, I internalized a stereotypical, myth-laden and classist idea of race bound-up in white supremacist, patriarchal, homophobic power.

As a dark-skin [B]lack male growing up during the 1960s in a working class African American family in the South, I learned some life-survival lessons about the interconnection between gender, race, and class. In the modern history of race relations in the South where I was born, racially integrated schooling did not actually happen until 1968. A decade before, then President Dwight Eisenhower had to send federal troops to desegregate Central High School to allow nine black students to enter it located in Little Rock, the state capital of Arkansas. I grew up in a racialized environment overtly marked by those (whites) who had and those ([B]lacks) who did not. In my hometown, it was starkly clear that whites generally possessed economic power. While there existed no stereotypical train tracks [separating] whites from [B]lacks in my town, the visual racial divide was clear to all.

There were no other "colored" folk (read Asian, Latina/o, and or "Native" American) to complicate the [B]lack/white racial binary and the entrenched class politics it represented. If there were working class and/or poor whites in town, they were overtly visible. However, from what I observed growing up in a racially segregated environment, the privilege of white skin afforded individuals who possessed it access to the best jobs, housing, education, health care, social, and economic services. Class was also racialized through gender. Blacks represented the lower "service" class folks—as maids, porters, and cooks. If a [B]lack middle class existed, it was clearly not visible (1-2).

I have accepted writing about freedom for the oppressed as a life-calling. I write to live. This is my sentence for life. In the course of my scholarly and pedagogical journey writing article after article, chapter after chapter, book after book continues to be my path to self-recovery. In these writings, I have included sentence after sentence to document my survival as a Black male in the U.S.—holistically in mind, body, and soul. Writing to survive systemic and institutionalized oppression, particularly related to experiences of it historically in the lives of Black folks, has been self-liberating. At the same time, I honestly admit that writing in opposition to the institutionalization of racism has not been easy. However, as I have stated, writing about the invisibility of my Blackness in the evolution of my professional career would lead me to a path of self-recovery. At the same time, I have realized that fear of teaching about the history *and* herstory of anti-Black racism is an off-track, distracting detour. My practice of anti-racist pedagogy challenges me to hold onto what I had been *called* to do—believing in the life-changing power of anti-oppressive "chat" for "CHAT" (Community Healing through Activist Transformation), in and outside the college classroom.

In "The Transformation of Silence into Language and Action," one of the most compelling chapters in *Sister Outsider*, Audre Lorde asks several provocative questions: 'What are the words you do not yet have? What do you need to say? What are the tyrannies you swallow day by day and attempt to make your own, until you will sicken and die of them, still in silence?" (41). Having willfully taken on the task of writing for life in love of social justice for the oppressed—I need liberatory and transformative words that move me and my students from silence to voice. For without them, my support for activist alliance building in resistance to oppression and domination would remain bound up in the deadly trap of silence. I am determined to remain sentenced for life—writing in the freedom of self-recovery for the oppressed.

Deeply inspired by Lorde's writings in *Sister Outsider* (1984), I would create the title of my first book as a play on her book's title. Pointedly, it would be the personal reflections she documents in *Sister Outsider* that would compel me in *Black Male Outsider, a Memoir: Teaching as a Pro-Feminist Man* (2008) to be openly vulnerable in opposition to hetero-masculinist notions of manhood—especially as a Black man. In "The Transformation of Silence into Language and Action," Lorde begins writing about her feelings having to deal with breast cancer and that there "was a 60 to 80 percent change that the tumor was malignant." Contemplating the life-threatening implications of it the possible outcomes—even though "[t]he surgery was completed, and the growth was benign"—she says:

> I was forced to look upon myself with my living with a harsh and urgent clarity that has left me still shaken but much stronger … Some of what I experienced during that time has helped elucidate for me much of what I feel concerning the transformation of silence into language and action.
>
> In becoming forcibly and essentially aware of my mortality, and of what I wished and wanted for my life, however short it might be, priorities and omissions became strongly etched in a merciless light, and what I most regretted were my silences. Of what had I *ever* been afraid? To question or to speak as I believed could have meant pain, or death. But we all hurt in so many different ways, all the time, and pain will either change or end. Death, on the other hand, is the final silence … And I began to recognize a source of power within that comes from the knowledge that while it is most desirable not to be afraid, learning to put fear into a perspective game me great strength … My silences had not protected me. Your silence will not protect you (40-41).

In hindsight, remembering Lorde's reflections about her having "most regretted" silences in regard to the possibility of death, I contemplate my own mental, emotional, and physical health. Particularly related to the traumatic, visual evidence of the death of George Floyd murdered by a white police officer on May 25, 2020 in Minneapolis, Minnesota—I speak prayer for my survival.

Confronting the deadening power of silence, Audre Lorde speaks truth to power as "we all hurt in so many different ways, all the time, and pain will either change or end. Death, on the other hand, is the final silence." Yet for all of us who witnessed Floyd's murder via mass media—"8 minutes and 46 seconds" would become the signifier for many who joined together to protest his death that would become the representation of the "transformation of silence." Every time I read Audre Lorde's poem "Litany for Survival," I contemplate what it means for Blacks in the U.S. to have survived the history and our ongoing struggle against racism. In the poem one repeated line stands out for me: "we were never meant to survive." Moreover, in the excerpt from the poem I include that follows (as reprinted on page 1924 in *The Norton Anthology of African American Literature*), it is clear that Lorde speaks truth to power, telling us that being "afraid" is not the emotional path to our freedom:

> ...when we are loved we are afraid
> love will vanish
> when we are alone we are afraid
> love will never return
> and when we speak we are afraid
> our words will not be heard
> nor welcomed
> but when we are silent
> we are still afraid
> So it is better to speak
> remembering
> we were never meant to survive.

These words have spoken to me over and over again. At the same time, from the first time I read this poem over two decades ago, the words "So it is better to speak" have continually challenged me to confront my fear of being a *Black man* in the U.S., founded upon the enslavement of African Black bodies. Time and time again, I have confronted ways I have felt "afraid" to express publicly feelings of emptiness coded in feelings of an absence of love for my humanity. There have been times that I have been "afraid" to speak out and write boldly in resistance to Anti-Black oppression. In truth, in a historical PWI context, I have felt many times that my "words will not be heard nor welcomed." I openly admit that even when I am "silent," I am "still afraid." As Audre Lorde speaks to me in her "Litany for Survival," even though "we were never meant to survive," it is *still* "better to speak." I must believe that Black lives still matter:

"Black Lives (Still) Matter"—In Spoken-Word(s)

See the writing on my sign—***BLACK LIVES MATTER!*** For real! Why? What makes a Black life so important to my life?

Hear me speak—*Black* lives didn't start out meaning anything valuable in these here "United States"—except as bodies to work the fields of the white master. The lack of Black lives today on the streets of America clearly makes little difference when Black bodies are being done away with so frequently—in 8 minutes and 46 seconds.

You have some questions for me? Yes! Why does that matter? Why must we always, hear about it? But why only 28 days out of the year to celebrate *Black* survival?

Hear me speak—*color* makes a critical difference when it comes to my *Black* body. *I* see *Black* bodies all the time, but who really cares about the color of my skin. Our folks say, "Black don't crack." This is how we made it over. But when you shoot at me, I do crack. When I drink poisoned water for years, my body don't crack. Being *Black* cost the price of my body. It ain't as cheap as you think. Asked the *KKK* if **Black Lives Matter** really matter. Why should anybody love me? The One who die on the cross for men and you really was colored. You say, "He was not Black." You vying for a seat at the top of the racial ladder. It's still all about white supremacy. And you say, "Black don't crack?" Really? Everybody knows, you colored folks know how to get over. You sing, dance, throw footballs, catch 'em—live for 'em. You know how to dunk—all ya'll tall as Shaquille. Ya'll know how to cook—chitlins, pig fits, hog mawhs—what you complaining about. Keep eatin', keep drinkin', keep steppin'. Ya'll know how to work it.

I have some questions for you. Would you be willing to take a bullet for me? Be gunned down in the street? Run over on my bicycle because you were speeding down the road. You said you didn't see me. What do I need to do for you to see me? Change the color of my skin?

Is this *Matter* really worth discussing? What's the *Matter* you ask? I am **Matter!** I live, love, move, and have my being in this **black** body. That's what *matters.* Does that *matter* to you? Or do you think that what *matters* is all about how much money you can make off my **Black** body? Be honest—that what really *matters.*

Hear me speak—Every cell, muscle, and bone in my Black body is made up of divine *matter.* I was created out of the *matter* of the only ONE who really *Matters.* Because I *matter* to the Creator, it really doesn't *matter* what you think of me. I know one thing—I was born to *matter!* That's all that counts in this *matter.* You might think I'm making too much out of this *matter,* but I know that in my Creator's sight—*Black Lives Matter!*

Hear me speak—What you think of me may never change, but what the Creator imagined in me will never change. The One who created me first loved me. But in the end, you say: "All lives matter!" Really—even those lives of the oppressed you live to shatter? Remember that *ultimately, it was that Brother hung on the cross centuries ago that took the deadly hit for all of us—BIPOC and white-identified folks! However, don't forget that **BLACK LIVES (STILL) MATTER!***

"Where We Must Go from Here"

A Revolutionary Blueprint: *Killing Rage: Ending Racism*

In "Beloved Community: A World Without Racism," the final chapter of *Killing Rage: Ending Racism* (1995), bell hooks writes:

> Like all *beloved communities* we affirm our differences. It is this generous spirit of affirmation that gives us the courage to challenge one another, to work through misunderstandings, especially those that have to do with race and racism. In a *beloved community* solidarity and trust are grounded in profound commitment to a shared vision. Those of us who are always anti-racist long for a world in which everyone can form a *beloved community* where borders can be crossed and cultural hybridity celebrated. Anyone can begin to live in an anti-racist world. If that longing guides our vision and our actions, the new culture will be born and anti-racist communities of resistance will emerge everywhere. That is where we must go from here (272).

As she references "we" and "us" more than once, she unequivocally articulates that in "all *beloved communities*" there must be an "affirm[ation] of our differences." In this contextual lens, it means that the "we" she credits must be "[courageous enough] to challenge one another, to work through misunderstandings, especially those that have to do with race and racism." Thus, the "we" and the "us" hooks refers to must include all folk willing to engage what most likely will be complex, complicated, difficult, and challenging conversations about what it means for the "us" who are anti-racist—"always long[ing] to live in an anti-racist world." In other words, this means "we" must put our words into action crossing boundaries and embracing "cultural hybridity." In this celebratory movement toward uplifting joy for difference in mind, body, and soul—"Anyone can begin to live in an anti-racist world." bell hooks grounds this idea in Dr. Martin Luther King, Jr.'s vision of a world void of racism.

Living in an Anti-Racist World—"The Life We Save is Our Own"

While bell hooks' book *Killing Rage: Ending Racism* was published over two decades ago—considering the violent and literally deadening implications of racism and white supremacy in the U.S. in this contemporary moment—there remains the revolutionary need for activist demonstration and critical dialogue for social justice to end racism. In hooks' thoughtful insight into what it means to "live in an anti-racist world," she strategically connects the personal to the political. In line with Dr. King's revolutionary vision of a "beloved community" and the insightful comprehension of it as envisioned by hooks, I imagine its realization in the writers' voices in *Liberation for the Oppressed*. I believe their writings will stand the test of time as they collectively advocate anti-racist activism for social justice. The writings in this book act to interconnect the personal to political. They also show how all people committed to social justice can employ their professional work in community partnership for labor toward building a beloved community. Moreover, the individuals' *soul* works in this book not only expose the real deadly effects of racism, but they also call out the hurtful outcomes of sexism, classism, homophobia, and ableism interconnected to it. In solidarity, our words actively re-enforce what it means to write, to live, and to act for social justice. As Dr. King envisioned, "Our goal is to create a beloved community and this will require a qualitative change in our souls as well as a qualitative change in our lives" (www.quotetab.com).

Works Cited

hooks, bell. *Killing Rage: Ending Racism.* Henry Holt and Co., 1995

Lemons, Gary. *Black Male Outsider, a Memoir: Teaching as a Feminist Man.* State University of New York Press, 2008.

---. *Caught Up in the Spirit! Teaching for Womanist Liberation.* Nova Science Publishers, 2017.

Lorde, Audre. *Sister Outsider: Essays and Speeches.* Crossing Press, 1984.

---. "Litany for Survival." *The Norton Anthology of African American Literature,* edited by Henry Louis Gates, Jr. and Nellie Y. McKay, W.W. Norton & Co., 2004, p. 1923-24.

Walker, Alice. *In Search of Our Mothers' Gardens: Womanist Prose,* Harcourt Brace & Co., 1983.

9

A Call to End the Idealization of *Whiteness:*
The Assassination of Racist Assimilationism
Brittany Powell

I remember sitting in Professor James E. Tokely's "Civil Rights in the U.S." class when I first heard Nina Simone's "Four Women." As Tampa, Florida's first Black Poet Laureate, he had a way of stirring something inside my soul in each lecture. Although I was no stranger to Simone, I had somehow never heard this song during my aunt and uncle's late-night card games at their juke joint tucked off a backroad in rural Georgia. I was sitting in a lecture hall ready to take notes on the day's lecture, when I heard her earthy voice belt out, "My skin is black, my arms are long, my hair is wooly, my back is strong, strong enough to take the pain, inflicted again and again." I looked around to see if anyone was looking at me because it was apparent the Nina Simone was singing to me about me. That day was the start of a long journey of not only understanding my Blackness but truly desiring and being in love with my Blackness. Until recently, I could not articulate the change that has happened in me since that day, but almost twenty years later, I realize that was the day that I began rejecting the lie of anti-Blackness.

Like many other Black people, I thought that integration required a degree of assimilation. I believed that to integrate into white society, I had to assimilate culturally into white society and become as indistinguishable with members of the white community as I could. However, racial assimilation requires a denial of whom one is culturally while upholding the domination of white supremacy. Those inside white society or those who strive to achieve white societal norms are not charged with changing the damaging aspects of their culture. In her book *Killing Rage: Ending Racism* (1995), bell hooks begins by discussing Black rage and the detrimental effects of realizing that racial assimilation did not exempt wealthy and privileged Blacks from racism. The underhanded psychological damage of assimilation is to believe that one who racially assimilates is somehow different from those who do not. When people of color make these changes and then find out that their time spent "acquiescing to white power to achieve—assimilating, changing themselves, suppressing true feelings" is still met with exclusion and unequal treatments, they become enraged (hooks 27). This essay attempts to dispel the belief that racial assimilation is a tool to achieve racial equality and success. To racially dismantle white supremacy, BIPOC (Black Indigenous People of Color) must call into question the historical and contemporary practice of racial assimilationism conceptualized in the idealization of *whiteness*.

Black into White: The Key to Success?

There was a time when I believed that racial assimilation into whiteness was the key to success. I bought into the lie that as long as my culture, identity, and ethnicity were secondary, it would bring me some approval in a white supremacist society. The need to seek approval from white society is why I pity people like Candace Owens, the Hodge Twins, or any other Black conservative voice that is willing to sell out their own people to make money. They believe if they play the game correctly, then they will get rewarded. In the essay "Marketing Blackness" in *Killing Rage: Ending Racism* bell hooks describes these types of people as "black thinkers who have no commitment to diverse black communities, who may regard black folks who are not of their class with contempt and disrespect" (178). Black people who have no commitment to Black communities are dangerous to each other. What makes Black Americans who think this way so dangerous is that they are useful tools for racists and those who support white supremacy. They uphold all the negative stereotypes about Black people while presenting themselves and Black people who think like them as the model minority. They make no impact on the progress to dismantle white supremacy but instead reinforce white supremacist ideals. These are the people that mass media, especially conservative mass media, like to anoint as the spokesperson for the Black community (178). Conservative media continually seek out assimilated Black people to uphold their beliefs that if the rest of the Blacks just believed and acted in a way that is acceptable to white society, there would be fewer or no racial issues in America. These Black voices strongly believe that if Black Americans just "act a certain way," Black people as a whole would be more successful. They think that the only issues of racial inequality are self-inflicted by Black people. Blaming Black people who do not willfully assimilate into whiteness is the exact mentality that those who uphold white supremacy want us to believe. Suppose Black people accept the narrative that the issues with racial inequality are exclusively the responsibility of the Black community. In that case, white people could willfully continue their reign of domination and would not be held accountable for racists actions.

In the summer of 2020, Black conservative commentators like Candace Owens spoke out against the protests after the death of George Floyd. Not only did she and others condemn the protests, they also used George Floyd as an example of what they believed is wrong with the Black community. Conservative commentator Glen Beck, during his program, asked Candance Owens if Floyd is "a symbol for Black America today." Owens responded that Floyd "is a symbol of a broken culture in Black America today … how we contribute to our own demise." On her Twitter account she ranted that although she hoped Floyd's family received justice, she believed that the Black community was making Floyd into a hero. "We are embarring in the regard," Owens said, "Nobody wants to tell the truth in Black America. Our biggest problem is us." Owens' statements not only downplay the role of racism in the death of Floyd and policing in America, they also absolve and provide justification for racism. White conservatives take statements like Owens' as justification for the mistreatment of Black Americans. The narrative that Floyd was a criminal who did not deserved to be a representation racial injustice could be heard from living rooms, social media, to mainstream media. Instead of discussing and trying to find solutions to the racism and brutality that caused his death and the deaths of so many other Black men and women at the hands of police officers, conservatives discussed Floyd's character and prior criminality history and used that to dismiss the conversation around systemic racism.

So far, the narrative of racial assimilation and integration has been believed by some people of all races—people who hold whiteness as the standard of that which is good and normal, and people who uphold white supremacy rather intentionally or unintentionally. In her talks with audiences across the United States, bell hooks observed that many white and non-whites insist that this is not a white supremacist society (*Killing Rage* 187). Regardless of race, many conservative and integrationist whites and BIPOC believe that Martin Luther King, Jr.'s dream of racial integration has been realized, and any discussion of it by whites. They also believe that BIPOC individuals that have studied, researched, or believe that racial inequality continues to exist are embracing victimhood. The socialized, post-racial belief is that racism is not the problem it once was because Americans have abolished slavery and made it illegal to discriminate overtly. Yet, white supremacy continues to shape American perspectives and systems (*Killing Rage* 188). The United States Senator Tim Scott and Vice-President Kamala Harris can be considered at the opposite spectrum of the political racial spectrum. Scott is a conservative Republican and Harris has been characterized as a liberal Democrat. Yet, they both recently stated that American is not a racist country. While their statements may be an attempt to unite a polarized country, their denial of the existence of racism undermines the history of civil rights efforts that demonstrated the need for racial equality. Post-racial ideology can, in fact, embolden those who consciously or subconsciously uphold white supremacy.

Racial integrationists like Scott and Harris are critics of past and present racist discrimination; they support the American tradition of individual rights, freedom of speech, equality of opportunity, democratic government, and the rule of law (Shelton and Emerson, 2009). Racial integrationists also do not believe that American society is inherently racist; they believe that whites must recognize Blacks as equal citizens and have a moral obligation to uphold the ideas of *The Declaration of Independence* "that all men are created equal" (Shelton and Emerson, 2009). In the essay "Whiteness in the Black Imagination" in *Killing Rage: Ending Racism,* hooks explains how these ideas are used to perpetuate white supremacy: "White and black people alike believe that racism no longer exists. This erasure, however mythic, diffuses the representation of whiteness as terror in the black imagination. It allows for assimilation and forgetfulness" (47). Racial assimilationism can allow for forgetfulness when white and BIPOC refuse to acknowledge the racism steeped within American society.

Racial Integration vs. Racial Assimilation: The Issue of Conflation

The issue with racial integration is that it is often conflated with racial assimilation. Integration allows all racial or ethnic groups to participate in all aspects of national life without being handicapped by their color (Mageli, 2019). On the other hand, racial assimilation requires one to forego their ethnic and racial identity in order to resemble the dominant culture, that is to be white. Successful racial assimilation allows one to become indistinguishable from members of the dominant group. As Black people, we were told the lie of assimilation as the key to equality. We were told by educators, media, politicians, and many in white society that if we just confirmed to the rules of white society that we would achieve the personhood that was the Civil Rights Era's goal. However, racial assimilating means conforming to a society that still holds on to white supremacist ideals. As Black people, we will always be seen for our Blackness. Racial assimilation into a society that still holds on to white supremacist ideals will not bring about racial equality. Until white supremacy is dismantled from the hearts of individuals and the fabric of our society, racial assimilation is ineffective. Therefore, no amount of racial assimilation will ever allow BIPOC to be seen as equal to whites. Even Black people who assimilate into whiteness through the economic hierarchy are still seen through their Blackness. Even GOP Senator Tim Scott admitted in an opinion editorial in *USA Today* stating: "I am not immune to being stopped [by police] while driving at home in South Carolina or even walking onto the ground of the Capitol." Scott has assimilated both economically and politically, yet that does stop him for being racially profiled.

Racial integrationist ideology can also be used as a tool to deny BIPOC communities to create spaces that promote cultural identity specifically for them. However, opponents of them inaccurately label these spaces as "self-segregation" or "reverse racism." While it has become "cool" for white folks to hang out with Black people and express pleasure in Black culture, there remain whites who are not dedicated to unlearning racism. Many white people show their disinterest in unlearning racism when they fight against anti-racist initiatives and dismiss the impact of systemic racism. Therefore, it makes sense for Black people and other people of color to protect themselves from objectivity (157). This call for racial integration is not brought up in predominantly white spaces such as neighborhoods, schools, businesses, and social organizations. These predominantly white spaces are not seen as racially segregated environments even though they produce social inequalities in our society (Farina, 2009). Instead, this critique is reserved for when people of color create spaces for themselves. Since whiteness has been the standard norm that everyone (including people of color) should live by when white and BIPOC assimilationists argue that spaces designed for people of color are signs of anti-integration, what they really mean is that these spaces do not call for the assimilation of people of color into whiteness (Farina, 2009). The conversation gets diverted to the need for people of color to assimilate into whiteness versus being a part of but not consumed by white societal norms.

According to bell hooks, assimilationism was a way to dismantle the radical revolution of Black consciousness that sprang from the Civil Rights Movement. The word "assimilation" became popular in the late 1960s and early 1970s as a way to describe Black people's complicity and internalization of white supremacy (*Killing Rage* 189). When Black people chanted, "Black is beautiful" and "Say it loud, I'm Black, and I'm proud," these revolutionary words threatened to topple the house that white supremacy built. Since blatant discrimination and overt racism are now frowned upon by mainstream society, there had to be a new way to undermine the revolutionary struggle. This new way encouraged BIPOC communities to assimilate into whiteness without acknowledging the need to deconstruct the foundation of it built on white supremacy.

Claiming My Blackness: The End to Racial Assimilationist Thinking

My growth away from assimilationist thinking, like any other type of development, happened in stages. First, I rejected the lie of Black inferiority. I entered college proud of my people and our history. Yet, I still believed the lie of equality meant assimilating. I thought that somehow, we as Black people had to make our Blackness palatable for the rest of society, especially white folks. Years of being in predominantly white spaces chipped away at the belief that if I talked like them, wore my hair like them, dressed better than them, was more intelligent than them, they would see my Blackness as equal. Racially conscious Black women shift or change who they are and how they present themselves as a response to racial and gender stereotypes, biases, and racist mistreatment they face (Shorter-Gooden, 2004). This shifting is also a coping mechanism in dealing with a society that rewards conformity, especially conformity of "minorities" to whiteness. In addition, hooks explains that when Black people enter social contexts that remain unchanged and in no way stripped of the framework of white supremacy, we are pressured to assimilate (*Killing Rage* 187). Racial assimilation is rewarded, whereas affirming Blackness is punished.

In a research based on the African American Women's Voices Project conducted by Dr. Kumea Shorter-Gooden and Charisse Jones explain how Black women 'shift' to navigate racial and gender bigotry in the U.S. This research shows that many Black women in the U.S. often feel pressured to present a face to the world that is acceptable to others even though it may be at odds with their Black identity. Many Black women may feel pressured to conform to codes set by a dominate white society. In doing so, they feel they must modulate their language, their behavior, and even their personal appearance to make whites feel more comfortable in their presence (Shorter-Gooden, 2004). Historically, as ideas of racial equality seemed to progress in the U.S., Black people were racially indoctrinated to believe that if we toned down our *Blackness* and conform more to white societal expectations, we would achieve social justice. But that was a lie. So, what is the truth? My journey to dismantle the lie of the value of racial assimilationism interconnected to the promotion of white privilege(s) would lead me to understand the truth. To liberate the racially oppressed in BIPOC communities, our society must no longer endorse ideas of racial assimilationism to end racism inequality. Promoting racial assimilationist ideology is an ineffective tool for radically dismantling white supremacy.

Rev. Dr. Martin Luther King, Jr. Day became a federal holiday one year after I was born. I grew up with the narrative that all Dr. King wanted was for little brown boys and girls to go to school with little white girls and boys. Now we have achieved that the world is a place of harmony? While Dr. King was fighting for integration, others were hoping for assimilation. However, racial assimilation has not brought about a positive change in the lives of Black people overall. While assimilationism has benefited some BIPOC individuals, especially those who not only assimilate but disregard their race, it has not radically changed the lives of all Black people overall. Instead, it has continued to function as a social policy that upholds white supremacy. As bell hooks says, "[It is ideally] one that would serve to deflect the call for a radical transformation of black consciousness" (*Killing Rage* 189). Instead of Black people being led to focus on building their own community and power, they were encouraged to assimilate into white culture. In reality assimilationist idealism drastically countered the political stance represented by the Black Power and Black Nationalists movements. To make real progress toward liberation and racial equality, BIPOC must identify how assimilation shows up in our everyday lives and then act to dismantle its idealism.

The day I first heard Nina Simone's "Four Women," I slowly began to break the shackles of assimilationist thinking. The first step was refuting the lie that my dark skin was a roadblock to beauty and femininity. The second step was dismantling the lie that assimilation was the only way to achieve success. As a child of the nineties, I grew up watching television shows like *The Cosby Show, A Different World, Living Single, Moesha,* and all the other Black comedy shows during the late nineties/early 2000s where being Black was in vogue. By then, the fight for equality during Civil Rights movement was something of the past. Mainstream media, Black activists, and everyday Black folks taught our generation that as long as we "get a good education and make something of ourselves," that the struggles of the past would bear fruit. In schools, we were successfully indoctrinated to believe that all Dr. King wanted was the realization of racial integration. Since integration was achieved, Blacks can now be integrated into white American culture, and it was our job as Black people to do our best to assimilate. As hooks argues, "… few black activists were vigilant enough to see that the concrete rewards for assimilation would undermine subversive oppositional ways of seeing blackness" (*Killing Rage* 123). The drive to assimilate has led Black people and other people of color to hide their racial identity and helps feed into the dangerous idea of "colorblindness." When Black people and people of color assimilate, it requires them to deny or downplay one of their most important aspects: their ancestral legacy. This denial by Black people and other people of color gives white people the room to ignore, discount, and deny that racism and white supremacy are real, ongoing issues that must be addressed.

According to bell hooks, many times to uphold the system of white supremacy, there are white people who will tout the achievements of Black people who have assimilated as proof of a just system. Black people focused on improving class mobility, on making it in the white world, assumed the attitudes and values of internalized racism (*Killing Rage* 123). Blackness has been so successfully undermined. As documented in a study published in *The Harvard Gazette*, fifty percent of white Americans believe that discrimination is as bad against whites as it is against people of color. Also, while most Americans understand that hard work does not equal success, 50 percent of whites believe that people of color would be more successful "if they only tried harder" (Simon, 2020). White people are not the only ones who believe in this lie. Many Blacks and people of color believe in this lie; they think that because they have assimilated and acquired some measure of success, others would be in the same position if they just tried harder. While I have never believed this myself, I know quite a few Blacks and people of color who do.

Exposing Classism in Black Communities

One way racial assimilationism shows up in Black communities is by pitting middle and upper-class Black people against poor Black people. Those who have achieved financial success sometimes believe that their proximity to whiteness via class protects them from discrimination. Some middle and upper-class Black people and even Black immigrants feel that they only face discrimination or racial stereotypes because they are put in the same category as poor Blacks. To avoid this discrimination, some Blacks try to separate themselves from the plight of poor Black people. These Black folks blame poor Black people for the cruel treatment they may get from white people. This scapegoating blames the victim rather than targeting the white supremacist structure (*Killing Rage* 199). Throughout history, white people have used Black people to subvert any fight for liberation, from slave revolts to the Civil Rights movement. While using spokespeople like Candace Owens or the Hodge Twins might have the desired impact, allowing some Blacks to participate in mainstream capitalism has been the most successful tool to divide us. As more and more Black people benefited from capitalism, the more repressed the militant black movement became (*Killing Rage* 252).

Many of the Black Indigenous People of Color who believe in the notion of "just try harder" or "pulling yourself up by the bootstraps" also see themselves as progressive. However, to be progressive does not mean one is divorced from colonized ways of thinking. Many BIPOC consider themselves progressive while maintaining a colonized way of thinking. Their privilege allows them to diminish Black people, often in the underclass and who are poor (*Killing Rage* 166). These "assimilationist Negros," a phrase coined by Lorraine Hansberry in her play *A Raisin in the Sun*, are Black when it's only convenient for them to be. After George Floyd's death, I noticed a few Black and women of color who prided themselves on their ability to assimilate into white society suddenly come out to speak about their experience of being a Black woman. They facilitated book discussions of Robin DiAngelo's book *White Fragility*. They attended rallies while making sure they separated themselves from the 'thugs who got out of hand and destroyed hard-earned business owners' property.' They made sure they were recognized as a Black-owned business when the discussion centered around patronizing more Black-owned businesses. When the fad of Blackness wore off, so did their lukewarm involvement in the Black community.

Decolonized Black people find radical ways to dismantle white supremacy. The work to dismantle white supremacy is ongoing. As radio talk show host and activist Joe Madison states frequently that this work is more than a moment; it is a movement. My first step to decolonize my mind was to stop believing what made me Black was negative. I rediscovered my love of Black men. To be honest, that did not take long to do. The next stage was embracing my kinks and being unapologetically Black, even when I am in predominantly white spaces. And while I enjoy a comfortable, middle-class lifestyle and have obtained advanced degrees, that doesn't stop me from understanding the plight of and fighting for other Black people who are not in the same position. Being decolonized is to push beyond the comforts of assimilation and being willing to confront and dismantle the systems of white supremacy that still exist today.

I was born in the projects of a small Florida town. Although my parents were legally married for most of my childhood, my father was in and out of my life due to a drug habit. My mom was essentially a single mom, and even when there were two incomes, we were still a working-poor family. While I have achieved a middle-class lifestyle now, my upbringing puts me in a unique position. I know that my middle-class status now was more about taking advantage of the opportunities presented to me and not just me "pulling myself up by my bootstraps." I understand that I am no more intelligent, determined, or able than any other poor or working-class Black person. I often tell my students that I would not have gone to college if I had not had the opportunity to attend the Project Upward Bound program. Project Upward Bound was a program for kids on free or reduced lunch and/or first-generation college graduates. I was given a hand-up. While it would be easy for me to ignore my working-poor class background, I use it as a tool to drive me to fight for liberation for all people.

Using my background as a tool means engaging and being active in the community that nurtured me and not in a paternalistic, savior way. I am here to serve the community; however, they need me to help them because there is no individual liberation without collective liberation at the end of the day. Fortunately, not all successful Black people feel the need to assimilate. Despite whatever mainstream success they may have achieved, many higher-status Black people seek to preserve their Blackness by supporting separatist strategies on matters specific to Black culture (Shelton and Emerson, 2009). The urge to maintain a connection with Black culture amid mainstream success is why social groups like Jack and Jill of America or Mocha Moms were developed, to keep Black families connected to their Black identity.

Another trick of racial assimilation is the belief that interracial relationships will lead to a more "browning" of America and, therefore, more acceptance of all races. The idea that love has no color is as dangerous as the notion of "colorblindness." The generation before me was taught to be "colorblind." This idea of "colorblindness" has made it harder or nearly impossible for some whites and people of color to identify when there are issues of racism. Colorblindness leaves you blind to racial discrimination. The notion of colorblindness makes it harder for you to identify and understand race issues because you do not acknowledge race as something that is a part of the human experience. In his book, *How to be an Antiracist* (2019), Ibram X. Kendi explains that assimilationists believe that if we stop identifying race, then racism will go away. However, they do not realize that we will not be able to identify racial inequality if we stop using racial categories. This inability to identify racial disparities will (and has led to) a world of inequality none of us can see, let alone resist (Kendi). This awareness has been fostered since the time many of us were toddlers. According to recent research by the American Psychological Association (APA), children as young as two or three develop racist beliefs. Research has also shown that children can think about complex topics at a very young age. Therefore, the notion of raising children to be "colorblind" is not possible. Young children have already developed racial beliefs. To combat toddlers from developing such harmful beliefs, anti-racist BIPOC and white parents have to do work to dismantle our own white supremacist beliefs and actively be antiracists. The APA suggests that we begin discussing race with our children at the age of five.

The Danger of Colorblindness: Race Makes No Difference

While everyone should all strive to love no matter the color of one's skin, to say that race is not a factor in forming relationships makes the idea of being colorblind dangerous. Recently, Hurbert Davis was asked how he felt about being the first Black basketball head coach at the University of North Carolina. He acknowledges the significance of his position, then stated that he is proud to be African-American and is proud of his white wife and his biracial children are a product of both of them. The fact that he felt the need to qualify his historical position with his proximity to whiteness shows the failure to think that interracial relationships would lead to the destruction of white supremacy. Nicholas Ochs and John Kinsman, both members of the far-right extremist group The Proud Boys, are reportedly married to Black women. This far-right extremist group has been designated a hate group in America and a terrorist group in Canada, yet in the case of Kinsman, pictures of him with his Black wife and biracial children were offered up as proof that he is not racist.

Being in an intimate interracial relationship does not absolve one from having internalized racism. In order to have an impact on racial attitudes, one needs to be exposed to antiracist ideology—according to Erin Pryor in "Love Sees No Color: The Pervasiveness of Color-Blindism Within Black-White Intimate Interracial Relationships" (2018). In this article, as a study of interracial couples, Pryor states: "They can interact with people of other races and even enter into interracial relationships without having to consider or think about race"—finding that whites navigate life and participate in society without paying close attention to minority groups. In interracial relationships, whites maintain a "colorblind ideology" that reinforces the existing racially unequal status quo and preserves white supremacy (Bonilla-Silva 2001, 2003; Carr 1997; Doane 2003; Gallagher 2003; Lewis 2003). Yet Black partners cannot be blind to race. As many Black people are very much aware of their "minority" status, "colorblindness" is a fundamental principle of racial assimilationism. It means that to participate successfully in a white-dominated society, Blacks must adopt mainstream racialized beliefs and practices (Pryor, 2018). Therefore this "colorblind logic" works as a central strategy for success. When Blacks and people of color predominantly date white people or outside of their race, one has to look at their reasons. Is it that they are in situations where they are surrounded by those who do not look like them, so they have no choice if they want companionship? Have they internalized anti-Black stereotypes? Is this racial fetishization?

In my own family, my Black brother married a white woman whose family had issues with race. My brother has only dated white women and seems to be more comfortable around whiteness. In addition, my brother has struggled with his own issues with colorism in the Black community. In an attempt to raise their children to be "colorblind" my brother and his wife inadvertently missed the opportunity to raise their children to affirm their own Blackness. Their interaction with their Black family once a year was not enough to dismantle the stereotypes of Blackness and anti-Blackness they internalized from white society and their white family members. Recently their teenage boys confessed they do not like to date Black girls because they remind them of the Black women in their family. However, it is not the Black women in their family who have done them harm but instead the stereotypes they have been told about Black women. We often see these stereotypes repeated in the media: Black women are loud, aggressive, mean, and controlling. In addition, their "colorblind" upbringing has been in predominately white spaces. While they try their best to raise confident Black men, my brother and his wife experienced blind spots in their parenting.

Even platonic friendships are affected by "colorblind ideology" and assimilationist thinking. I have a lot of white friends and know many white people, yet when for many of the white people I know (almost all of them), I am the only Black person or person of color that they know. The Public Religion Research Institute study found that three-quarters of white people don't have any non-white friends. On average, they had only one friend representing each racial demographic. In her essay "Where Is the Love: Political Bonding Between Black and White Women" in *Killing Rage: Ending Racism,* hooks discusses the hurdles of cross-racial friendships. One significant barrier is that individual white women tend to be unaware of how the history of racism has institutionalized structures of racial apartheid and inequality. In other words, they are unaware of or do not acknowledge systemic racism. Secondly, hooks argues that "racist/sexist division of sexual competition for men that deem white women more desirable, more worthy of respect and regard than black women" creates a barrier to cross-racial relationships among Black and white women (219). In an interview with *The New York Times*, author Aminatou Sow explained, "There is not a way to be intimately close with people if you refuse to engage in the truth of how the world is organized" (July 2020).

I see the struggle of cross-racial friendships in elementary-aged children as well. Psychologist Beverly Daniel Tatum points out that if a white child has a friend of color, it is likely that the friend is a minority in a primarily white community. When my children are invited to a white classmate's party, they are almost always the only Black children in attendance. My children are the only experiences many white kids have with Black people. There are white people love to point out how their children play with kids no matter the color of their skin, and kids are colorblind, yet their own friendship circle is almost wholly white. Children see these cues and other cues about race from their parents. By adolescence, their friendships begin to be less and less diverse.

When I arrange birthday parties for my children at our home, one will see that children of different races and ethnicities are invited to come. My girls value their friendships for their Indian, Japanese, Chinese, and Latino/a friends so much that they expect us (as parents) to participate in their cultural celebrations as if we are also a part of that culture. They know when it's Chinese New Year just as much as they know about Black History Month. They get excited about Diwali just as much as they are excited about Kwanza. But my children cannot be the only Black friend for every white child in their classroom. Surrounding oneself with people from other races and ethnicities takes intentional work that many adults are unwilling to cultivate. These friendships should not be just a box to check off in your diversity and inclusion checklist but should be based on common interest and mutual bonding. As pastor and author David W. Swanson has said, "You have to choose to prioritize racial justice, even when it's outside of your comfort zone" (Wong, 2020). According to Swanson, white people struggle with cross-racial friendships because they do not need to be cross-culturally competent in this society. It takes more than cross-racial friendships or romantic relationships to combat racial injustices. When BIPOC assimilate to maintain these relationships, it is damaging to them and white individuals who do not see how they take part in upholding white supremacy.

Becoming the Model "Minority": The Truth Be Told

We should all understand our biases and stereotypes and examine how they affect our platonic and intimate relationships. A few years ago, I had lunch with a white female neighbor. I had found out through her social media postings that she was a die-hard Trump supporter. I had lunch with her to find out how she could support a political candidate who made what many would argue as racists statements about Mexican immigrants. This neighbor was married to a man who immigrated from South America. During the discussion, she extolled all of the racist stereotypes and tropes that conservative media outlets had promoted. When I asked how these applied to her husband, she told me that he was different. He wasn't like all the other "freeloading immigrants," including her in-laws. He was a model immigrant. In an online support group that I am in for culturally fluent families, there have been a few occasions when white women disparage Black people, more specifically Black women, while holding up their Black partner as the model minority. In these cases, racial assimilation did not change the structure of white supremacy; it upheld the idea of them versus us. Even though these white people were in intimate relationships with people outside of their race, they still held on to their racists' beliefs. In cases like these, the idea that "love has no color" limits love to only those with whom you are in personal relationships. In these cases, the idea of "love has no color" does not dismantle white supremacy.

Some Black women have been known to date outside of their race because they struggle with internalized European, white beauty standards. We should all strive to love each other, no matter how they look on the outside, right? However, we need to examine how our attraction plays into our racial identity. When I started dating, I had a thing for white boys. To be honest, I had a thing for any boy that wasn't Black. Black men represented everything that had hurt me. Also, if I married someone outside of my race, my children would not have to hear the backhanded insult of, "You're pretty to be so dark." For as long as I can remember, I have heard what a pretty dark child I was. As a kid, I thought it was funny that people, especially Black people were surprised that I was pretty and dark-skinned, as if they two were supposed never to inhabit one's body at the same time. But the more I heard, "She looks just like Barney Fife (the nickname for my father), color and all," the more I realized that this meant these attributes were a hindrance to my beauty. My father is a permanent sun-kissed, deep chocolate brown. My mother, on the other hand, was the color of a Georgia pecan. Even as an eight-year-old, I knew that the skin I inherited from my father somehow took away from my "prettiness" and my femininity, no matter how adults tried to hide it inside of a compliment. As bell hooks states in *Killing Rage: Ending Racism*, "Dark skin is stereotypically coded in the racist, sexist, and/or colonized imagination as masculine ... Introspectively of people's sexual preferences, the color-caste hierarchy functions to diminish the desirability of darker-skinned females" (129). As a young girl, I thought that if I married a man outside of my race, my children would look like the light-skinned Black girls with the long, relaxed hair that I saw on my television screens.

In the meantime, I could try to assimilate as much into white society as I could. I stopped wearing my hair in braids in high school and began to relax my hair and wear extensions and wigs. While I was comfortable with my dark skin, even if others were not, I was not pleased with all aspects of my Blackness. It is well-known with people of color, not just Black people, that as hooks points out, "Light skin and long straight hair continue to be traits that define a female as beautiful and desirable in the white racist white imagination and in the colonized black mindset" (127) That colonized mentality of needing straight hair to be seen as a fully beautiful woman did not change until I was about to become a mother. It took me over twenty years to understand that I am beautiful, with the hair that grows naturally out of my head is an example of the depths of colonized thinking. When I was in college, a Black girlfriend of mine cut-off all of her hair and went natural. I was jealous of her freedom to embrace her beauty, but I also worried that she would not be able to get a job, let alone a career in media, because of her natural hair. Last year, she confessed how deeply insecure she had been after the big chop and how it took her years to define herself as beautiful afterward. In 2020 I binged watched two seasons of an Indian television series called *For More Shots Please!* I was excited to see other women of color get a show about friendship, love, sex, and all the messy complexities of life. While the show tackles some heavy issues such as homophobia and slut-shaming, I was disappointed that the entire cast was made up of very fair-skinned Indian men and women as if darker-skinned Indian people didn't exist at all. The colonized belief of white as better, more desirable is an issue that permeates the psyche worldwide.

In "Black Beauty and Black Power," also an essay in *Killing Rage,* hooks boldly states that "[t]he affirmation of assimilation, as well as racist white aesthetic standards, became one of the most effective ways to undermine efforts to transform internalized racism in the psyches of the black masses" (126). My need to assimilate led me to shun the historically Black college, (or HBCU) that I was accepted to and purposely attend a predominantly white institution (PWI). By my sophomore year of college, I regretted my decision and actively sought out spaces where I could be comfortable in my Blackness, including minoring in Africana Studies. My oldest sister, on the other hand, attended an HBCU. She joined a Black sorority and married an HBCU, Black fraternity member. Except for her job, her world revolves around Blackness. Yet, she can still be heard scolding her daughter for her natural hair and tattoos or admonishing her son for being outside for so long that his deep caramel skin turns into a milk chocolate hue. Whenever my niece or nephew has brought home someone who is not BIPOC or mentions their attraction to someone outside of their race, especially a white person, my sister wonders why they don't see the beauty in having Black mates. Like hooks urges, "collectively and individually we must all assume accountability for the resurgence of color-caste hierarchies in black life" (126).

Now that I am a mother, this is something I am vigilant about. I knew that my children would be dark-skinned since I married a man even darker than I. Our first child we named Layla, which means "night" because we wanted her to embrace her darkness from the moment she left the womb. Layla is dark with kinky hair that she loves to wear in an afro or braided. People always comment on how smart she is. Maya, to my surprised, inherited the Georgia pecan skin of my mother. She loves her bouncy, loose curls but often opts for beads and braids so she can swing her hair. People always comment on how pretty she is. As a mother, I have to counteract the narrative that Layla can only be seen as smart because of her dark skin, and Maya is pretty because of her lighter brown skin.

"Love Has No Color"—Assimilationist Idealism and (White) Christianity

One of the biggest promoters of "love has no color" while covertly promoting assimilation is Christianity, as interpreted in the context of white supremacy. I grew up in the Black church, where my Blackness was always affirmed and celebrated. When I moved to a predominately white suburb, I could not find a local Black church, so I decided to attend the highly recommended a racially diverse church. I believed the lie that all Christians believe that we are all one in Christ. I quickly noticed at the church very few Black and people of color in leadership positions, even though the church boasted about having a racially mixed congregation. I never felt comfortable there. During each local, state, and national election cycle—while I was a member of the church—the sermons I listened to were coded with dog-whistle, racists language like "We back the Blue" with no mention of the unjustified murders of unarmed Black men and women. Some of the church's pastors boldly preached from their pulpits how our nation's first Black president was a Muslim terrorist.

While the lead pastor at this "multicultural mega-church" refused to come out and encourage parishioners to vote for Trump, but instead to vote with a Christian heart, he refused to condemn the racist language coming from then-presidential candidate Donald Trump. I was saddened that this pastor declined to address the racism. When over eighty-percent of white evangelicals pulled the lever for Donald Trump, (Martínez and Smith, 2016), I knew I would no longer trust my white brother or sister in Christ to be an ally in fighting for racial equality. Worse yet, they did not recognize their role in upholding white supremacy and how that affects their Black brothers and sisters in Christ. After the murder of George Floyd, the church posted messages on its social media about how the church's members were standing with Black Americans in racial solidarity. But by then, it was too late. At least three other Black families I knew of and I had left the church to join a predominantly Black church. For years the church ignored racial tension both locally and nationally, but once it became popular to speak out against racism, the church finally found its voice.

I have always struggled with white-dominated Christianity's racist history. Much of Christian history saw no conflict between the faith and slavery. White supremacists often used the Bible to justify slavery. Scriptures like: "Servants, be obedient to them that are your masters according to the flesh, with fear and trembling, in singleness of your heart, as unto Christ (Ephesians, 6:5 King James Version) and the story of the descendants of Ham in the book of Genesis, served as biblical support of slavery. hooks argues that "white-dominated Christians now use a rhetoric of multiculturalism to invite non-white people to believe that racism can be overcome through a shared fundamentalist encounter" (*Killing Rage* 202). Meanwhile, recent public opinion polls show that white Christians are consistently more likely than non-religious whites to deny the existence of systemic racism. A survey by the Barna Research Group revealed that white evangelical Republicans are less likely to think race is a problem but more likely to think they are a victim of reverse racism (Jemar Tisby, *Color of Compromise: The Truth about the American Church's Complicity in Racism*, 2019).

As they did in the past, conservative white people have been using Christianity and the belief that we are all one in the body of Christ to keep Black people docile and in bondage. In *Color of Compromise*, Jemar Tisby argues that when faced with racial inequality, the American church practices a complicit Christianity rather than a courageous Christianity. Also, in *Color of Compromise* Historian Carolyn DuPont took it one step further by stating, "Not only did white Christians fail to fight *for* black equality, they often labored mightily *against* it. Many white Christians believe that racism only includes overt acts such as Jim Crow Laws or calling someone the "n-word." However, racism is more than those overt acts. Being complicit and silent in the face of injustice or supporting the status quo is supporting racism and white supremacy.

The belief of many white evangelicals and some BIPOC evangelicals is that if we worship together and assimilate through the body of Christ, then race will not be an issue. A study of multiracial congregations conducted by Carolyn B. Helsel in *Anxious to Talk about It: Helping White Christians Talk about Racism* (2019) showed that whites continued to remain dominant in power positions, even when their percentage of overall membership declined to the point of being a minority within their churches. Although the mega-church that I attended boasted about its diversity, the lack of Blacks and people of color holding high positions within the church was more of a testimony for their beliefs of equality. The Black pastor of my new church often talks about how some white pastors tried to discourage him from starting a predominantly Black church. The thought was that a church that focused on the Black community would not be successful. My pastor pushed back on this notion because he saw a need for Black people to have a safe space that they will be able to worship. My new pastor does not shy away from issues of race and racial inequality.

While my pastor welcomes integration, he also understands the damaging effects of racial assimilation. As hooks states in *Killing Rage: Ending Racism*, "Resisting the pressure to assimilate is part of our struggle to end white supremacy" (187). White, evangelical Christianity requires Black and other people of color to assimilate into their white religious culture. Avoiding discussions or race, or worse yet believing they are unnecessary, requires Christians of color to disregard issues of race and injustice that may impact them in order to assimilate into the ideas of white evangelical Christianity. In recent years, I have seen the desire to assimilate into white identity increase in Black people and other people of color because these are the messages they are getting from white pastors of multiracial churches. These messages of racial assimilation, rather direct or indirect, have caused Blacks and people of color to no longer see the need to fight for their own racial equality but rather to uphold white supremacy.

For many white Christians, 'we are all God's children' until someone mentions race. When Christians of all races try to speak out for equality, the backlash is swift and severe. This was apparent in 2016 when Black Christian artist Lecrae came under fire for a tweet on America's Independence Day. He tweeted a photo of slaves with the caption "My family on July 4th, 1776." White conservatives came out in droves to condemn and call for boycotts. The tweet received more than 15,000 retweets and 23,000 likes (Tisby, 2019). Some followers questioned Lecrae's patriotism, while others accused him of making everything about race instead of the Gospel. Shortly after this incident, a Black Christian penned an opinion piece chastising Lecrae for being more of a social justice warrior than a soldier for the Lord. This opinion is the product of assimilation into white Christianity that believes one's fight for racial equality cannot work together with an individual's religious beliefs. The same people who criticize Christians who fight for social justice and equality are the same Christians who now revere Dr. King. The same white evangelicals who criticized Dr. King for his fight for equality when he was alive are the same white evangelicals who urge Black Americans to be more like Dr. King now.

Black Christians are not the only ones under attack for speaking out against racism in the church. When the Southern Baptist Convention Ethics and Religious Liberty Commission president, Russell Moore, opposed Donald Trump and suggested that evangelicals would lose credibility among Black people by supporting Trump, his position became jeopardized (Tisby, 2019). Moore has since resigned his position whether or not it had anything to do with being labeled a liberal and "a source of significant distraction." When Christians, regardless of color, speak out against racial inequality, they are often ironically seen as less Christ-like.

In her book, *I'm Still Here: Black Dignity in a World Made for Whiteness* (2018), Austin Channing Brown describes her frustration when white Christians expect her racially to assimilate in the name of Christianity: "White people who expect me to be white have not yet realized that their cultural way of being is not in fact the result of goodness, rightness, or God's blessings" (20). Brown candidly talks about her struggles of being a Black Christian woman in predominantly white organizations, including churches. Brown explains that she is "trying to clarify what it is like to exist in a Black body in an organization that doesn't understand it is not only Christian but also white" (20). Brown admits that even though the church "has been the oppressor as often as it has been the champion of the oppressed, I can't let go of my belief in the church—in a universal body of belonging, in a community that reaches toward a love in a world so often filled with hate" (21). In other words, according to Brown, people can criticize the institution they love for its commitment to white supremacy. Other Christians of color, including music artists, have also been vocal about the critique of the church that they love. As Christian rap artist KB states in his song, "Long Live the Champion," "Yes, I love the kingdom more than I love my nation, Yes, I love my neighbor more than I love his papers."

My relationship with Christ has deepened now that I am back in a Black church. There is something about the sense of belonging that allows me to worship and connect with God on a deeper level. The Black church is also where most of the Civil Rights movement was birth. The Black church served as a place to save souls and ground zero for fighting for equality. Racial integration has led to the disappearance of more and more Black only spaces. Instead of being a necessity born out of overt racism, Black only spaces are now needed as a safe space from covert racism.

It has been said that the Dr. King once told Harry Belafonte that he felt like he was integrating his people into a burning building (France-Williams, 2020). Until we all deconstruct and destroy white supremacy, racial assimilation accelerates the burning building. Austin Channing Brown suggests that "to assimilate into whiteness is to be empty, malleable so that Blackness can be shaped into whatever is necessary … It sees potential, possibility, a future where Black people could share some of the benefits of whiteness if only we try hard enough to mimic it" (*I'm Still Here* 79). Assimilationism has been sold as a tool of racial integration. However, racial assimilation has only led to Blacks and people of color upholding white supremacy instead of fighting to change the system. Assimilationism is the absorption of people, ideas, or culture into broader, racially generalized society. Once BIPOC are absorbed, we have lost our individuality. In *I'm Still Here,* Brown asserts that while the notion of racial assimilation should be like a delicious melting pot, what happens when the ingredients are added to a poisoned soup base? White supremacy is like a poison that seeps into your mind, drip by drip. America's melting pot has been poisoned with white supremacy, yet BIPOC are expected to assimilate into the poisonous ideology of white supremacy.

The Need for Radical, Anti-Racist Tools to End Racism

Some Liberal whites and assimilated BIPOC would argue that reimagining racial assimilationism in this new era of immigration is necessary. However, our nation has developed a destructive pattern of taking an old idea and retooling it without fixing the underlying issues. The underlying problem with assimilation is white supremacy. hooks describes assimilation as a strategy that provided social legitimation for the shift in allegiance. For middle-class Black people, the shift in allegiance is less about race and more about maintaining class status. Allowing Black to participate in American capitalism via assimilation does not destroy white supremacy but instead creates a chasm between the economically advantaged and the economic disadvantaged (*Killing Rage* 186). Assimilation has caused some Black people to absorb white society's ideas of capitalism and individualism to the point that they no longer identify with Blackness. At the same time, some actively support white supremacy under the notion that they are somehow different or better than other Black people. However, the majority of mainstream successful Black people still have a deep commitment to Black social heritage (Shelton and Emerson, 2009). Those who maintain their commitment to Blackness, on the other hand, still find it necessary to shift racially aligned with whiteness in order to fit into mainstream society.

Interracial relationships also have little effect on white supremacy since they can foster even deeper beliefs of inferiority and stereotypes of Black identity if they are not acknowledged and changed. In interracial relationships, rather intimate or platonic, assimilation does not necessarily combat the feelings of racial inferiority but can maintain racially unequal status quo and preserve white supremacy (Bonilla-Silva 2001, 2003; Carr 1997; Doane 2003; Gallagher 2003; Lewis 2003). Unless the white people in these relationships commit to not being racists but to be antiracists and do the work to understand the experiences of Blacks and people of color, interracial relationships will do nothing in the fight against white supremacy. Cross-racial relationships can reduce the widening racial divide but only if people mutually learn from each other and listen with humility (Wong, 2020). Therefore, when racial assimilation calls for one to downplay or deny cultural differences or focus on sameness, assimilation acts as a barrier to developing deep and authentic relationships and understanding of another person's cultural differences. Having cross-racial relationships will not automatically eliminate racism and white supremacy. There needs to be more work for critical consciousness done on all parts.

According to bell hooks, assimilationism has been used as a social policy strategically to act as a counter-defense to the call for a racial transformation of Black consciousness. She insists that it was not enough for Black people to be given rights to integrate into white society and organizations. They also in the struggle for racial justice had to become "honorary whites" to succeed (*Killing Rage* 189). However, Black people's historical assimilation trajectories do not follow the "straight-line" that is common among many racial, ethnic, and religious groups (Gans, 1979). Blacks who achieve some success cannot wholly abandon their racial identities, and racial discrimination prohibits them from fully melting into the mainstream (Shelton and Emerson, 2009). The struggle to become a "honorary white" is played out when Senator Tim Scott discusses his experiences of getting racially profiled by the police, but yet he still refuses to admit that America is a racist country because that admission would jeopardize his political standing as the only Black Republican United States senator. Relationships, religion, or economic success through racial assimilationism for Black people is counterproductive if the culture being longed for and/or desired is steeped in white supremacy. The answer to racial liberation for the oppressed cannot be solved until BIPOC and white allies stop expecting assimilation to solve racial inequality and start embracing real radical change for racial justice. Until we kill the deadly plague of white supremacist ideology within our nation, assimilationist idealism will continue to be a deadly tool aimed to destroy real racial progress in the U.S.

Works Cited

American Psychological Association. (2020, August 27). "Children notice race several years before adults want to talk about it" [Press release]. http://www.apa.org/news/press/releases/2020/08/children-notice-race

Bonilla-Silva, Eduardo. *White Supremacy and Racism in the Post-Civil Rights Era*. Boulder, CO: L. Rienner, 2001.

Bonilla-Silva, Eduardo. 2003. *Racism Without Racists: Color-blind Racism and the Persistence of Racial Inequality in the United States*. Maryland: Rowan and Little Field Publisher, Inc.

Brown, Austin Channing. *I'm Still Here: Black Dignity in a World Made for Whiteness*. Convergent Books. New York, NY. 2018.

Carr, Leslie G. *Colorblind Racism*. Thousand Oaks, CA: Sage. 1997.

Doane, Ashley W. "Rethinking Whiteness Studies." Pp. 3-18 in *White Out: The Continuing Significance of Racism*, eds. Ashley W. Doane and Eduardo Bonilla-Silva. New York: Routledge. 2003.

France-Williams A D. *Ghost Ship: Institutional Racism and the Church of England*. SCM Press, 2020.

Gallagher, Charles A. "Colorblind Privilege: The Social and Political Functions of Erasing the Color Line in Post-Race America." *Race, Gender & Class* 10 (4):22-37. 2003.

Gans, H. "Symbolic ethnicity: the future of ethnic groups and cultures in America." *Ethnic and Racial Studies*, 2, 1–20. 1979.

Helsel. Carolyn B. *Anxious to Talk about It: Helping White People Talk Faithfully about Racism*. ChalicePress.com, 2nd ed., 2019.

hooks, bell. *Killing Rage: Ending Racism*. New York, NY: Henry Holt and Company. 1995.

Jones, Charisse, and Kumea Shorter-Gooden. *Shifting: The Double Lives of Black Women in America*. Perennial, 2004.

Lewis, Amanda. "What Group? Studying Whites and Whiteness in the Era of 'Colorblindness.'" *Sociological Theory* 22: 623-646. 2003.

Mageli, Paul D. "Integration." *Salem Press Encyclopedia*, Salem Press. Research Starters, *EBSCOhost*. 2019. http://ezproxy.lib.usf.edu/login?url=https://search.ebscohost.com/login.aspx?direct=true&db=ers&AN=93788033&site=eds-live.

Martínez, Jessica and Gregory A. Smith. "How the Faithful Voted: A preliminary 2016 analysis," Pew Research Center. 2016, https://www.pewresearch.org/fact-tank/2016/11/09/how-the-faithful-voted-a-preliminary-2016-analysis/.

Farinia, Navid. *Debating Integration vs. Assimilation, Cornell Daily Sun, The: Cornell University (Ithaca, NY), August 27, 2009.* https://infoweb-newsbank-com.ezproxy.lib.usf.edu/apps/news/document-view?p=WORLDNEWS&docref=news/146341409545A9D8. Accessed 26 May 2021.

Kendi, Ibram. X. *How to Be an Antiracist*. New York, NY: Random House. 2019.

Pryor, Erin. "Love Sees No Color: The Pervasiveness of Color-Blindism Within Black-White Intimate Interracial Relationships." *Michigan Sociological Review*, vol. 32, Michigan Sociological Association, pp. 92–130. 2018.

Shelton, Jason E., and Michael O. Emerson. "Extending the Debate over Nationalism Versus Integration: How Cultural Commitments and Assimilation Trajectories Influence Beliefs About Black Power." *Journal of African American Studies*, vol. 14, no. 3, Springer Nature, Sept. 2010, pp. 312–36. *EBSCOhost*, doi:10.1007/s12111-009-9112-7.

Simon, C. "Facing the denial of American racism." Retrieved April 01, 2021, from https://news.harvard.edu/gazette/story/2020/06/facing-the-denial-of-american-racism/ 2020, June 12.

Tatum, Beverly Daniel. *Why Are All the Black Kids Sitting Together in the Cafeteria?* Penguin Books, 2021.

Tisby, Jemar. *Color of Compromise: The Truth about the American Church's Complicity in Racism.* Zondervan, 2020.

Wong, Brittany. "Why White People Are Bad at Interracial Friendships (And How to Do Better)." *HuffPost*, 4 Sept. 2020, https://www.huffpost.com/entry/close-interraacial-friendships_1_5f5122c8c5b6946f3eaed704.

10

Killing Rage on the Page: A White Female Reader Interrogates Whiteness and Engages Community
Tiffanie Kelley

[W]hy am I as I am? To understand that of any person, his whole life, from birth, must be reviewed. All of our experiences fuse into our personality. Everything that ever happened to us is an ingredient.

Malcolm X and Alex Haley, *The Autobiography of Malcolm X*

In her text *Killing Rage: Ending Racism* (1995), bell hooks confronts stereotypes of Black rage, and calls for a "counter-hegemonic 'race talk'" in which persons from every race, gender, and class can challenge pervasive methods of "neo-colonial white supremacy" (5). A provocative Black activist that hooks reflects on in the text is Malcolm X, who, she argues, is a prime example of the ways mass media can "collaps[e]" the nuances *of* and motivations *for* Black rage (13). As a white woman from the rural, working-class South, I did not know much about Malcolm X in comparison to Dr. Martin Luther King, Jr.—only that X was a militant contemporary to King's non-violent activism. Otherwise, I knew nothing about him. However, in graduate school Malcolm X became an important voice in my scholarship. His posthumous life narrative, *The Autobiography of Malcolm X* (1965), taught me about X's complex lived experience from childhood to his premature death in 1965.

In this essay, I reflect on hooks' assessment of Black rage and my position as white female reader. I respond to her critique white-authored scholarship in the first three essays of *Killing Rage*. Additionally, I reflect on my own connections, as a white woman, to Malcolm X and his dictated life narrative *The Autobiography of Malcolm X* (1965) as well contemporary young adult fiction. As I reflect on myself in this essay, I use an intersectional lens informed by theory from two recent texts: Anna Carastathis's *Intersectionality: Origins, Contestations, Horizons* (2016) and Patricia Hill Collins's and Sirma Bilge's *Intersectionality (Key Concepts Series)* (2020).

In/visibility and Subjectivity: Knowing When to Speak and When to Listen

In "Killing Rage: Militant Resistance," the opening essay of *Killing Rage: Ending Racism*, hooks describes the connection between subjectivity and rage, and specifically highlights (neo)colonialist interpretations of Black rage in the civil rights era and its residual effects in the 1980s and early 90s. Rage, for hooks, denotes the Black person's presence, because they refuse to passively accept oppression. That is, white societal expectations on Black people to repress their rage (in any and all situations) have uniquely colonial undertones: a colonizer/colonized dynamic is at play (12). Malcolm X, hooks argues, was frequently criticized for his activism because he refused to be passive (13). He was direct about his grievances with white supremacy in American society and government. His activism demonstrates the constructive role that rage plays in anti-racist discourse: "his passionate ethical commitment to justice served as the *catalyst* for his rage" (my emphasis, hooks 13).

I'm reminded of Jacqueline Jones Royster's powerful essay on BIPOC voices and subjectivity "When the First Voice You Hear Is Not Your Own" (1996). Royster describes her experience of listening to white voices discuss BIPOC history and experience, as if they are authorities on the subject. It is precisely white theorists' treatment of BIPOC communities as "subject matter" that Royster takes issue with (30). Like hooks, she asserts that this method of white-centric discourse reinforces colonialism in theory and practice (30-31). Royster explains that this is ultimately an issue about "the right to inquiry and discovery" in academic and mainstream discourses (31). She describes feeling a "visceral" rage at this practice: "I am made to look over a precipice," and "[find] it extremely difficult to allow the voices and experiences of people that I care about deeply to be taken and handled so carelessly and *without accountability* by strangers" (my emphasis, 31). Royster connects white theorizing of BIPOC communities to the violent discovery of North America by Christopher Columbus (31). That is, white-centric theory and praxis, similar to physical acts of colonialism, assumes ownership over BIPOC communities.

Royster calls BIPOC communities "home places" (32) and white theorists "voyeurs, tourists, and trespassers" (34). Through her spatial metaphor, she emphasizes the importance of embodiment in discourse communities, asserting "point of view matters and that we must be trained to respect points of view other than our own" (32). Moreover, when white people speak as authorities on BIPOC communities, they perpetuate colonial methods of discourse.

As a white female scholar from a working-class background, I must be more reflective and self-aware. When white scholars treat BIPOC people as subject matter, we render their experiences invisible.[1] White scholars exist at different intersections than BIPOC scholars. We can engage in personal and scholarly conversations with our BIPOC friends, but we can never be authorities on other human beings lived experiences—nor should we be. Our relationships and work require intersectional thinking and practice.[2] Consider Patricia Hill Collins' and Sirma Bilge's "working definition" in their comprehensive text *Intersectionality (Key Concepts Series)*:

> Intersectionality investigates how intersecting power relations influence social relations across diverse societies as well as individual experiences in everyday life. As an analytic tool, intersectionality views categories of race, class, gender, sexuality, class, nation, ability, ethnicity, and age—among others—as interrelated and mutually shaping one another. *Intersectionality is a way of understanding and explaining complexity in the world, in people, and in human experiences.* (emphasis added, 221)

Identities are not one-dimensional. Nor are they additive—rather, they are complex. Each context includes a variation of power dynamics so that "an individual may be an oppressor, a member of an oppressed group, or simultaneously oppressor and oppressed" (Hill Collins and Bilge, 3). Moreover, identity categories are not hierarchical because they occur simultaneously at a multiplicity of intersections.

In Search for a Safe Haven: X's *Autobiography* and the Freedom to Be

I consider X's *Autobiography* one of my favorite books, so I was particularly struck by hooks' emphasis on X in her essays. I read *The Autobiography of Malcolm X* for the first time in a graduate seminar on American life narrative in Fall 2018. I was moved by X's honesty and his commitment to developing his self-image, not just in resistance to white supremacist oppression but also when he experiences betrayal by his family and friends within the Nation of Islam (NOI). As a white woman from a working-class background, who also grew up in a fundamentalist church in rural North Florida, I deeply connected to X's experiences in the NOI. Specifically, I know what it is like to be part of a religion that makes you feel protected and *seen* by the other people in that religion, even if only for a brief time.

I started going to church regularly when I was ten years old, which is also when I started middle school at that church's private school. I was no longer attending public school because my mother feared for my safety. I was being bullied almost every day during P.E. at primary school because me and my best friend, who was a girl, were kissing. We would meet by a tall pine tree and a group of Black girls would break us up and would sometimes make fun of us. To this day, I remember telling my mother that I was being bullied because of my weight, and it's possible that that was another reason, but I recall the girls taking issue with me and my best friend kissing. My mother talked to the teachers who oversaw all the kids during P.E. and told them what was happening. I also remember trying to explain to these teachers that I was being mocked, and the teachers made fun of the way I was trying to explain myself. The issue didn't resolve itself until I finally fought back. On that day, I remember two girls holding my arms back while a third girl punched me in the stomach. I broke free of their grasp, and I pulled the first person's hair I could reach and fought back the best I could. I don't recall them hitting me after that day. I'm not proud of this moment, but I also wanted to defend myself.

I share these memories because even though I initially didn't want to switch schools, I eventually felt a sense of protection at the private school that was absent at primary school. Of course, looking back at these memories, the trade-off would be that the religious environment would be just as harmful in other ways. Within a few years, I would repress my sexuality and speak hatefully about queer sexuality until I was twenty-two years old. That is, I experienced homophobia early in my childhood, but I also perpetuated homophobia in my youth and young adulthood.

Purity culture was infused into weekly youth meetings and the curriculum at the school. I was taught early and often to avoid premarital sex and promiscuous attire, and I was frequently reminded of my responsibility to prevent men from having lustful thoughts. My religious upbringing was sexist and patriarchal. I adhered to these standards because I wanted to please the adults around me. However, by doing so, I internalized these values.

Having denounced my faith for ten years now, I am anxious as I reflect on the indoctrination I encountered on a daily basis. These sexist patriarchal standards represent an unsettling way of life, but they were normal to me when I was growing up, as was the emotionally-charged services that were typical to church and sometimes school, too.

The church was predominately white, nondenominational, and charismatic,[3] meaning that services were intense. Worship consisted of music and demonstrative participation from the congregation: clapping and, sometimes, dancing; standing, sitting, or laying close to the alter; raising your hands; and speaking in tongues. After their message, it was common for preachers and guest speakers to have an alter call

142

for prayer requests, which many times escalated into worship services. During these kinds of services, a congregation member might prostrate themselves or laugh uncontrollably.[4] These practices occurred at kids camps and youth camps,[5] and occasionally at school.[6]

I describe these practices with ambivalence because, looking back, most of the congregation, myself included, had an unhealthy dependence on outward expressions of worship, that ultimately became manipulative. I recall a night service at youth camp when the youth pastor invited us to ask for prayer. When people did not respond, his colleague interjected and elicited our participation by telling us that if we had not read our Bible in six months then we needed prayer. As he listed more examples of why our faith was in peril, more youth, including myself, came forward asking for prayer.

I do not suggest that all faiths with expressive practices are innately manipulative. Rather, my aim is to demonstrate that, at the church where I grew up, devotion and efficacy was measured by your emotional response to a given message. Matched with homophobia and the toxic purity culture, the pressure to perform was overwhelming.

The religious indoctrination and emotional manipulation typical to this church prompted me to renounce my faith in 2011. I struggled to express my anger and disorientation. On both a physical and mental level, I left a space in which I had been socialized and indoctrinated for just over a decade. At the time, this was half of my life and there were not many people who validated my experiences, because they were still a part of the church or devout Christians. I did not know, yet, how to deconstruct the church's indoctrination,[7] and I would not find the Exvangelical[8] movement on Twitter for another five years. Ultimately, when I read life narratives that challenged religious oppression, like X's *Autobiography*, I felt seen.

My mid to late twenties have been a hard journey of confronting my nuanced experiences with religion. For a time, it was a safe haven from the homophobic bullying I experienced in primary school, but I eventually became a devout Christian within just a few years and experienced many benefits while I was in high school. I loved music and started playing acoustic guitar on the worship team when I was fifteen. Within a year, I was also lead-singing for the youth band, occasionally playing guitar in the band as well. I was thriving in the community and practicing my hobbies every chance I could get. I had several friends with whom I played music and wrote songs; and me and another friend who played electric guitar started our own music duo where we played small gigs in town.

My experiences in primary school seemed very far away. And so, when I left the church in 2011, I was confused and angry. I knew that the ways I thought and viewed the world had to change, but music remained a big part of my life. I felt that I had to give everything up, including my love of music. I wanted to reject everything about church and start over with a blank slate. Singing, writing songs, playing guitar—it all reminded me of a community from which I was estranged. I didn't know which parts of my identity I could keep or give up because it had been corrupted by the church.

Reading X's *Autobiography* in 2018, I resonated with many of X's religious experiences, both within the NOI and after his excommunication. X tells Haley that during his first conversion (to the NOI), "[he] was going through the hardest thing," and "also the greatest thing, for any human being to do[:] *to accept that which is within you, and around you* (my emphasis, X and Haley 258). In the second essay of *Killing Rage*, "Beyond Black Rage: Ending Racism," hooks explores the ways in which black rage has been weaponized by mass media to stereotype black identity. She argues for a more "complex and multidimensional" discussion on the "nature of black rage" (27). Elijah Muhammed's teachings introduced to X a new way of seeing himself in relation to the world. X was empowered. He became aware of the ways in which white supremacy was central to the American cultural imaginary. And, though X would later revise his philosophy of race (whiteness versus the white devil), this conversion was significant to the development of his self-image. This quote applies to X's life, even after he is excommunicated, because he would again reconsider his self-image and the world around him *outside* of the NOI. As a white woman, I will never know the experience of a Black man coming to voice in a religion that helped him challenge white supremacy.

However, as an exvangelical,[9] I am familiar with the process of reflecting on religious experiences that somehow both empowered you *and* oppressed. I have been in mental health therapy for two years now, and I am still deconstructing my childhood religious indoctrination. It is never easy, but I think it is now less shocking. The first time you wake up to the reality of your indoctrination, it's jarring. You're figuring out how you feel and why you feel that way. You start wondering who you can trust, and if you can even trust yourself. More than anything, you feel a visceral anger and a profound sense of loss. I will never know what it is like to be oppressed because of the color of my skin. That is a fear and a rage I will never know. X's religious experiences in the NOI and in Orthodox Islam are intricately linked to his Black rights activism. That is, X's *Autobiography* describes just one Black man's experience of coming to critical consciousness in a "cultural climate where the psychological impact of racism" is completely ignored (hooks 26). His *Autobiography* is a justification of his rage and a representation of his self-recovery.

Travelling on a Theoretical "Journey" to Decolonization for Critical Self-Reflection

In essay three "Representations of Whiteness in the Black Imagination," hooks analyzes black theorization and the politics of location (41-50). hooks responds to Edward Said's essay "Travelling Theory" and agrees with the idea of thinking outside the present, "moving into the past" and beyond "fixed locations" (41-2). However, she questions use of the word 'travel' for its colonialist implications:

> "[t]ravel" is not a word that can be easily evoked to talk about the Middle Passage, the Trail of Tears, the landing of Chinese immigrants, the forced relocation of Japanese Americans, or the plight of the homeless…. it is crucial that we recognize that the hegemony of one experience of travel can make it impossible to articulate another or for it to be heard. From certain standpoints, to travel is to encounter the terrorizing force of white supremacy. (43-44)

When scholars theorize space and movement and the intersections of a given identity, then, they should utilize a "theory of journey" rather than a theory of travel: the journey "expose[s] the extent to which holding on to the concept of 'travel' as we know it is also a way to hold on to imperialism" (43). Using a theory of journey makes theorization an act of decolonization. Malcolm X isn't specifically mentioned in this essay as he is in other parts of *Killing Rage*, but I feel a theory of journey could be a useful lens for understanding his *Autobiography*. Indeed, the narrative "follows the childhood, conversions, and *travels* of the titular subject who negotiates how his experiences shape his identity as a black rights activist" (Kelley 8). I used the word 'travels' in my master's thesis to describe X's moves throughout his narrative. Even though some of those moves were made by X for his own spiritual development, such as his trip to Mecca after converting to Orthodox Islam, many were not. X's narrative represents complex power dynamics and varying relationships to different spaces. If I could revise my chapter on X, I would use Said's theory of travel in conjunction with hooks' theory of journey to further explore X's development of his self-knowledge.

In my autocritographical journey and study of *Talking Back: Thinking Feminist, Thinking Black* (1989) by bell hooks, I reflect on her essay collection in this book. *Talking Back* prompted me to consider the ways in which I theorized self-knowledge and addiction in my master's thesis *Life Narratives as Technologies of Self: Explorations of Agency in A Son of Forest and The Autobiography of Malcolm X* (2020). *Killing Rage* has been just as important for looking back on my research. hooks' discussion of rage in connection to Malcolm X's public image and his *Autobiography* were particularly important to me because I, too, feel that his *Autobiography* is a powerful depiction of the ways in which in his rage was a constructive force for his activism and for raising his critical consciousness. Studying writings by hooks has been pivotal for revising my research interests. Specifically, *Ain't I a Woman*, *Talking Back*, and *Killing Rage* will be key texts on the reading lists for my Ph.D. portfolio. *Teaching to Transgress* (1994) will be a significant text in the introduction to my dissertation because of its impact on the trajectory of my research interests. Even though X's *Autobiography* won't be included in my Ph.D. projects, hooks' words constantly prompt me to think of his life and text in new ways.

In truth, texts by hooks have forever altered the ways I see myself embodied in the world. *Killing Rage: Ending Racism* (1995) certainly qualifies as one of those texts. I was struck by hooks' explorations of solidarity. She considers the ways in which white people identify with BIPOC people in both constructive and harmful ways. I kept thinking of my favorite novel-in-verse *The Poet X* (2018), by Elizabeth Acevedo, in which the main character Xiomara comes to voice when she joins the slam poetry club at her high school. Her commitment to poetry and her mother's devotion to Catholicism are frequently at odds in the novel because her mother wants her to complete confirmation classes, which sometimes interfere with poetry club meetings. Eventually, an outburst from Xiomara's mother ends in a burned poetry notebook and a fractured mother-daughter relationship. However, the novel ends with the two of them seeking help from her mother's pastor to mend their relationship, and Xiomara continues to write and perform poetry. As much as I relate to the main character in this narrative, we differ in many ways. I reflect on my connection to Elizabeth Acevedo's narratives as I also reflect on hooks' exploration of solidarity and embodiment.

I begin with a brief excerpt from a chapter of *The Poet X*, entitled "Church Mass," in which Xiomara reflects on her embodiment (or lack thereof) in the church (Acevedo 58-59):

When the only girl I'm supposed to be
was an impregnated virgin
who was probably scared shitless.
When I'm told fear and fire
are all this life will hold for me.

When I look around the church
and none of the depictions of angels
or Jesus or Mary, not one of the disciples
look like me: morenita and big and angry.

When I'm told to have faith
in the father the son
in men and men are the first ones

to make me feel so small.

That's when I feel like a fake.
Because I nod, and clap, and "Amén" and "Aleluya,"
all the while feeling like this house his house
is no longer one I want to rent.

I know what it's like to feel apprehensive about expressing yourself, in spite of the demands of your religious upbringing to be an upright woman. In the church I grew up, a complement you might hear if you were a respectable woman was that you were a "Proverbs 31 Woman." I don't imply that it's wrong to embody the values of any spiritual text. If I were still Christian, I might appreciate the comparison because someone had acknowledged the way I represented biblical values. However, like Xiomara, I feel isolated by the ways in which virtuous womanhood is put on a pedestal in the church. It's as though there's only one right way to be a godly woman. And I, too, take issue with the trinity and the fact that it only comprises men even though a woman gave birth to Jesus. And yet, as a white woman who grew up in a predominately white evangelical church in the South, scripture and American exceptionalism were taught hand-in-hand. This amalgam of American evangelicalism, patriotism, and white supremacist patriarchy privileges white congregation members. Mine and Xiomara's religious experiences diverge at intersections of race and culture. As Xiomara states, "none of the depictions of angels / or Jesus or Mary, not one of the disciples / look like [her]: morenita and big and angry" (Acevedo 58). Her pastor gives "mangled Spanish sermons" and the women in the Bible aren't Black (Acevedo 58). Where my religious upbringing overlapped with the white American patriotism typical of Southern culture, Catholicism conflicts with Xiomara's Black and Dominican culture. That is, Xiomara feels isolated because of gender *and* race *and* culture.

The Poet X is one of my favorite books because I feel a deep solidarity with Xiomara as a poet and a woman. And yet, I respect our differences, too. As a white woman, I don't know what it's like to feel unrepresented based on my skin color and my culture. And Xiomara's experience matches that of many BIPOC women who experience gender, racial, *and* cultural oppression. Though much of our experiences overlap, mine and Xiomara's embodiment in the church is considerably different. If compare mine and Xiomara's experiences and conclude that they are generally the same experience because we're both women, I reinforce white-supremacist notions feminism.

In her essay "Revolutionary Feminism: An Anti-Racist Agenda" in *Killing Rage: Ending Racism*, hooks explores solidarity within and across feminist movements. She critiques white-power feminists who refuse to practice intersectionality or "interrogate their racial identity and racial privilege" (99-100). BIPOC, especially Black women, then, associate feminism with "bourgeois white women" and fear that solidarity with white feminists will make them out to be "race traitor[s]" (100). Ultimately, if we are to make "meaningful and powerful expression[s] of solidarity and sisterhood," white women must challenge "the racism of their white peers" (102-03). I know hooks is calling for white feminists to have constructive antiracist dialogues with their white peers. But I'd like to extend that idea and encourage white women like myself to continue reflecting on their thoughts and actions—particularly related to issues of racism. This, too, is a powerful expression of solidarity. Coming to critical consciousness doesn't mean we, as white women, no longer say or do racist things. It just means we might be more conscious of when and how we're doing it, and, hopefully, we're more receptive to change; additionally, we're also, hopefully, more receptive to criticism and dialogue with our white and BIPOC peers.

Reflecting on My White Privilege and the Role of Higher Education

One way I can reflect on myself is my positionality as a white female reader. I have an emotional connection to Xiomara in *The Poet X* because of the solidarity I feel with her as a poet and a woman. But as I reflect on this novel in light of bell hooks' words, I know, too, that my solidarity with Xiomara is nuanced. My experiences and identities are not interchangeable with Xiomara, who is black and Dominican and lives in Harlem. That is, I respect both our similarities *and* differences. My solidarity with her isn't contingent upon our sameness. I would be upholding white supremacist values if I only read books and related to characters that were exactly the same as me. It would also be dehumanizing to Xiomara if I relate to her— a Black, Dominican woman—and claim that we are essentially the same person, because I would be rendering a part of her identity invisible.

The same can be said for my connection to Malcolm X. My religious indoctrination was gendered and *racialized.* As such, my connection to X must be viewed through an intersectional lens. As a white woman, I was the scapegoat for purity culture, and as a long-time member of the church I felt pressured to perform at all times. However, my religious experiences are different than those of X, whose religious zeal and activism for Black Americans made him the target of racism in the 1950s and 60s.

Choosing Antiracism: Raising Critical Consciousness

I purposefully mention here that my journey into critical consciousness occurred by accident. Until the last few years, I treated anti-racist education as an option. Being immersed[10] in higher education since 2015, I have been exposed to new people and perspectives, and diverse texts by the nature of the institutions I attended. I have read and enjoyed Black-authored fiction and poetry and wrote essays about black literature. But I still haven't made anti-racism a priority. In my recent autocritographical writings, I reflect on the ways in which I should center anti-racism in my teaching philosophy; I also reflect on my use of white-authored, Eurocentric theory to write about black literature. That is, I'm unsure when I would have taken any initiative to be an anti-racist were it not for higher education. I fear I would have been one of those white people who claim racism isn't as much of an issue anymore because 'slavery has been over for 150 years.' This kind of thinking is prevalent in the South, or at least in some of the circles in which I grew up.

Additionally, thinking of my previous reflections on my childhood, I was immersed in white supremacist culture from a young age, and higher education is the primary reason I came to question my faith and my limited worldview. Without higher education, I fear I would have a similar mindset to the person I was in the mid to late 2000s. I, therefore, need to consider the ways in which my relationship to education has shifted between private, predominately white schools and a public, predominately white university. It's worth noting here that the public universities I've attended since 2013 have been more diverse than my private education, but they are still predominately white institutions overall. Am I, for example, co-dependent on higher education to help my think differently about the world around me? Since moving away from college in 2009 ultimately resulted in my deconstruction from harmful religious affiliations, perhaps, I assume that college has the potential to change for better, most of the time. But I was a white woman from a working-class background. How differently would I feel if I were Black? In *Killing Rage,* bell hooks notes that "integrated education structures" as spaces where white people have historically "colonize[d] the minds and imaginations of black folks" (109). Moving to a new location and attending college helped me think differently about my embodiment in the world, separate from church. But it did not prompt me to think as critically about my racial identity and privilege.

Also, in *Killing Rage* in the essay "Teaching Resistance: The Racial Politics of Mass Media," hooks asserts that "racial integration" was the strategy for "maintain[ing] … neo-colonial white supremacy…. Gone was any separate space apart from whites where organized militant resistance could emerge" (109-110). Here, my privilege is evident. I finally felt empowered when I had (literal) space to consider who I was irrespective of my having grown up in a small church space. This isn't to say that BIPOC college students don't have similar experiences. That would be incorrect and racist. What I mean, though, is that I didn't experience microaggressions or other forms of racism because of the color of my skin. I also didn't feel underrepresented at a pre-dominantly white institution. So, when I think that my anti-racist education occurred by accident, I feel embarrassed because it demonstrates my own ignorance and privilege. I don't know that it happened by accident, but I will correct that statement now and say that it happened through a slow, slow process of coming to terms with my religion, sexuality, and *then* my racial identity. My journey toward critical race consciousness represents the experiences and texts that have made me the critical anti-racist thinker I am today.

Becoming an Antiracist Ally: Education for Liberation

In the essay "Loving Blackness as Political Resistance" in *Killing Rage: Ending Racism*, bell hooks engages with *A Black Theology of Liberation* (1970) in which its author, James Cone, "call[s] for" a "critical interrogation of 'whiteness' while simultaneously problematizing constructions of white identity within white supremacist culture" (148-149). hooks responds to Cone's text, noting that—

> many white folks active in anti-racist struggle today are able to acknowledge that all whites (as well as everyone within white supremacist culture) have learned to overvalue 'whiteness' even as they simultaneously learn to devalue blackness. They understand the need, at least intellectually, to alter their thinking. Central to this process of unlearning white supremacist attitudes and values is *the deconstruction of the category 'whiteness.'* (my emphasis, 150)

This is such as an important concept. As an anti-racist, I must think critically about my racial identity and its relationship to a 400 years long history of colonial oppression against BIPOC folks. When I consider my own embodiment in my culture and society, what does that embodiment say about my relationship to education? To the law? But critically thinking of my own embodiment in the world and questioning whiteness isn't enough. hooks also asserts in *Killing Rage* that we must "learn to identify with and love blackness" as well (151). If we attempt to be colorblind or ignore each other's differences, we're simply reinforcing neo-colonial white supremacy. Rather, we can "learn how to identify with" each other's "difference[s]— to see it as a basis for solidarity" (151). Here, I do feel I've done something right. Many of my favorite authors are BIPOC. Alongside Elizabeth Acevedo, I also love Jacqueline Woodson, Talia Hibbert, Danez Smith, and Upile Chisala. For the past four years, I've made it a priority to read more BIPOC authors and stories in my free time. I continue to do so now, and I'm always finding new favorite books and authors.

I have highlighted Elizabeth Acevedo in this essay because I truly love the narratives she creates. I love her explorations of religion, sexuality, community, race, and family. Her stories center on one or more characters and their embodiment in a world that can feel so isolating but is also so full of potential. As a white woman who grew in the rural South, I understand that feeling very well. But I also know that my similarities end where Acevedo's Afro-Latinx, Catholic characters experiences in New York City begin. I feel it is only appropriate to end this section with a quote from

Acevedo's most recent novel-in-verse *Clap When You Land* (2020), in which two sisters meet for the first due to the sudden death of their father:

> There is another girl
> on this planet
> who is my kin.
>
> My father
> lied to me
> every day of my life.
>
> I am not alone
> but the only family
> I have besides Tía
> are all strangers to me.
> I want to put my fingers
> against my sister's cheek.
>
> I want to put my face
> in her neck & ask
> if she hurts the way I do.
>
> who would understand
> my heart right now?
> If I find her
>
> would I find a breathing piece
> of myself I had not known
> was missing?

Interrogating the Toxicity of Colorblindness—Every Day

During one week in a graduate literature course on theory and criticism I took in spring 2021, taught by USF English professor Dr. John Lennon, students discussed several writings on intersectionality[11] in relation to domestic violence, politics, and academic disciplines. Having read them after reflecting on several of bell hooks' texts, these writings were especially enlightening. For example in one of them, *Seeing*

Race Again, I was compelled by the author's call to counter colorblindness, which "requires an interrogation into the disciplinary, cultural, and historical dynamics that sustain a disaggregated, partial, and parochial knowledge base about [the topic of race itself]" (Crenshaw et. al. 5). Given the infinite ways in which constructions of race and whiteness are embedded into every aspect of society and its institutions, we as anti-racist allies must be persistent raising our critical consciousness. That is, we must choose to do so every day. As I finished reading *Killing Rage: Ending Racism*, I had several experiences that reminded me why colorblindness is toxic and why unconditional allyship is a daily choice. I practice intersectionality as a reader, and my values have been put to the test. As I reflect on reading the final essays in *Killing Rage*, the process called me to remember why I decided to stop reading a book series I had begun some time ago. In the last essays of hooks' book, she further exposes the ways in which white supremacy is integral to enculturation and related to one's daily actions and ways of thinking.

In "Overcoming White Supremacy: A Comment," hooks writes about the importance of language and authenticity if people are going to practice anti-racism in their lives. She notes that

> [w]hen liberal whites fail to understand how they can and/or do embody white supremacist values and beliefs even though they may not embrace racism as prejudice or control …, *they cannot recognize the ways their actions support and affirm* the very structure of racist domination and oppression that they profess to wish to see eradicated (my emphasis, 185).

Whites who identify as anti-racist allies have to be conscious about our positions in a white supremacist society. And once we're conscious of those positions, *we have to name them*. Even if we are not actively trying to be racist, there are still ways in which we are complicit in perpetuating white supremacist values (hooks 187). For white people like myself, we inherit varying levels of privilege, depending on class, *just because of the color of our skin*. It therefore takes a conscious effort to acknowledge that privilege and consider our positionality in a given situation. I was especially compelled by hooks' assertion to use the terms "white supremacy" (187) and "assimilation" (188-189). These terms indicate the ways in which success in a white supremacist patriarchal society is contingent upon one's relationship to whiteness (189). It follows, then, that assimilation is a dehumanizing process for

BIPOC. As hooks notes, their success depends on parts of who they are in order to perform whiteness (189).

As a white female ally from a working-class background, intersectionality has become an important value in my academic and personal education on anti-racism; so, I was glad to learn more about the ways in which intersectionality is needed in other areas of North American society. I have been inspired to discuss ideas for raising critical consciousness with my colleagues. During one week in Dr. Lennon's theory and criticism class, students divided into small groups to discuss the readings. My group was predominately white and there weren't Black students present. Several peers asked similar questions to the effect of: "Now that we know this information, how do we make authentic changes in our daily lives?" Three of us shared some experiences of discussing (or, struggling to discuss) race in our classroom, and considered how we might make these changes as educators. My colleague Lydia posed this question to the class when we returned from small groups.

Little did I know, I would get the chance to put these ideas into practice just hours after that particular session ended. I logged on to Twitter, as I usually do. As I scrolled, I noticed that a white young adult author I follow, Emily A. Duncan, was trending on Book Twitter.[12] I've been an avid supporter of Duncan's debut gothic fantasy *Wicked Saints* (2019), which explores religious and political intrigue in an imaginary world inspired by Russian and Polish history and mythology. I recently re-read the first two books in this series with some friends in anticipation for the release of the final book in the trilogy, which recently released. I also preordered a gift set from a small business that included the third novel *Blessed Monsters* (2021), signed by the author, along with merchandise inspired by the series.

I started following Duncan's Twitter account in March 2020 after reading her debut novel. Since then, I've noticed that Duncan either primarily posts or retweets art and concepts about upcoming works and their opinions on *Star Wars*. So, I was in shock as I learned the negative reasons for Duncan's attention on Book Twitter. They were initially trending because they were outed for harassing an Asian author, Hafsah Faizal, who debuted in the same year as Duncan. This alone was disconcerting, but I kept reading tweets by both white and BIPOC users. I learned that in 2019, Duncan has also bullied Twitter users. Reviewers have also criticized the antisemitism they claimed were deliberate in the world-building and characters of Duncan's debut series, which I hadn't noticed. For two days, I listened to other reviewers in the bookish community, primarily on Twitter but occasionally on Instagram. I read Twitter threads describing blood libel[13] as well as Jewish history[14] in early modern eastern Europe.

In *Killing Rage: Ending Racism,* hooks' essay "Keeping a Legacy of Shared Struggle" seems relevant to the events on Book Twitter that week. In this essay, hooks reflects on antisemitism in the South and within the Black community in the North, as well as the writings in Elly Bulkin's text *Yours in Struggle: Three Feminist Perspectives on Anti-Semitism and Racism* (1984). In particular, hooks writes that white supremacist patriarchal culture implies isn't just inherently racist and sexist, but also anti-Semitic (206). This is due to the

> profound link between white fascism and black fascism, white conservatism and black conservation. Black folks who are anti-Semitic are not just under the influence of "crazed" Black male leaders; they are also guided by the anti-Semitism that is *rampant in the culture as a whole.* (my emphasis, 209).

I shouldn't be surprised by hooks words. And yet, I am. Growing up in a predominantly white evangelical religious culture, Jewish culture is highly respected. And so, similar to hooks' religious experience, anti-Semitism was not part of my reality growing up. My adulthood, and the current anti-Semitic events, reveal the ways in which anti-Semitism is still very much rampant in the U.S. I'm reminded again of the deficit in my own worldview and education, and I am committed to being a reader who is self-aware of her own biases and shortcomings and ready to do better for herself and her BIPOC friends and colleagues.

Other social media users have shared evidence of Duncan's connection to the nationalistic philosophy of rodnovery.[15] I'm not saying that authors cannot write about and challenge nationalistic ideas in their texts. Plenty of authors do so. However, the evidence is clear that Duncan perpetuates racism in word and practice. I've also read Twitter threads by Asian authors Hafsah Faizal, who shared her experience with Duncan, and Rin Chupeco, who shared similar experiences as Asian author coming up in the publishing industry in 2012. I've always felt that the "bookish" community is, for the most part, a diverse and welcoming community. But it's a community that exists primarily in a white supremacist patriarchal society. Publishers also exists in that same society. And so, racism and anti-semitism are very present within the community, whether readers and authors realize it or not.

During a Monday evening in 2021, I emailed the company from which I ordered Emily A. Duncan's third novel *Blessed Monsters* (2021), asking for a refund on my purchase. The chances were slim since the books would be released on Tuesday the next day, but since then I've been given a full refund; and the brand has offered refunds to all subscribers who purchased Duncan's book. On that Tuesday evening, Duncan shared an apology on Twitter[16] and Instagram which made me feel justified in my decision to stop supporting them on social media and in my personal life. Duncan admitted to all allegations against them: bullying and harassment towards Twitter users and Asian authors, and the antisemitism inherent in her novels. I was reminded of this quote in the final essay of *Killing Rage*, "Beloved Community: a World without Racism"—

> In the past the affirmation of white supremacy in everyday life was declared via assertions of hatred and/or power …; *in our contemporary times white belief in black inferiority is most often registered by the assertion of power.* (my emphasis, 268)

Duncan's contract with their publisher was a six-figure deal, and she was attacking white and BIPOC in the community who had nowhere near the influence and power they had.

I chose to reflect on this incident in this autocritography because it's important that I continue to reflect on my thoughts and actions. Coming to critical consciousness doesn't mean we, as white women, no longer say or do racist things. It just means we might be more conscious of when and how we're doing it, and, hopefully, we're more receptive to change; additionally, we're also, hopefully, more receptive to criticism and dialogue with our white and BIPOC peers.

I feel this is an important part of choosing to be anti-racist every day. When I realize I've been complicit in the perpetuation of racism, that is, when I learn something that changes that way I previously thought about an issue or topic related to white supremacy—I must change my way of thinking. More importantly, I must listen to and dialogue with all the people who are bringing these issues to light for freedom for the oppressed. As Jacqueline Jones Royster writes in her essay "When the First Voice You Hear is Not Your Own":

> We need to get over our tendencies to be too possessive and to resist locking ourselves into the tunnels of our own visions and direct experience. As community

members, we must learn to have new faith in the advantage of sharing. As strangers, we must learn to treat the loved people and places of Others with care and to understand that, when we do not act respect- fully and responsibly, we leave ourselves rightly open to wrath. The challenge is not to work with a fear of abuse or a fear of retaliation, however. The challenge is to teach, to engage in research, to write, and to speak with Others with the determination to operate not only with professional and personal integrity, but also with the specific knowledge that communities and their ancestors are watching. (33)

If I'm going to change the ways I listen to and engage with my BIPOC colleagues, I have to decolonize the ways in which I participate in discourse communities. It is imperative that I raise my critical consciousness and practice anti-racism in my scholarship. Moreover, I want my scholarship to be ethical and engaging. I should not be conflating "subject matter" with individuals (Royster 32). To do so would mean that I am upholding white supremacist capitalist imperialist values in the academy. I must reflect on my choices and consider the methods by which I engage topics and dialogue with individuals.

Notes

[1] Here, I invoke Anna Carastathis' words in her text *Intersectionality: Origins, Contestations, Horizons*: "[i]intersectionality reveals the absence of concepts adequate to the lived experiences of simultaneous oppressions" (118).

[2] Intersectional work always involves a social justice component. Self-reflection and ethical scholarship are two ways white scholars can practice intersectionality.

[3] Pentecostal churches such as Assembly of God and Church of God are the denominations that most closely compare to the church of my youth and young adulthood.

[4] This is called being "slain" or "slaying in the spirit." When occurs, the people praying for this person will "catch" them and lower them to the ground, so they are not hurt. Laughing uncontrollably refers to being "drunk in the spirit." You can view an example of this on a large scale in the documentary *Lakeland: The Movie* (unrated, 2012). On YouTube the title is "Lakeland: The Movie (Documentary film on Todd Bentley & the Florida Outpouring)": https://www.youtube.com/watch?v=UDEsXVUQeLo&t=0s. Roy Peterson, a UK filmmaker and blogger, spent two years on this documentary. My family never went to this revival, but several members of my church travelled to Lakeland, FL several times to attend it.

[5] I attended three kids camps before I became a counselor when I was a fourteen and attended seven or eight of the youth camps. The documentary *Jesus Camp* (2006, PG-13), directed by Heidi Ewing and Rachel Grady, is a n accurate example of the kids and youth camps I attended in the 2000s.

[6] Though it only happened once, I recall a time in middle school where some students were listening to a CD of worship music in the sanctuary, and the room slowly erupted into laughter. It started with just a few people laughing to themselves, but their actions seemed to be contagious. I, too, was part of this group. Admittedly, I recall being confused as to why everyone was laughing, but I joined in because I thought it was funny and, perhaps, I was supposed to be following along.

[7] Deconstruction is a common term in this community and refers to the process of unlearning harmful religious doctrines.

[8] On Twitter, you can search the hashtag #exvangelical, and you will find a multitude of accounts (with this hashtag in their bio), tweets, and subtweets discussing experiences, usually toxic, growing up in evangelical, sometimes fundamentalist, churches. The hashtag is not meant to single out spiritual or non-spiritual people, but rather to bring together people who are questioning their faith or deconstructing their religious indoctrination. Another hashtag #EmptyThePews is also common in this community, but most 'members,' including me, call themselves exvangelicals or exvies.

[9] This is a community mainly on Twitter, but also can be found on Instagram, that uses the hashtag #exvangelical to share stories of doubt, recovery, and deconstruction from the Evangelical movement.

[10] Immersed as in: being a full-time student or working within the university while also attending the university.

[11] Specifically, we read the introduction to Kimberlé Crenshaw's *Mapping the Margins: Intersectionality, Identity Politics, and Violence Against Women of Color* (2008); the introduction to the collaborative text *Seeing Race Again* (2019); Crenshaw's essay "How Colorblindness Flourished in the Age of Obama"; and George Lipsitz's essay "The Sounds of Silence."

[12] Book Twitter is a community of readers, and sometimes authors, on Twitter who share memes and opinions on books; share book recommendations; and debrief issues in the publishing industry and within the bookish community at large.

[13] From the Twitter account @novatjerneld.

[14] From the Twitter account @anon25096638.

[15] The Instagram account @bookish.you.should.know shared a sequence of Duncan's tweets from February 27, 2019 as evidence. I reviewed this Twitter thread myself, and it appears Duncan used this philosophy in developing the world and plot of their debut series.

[16] Transcription of Duncan's apology, posted to Twitter at 5:59pm on Tuesday April 7, 2021, reads: "I want to issue an apology, especially to my BIPOC colleagues in publishing whom my words and actions have harmed. I have made remarks in various places that were hurtful and mean and through my privilege I did not see that I was using my status to hurt others, but I was. There is no excuse for it, it was racist. I am

deeply sorry, and while I do not expect forgiveness, I do want to speak directly to those I've harmed. My words and my behavior were inappropriate and I did not see when friends were trying to call me in. It was and remains reprehensible, and I apologize for it. To those specific individuals that I have hurt, I would like to personally apologize, but only if you are willing, comfortable, and would feel safe hearing from me, and I understand if not. [paragraph break] I also want to apologize for an instance of poor behavior on Twitter where I was cavalier about a very serious topic. My callousness caused harm and I should have both recognized spoken on it much earlier than this. [paragraph break] In terms of criticisms that an element of my book included an anti-Semitic plot, I did recognize the significance while researching and tried to handle this in a sensitive way, but I fell short. I am sorry for the harm this has caused. I will take more care when writing outside of my own experience and understanding. [paragraph break] In making amends, what damage is done cannot be undone. I will be taking an extended leave of social media because I recognize that I have a lot of work to do on addressing and rectifying my behavior, including working on conducting myself in a more respectful and mindful manner toward both my peers and my audience, and I want to give my full focus and attention to this."

Works Cited

Acevedo, Elizabeth. *Clap When You Land*. Harper Teen: New York, 2020

--- *The Poet X*. Harper Teen: New York, 2018.

Carastathis, Anna. *Intersectionality: Origins, Contestations, Horizons,* Lincoln: U of Nebraska Press, 2016.

Crenshaw, Kimberlé Williams et. al. *Seeing Race Again.* University of California Press: Oakland, 2019.

Hill Collins, Patricia., and Sirma Bilge. *Intersectionality*, 2nd ed. Newark: Polity Press, 2020.

hooks, bell. *Killing Rage: Ending Racism*. Henry Holt and Company: New York, 1995.

Kelley, Tiffanie. *Life Narratives as Technologies of Self: Explorations of Agency in A Son of Forest and The Autobiography of Malcolm X*. 2020. U of Central Florida, Master's Thesis.

Royster, Jacqueline Jones. "When the First Voice You Hear is Not Your Own." *College Composition and Communication*, vol. 47, no. 1, 1996, pp. 29-40. *JSTOR*, https://www.jstor.org/stable/358272. Accessed 18 June 2021.

X, Malcolm and Alex Haley. *The Autobiography of Malcolm X.* 1965, Modern Classics edition, Introduction by Paul Gilroy, Penguin Books: London, 2001. hooks, bell. *Killing Rage: Ending Racism*. Henry Holt and Company: New York, 1995.

11

Exposing the Invisible Maladies in the Lives
of South Asian Communities
Manjari Thakur

Scientifically, considering the deadly effects of the COVID-19 during the pandemic, each one of us has been confined to our homes, our rooms, and our own bubbles. We have been trapped within our own lives for months with no end in sight. We are still afraid to leave our homes for the safety of our relatives and the people we love. We are also terrified that other people might bring us harm by being in contact with us. Being isolated is no way to live, for fear, anxiety, and isolation become our only companions. Now imagine isolating and living a quarantined life for the rest of your life, not because of the COVID-19 pandemic and our shifting realities but because of the hesitation to walk outside the door only to be attacked racially. This attack comes into action solely by the way you look and speak. Imagine living such a life in a country that is not yours and the torment it brings. This inescapable torment is the current reality of the Asian community in this "white supremacist capitalist patriarchal society" (hooks, *Teaching Community: A Pedagogy of Hope* 26). Considering what is happening around us almost every day, through this essay, I will take you on a journey that is represented as a "normal" day in the lives of Black Indigenous People of Color (BIPOC). I will focus on my own path of inner-healing "killing rage" towards television and mass media that normalized racism in my everyday personal and professional experiences. Having become critically conscious of the deadly effects of white supremacy, I expose ways through which many of us have become complicit in the perpetuation of it. I will also demonstrate the ways we, as Indians in the U.S., pursue the "American Dream"—especially related to how individuals in the Indian community act to remain invisible or to assimilate into whiteness only to be marginalized because of their racial "other"ness.

I begin this essay by identifying myself before I delve deep into the enthralling antiracist work bell hooks writes about in *Killing Rage: Ending Racism*. Who am I, you ask? I am a straight, rebellious woman of Indian descent, born and raised in New Delhi, who has also lived in the UK, Europe, and now living in the U.S. I am in my first year of the Ph.D. program in Literature at the University of South Florida, where I am also a Graduate Assistant. I suppose, only by identifying myself as a whole person, I am able to identify myself more with bell hooks' work. I belong to the Asian community in America. The term 'Asian community' "encompasses a broad array of nationalities and accompanying differences" (Yoo and Kuo, 2021). I am the Indian next door—the one you see almost every day in your normal life. And I am aware that I look different from the images that are usually associated with the Indian community—like shown through the character of Apu in *The Simpsons*. So, look at all the people behind these made-up images, by unhinging opinions already formed. Look at the routes that have broken and built me as a person, and us, Asians, as a community, to discover the histories that have gone into the building of our identities, and to understand the nuances of our engagement with the world around us. Because—

> We are more than the mere stereotypes and fetishes,
> Our pain is real like yours.
> So wake up and say,
> I see you, I hear you
> I hold you in my heart.

Repeat these words again and again because our voices and our stories matter, and do not feel like you have to state your own trauma when you listen to someone's voice that is not 'white'. As seen apparently by the latest attacks, Southeast Asian women are so often seen and treated as objects, as trophies and this is the very problem that we are facing today. This is the type of violence that emerges through microaggression. Sue et al. in "Racial microaggressions in everyday life: Implications for counseling" defines microaggression as "brief and commonplace daily verbal, behavioral and environmental indignities, whether intentional or unintentional, that communicate hostile, derogatory or negative racial slights and insults that potentially have a harmful or unpleasant psychological impact on the target person or group" (11). To simply put it in words, microaggressions are the everyday denigrated discriminatory actions against the members of a marginalized group. This microaggression leads to the type of violence that includes the intersectionality of how Asian/Southeast Asian/women of color are treated, which further includes their trafficking, dating back to the colonization of India and mass-migration of Indians to the U.S. However, as Anne Anlin Cheng writes for *The New York Times*, "When it comes to Asian American grief, do Americans want to know?" There are very few who want to read about the race issue and the subjects related to women of color—a few who share bell hooks thought that there has been "a long tradition of sexist and racist thinking which has always represented race and racism as male turf, as hard politics, a playing field where women do not really belong" (*Killing Rage: Ending Racism* 1). Nonetheless, no one can be in more denial than the man who regardless of numerous pieces of evidence in front of him thinks that racism and sexism and all the pain in this world do not exist. Yet, here I am, and like hooks, "I find myself reluctant to "talk race" because it hurts," but I will do it nonetheless (*Killing Rage: Ending Racism* 3).

I remember reading writings by bell hooks for the first time. I started with *Ain't I a Woman: Black Woman and Feminism,* and it crushed my soul. I believe that my reaction/response to reading this canonical text can never be expressed in simple words as the book made me realize that I know so little, almost nothing, about the history of Black womanhood. I also realized that there may be many like me out there on this planet who probably do not know many racially marginalized groups and their daily lives. After reading *Ain't I a Woman?* I started reading *Talking Back: Thinking Feminist, Thinking Black,* which further made me realize that being an Indian woman is like being on a stage all the time, wherever, and whenever we are, we are always performing a role, and the masks on our faces are caked with the remains of every role we've struggled to shed. The shadows never leave us—wife, mother, sister, daughter. Our identities are patchwork quilts of everything we fall short of, and every day is designed to remind us of that. There are blank forms that glare at us, responsibilities that tower over us—we are told to measure our worth in relation to someone else, someone who can choose to deny us our identity, our rights as if we don't exist as a whole. However, it is not just Indian women but females of the BIPOC communities who are still carving out their identities in this world of patriarchal domination by white men and men of color.

After reading *Talking Back*, I couldn't stop myself from reading bell hooks' riveting and canonical works. I always think of her work as a personal challenge to me. Even though she writes beautifully and in a conversational tone, it can be deceptive and complex at times. Even though she is dialoguing with me, sharing her ideas and her ways of "killing rage," especially related to racism, holding my hand through these difficult times, it remains a challenge for me. At times, her work is re-affirming, and at other times, it is painful to read. Perhaps, being uncomfortable and feeling the pain that is related to the conversations about racism is what *all of us* need today. Each book by hooks I have read leaves me with a sense that pushes me beyond my comfort zone—that forces me to shout and tell my stories and look at the world directly in the eyes of those that do not want me to exist. However, when I read bell hooks' works, I never leave any of them feeling a little lost or clueless as to what needs to change in me or in society, nor am I ever unaware of the realities and complications of human beings she puts forward.

The Painful Difficulty of Reading *Killing Rage: Ending Racism*

I must admit, however, that reading *Killing Rage: Ending Racism* often left me clueless. It took a while to read because this book is difficult, dense, painful, and true. This book has provided me with the vocabulary to finally define the pain and anger I have felt in the past, and am facing now. Each essay within this book touches upon a subject that relates directly to me as a brown, Indian woman. It is almost astonishing that bell hooks wrote this book almost 30 years ago, but it stands so true to today's climate. It is as if she just finished writing this book. The issues she so eloquently wrote about when I was born, are still relevant to the world I am living in, and relevant to me as a grown woman of color at age 27. She, through her essays, establishes her main idea—her argument that feminism and racism go hand in hand, and we must consider these issues together to challenge and eradicate the basis of racism.

I am not saying that her work is confusing, rather this book is thoughtful, clear, insightful, and provides a nuanced consideration of race and BIPOC liberation which takes us "beyond the black-and-white binary of racial discussions in America, to understand how white supremacy pits minority against minority" (Yoo and Kuo, 2021). Yet, *Killing Rage: Ending Racism* leaves me clueless about my status in this foreign land I think of as the United States of America. It's not that her work is alien to me, rather it is too familiar and hurtful to talk about, because, like hooks, I think "some days it is just hard to accept that racism can still be such a powerful dominating force in all our lives" (263).

Each essay in *Killing Rage* is sharp and unapologetic, but after each essay that I read, I cannot figure out what exactly to do with the countless timeless issues that seem all the more timeless in the wake of reckoning with my feelings with regard to "whiteness", and as hooks says "the enemy [is] not white people. It [is] white supremacy" (196). When in this foreign land someone, who does not belong to the Asian community sees me, they recognize my color, my race, and they want to know about my history, my social position, and economic worth so that they can figure out to what extent they will be racist. These are some of the factors that comprise my value, give the totality of my life, and my freedom. Thus, after finishing the book I could not figure out how I can either hide from the eye-sight of whiteness or show my "killing rage" only to be marginalized for long. I am told time and time again that people around me, including myself, and people belonging to my community suffer from racism, and I can feel my own rage grow each day. This rage does not come from anything else, but the mere fact that racism is a part of our lives. This rage stems from the fact that it is so easy for us to be pushed aside to make way for "the white man". This rage comes from the stereotypes I hear every day.

However, when I express this rage, I am told that my pain isn't real—people who are attacked aren't related to me, so how can my pain be real? Do I have to be related to them to feel the pain? Isn't having a human relationship enough? In *Killing Rage: Ending Racism*, hooks talks about the rage and imbalance that we see in today's world—trauma within the BIPOC communities, stereotypes, internalized racism in mass media, and the friendship between black and white people. These spectra of topics covered by bell hooks in the various chapters in *Killing Race* are looked at to create a positive plan for the future rather than dwelling on creating a victim identity and what has happened before. She writes about her past experiences to bring forward the issues she faced almost 30 years back, but are still prevalent in today's world. She pinpoints her "killing rage" towards things that reinscribe racism still today. I want to write about happier things but that feels inappropriate given the timeless issues we are in. Even so, I will write about issues of racism, the sadness that comes with it, and I will write about how sorrow has absorbed itself into me and I am drenched in its syrupy affection. I will focus on my "killing rage" and I will take you on this with me journey that is considered a "normal" day in the lives of Black Indigenous People of Color.

bell hooks asks us to not remain repressed, contained, or trapped within our rage, and we must not. Her writings critique racism and stereotypes and yet remain optimistic in the belief that the future can be envisioned without racism. No matter our difference across boundaries of race, gender, class, sexuality, ability, and/or culture—we still are a part of the problem of white supremacy, and we need to have critical strategies to deal with this "killing rage" within us to change the world we live in. However, as stated earlier, I have been a part of this world for almost three decades, and from 2020 to 2021, I find myself trapped in the U.S., not only due to the pandemic but also because of racism. "Killing rage" that is within all of us comes from the world we live in, and the people we see around us. As I have also stated, I want to write about happier things, things that make me happy but it feels inappropriate because I am surrounded by the tragedy of being a woman and a woman of color. Considering the complexities associated with my identity, I will instead focus on the day-to-day incidents of my life.

My Day-to-Day Life Incidents

Incident 1: When I was born, my parents very lovingly gave me a name that meant the world to them. It's Manjari *(m-uh-n-j-uh-r-ee)*. It means purity and sanctity of basil flowers. I love my name, but then I moved to different countries where my name is considered exotic, where my skin color is also viewed as exotic. In these countries, I tried to explain to everyone around me who was white how to spell and say my name. To my dismay, many of them around me ignored the way my name should be said. Instead, they invented a new way of pronouncing it or simply laughed it off. I was called mun-JAARI, MAN-Jerry, or the worst, Mun-jury. I have spent my entire adult life in the UK, Europe, and now in the US, but I realized years back that it is much easier to have a name that is not an inconvenience to others. Now I prefer to be called "M" because I hate dealing with the burden of correcting people each time they laugh at my name or pronounce it wrong. I hated the shame I felt every time a new professor would butcher my name. I go by "M" because I don't want to deal with the disrespect, but most of all, I don't want the inconvenience—inconvenience to others. This may seem like a small thing, but it is not. Our names are our identity. It is our heritage. It is what we are left with that reminds us who we are, and where we come from. So, yes, learn to say one's name right, and perhaps by doing so you will make a difference in that person's life.

Incident 2: The year 2016. Brexit results announced. I decide to go out and get groceries for the week. I step out and start walking. What do I see? A group of white men walking towards me, and another group of white men and *women* in their car, driving towards me. They stop. They stare. They take out their cricket bat. They open their mouth and say "Get the fuck out of our country, you bitch." One white woman got out of the car and almost spat on me. Another man opened his mouth and said, "This is our country. We will take it back. If you stay, you will be raped." No one came to help me. Even though my body was boiling with rage like bell hooks my "rage was merely a sign of powerlessness" (*Killing Rage* 12). I started walking and then running back to my apartment. I did not go out for almost a week. I stayed in without any groceries. I stayed hungry.

From this experience, I learned that I must stand up for people's human rights. I must believe, support, and protect people. The Asian community sees violence on a daily basis. Asian women in the Western world are often seen as erotic and exotic objects, especially through media portrayal. Words such as dusky, docile, and quiet signify how Western societies fetishize Asian woman's bodies. Help us stop this racism and fetishization.

Incident 3: March 2021. I wanted to have a relaxed day, so I decided to go to the beach in Florida. There I am reading my book in my own happy zone, suddenly a group of white men sitting not so far from me yelled. "Yo, is your husband making the bomb at home!" followed by the voice of the other white man: "Don't annoy her, she will sleep with you without you annoying her." I, like hooks, believe "that one fantasy of whiteness is that the threatening Other is always a terrorist" (*Killing Rage* 44), and I think we will always be terrorists in their eyes unless we are "in the absence of the reality of whiteness" (*Killing Rage* 45). So, what do I do next? I get up and leave. It is the easiest thing to do, get up and leave, for what else can I do in a country that is not mine. I believe by this time, after coming face to face with thousands of such incidents, it doesn't affect my thick brown skin. I have always known about racism and its impact on people across racial, ethnic, and cultural identities, and I have always known the ways racist thinking is prevalent in today's world. However, it was only after I moved to other countries that I saw it closely—face to face. Again, like bell hooks, being "close to white folks, I am forced to witness firsthand their willful ignorance about the impact of race and racism. The harsh absolutism of their denial" (*Killing Rage* 17). It disheartens me, yes, but can I do anything else than feeling upset? As an antiracist ally, if you see anyone around you who is hearing such racist comments, or who is having racial slurs directed at them, stand up for them.

Incident 4: I cook food that reminds me of my home country, and people around me who are not Asians or Indians tell me, "Your food smells." And we take it lightly or laugh it off because "[i]f we pretend racism doesn't exist, that we do not know what it is or how to change it – it never has to go away" (*Killing Rage* 4), but the smell will go away with all the laughs.

These mentioned incidents are just a few I feel comfortable writing about so openly, but there are so many more I don't even want to relive in my memory. Even though these incidents took place outside my home country, many incidents happened within my own culture. To begin with, India won its freedom from British *Raj* in 1947 (it has *just* been 74 years since our fight for independence). Before 1947, my country India was colonized by "white supremacist capitalist patriarchs" (hooks, *Teaching to*

Transgress 26) who brought with them a culture that never left. We (read: Indians, a part of South Asian communities) cling to these cultures, traditions, and principles as if our country was born with these beliefs. Also, to retain these dogmas, we relate more to the white voice—it is hidden inside all of us. We respond more to it. We only answer to it and we are racially colonized because of it. Hira Singh and M.A Kalam in "India's Race Problem: Ignorance and Denial," mentions that: "Ignorance is not the whole story of India's race consciousness. It is a duality marked by a reverential attitude towards whites and its very opposite towards blacks that is pervasive among Indians cutting across class, caste, regional and religious lines which defines the common sense of India's race consciousness" (75). The colonization of India left a "dis-ease" (*Teaching to Transgress* 15) that forced us to behave like white people, which ultimately segregated the classes within our culture—and it was not just the segregation of classes, but also the segregation of skin color. I, a non-white, female of color, have lived 19 years of my life in India and I am ashamed to say that colonization has ingrained in us the idea to be white, act white, and resist everything that is not white. Whiteness prevails in my community not in actual terms of skin color but in terms of ideology that has taken over us after colonization, and sadly it has taken over the Indian education system too.

Teaching Colonization for Assimilation

The education system in India is based on the British education system that eradicates the very history of India and Indian people because there was this "emergence of neo-colonial white supremacy" (*Killing Rage* 109) that shaped our education system to maintain the domination of white people. bell hooks mention that "placed in positions of authority in educational structures and on the job, white people could oversee and eradicate organized resistance" (109), and in a similar way when white people left India years back, they left their media, their structured white institutions to shape and mold us. Mass media plays an important role in our life— before a child can even learn how to spell their name, they would know how to turn on the television and that is the kind of impact television has always had in our lives because it was a tool used by white patriarchs as "television and mass media were the other great neo-colonial weapons" (*Killing Rage* 110).

Growing up in a heterosexual, patriarchal, orthodox family I was told to learn English, and one of the ways to do it was to watch BBC, English movies, shows, and read newspapers. It was through mass media that I learned how to speak the way I do today and this way "white supremacist values were projected into our living rooms, into the most intimate spaces of our lives by mass media" (*Killing Rage* 110). In my childhood days, it was this whiteness that I craved to assimilate with people I didn't know then—I just knew how they would look—white. Various movies were presented to me to understand what "life" really looks like, it created "the longing to have access to material rewards granted whites (the luxury and comfort represented in advertising and television)" (*Killing Rage* 110). It created a world for me that was full of rainbows and sunshine, but no one ever mentioned to me that under these rainbows are dark clouds that drown human emotions and flood the lives of marginalized groups.

While growing up, I attended many international schools, as my father wanted to make sure that I learn the language of the colonizer to have a better future. When I was in these international schools, multiple racist incidents took place—ones that scarred me and stayed with me were where the racial discrimination was based on food (food that did not smell like the English breakfast), and where talking in one language and accent was made fun of! Fear for speaking in a language that I knew and have learned, was the site of segregation, of the otherness in this school. Moreover, it was there where I first learned about segregation and what it meant. We had students from all cultures and of all skin colors and it was customary to segregate us. For instance, on school trips, the non-white (mostly Indians) and white students had a different bus, and black students had a different bus. In school itself, we had separate rooms. Black people in one, and white and non-white students in the other. I remember when one girl who was biracial (Indian and Black) asked why were we segregated, and that's when it hit me and snapped me out of what I was unconsciously being a part of. Another incident that took place within the premises of this particular institution was when I was made fun of my dark skin, and to be clear everyone in India is almost as the same color as me, a shade lighter or a shade darker. I was constantly told to put the controversial "Fair and Lovely" cream on my face, to look fair—to elaborate on this, it is a product of a white (colonized), capitalist society that is obsessed with skin color. The idea was to look fair and to speak in an accent that we were 'looted' in. Not that I could do anything about it, but I made sure to leave that school and go back to the private school that focused more on education for freedom.

Through conscious and subconscious internalized biases, members of the Indian community act in varied ways to maintain their closeness to whiteness and privilege which can be seen in the educational practices, and to further say, even in dating/marriage practices. It is far more common and acceptable to read a work by a white male/female, and it is "easier" to date/marry a white individual than it is to engage in any form with Black individuals (be it reading their work, or working on their histories). Partnerships (of any kind) with white people maintain and preserve the white side-by-side privilege that India has, whereas alliance with Black individuals is seen as a "threat to white authority" (hooks, *Teaching to Transgress* 3).

As a product of a society that is deeply influenced by colorism, Indians are strongly discouraged from speaking incorrectly, when I say "speaking," I talk about the English language and the accent. We are discouraged from engaging in affiliations of any kind with black people, this also includes education about black history, having courses in college that talk about African Americans. An individual's worth in the Indian community is based on their skin tone/color (for example a dark-skinned woman is deemed undesirable despite her successes). Studying about Black communities, and working on them is in direct contrast to upholding ideologies that support whiteness. As a product of systemic racism, Indians are afforded opportunists and these opportunities allow the dominant group (white ideologists) to suggest that systemic inequalities do not exist and our community remains more proximal to the white spaces. Due to the closeness of the Indian community with white peers, there is also an uprising of racial fetishism and objectification that comes from the inherent racist culture of India, which further contributes to the rape culture that unfortunately India is known for, which tolerates and even validates sexual violence perpetrated upon black, dark-skinned, female bodies.

Mass Media and Indian Stereotypes

On one hand, it was through mass media that we, Indians, learned to speak a language that is not ours, absorbed to integrate with other cultures. On the other hand, what we learned through such movies and shows were nothing but typical stereotypes of various ethnicities and countries. As bell hooks points out in *Killing Rage: Ending Racism,* "For the most part television and movies depict a world where blacks and whites coexist in harmony although the subtext is clear" (113)—the subtext of depicting stereotypes. Movies offer an important role in influencing ethnic and national identities, especially in the absence of any face-to-face interactions with these groups. They help to create and spread international stereotypes. For instance, it would not be surprising if many Americans learn about Indians through films such as *A Passage to India*, *Indiana Jones: Temple of Doom*, and *Slumdog Millionaire*, for this, is the way India is received by many in the West. Often when I am traveling to the West, I hear questions from people I meet when I am in a new city: "Isn't India a very poor country with slums everywhere?" Everyone must be a vegetarian there?" "Do you worship cows and why do they roam around in streets?" and the late being the fascination of the west with the spiritual side of India, "Do you also practice yoga?". Where do these questions emerge from? They most likely originate from the "yellow-filter, slum-showing" effects in numerous Hollywood movies.

Indians have been very famous (read: infamous) when it comes to their portrayal in mass media. I can count famous movies and shows where we are shown as uneducated, slum-born filthy people. For instance, *The Simpsons* introduced a "dark, orange-colored" Apu, in their all-yellow-skinned people universe, as one of the main characters back in 1990, with a horrible accent—and it took over 30 years for the show's creators to understand the underlying racism in it. We live in a place where a French person's accent and voice are considered to be amazingly beautiful, but a "hello" from an Indian person would make people laugh. Many would say ironically that the world we live in has definitely gotten better. We have moved past the savage depiction in *Indiana Jones and the Temple of Doom* where our people were seen eating snakes and monkey brains to *Slumdog Millionaire* where everyone is born in a slum and is a beggar on the road. To add to it, nowadays the depiction of Indian females is probably the worse. As hooks notes in *Killing Rage: Ending Racism,* we are shown as either a "nanny" or "servant" and it "does not disturb most viewers at this moment," whereas "the fact that a black [woman of color] woman can be cast in a dramatically compelling leading role as a servant does not intervene on racist/sexist stereotypes, it reinscribes them" (13). Similarly, we are also depicted as "the exotic-dusky woman" everyone wants to be with, and it is these stereotypes that lead to the fetishization of Asian women in the U.S. I am currently living in the U.S., where I am forced "to believe in our inherent inferiority" (110) due to my skin color and words that come out of my mouth, and through such depiction of my community, "mass media bring white supremacy into our lives, constantly reminding us of our marginalized status" (110).

I have always seen my father work hard so that his kids could pursue the "American Dream". Though his initial preference was his son, to educate him, and to get his life together, he slowly came to terms with the fact that I wanted to study too. He worked hard for me as well, and wanted and still wants me to be "white", even though as I employ bell hooks' words here: "skin color was the body marking that separated and divided", he still wants me to "pass into whiteness" (*Killing Rage* 240). For, we all, and when I say "we," I mean Indians, are taught from the beginning that life is much better as a white person. My father and forefathers have seen it with their eyes, that with being a skin tone lighter, people can just colonize a country and take everything from people who are a tone darker. Britishers not only colonized our country, but they also colonized our minds, and now my father hopes that I will assimilate into this white-ness so that my life becomes easy, but racial assimilationism is a two-edged sword. To add to this, my family members were never really surrounded by Black people. We definitely read briefly about black people in our history books and were taught that being Black would mean being punished, so it was/is always better to be white. I remember the first time I saw a Black person. I was 14. Can you imagine living 14 years of your life and not knowing that there exists another race of beautiful people in a color that is not white? And I only saw that Black person because I stepped out of my country, so can you imagine there still exists people in my country who, perhaps, are not aware of different races, gender, and people. This stems partly from the problematic depiction of black people in mass media or no depiction at all. When I was small, I don't recall watching movies or TV series that had people of any other color but white. Therefore, white was what we aimed for. White-ness and the "American Dream" became synonymous.

Whiteness and the "American Dream"

Moreover, this "American Dream" comes with numerous pitfalls. When I was applying for the visa to come to the U.S, I was told that I needed to have a huge sum in my bank account, so that I could show the visa office that I am rich and, thus, it would take me in. My merit, my degrees, and my research as an academic scholar were rendered useless, for the Americans just wanted to know my financial background and what I would bring with me to the States. When I reached the visa office and submitted my documents, they told me after looking at my bank account that I got the visa. No questions were asked, except whether 'I would come back to India after completion of my course work', to which I said, "Yes." To my right, was another student and the visa interviewer asked him the same question to which he said, "No, I will work in the States." And he was denied a visa right then and there. The point of this story is not to tell how the visa office works but how we are unwanted in this land right from the beginning. There have always been deliberate attempts at preserving the White race and white supremacy within the U.S. by racializing the borders. Immigrants are commonly accepted if they are wealthy, or as cheap laborers for the economic growth of the U.S. Therefore, there is a trend to grant visas only to those who will help with technology and medical innovations but will go back to their homelands the moment that innovation is complete. White supremacists do not want anyone else to enter "their" country, especially anyone who is not white, thus, there is a reluctance to accept refugees, and people from other cultures—particularly Muslims.

When we finally enter the U.S. either as cheap laborers or as students, we face obvious and subtle forms of racism and discrimination. We hear over and over that we need to assimilate and speak English in public. There is also a deep-seated perception that all people of color are foreign no matter how long they've lived in the United States or how 'assimilated' they are because we are often measured by white people both in terms of physical and cultural differences. Some people of color who did not identify as African American are born here and have their roots in America that date back decades, but they are still asked, especially if they have dark skin where they are and their family is from. Or sometimes they are slyly praised for their ability to speak good English as if it is an achievement because our skin is brown and we may have an Asian surname. Even when we do everything "right" to Americanize, there is always something about American identity that reminds us, we are not white. On the contrary, to assimilate many of us try to adopt white supremacist values characterized in the media and the dominant white institutions, and many of us believe we are inferior because we are not white. This results in self-hatred. When we try to assimilate "properly", we are told by the very people who asked us to speak their language, to behave the way they do, that we are 'Oreos' or 'bananas'—colored on the outside and white on the inside, and ideologically we will never be white. After listening to such comments, there are those of us who are reluctant to do anything and be a part of the anti-racist struggle. As hooks states in *Killing Rage: Ending Racism,* there are BIPOC who "are reluctant to commit themselves fully and deeply to an anti-racist struggle that is ongoing because there is such a pervasive feeling of hopelessness—a conviction that nothing will ever change" (271).

In chapter 8 of *Teaching Community: A Pedagogy of Hope*, which bell hooks titles "Moving beyond Shame," she talks about the dominator culture and how in varied phases, it invokes a feeling of internalized racial shame. She says, "One of the ways racism colonizes the minds and imaginations of black people is through systematic shaming" (94). Though this is true, the shaming also extends to different cultures, people of color, and ethnicities. Moreover, this shaming comes in varied forms for me. Initially, it was the shame of being in a culture (India) that invests and prays to a *Devi* (goddess) but suppresses the very being of a female when a girl child is born. Then the shaming grows with one's age. It was then the shaming of menstrual blood. Furthermore, it was the shaming of living in the dominator's culture. Food, which is a memory-keeper for me, turned into a horror story for me, as it was also used as a tool to shame me and to reduce my identity and status as a racialized outsider in a culture of whiteness. It doesn't stop there. The shaming continues within my academic experience in higher education. Feelings of marginalization continue to push the "other" to the other side. We, people of color are told time and time again, by white supremacists who teach in universities, schools, offices, how our history is not valid, how it is unimportant, and perhaps not a subject to ponder over. If this is not shaming, then what is? During my MA in the UK, I wrote a beautiful poem for a creative writing class, and I painted a canvas for my other course in the same university only to hear from my colleagues and professors that, "Oh, we didn't know Indians are capable of doing this." I relate to hooks' unnerving experience where she "had to face the skepticism of white teachers and student peers who found a smart black person anomaly" (*Teaching Community* 97). Is being capable enough to read, write, and talk about topics that are considered political or to be smart, is to be an anomaly? Or is this just an extension of shaming, because the stereotypes tell that Indian females can't be smart. They'd rather look after someone's baby.

We already come from a place where mass media has been the primary vehicle for shaming (*Teaching Community* 94). We have learned from the beginning that the color of our skin will segregate us as we are alive. We, as female Indians, or South Asians are always equated to the negative characteristics or "nanny stereotypes", as this is made apparent through various movies and novels. This is the way "mass media assaults the self-esteem" of African Americans and other people of color as well. When I was studying in the UK, I had my own little community of Asian people, and we would hang out after our classes or travel together, but whenever we walked outside our university area, our community would be looked at as "other and harmful". The daggering stares made us aware of how different we looked from the white skin. We enter an unknown land with an emotion of already being scared to be in a place where we don't know anyone, and in my experience, it is these spaces where, as bell hooks notes in *Killing Rage: Ending Racism* that "shaming as a weapon of psychological terrorism can damage fragile self-esteem in ways that are irreparable" (99). The political circumstances don't help either.

One of my friends from China was assaulted recently in the UK, while he was on his way home. He was assaulted simply because he is from China and apparently because there are people who believe that this nation's citizens should be blamed for the existence of COVID-19. The news distressed me, which was followed by the news of the Atlanta attack on Asian American women. These women created their own community with hope, and love only to be deadly attacked by a white man. This incident is horrifying but not surprising, as it is a part of the racially targeted violence against the Asians that rose during the pandemic. These attacks are a continuation of the long history of the erasure, dehumanization, and hyper-sexualization of Asian women, as they are often considered disposable—especially when our immigration status, socioeconomic status, our cultures, and languages are heavily policed. Additionally, these attacks are not new, for there has been a history of anti-Asian racism. Tessler et al. in their article "The Anxiety of Being Asian American" mentions how white supremacists equate non-white bodies as unclean and impure. She further mentions how "the bubonic plague was framed as a racial disease which only Asian bodies could be infected by whereas white bodies were seen as immune" (2020). Similarly, they are considered as a threat and were called a "yellow peril". We are pushed outside of the circle of 'who is deemed valuable' by white supremacists. The attacks can be categorized as racial misogyny and racial capitalism. These attacks shame the Asian community, as now members of it are afraid to even step outside in public spaces. The media rather continues to shame them by talking about their profession, like in the case of the Atlanta shooting—where the victims were "characterized as a problem that needed to be eliminated" (Nguyen, 2021). It is not a made-up story when white people shame Asian Americans for their food, as noted by Mei Fong in her article "When the Cafeteria Becomes. A Cultural Battlefield," about the lunchbox shaming. She mentions that the "taunts and embarrassments don't end with grade school. A quick search yields online forums devoted to discussing the kind of lunches you should, and shouldn't, bring to the office. Not surprisingly, a lot of the foods employees are discouraged from bringing to work are dishes beloved by immigrants. This is the reality of many Asians living in the U.S. who are marginalized.

"Killing Rage" Inside Us

bell hooks for me is one of the authors that I turn to for matters of feminism, womanism, and teaching practices. However, after finishing reading *Killing Rage: Ending Racism,* I am sure I will return to more of her writings on matters of racism. Anti-racist allies need to understand that we all have "killing rage" inside us, and bell hooks wants us to turn that rage into critical consciousness, knowledge, and powerful arguments to challenge the structures that create oppression and marginalize BIPOC communities. In *Killing Rage: Ending Racism,* she is asking her readers to sit in discomfort and face the white supremacist capitalist patriarchal society we all have been reared in. However, she also reminds us that being anti-racist is a choice, and we can learn to decolonize our minds and lives and build a beloved community. hooks says, "Those of us who are always anti-racist long for a world in which everyone can form a beloved community where border can be crossed and cultural hybridity celebrated. Anyone can begin to make such a community by truly seeking to live in an anti-racist world" (272). I believe, her anti-racist work is essential for people, and her work is needed. As a South Asian female, I wish I had been taught from the beginning that we deserve kindness, decency, respect, and affection just as much as white people do. As I have stated, instead I was taught that Indians are lucky that we are not born black and we should be grateful for that. We need to work toward creating a beloved community where no one is taught this. We need to learn how to work toward building communities of inclusion beyond the boundaries of systemic and institutionalized oppression because we would have decolonized our minds, and "that is where we must go from here" (272).

In a time when fear has plagued many of the communities of Asian Americans, blacks, and people of color (as well as varied ethnicities) due to the overwhelming cases of anti-Asian hate crimes and violence—we must continue to embrace our racial, cultural, and ethnic differences and come together as a community built on love, and come together now more than ever. The world needs more love than hate, now more than ever. This is the world hooks is talking about in *Killing Rage: Ending Racism.*

bell hooks' asks her readers to remain disheartened until we fix what is wrong in our society. *Killing Rage: Ending Racism* shares her words, her painful experiences to help us understand the plight of marginalized people, to help us bring to the center who we are. As a woman of Indian descent, I am not alone and these problems of racism are not just mine. I am not the only woman, the only Indian woman, or the only Asian woman who feels these emotions. There are many out there, and while I have the liberty and the freedom to express my pain and my "killing rage" through my writing, others don't. As hooks says, "For some, talking race means moving past the pain to speak, not getting caught, trapped silenced by the sadness and sorrow" (5). While I have friends who mention that they will stand for me, there are others on the margins out there who don't have such friends. While I might have gotten used to being the "other", there is someone out there who is facing it for the first time. There is someone out there who is having this killing rage inside them right now. For eons, we, Indians a part of the Asian community, have stayed invisible to stay safe and alive. Finally, as bell hooks points out in *Killing Rage: Ending Racism* for long "safety resided in the pretense of invisibility" (36). But I am determined to stay visible and share my activism as an anti-racist ally; for this work can help someone on the margin of society to work toward "killing rage" inside them.

Works Cited

Cheng, A., 2021. *Opinion | What This Wave of Anti-Asian Violence Reveals About America.* [online] Nytimes.com. https://www.nytimes.com/2021/02/21/opinion/anti-asian-violence.html [Accessed 20 June 2021].

Holcombe, M., Yan, H. and Vera, A., 2021. *Victims of the spa shootings highlight the vulnerability of working-class Asian women as more Asian Americans get attacked.* [online] CNN. https://www.cnn.com/2021/03/18/us/metro-atlanta-shootings-thursday/index.html [Accessed 1 June 2021].

hooks, bell. *Killing Rage: Ending Racism.* Henry Holt and Company, New York, 1995.

---. *Teaching Community: A Pedagogy of Hope.* Routledge, Taylor & Francis, New York, 2003.

---. *Teaching to Transgress: Education As The Practice Of Freedom.* Routledge, Taylor & Francis, New York, 1994.

Singh, Hira, and M.A. Kalam. "India's Race Problem: Ignorance and Denial." *Social Scientist*, vol. 45, no. 9/10, 2017, pp. 75–78. *JSTOR*, www.jstor.org/stable/26380455. Accessed 1 June 2021.

Sue, D. W. et al. "Racial microaggressions in everyday life: implications for clinical practice." *The American psychologist* (2007): 72–79.

Tessler, Hannah et al. "The Anxiety of Being Asian American: Hate Crimes and Negative Biases During the COVID-19 Pandemic." *American journal of criminal justice: AJCJ*, 1-11. 10 Jun. 2020, doi:10.1007/s12103-020-09541-5

Yoo, J. and Kuo, S., 2021. *A Literary Guide to Combat Anti-Asian Racism in America.* [online] Electric Literature. https://electricliterature.com/books-about-anti-asian-racism-in-america/ [Accessed 22 June 2021].

Part III
Killing Rage: Ending Racism
and the Love for Anti-Racist Alliance

If we, humans of all colors, races, classes, genders, and sexualities are holding our breath for change, we are suffocating ourselves.

Atika Chaudhary, "A Deeper Shade of Consciousness: *My Voice is My Resistance,*" *Building Womanist Coalitions: Writing and Teaching in the Spirit of Love* (2019)

What does transformation look like? What's the relationship between scholarship, research, pedagogy, and innovative social-justice work? How can we use words, ideas, writing, and reading to provoke progressive individual and collective change? How can we enact transformation in the various aspects of our lives—in our classrooms, our scholarship, our relationships, our daily practices?

AnaLouise Keating Foreword, "Womanism for All! The Transformational Power of Radical Love," *Building Womanist Coalitions*

As I am writing this on Martin Luther King, Jr., day, I use his words to amplify the power of love as the highest educator: 'I have decided to love. If you are seeking the highest good, I think you can find it through love … [S]he who loves has the key that unlocks to the meaning of ultimate reality'…. While our differences cannot and should not be erased, we can assiduously seek to strengthen the 'lie that binds our hearts …'

Scott Neumeister, *Let Love Lead on a Course to Freedom* (2019)

12
Learning Allyship for Racial Justice: The Work Never Ends
Nikki Lyssy

The work of becoming an ally for racial justice is an ongoing process, and if coming into critical consciousness has shown me anything over the past year, it is this: the work expands, the work grows, and the work never ends. Through the careful and intentional study of scholars and authors, bell hooks and others, as well as the careful examination of my own life experiences, I seek to interrogate the ways in which my allyship in the struggle against racism has come into being—and the work I have to continue to do as a heterosexual, blind, white woman interested in dismantling the white supremacist capitalist patriarchy.

I come from a line of strong, supportive women—women who lift each other up, who tear down walls of oppression, and seek to better the world. Even though growing up blind, I still had the advantages of being white and heterosexual in heteronormative society. Also, I was fortunate to grow up middle to upper-class, living a very comfortable lifestyle. I attended schools where I was given every opportunity to succeed—though it was not always easy, and there were those who assumed that I would not because of my blindness. In *Killing Rage: Ending Racism* (1995), bell hooks examine closely the intersections of feminism, class, and race in the second half of this groundbreaking book, as she explains in great detail the ways that white supremacy and feminism can breed complacency unless allies in the struggle for social justice come together and stand alongside the oppressed so liberation can occur for all.

Because I grew up surrounded by strong women, I was to become be a feminist—even if I did not call myself one until much later. However, in the revolutionary feminist courses I have taken in college over time, including one based on the writings of bell hooks, I have learned from her that "the crude racism and white supremacy that surfaces in feminism sends the message that solidarity between white women and Black women can never be a reality" (*Killing Rage*, 104). This system of a lack of willingness to truly see, hear, and empathize with each other ensures that the chains of white supremacy remain tightly wound around all human beings, that the only way to break those chains is to understand that the agenda of white supremacy is constantly perpetuated by mass media and culture. The way to shift the narrative, to support and nurture bonds between white women and Black women and women of color, is to be willing to lift our white voices and speak in ~~on~~ solidarity: "… those white women who are fundamentally committed to advocating revolutionary feminist thinking, which has in it a core anti-racist struggle, must dare to make their voices heard" (104). It is very important for me, as a white woman learning ethics of allyship, to ensure that my voice does not speak in place of the oppressed, but rather specifically to support Black women and women of color in a meaningful, intentional, genuine way.

In fact, bell hooks suggests that white women who speak up in support of Black women and women of color are often times not given recognition the way that racist white feminists are: "often the individual white women who have divested of white supremacy and do show themselves again and again to be allies in the struggle against racism, rarely receive the limelight. Mass media certainly rarely highlight their work" (104). It is only through committing to anti-racist work, through understanding that our voices, as white women, must be loud and unyielding in the struggle to end racism, that we can truly create feminist alliance where all voices—the loudest for liberation of the oppressed—are equally heard.

Unlearning Racism through Critical Consciousness

Coming into critical consciousness is a process that requires unlearning implicit biases that are part of the dominant structures and the media agenda set forth by a society founded upon white supremacist patriarchal capitalism which we have all internalized. Abigail Libers notes that "… what makes racism different from individual prejudice is who has institutional power. White people control our government systems and institutions in every sector, from law enforcement and education to health care and the media, leading to laws and policies that can advantage white people while disadvantaging everyone else" ("How to Unlearn Racism"). Acknowledging this societal composition and working to unlearn its strong grip is one way in which Libers seeks to understand her own role in a white supremacist society: "The process of unlearning is only the first step, and it needs to translate into a commitment to practices such as breaking white silence and bringing an antiracist lens to my work" ("How to Unlearn Racism"). My experience is somewhat similar to Libers, as I am truly interested in unlearning the myriad of ways in which white supremacy is normalized in everything from education to the workforce. Libers points out that the work of allyship is "only possible, and sustainable, by building empathy and feeling the ways in which racism is not just harmful for people of color—it hurts white people, too" ("How to Unlearn Racism"). In *Killing Rage: Ending Racism* it's a sentiment hooks echoes: "Many citizens of these United States long to live in a beloved community—where loving ties of care and knowing bind us together in our differences … most folks in this society have become so cynical so convinced that solidarity across racial differences can never be a reality, that they make no effort to build community" (264). It is through a fierce commitment to antiracist work that the cynicism can turn into optimism. hooks maintains that "Those of us who are not cynical, who still cherish the vision of *beloved community,* sustain our conviction that we need such bonding not because we cling to Utopian fantasies but because we have struggled all our lives to create this community" (264). Claiming to be a white ally for the oppressed is meaningless without the ongoing agenda to end racism in solidarity with BIPOC communities who have been forced to engage in this work alone for far too long.

In my own educational life journey, I have not been forced to consider the role that my whiteness plays in the person I am until I began to seek out classes in college and community opportunities to learn about how to become an ally. The fact that they would call attention to a whiteness that is so normalized made me uncomfortable to speak openly about it for years. It's a sentiment that scholar Crystal E. Newby characterizes in her 2020 article "So You Want to be an Antiracist?" forcing me to consider the ways in which my *color*-blindness often led me to remain silent when I should have spoken out against racism and white supremacy. Newby calls attention to the power of whiteness: "White supremacy has been imbedded into the very fabric of the United States since its inception" ("So You Want to be an Antiracist?). As a result, the history of the U.S. that I was taught growing up in school reflects this truth and leaves no room for the real and true story of what it means to live in a society where the white supremacist capitalist patriarchy remains fully intact. In unlearning racism, it is this work I for critical consciousness to end racism, the work of unlearning how to live beyond its deadly silencing structures, and to understand that according to Ibram X. Kendi in *How to Be an Antiracist* (2019): "… being an antiracist requires persistence self-awareness, constant self-criticism, and regular self-examination" (23).

Liberatory Feminism and Self-Awareness

I turn my attention back to feminist thinking as a critical source for the possibility of liberating allyship across racial, ethnic, and class differences, an arena where all women should be seen as equal but often times are not as long as systems of white supremacy, patriarchy, and classism remain unchecked. I was fortunate to grow up as an identical twin, so I shared everything with her from a birthday to a bedroom. Our parents raised their four daughters to be a close-knit bunch—so close, in fact, that my twin and I went to the same college, followed by my younger sisters, who also attended the same school. Of course, not all women may relate to my narrative experience. My sisters and I rarely competed against each other for attention. However, in a patriarchal society rooted in sexism and capitalism, "sisterhood" (whether biological, cultural, and/or political is always about competition for male approval. In the field of literary studies, scholarly and creative production related to publication, it is especially prevalent. In the writing world, where writers are constantly pitted against each other and competing for book deals, publishing opportunities, and jobs in academia are challenging for women—especially those who are Black and of color having to compete not only with white women, but white men and those of color as well. Considering this oppressive structure, in *Killing Rage: Ending Racism,* bell hooks argues "that we [progressive feminist allies must] create and sustain the conditions for solidarity and coalition-building by vigilantly challenging the ethic of competition, replacing it with communal ethic of collective benefit" (105). Solidarity for social justice along with a vision of feminist thinking committed to inclusion then becomes the new normal. In the visionary framework, it allows us all—across differences of race, gender, class, sexuality, and ability—to work together to dismantle the white supremacist capitalist patriarchy that pits women against men and women against women.

Furthermore, as a visionary Black feminist, bell hooks is interested in calling out various ways that unresolved mental trauma of racist aggressions imprint themselves on the minds and souls of BIPOC individuals, making it remarkably difficult—if not virtually impossible—for any alliance bridge-building for racial justice to begin. However, she states: "When African-Americans begin to name and confront this suffering in ways that are constructively healing, we will be better able to share our reality with those allies in struggle who are not black but are equally committed to transforming this society, to ending racist domination" (*Killing Rage* 144). Moreover, hooks points out that "The discourse of blackness is in no way connected to an effort to promote black self-determination it becomes simply another resource appropriated by the colonizer" (*Killing Rage* 178).

bell hooks clearly proclaims in *Killing Rage: Ending Racism* that we—those of us who identify as feminist allies—cannot have a discussion about race and feminism without considering the roles that class status plays in our lives. Failing to acknowledge the way role that class biases play out in a society—not only founded upon white supremacy and patriarchy interconnected to ways classism impacts people's everyday lives—simply perpetuates systemic and institutionalized oppression. By choosing to acknowledge the role that class plays in each of our lives, by repositioning ourselves in a system that seeks to keep white supremacy on top, we can change the narrative. This is allyship I have envisioned myself as being.

In Solidarity: BIPOC and White Allies Crossing Borders of Difference

bell hooks firmly suggests that self-actualization for Black folks—and anti-racist white folks as well—can only occur when each group interrogates their biases and is willing to work toward a new understanding of each other. She points out that "ironically, many changes in social policy and social attitudes that were once seen as ways to end social racial domination have served to reinforce and perpetuate white supremacy" (*Killing Rage* 186). Those who do not "see" race or class differences can conveniently continue to benefit from a white supremacist system that values material comfort and the comfort of the oppressor over the discomfort and dislodged experiences of the oppressed: "without an organized collective struggle that consistently reminds us of our of our common concerns, people of color often forget. Sadly, forgetting common concerns sets the stage for competing concerns" (*Killing Rage* 200). In competition for class resources, jobs, and opportunities within and outside of the workforce, hooks point out that "until racist antiblack sentiments are let go [even] by people of color, no transformation of white supremacy will take place" (*Killing Rage* 201).

As I have come into critical consciousness as a white woman for liberation of the oppressed, I understand that my racial privilege allows me access to certain opportunities that I may have taken for granted before. Characterized by hooks as "white supremacist thinking," she acknowledges in *Writing Beyond Race: Living Theory and Practice* that "in order to talk openly and honestly about race in the United States, it is helpful to begin with the understanding that it is white supremacist thinking and practice that has been the political foundation undergirding all systems of domination based on skin color and ethnicity" (3-4). Through calling out this problematic way of thinking, as white allies against systemic and institutionalized oppression, we can lean into the spirit of love.

I have always been comfortable identifying myself as a blind woman; I have always been proud of my identity as a blind woman. Only more recently am I able to comfortably call into question my whiteness, and in doing so, I hope to normalize the concept of white people talking about our whiteness and the gross disparities that present themselves when BIPOC are not part of the conversation. After all, as hooks notes in *Writing Beyond Race*, "Thinking about white supremacy as the foundation of race and racism is crucial because it allows us to see beyond skin color" (6).

Furthermore, my position as a white blind woman in academia is sadly a unique one. But I cannot help but wonder if dominator culture is partly to blame, as the silent culprit wherein it is easier to blame than to embrace. It's a concept hooks understands as she states in "Moving Past Blame: Embracing Diversity," chapter 3 of *Writing Beyond Race*: "Diversity if the reality of all of our lives … When we are more energized by the practice of blaming than we are by efforts to create transformation, we not only cannot find relief for suffering, but we are creating the conditions that help keep us stuck in the status quo" (26; 29). For years, I was part of an organization called the National Federation of the Blind, and while this group represented equality for all blind people, they also fell into patterns of blaming that drove me away eventually. The NFB's insistence that sighted employers simply do not want to hire blind people, or that blind people are not seen as equals by our sighted counterparts unless we "perform" our blindness a certain way, simply are not the actual case. I have been a member of two English departments—one as an undergraduate at the University of North Texas, and now as a graduate student at the University of South Florida—and have been met with unwavering support in both.

I firmly believe that if more blind individuals could simply transform their thought processes about our range of abilities to reflect our diversity as a necessary and important component to a successful workforce, I would not be one of the only ones in my chosen field of creative writing. hooks says it best when she writes, "Moving past the ideology of blame to a politics of accountability is a difficult move to make in a society where almost all political organizing, whether conservative or radical, is structured around the binary of 'good guys' versus 'bad guys'" (*Writing Beyond Race*, 30). Because we both were steeped in families where our blindness was not weaponized or viewed as a "disability", we grew and flourished. To be a person who is accountable is to be a person who engages with the world where all the cards are stacked against me, yet I still make a choice to believe that the only oppression that occurs is when I oppress myself. hooks says, "Accountability is a more expansive concept because it opens a field of possibility wherein we are compelled to move beyond blame to see where our responsibility lies" (30).

Additionally, hooks puts forth the idea that through love and genuine growth, discomfort and understanding, the interconnected systems of white supremacist patriarchal domination that prevail will eventually fall. I know Lauren does not want to be the only blind person in her law school cohort, much like I wish I was not the first blind person to pursue an MFA in the English department at the University of South Florida. We walk these roads with love and hope, praying others will follow and realize that through a spirit of love, domination and oppression can be conquered once and for all.

Dear bell hooks,

I write to you today with a full and open heart, and primarily to say thank you. Thank you for calling me into critical consciousness through your writings, especially your book *Writing Beyond Race: Theory in Practice.* You see, I am a white heterosexual-identified woman. I am also blind in the sense that I literally cannot see, but I hope to see in the greater sense of understanding how to be an ally. In this letter, I seek to identify the ways in which you have shown me to interrogate structures of class, white supremacy, and dominator culture—what you refer to collectively as "the white supremacist capitalist patriarchy" (36)—with love for my fellow humans. I want to prove to you, and to myself, that I can become part of dismantling these systems that seek to keep white supremacy intact, and it is through this book that I come to understand everything I have truly learned, and the work I still have to do, to fully claim my allyship for the betterment of Black Indigenous People of Color.

In your essay "A Path Away from Race: On Spiritual Conversion" (92-97) in *Writing Beyond Race,* in particular, you write about how Martin Luther King, Jr.'s vision for nonviolent resistance and a peaceful dismantling of systems of domination. You state that "King's vision that love was the most constructive way to create positive social change benefiting everyone was changing our culture" (96). You emphasize love as the agent which we all share and the way that "motivated by our belief in a love ethic, masses of Americans worked in the late 60s and the early 70s to unlearn the logic of domination and dominator culture" (96), and how it is through learning to truly embrace a spirit of love that we begin to view each other in a new light. Your description of the ways that conversion took place in your own life, how you "studied and wrote about ending domination in all its forms" and began to understand that "the politics of love could produce lasting and meaningful social change" stirs hope in my soul. No, I am not oppressed in the sense that you write about in regards to BIPOC communities, but I have a disability (a word I distinctly do not align with) in which I have truly learned that to love those who do not understand and to be willing to educate to bridge the gap is necessary if I am to succeed in the world.

Furthermore, bell, you have shown me that through creating dialogue and engaging critically with one another, we can create communities of caring. In your essay "Bonding Across Boundaries," you highlight the exciting dialogue that can occur when we are able and willing to reach across the boundaries of class, race, and culture to create bonds that connect each of us. You write beautifully of how "a positive politics of difference was the starting point for forming ties across boundaries, especially those imposed by systems of domination...By imperialist white supremacist capitalist patriarchy" (*Writing Beyond Race* 143). Through reaching across these boundaries, we begin to celebrate the things that make us each unique and to revel in our different experiences of living while forging a new path that leads to the self-liberatory experiences of our humanity. In *Writing Beyond Race: Living Theory and Practice,* you clearly state how critically important it is to speak out about making connections with people different from yourself. Unraveling unconscious notions of white supremacy from my mind and heart, bell, is the work I will spend the rest of my life doing. As a white woman, I know I have a long way to go, but I hope spending time with your ideas and books is the first step to unearthing the type of ally I seek and have begun working to be.

Finally, your ideas about the role that conflict plays in relationships grounded in love—in the ability to interconnect in spite of our differences—are awe-inspiring, especially when you speak of your parents with such tenderness. The structures of class and capitalism are in particular responsible for the fact that I grew up surrounded by predominately white people until I moved four hours north to college and began to interact with people who were Black, brown, Hispanic, Asian—people with whom I share wonderful conversations and relationships with across these boundaries. I want to always work for change by surrounding myself with individuals who push me to examine my whiteness and continue to cross boundaries imposed by the white supremacist capitalist patriarchal structures that we as feminist allies are all trying to shake off for good.

I close this letter by saying again, thank you. I am embarrassed to say that, were it not for your writings, I may not have come as fully into critical consciousness as I now am, and my work has only just started.

Most sincerely,

Nikki

Works Cited

hooks, bell. *Writing Beyond Race: Living Theory in Practice*. Taylor and Francis Group, 2013.

---. *Killing Rage: Ending Racism.* MacMillan, New York City, 1995.

Libers, Abigail. "How to Unlearn Racism." *Scientific American*, vol. 323, issue 4, 2020, p. 58-63. Accessed May 31, 2021.

Newby, Crystal E. "So You Want to be an Antiracist?" *Journal of College Admission*, Fall 2020, issue 429, p. 27-28. Accessed May 31, 2021.

Kendi, Ibram X. *How to Be an Antiracist*. Random House, New York, 2019.

13

A Bridge to Walk Across: The Role of Literary Critique In Challenging Intersecting Systems of Oppression, Jesse Gilleland

In Fall of 2020, I began as a graduate student at the University of South Florida in an English literature M.A. program during the height of a global COVID-19 pandemic with very little idea of what period or field of literary study I wanted to focus on. During my time as an undergraduate student in a creative writing program, I had taken a handful of literature classes ranging from a survey of Western poetry to a course entirely on the British modernist movement, all of which I found interesting. I knew that I had a passion for literary critique and analysis, but I had not yet realized the transgressive and radical power of literary study when harnessed for social justice. I was exposed to very few radical writers and instead was primarily confined to the traditional Western canon of "great white men," with a few white women thrown into the mix for diversity's sake. I could count on one hand the writers of color that I was exposed to in the classroom during my undergraduate years, and the role of systematic oppression in the texts that I studied was rarely mentioned. As a white person, the lack of BIPOC writers in my literature classes was far too easy to overlook, and it would not be until later that I realized what a devastating failure it was on my own part that I had not actively sought out the writings of people of color to challenge the stranglehold that white supremacy has on the literary canon.

In my first semester in the graduate literature program, I took a course on 18th and 19th century African American women's literature. There were no Black students in the classroom, and most of us had never read or even heard of most of the works that we would be reading, aside from the autobiography of Sojourner Truth. It was during this course that I realized how drastically my understandings of literature had been limited by taking courses that solely focused on white authors. One of the novels that we read was Harriet Wilson's *Our Nig: Sketches from the Life of a Free Black*, the first known novel by a Black woman published in America. The novel served as a fictionalized autobiography of Wilson's early life as an indentured servant in the house of a white family in New Hampshire. Throughout the novel the protagonist, Frado, who is based on Wilson, is abused physically, emotionally, mentally, and spiritually by the white woman that she works for. I wrote my seminar paper for this course on how white women in the 19th century based their femininity off the labor of Black women and then upheld the ideals of the "cult of true womanhood," the ideology that a true woman must be pious, pure, demure, and submissive. The cult demanded that a "true" woman never work and only ever remain a symbol of spiritual perfection and feminine obedience in the household; no Black woman would ever be able to attain "true" womanhood according to these standards and would instead only ever serve to help white women live out their own fantasies of feminine identity.

As a white trans person who was assigned female at birth, I knew that white privilege was something that I had. However, I conceptualized that privilege as something that people of color were lacking, and not something that I, instead, possessed. Over the course of my African American women's literature class and through the writing of my seminar paper, I realized this was not the case: white people actively and purposefully brought white privilege into existence through the subjugation of people of color. It is not simply something BIPOC do not have, but something that we as white people constructed for ourselves through their systematic oppression. The privilege that white women possess, then, is constructed in opposition to the womanhood of women of color, and Black women in particular. In *Killing Rage: Ending Racism* bell hooks discusses the relationship between gender and race and how the intersection between the two affects Black women. She writes that because of the intersections between gender and race, Black women experience forms of racism and sexism unique to only those who inhabit both Blackness and womanhood. Through the work of bell hooks in *Killing Rage*, I explore the ways in which white women's femininity is defined in juxtaposition to the femininity of Black women, the effect this has had on Black women's relationships with their femininity and with feminism, and how this racial gender hierarchy is maintained even in supposedly progressive spaces. Furthermore, I explore how literary analysis can be a strategic tool to explore the intersections of race and gender and to challenge oppressive institutions that dominate people on the basis of race, sex, sexuality, and gender identity.

Repressed Anger Across Differences of Race, Sexuality, and Gender

In one of my undergraduate classes on British modernist literature, one of our assignments was to do a presentation on an academic article about one of the books we read for the class. I chose the article "Anger, Anxiety, Abstraction: Virginia Woolf's "Submerged Truth"" by Kathleen M. Helal that analyzes the relationship between gender and repressed anger in Virginia Woolf's work. I was drawn to this article because, as a white nonbinary person who was raised and socially conditioned as a white *woman*, I was taught that the anger I felt at my treatment in society was unladylike and unbecoming. I had long repressed those feelings out of fear of being perceived as ugly and unlovable, and seeing this repressed anger reflected in the work of such a famous and successful white feminist author gave me a sense of solidarity. However, towards the end of the article was a critique of Virginia Woolf's white feminism that argued that while Woolf, who has made many documented racist comments in the past both in her novels and in her private writings, and other white feminists "associate anger with anxiety and abstraction, Black feminists have found it to be an extremely effective political tool" (Helal 91). In my assignment on the article, I brushed this critique aside by pointing to the similarities between white and Black feminists that state that all women regardless of race are taught to repress anger, lest they experience social backlash.

What I failed to do in this instance was to critique the racial differences between the socialization of women and anger, and to take into greater consideration the way that Black women's anger is repressed not only because of their gender but also because of their race. The 'angry black woman' is one of the most prolific stereotypes that abound about Black women in our current day; it is an image that portrays Black women as hysterical, illogical, and dangerous. It is society's way of saying that Black women will not be taken seriously by white society if they do not repress their anger. In actuality, Black women have every right to be angry at their lot in society as the victims of both racism and sexism. In *Killing Rage: Ending Racism* bell hooks discusses the relationship between sexism, racism, and the anger that one feels as the subject of such oppression. She writes of the power of such rage when it is properly examined and channeled into social justice instead of repressed, denied, and misdirected. hooks writes that rage "[has] the potential not only to destroy but also to construct … I understand rage to be a necessary aspect of resistance struggle. Rage can act as a catalyst inspiring courageous action" (16). She emphasizes the transformative power of anger when directed by the oppressed at the oppressor in response to extreme injustice and inequality.

Anger at institutionalized oppression pulls one out of denial and forces one out of complicity and docile acceptance of the status quo, which challenges white supremacist capitalist patriarchy. It is in white people's best interest that Black women do not recognize and channel their anger, so we (white people) misrepresent Black women as irrational in order to belittle their rightful anger at a system that treats them unfairly. bell hooks writes, "A black person unashamed of her rage, using it as a catalyst to develop critical consciousness, to come to full decolonized self-actualization, had no real place in the existing social structure" (16). Black women expressing rightful indignation at their subordination in society are silenced by racists that insist that Black people should accept their lot in life, by sexists that say women must repress their anger and be submissive to be true women, and by all of white supremacist capitalist patriarchy that says that angry Black women have no place in civil society.

White women and white people assigned-female-at-birth have also been told that their anger has no place in society, but their anger has not also been subordinated based on their race. White rage, especially when directed at individuals in BIPOC communities, has always had a place in society regardless of gender and will continue to have that place in society. As bell hooks discusses in her first book, *Ain't I a Woman: Black Women and Feminism*, white women have historically taken out their anger on Black women when it has not been socially accepted elsewhere, whether that anger be directed on enslaved women, Black women who they employ as domestic workers in their homes, or Black students in their feminist classrooms who dare to bring up issues of race instead of focusing solely on the plight of white women. In *Killing Rage*, hooks writes, "The black rage that white power wants to suppress … is the rage of the downtrodden and oppressed that could be mobilized to mount militant resistance to white supremacy" (29). White women benefit from white supremacist patriarchy forcing Black women to repress their anger, because if this anger was not repressed, white women would have to come to terms with the harm that they have caused Black women and how this harm has upheld white supremacy for their own benefit.

Racism and the Cult of True Womanhood

The legacy of white women's exploitation of Black women is what I attempted to expose in my paper on the work of Harriet Wilson. I began my paper by discussing bell hooks' essay "Holding my Sister's Hand: Feminist Solidarity" in her book *Teaching to Transgress: Education as the Practice of Freedom.* She discusses the historically strained relationships between Black and white women and how the legacy of slavery and segregation continue to impact the relationships between women across race and class differences today. hooks writes in *Teaching to Transgress* that "white women's class and race privilege was reinforced by the maintenance of a system where black women were the objects of white male sexual subjugation and abuse" (96) because white women would always rank above Black women as long as Black women were the objects of domination. Moreover, she argues, "contemporary discussions of the historical relationships between white and black women must include acknowledgement of the bitterness black slave women felt towards white women" (96). While the narrative of Harriet Wilson's *Our Nig* centers on a free Black woman, the main character's experiences as an indentured Black woman *servant* at the mercy of a vicious white woman exemplifies these historical tensions.

Throughout the novel, the mixed-race main character, Frado, is horrifically abused by Mrs. Bellmont after being abandoned at her home by her impoverished white mother at a very young age. Despite having a reputation as a "she-devil" who treats all of her servants terribly, Mrs. Bellmont is still considered an upstanding citizen in the small New Hampshire town in which she lives. By forcing Frado to take on all of the housework, Mrs. Bellmont is able to attain ideal femininity as purported by the cult of true womanhood that was rampant at the time the novel was published in 1859. The novel exposes the unachievable nature of the cult of true womanhood by illustrating how it is impossible to become a woman who never works but still maintains the household and dresses in elegant, expensive outfits without the exploitation of poor women of color, directly undermining the harmless and meek attitudes that a "true" woman was expected to have. "True" womanhood as it was understood in the 19th century was impossible within the exploitative and oppressive white supremacist capitalist patriarchal system that tirelessly worked to oppression the poor and people of color even in the private sphere of the home. Literary analysis of this text allows scholars to take a closer look at the historical relationships between Black and white women from the perspective of a Black woman and enables us to trace the legacies of those relationships to today, giving us a better understanding of both racism and sexism alike. This knowledge offers us opportunities as feminists to better understand one another and to begin the process of healing from great historical traumas.

Gatekeeping Objectivity, the Politics of Silence, and Feminist Individualism

However, as bell hooks reminds us in her later work *Teaching Community: A Pedagogy of Hope*, both political and academic discussion have long been gatekept by the guiding hand of "objectivity." The elite classes say that in order to have a valid point, one must remind unbiased and emotionally distanced from their own argument. This directly benefits those who are not victims of systematic oppression and who do not have personal stake in the topics they are debating. A white man debating the intersectional oppression that Black women face is fundamentally less invested in the outcome of said debate than a Black woman who faces the consequences of such oppression on a daily basis and is personally affected by the outcome of such debates. This goes hand-in-hand with conservative white people who argue that one should be able to be friends with someone regardless of their politics, because to them politics are an opinion the same as their preferred pizza toping, not a harsh reality that can have life-changing (and in the case of some legislation, life-ending) consequences for BIPOC communities that are more directly affected by supposedly neutral, conservative politics. For many people (especially BIPOC, LGBTQ people, disabled people, poor people, etc.), it is unthinkable to live a life so privileged as to not be personally affected by politics. To experience intense emotion such as rage, fear, and sorrow in the face of such injustice is an entirely natural reaction. It is those who are in the most pain who need most to be heard, but the standard of "objectivity" continues to be used to silence the voices of the oppressed.

Most white women and white members of other oppressed groups, such as the LGBTQ community and the disabled community, have experienced silencing on the basis of showing too much emotion, being labeled hysterical, or being told we weren't "objective" enough for our thoughts to be taken seriously. Our shared anger at this silencing could serve as a rallying point between oppressed white people and Black women as long as we embrace solidarity instead of victimhood. bell hooks writes in *Killing Rage* that the women's liberation movement that followed the black civil rights struggle, led primarily by white women, was able to utilize victimhood because of their white privilege: "Without witnessing the assassination of any of the leaders of the feminist movement, without any police brutality, without a mass movement for social justice, white women were able to collectively redress wrongs enacted by a system of gender discrimination. The rhetoric of victimhood worked for white women" when it would have never worked for black women (54). However, she also warns of the dangers of embracing victimhood, arguing that it can be "disempowering and disenabling" to think that one is a powerless victim of systems of oppression, and that "if shared victimhood was the reason to be feminist then women who were empowered, who were not victims, would not embrace feminism" (51). The rhetoric of victimhood was successful in the face of white women's liberation because white women were already seen as victims, as the cult of true womanhood had demanded that women be meek and helpless. Their embracement of the 'damsel in distress' role did not challenge traditional gender roles but instead appealed to them, making their case more palatable to the patriarchy. Such rhetoric of victimhood would not be so successful for Black women who are viewed by society to be "somehow more inherently treacherous, devious, lacking in morality and ethics than male counterparts … inherently predisposed on the basis of [their] gender to lie, cheat, and betray" (79).

Also in *Killing Rage: Ending Racism,* bell hooks writes in her essay, "Revolutionary Feminism: An Anti-Racist Agenda" that in the wake of the women's liberation movement, "It should have come as no surprise to any of us that those white women who were mainly concerned with gaining equal access to domains of white male privilege quickly ceased to espouse a radical political agenda which included dismantling of patriarchy as well as an anti-racist, anti-classist agenda" (99). Once many white women felt that they achieved individual career success, they did not see the need to continue to fight for radical change in society. The main issue that these white women had with white supremacist capitalist patriarchy was the patriarchy, and once they felt that this was no longer an insurmountable obstacle to their own personal and financial success, they became complacent within the white supremacist capitalist system. In fact, under contemporary neoliberalism many white women benefit from this system. They feel empowered by the fact that they can oppress people on the basis of race and class the same way that white men can, and in return, the system can masquerade as progressive because women can be CEOs of companies that exploit the labor of poor women of color and can be high-ranking intelligence officers who participate in the brutal torture of prisoners of color (Goldman).

White women can financially excel at the expense of poor women and women of color without a second thought as to how their actions might defy the basic tenets of feminism, because their understanding of feminism equates it with individual success. The modern woman is expected to take care of all housework and childcare, have a successful career, and be conventionally attractive (meaning living up to Western European beauty standards rooted in white supremacy), giving women a workload that is nearly impossible to handle. The women who *can* handle all of these expectations are middle and upper-class white women who can afford to pay for their children to attend daycare or can hire domestic workers to perform housework for them. This work then falls on low-class and working-class women, often women of color. These successful white women are then living up to their ideals of a powerful, wealthy femininity, or to quote the Broadway musical *Mean Girls*, "this is modern feminism talking / I expect to run the world in shoes I cannot walk in / I can be who I want to be and sexy" while exploiting the labor of poor white women and women of color. These women fail to critique the way that upholding the white supremacist capitalist system still reinforces patriarchy even when the person participating in that system is a woman. Embracing a violent, oppressive, dominating system will always continue to encourage oppression of women and violence against them. They position themselves at the apex of the feminist movement without seeing that their treatment of women of color and poor women is only a stone's throw away from how racist white women in the 19th century treated Black women in order to bolster their own femininity with the fruits of Black women's labor.

Once again in *Killing Rage,* bell hooks writes that, "It is this opportunistic appropriation of feminist thinking that consistently corrupts feminist politics, sending the clear message to the disenfranchised poor and working-class women and men of all races that feminist movement is not for them" (100). By embracing the image of the beautiful white woman in a position of power, cis heterosexual (cishet) upper-class white women are able to turn their backs on disenfranchised women and may fail to see that women will always be disproportionately exploited as long as the white supremacist capitalist system remains in place. For instance, the documentary film *Maquilapolis* released in 2006 showcases the lives of women working in American-owned factories in Tijuana near the Mexican American border. Impoverished women of color disproportionately make up the worker population of these factories, and many of these women are single mothers who moved their families to Tijuana because of the promise of factory work, only to find themselves living without electricity or running water in houses made out of garage doors. These women are constantly exposed to dangerous chemicals in the factories that can result in long-term health issues which they will then not be able to access or afford healthcare to treat. These chemicals are then dumped into the villages immediately surrounding the factories that the women live in, polluting the environment and potentially harming their families, as well. American white women embracing white supremacist capitalist imperialist systems only upholds the exploitation of women of color in countries that have less labor protection laws, whether that be Mexico, the Philippines, or Ethiopia. Through the labor of oppressed women, these white upper-class women construct a "feminism" not for the equality of all women, but for their own individualistic success at the expense of others. The message they send is clear: it doesn't matter if you oppress other women as long as you do it as well as a man would.

Internalized Classism and Capitalist Success

When white women portray the pinnacle of feminism as white, cishet able-bodied women succeeding financially in a capitalist system, they make it clear that their feminism is not intended to uplift the people of color, lower classes, and others who are exploited by the system. In *Killing Rage,* bell hooks explains that many Black people long to be rich and acquire material wealth because they have been taught by a racist and classist mass media that wealth is the only true sign of success and that being successful is the only way to achieve true happiness. She writes, "black folks across class are embracing a vision of life that sees well-being as connected only to material possessions ... we are all socialized by television to identify with the values and attitudes of the bourgeois and ruling classes" (255). This fervent belief in capitalist accumulation may prevent many people of color from realizing how they are exploited by the bourgeoisie and stop them from developing class consciousness, and conflating women's rights with women's financial success only exacerbates the issue. If one equates success with financial gain, then one will believe that a lack of money is a personal failure and not an intentional part of the system designed to work against anyone who is not already on top. She then notes that because the media shows white people embracing crime and immoral means in order to generate their own wealth, many Black people do not see the problem with doing the same. However, the white supremacist capitalist patriarchy does not reward *all* criminal and immoral behavior; while upper-class white people of all genders are rewarded financially for exploiting others, cutting legal corners, evading taxes, committing fraud, etc., the same system benefits from imprisoning people of color for these same acts. Imprisoning Black people not only divides Black communities and keeps them from organizing mass protest, but also allows white supremacist capitalism to exploit prison labor. By imprisoning large amounts of people of color, these imprisoned people will now be working for pennies an hour, as opposed to minimum wage workers outside of prison. Additionally, because felons are still barred from voting in many states, it also silences the Black vote at the polls and keeps African Americans from having more political influence; white supremacists then elect government officials who will engage in gerrymandering to further suppress Black votes, write racist laws into effect, ignore the needs of Black constituents, and divert more funding to police departments to imprison and brutalize even more BIPOC.

In *Killing Rage,* hooks also writes about how the pressures of capitalism drive white radicals away from progressive causes and back into the white supremacist capitalist patriarchal culture. She writes that because of the rise of housing costs, many young progressive people of all races and genders became afraid that if they did not find an economically lucrative job, they would not be able to survive outside of poverty. She states: "Radical white youth who had worked on civil rights struggles, protested the war in Vietnam, and even denounced US imperialism could not reconstruct their ties to prevailing systems of domination without creating a new layer of false consciousness" and began to believe that racism was no longer an issue now that segregation had supposedly been eliminated (190). While these radicals should have worked harder to resist the pressures of a racist, sexist, capitalist system, I would also argue that poverty is used by this system as an intentional tool against revolution. For decades, the minimum wage has stayed the same while inflation causes the cost of living to soar. Adequate housing and food have become more and more expensive, healthcare has been increasingly privatized, and expensive technology such as smartphones and computers have become necessities in order to survive in these contemporary times. In the Covid-19 pandemic, the rich and those with secure, intellectual jobs have been largely able to quarantine at home and preform their jobs remotely, while the poor and working-classes who work in grocery stores, restaurants, construction sites, and factories have not had this luxury since they have been deemed essential workers. Meanwhile, our essential workers are also largely the people who suffer from preexisting conditions and who cannot afford access to healthcare in the first place, as well as people of color who may experience discrimination at the hands of white doctors and nurses. Additionally, the necessity of working more and more hours at minimum wage jobs, the exposure to dangerous conditions in physical labor-based work, and the cheapness of unhealthy foods, such as fast food and TV dinners, creates an increasingly exhausted and unhealthy lower class that cannot muster the energy or take the time off of work to organize protest. Women who embrace and glorify capitalism only serve to uphold the oppressive system and undermine the feminism they claim to represent.

Colorism and the Aestheticization of Whiteness

In *Killing Rage: Ending Racism,* bell hooks also discusses the damage that white beauty standards for women have had on the Black community. She writes that in the history of racism and white supremacy in the U.S., lighter skinned Black women have always been deemed more attractive and, therefore, more valuable by white society.

While historically all enslaved Black women were in constant danger of being sexually exploited by white men, lighter-skinned Black women were especially targeted because they appeared closer to white women than did their darker-skinned counterparts. hooks writes that because racist white men saw these women as more sexually appealing and more valuable, this created a historical precedent for the color caste hierarchy in the Black community: "Light skin and long straight hair continue to be traits that define a female as beautiful and desirable in the racist white imagination and in the colonized black mindset. Darker-skinned black females must work to develop positive body self-esteem in a society that continually devalues their image" (127). These color caste hierarchies reinforce the idea that the white woman is the pinnacle of attractiveness and femininity. In a white supremacist, colonized context, Black women must make themselves appear as close to whiteness as possible in order to be seen as beautiful. While this idea is extremely damaging to the self-esteem of Black women, it is extremely uplifting to the self-esteem of white women who have been historically led to see themselves represented as the embodiment of physical beauty everywhere they look at the expense of Black women and women of color who do not meet that beauty standard.

White women's denigration of Black women's appearances in order to feel more attractive themselves is nothing new, as we can also see in Harriet Wilson's novel. At one point in the story, Wilson writes, "… she [Frado] was never permitted to shield her skin from the sun. She was not many shades darker than [Mrs. Bellmont's daughter] now; what a calamity it would be ever to hear the contrast spoken of. Mrs. Bellmont was determined the sun should have full power to darken the shade which nature had first bestowed upon her as best befitting" (22). This quote shows that Mrs. Bellmont is deliberately forcing Frado to work in the sun in order to darken her skin to make her appear less white, which would have made her less conventionally attractive according to the time period's racist beauty standards and would also make it clear to outsiders that she was not a part of the Bellmont family. However, this moment also exposes Mrs. Bellmont's anxieties around Frado's mixed racial identity and illustrates exactly how purposefully racial skin color hierarchies are constructed. Mrs. Bellmont also cuts Frado's hair off when she deems that Frado is getting too close to being seen as conventionally attractive, as shown when Frado tells one of the Bellmont sons what happened and he replies, "Thought you were getting handsome, did she?" (39). These scenes support the argument that hooks makes in *Teaching to Transgress: Education as the Practice of Freedom* that make colonized white women feel the need to "[protect] their fragile social positions and power within patriarchal culture by asserting their superiority over black women" (96) whether this be by upholding white supremacist beauty standards, by creating harmful stereotypes around black women, or by supporting white men's physical abuse and degradation of Black women.

bell hooks goes on in *Teaching to Transgress* to explain that Black women in contemporary times are often distrusting of white women because of the abuse they suffered at their hands during slavery and as domestic workers. She notes that in her conversations with many Black women, they were shocked by the lack of empathy white women felt in discussions about slavery such as the abuse Black women suffered at the hands of slaveowners or when their children were sold away from them through their enslavement (96-97). Historically, many white women saw Black women as sexual competition or as having the power to expose the white women's personal secrets that they encountered in their homes (107). hooks writes that, "Until white women can confront their fear and hatred of black women (and vice versa), until we can acknowledge the negative history which shapes and informs our contemporary interaction, there can be no honest, meaningful dialogue between the two groups" (102). When white people refuse to learn the history of racial oppression and instead choose to remain purposefully ignorant so that we do not have to face the harsh reality of racism and address the damage that white supremacy has caused, we only further perpetuate its traumatic and painful effects on BIPOC communities. When white women in particular refuse to educate themselves on the unique experiences of racism and sexism that Black women have experienced because of their identities as Black women, they further estrange Black women from the feminist movement and reinforce the idea that feminism is a "white women thing". A white women-centered feminism that does not take into account the oppression that Black women and other women of color face and that does not make space for them to have their voices heard is not true feminism, but instead a shallow reincarnation of white supremacy in a feminist context.

The Critical Need for LGBTQ Solidarity across Racial and Ethnic Differences

The feminist movement is not the only possibly progressive movement that must deal with issues of racial tension. In the LGBTQ community, racism has become increasingly problematic and unignorable as the community has grown in size and visibility in the last ten years. Much of the tension and conflict between white and

Black women that bell hooks describes in many of her works is applicable to the LGBTQ community. Many LGBTQ Black people and people of color are made to feel unsafe in queer spaces that are predominantly white, and so stick to their own queer BIPOC spaces to avoid this racism, which leads to divisions and segregation within the LGBTQ community. Many white LGBTQ people feel that that are not capable of being oppressors because they are victims of homophobia and/or transphobia, much as how cishet white women feel that they cannot be oppressors because they experience sexism. This belief enables white LGBTQ people to uncritically embrace racism and allows them to unapologetically espouse racism.

One of the most notable examples of overt racism in the LGBTQ community is that of the gay dating app Grindr, that up until 2020 allowed users to filter perspective partners by ethnicity and is infamously rife with racist bios in which their users write things such as "no blacks, no Latinos, no Asians" despite the fact that such language was banned in 2017 (Carlson et al). In their article, "Grindr is deleting its 'ethnicity filter'. But racism is still rife in online dating" Carlson et al explore the issue of racism on Grindr by interviewing several gay Asian Australian men about their experiences with the app and found that Grindr "was repeatedly singled out by research participants as a site where they regularly experienced sexual racism—both in user bios, and interactions with others." One interviewee is quoted as saying, "It scars you in a way that it affects you in [situations] beyond the Gay community … it affects your whole life." Not only are these experiences traumatizing, but they alienate members of the LGBTQ community who should have been made welcome. LGBTQ BIPOC who experience intersectional oppression based on race and sexuality and/or gender identity are in desperate need of a supportive community, but instead are finding LGBTQ spaces rife with white supremacy. Unless the queer community makes a purposeful effort to address these issues and to become a more welcoming space for BIPOC, our communities will continue to be exclusionary and will uphold the very tenets of white supremacist capitalist patriarchy that we claim to oppose.

White LGBTQ people also forget that trans BIPOC experience not only transphobia, homophobia, and sexism, but also racism that directly influences the other types of discrimination that they face, much like how hooks describes cis Black women experiencing a specific type of racism and sexism because they are both Black and women. According to the National LGBTQ Taskforce, "Black transgender and gender non-conforming people face some of the highest levels of discrimination of all transgender people" and that 41% had been homeless at least once in their life.

The report also stated that 31% were living in extreme poverty, and 20.2% had HIV (compared to 2.64% of all trans people). Since Black trans people historically played a major role in starting the gay rights movement, such as Marsha P. Johnson and Miss Major Griffin-Gracy who were involved in the Stonewall Riots, the entire LGBTQ community owes them gratitude, but not much of the gratitude is being shown as Black trans youths are left poor and on the street. If the trans community and the broader LGBTQ community is ever going to come together in true solidarity to achieve something revolutionary, we will have to cross class, gender, and racial boundaries in order to fully speak to each other and forge stronger bonds.

As a white trans bisexual person, my experiences with homophobia and transphobia often inform my understanding for the oppression other groups face. hooks writes that many white gay women who were committed to anti-racism said "that discrimination against them on the basis of sexuality helped bridge their understanding of the pain of race-based discrimination. Rather than assuming that this pain was identical to the pain they experienced, they accepted the 'bridge' as merely a base to walk across" (*Teaching Community* 62). When I talk about my own experiences with homophobia and transphobia in the context of oppression in a broader sense, I always fear that people will assume I am trying to speak over BIPOC and other marginalized groups, or that I will come off as believing that my oppression trumps all other forms of oppression and must take precedence in the conversation. My self-consciousness surrounding this stems from my knowledge that there any many white LGBTQ people who do firmly believe that because they experience homophobia or transphobia, they are absolved of all sin when it comes to racism, classism, sexism, or ableism. As bell hooks notes, "Many white people are unable to bridge this gap. They remain unable to look at the way in which whiteness and white power give them access to privilege to the role of dominator" (*Teaching Community* 62). So, while I find that my experiences with homophobia and transphobia allow me the unique opportunity as a white person to empathize and relate to other oppressed demographics, it is essential to keep in mind that my queer identity does not erase my whiteness or mean that I no longer benefit from white supremacy. I am still just as much white as I am bisexual or trans, and my white identity has had an equal impact on my life. It is just one that white people have been raised not to recognize, while BIPOC are forced to be aware of their racial identity on a constant, daily basis. White LGBTQ people need to come to an understanding that in order to truly fight homophobic and transphobic oppression, we must fight all forms of oppression that reinforce binary ways of thinking, inequality, and domination.

In fact, I believe that it is essential for white people to have some level of self-consciousness when comparing the oppression they may face, whether this be sexism, homophobic, transphobia, ableism, etc. with the racism that BIPOC face, because otherwise one may fall into the trap of believing themselves to be the expert on oppression and to silence the voices of BIPOC who may have different experiences and to blind oneself to one's own internalized racism. My own anxiety over my intentions being misconstrued prompts me to choose my words carefully, which is much more a strength than a hinderance when participating in important discussions about oppression, and it prompts me to carefully analyze my own intentions before speaking. This self-reflection is important for all people involved in progressive movements because, otherwise, we will not be able to unlearn harmful behavior and ways of thinking that have been instilled in us while growing up in the white supremacist capitalist patriarchal system.

Our suffering at the hands of oppressors should not be treated as a competition for who is the most oppressed, but, as hooks says, the bridge that we walk across. Discussions about the similarities and differences between our struggles can be a great source of learning to understand one another, to empathize, and to strategize how we can best join together to fight against the oppressive systems of domination at work in our society. Communication must be the basis for allyship—simply saying that one supports BIPOC communities but never speaking to them or actively advocating for their fight for equality is not enough. White women who claim to be feminist allies for all women but who do not listen to the voices of Black women and women of color or who only promote support for other white women do not uphold the true morals of feminism, and instead only support white supremacy masked in seemingly progressive ideology. White LGBTQ activists who only consort with other white queer people or worse, who actively exclude and harass BIPOC, are not fighting for our community but instead "white"-washing it and driving away the people in greatest need of our support. It is in the best interest of white supremacist capitalist patriarchy that we divide ourselves and build walls between our communities so that we cannot join together to overthrow the system. By antagonizing and silencing each other, we do the work of the system for it. But when we make room for each other at the table of life, when we come together in good faith to discuss the tremendous obstacles we face and the oppression that plagues our lives, we have the power to create real change in the benefit not only those in our own camp, but *all* people.

The study of literature can serve as the basis for such necessary conversation between oppressed peoples and as an anchor for discussions surrounding race, ethnicity, gender, sexuality, ability, etc. Analyzing the intersectionality of oppression can be easier through the lens of literary critique when one can turn to the words on the page in order to understand the experiences and viewpoints of the oppressed. It can also be used as a tool to challenge forms of bigotry that are perpetuated through literary works and to uncover the many ways that conscious and unconscious bias may present themselves in writing and art, so that we—as literary and social media scholars—may come to a deeper understanding of prejudicial ideologies. bell hooks illustrates the transgressive power of literary critique throughout her many works as she critiques books such as *The Help* or films such as *Crash* that ineffectively handle issues of racism, and when she discusses the life-transformative power of anti-oppressive experiences with her students in literature classrooms. In my experience, when performed as a radical act that challenges dominating systems of white supremacist capitalist patriarchy—literary scholarship has the power to shed light on the inhumane sides of humanity and to open the door to a brighter future in which a beloved community, based on love and egalitarianism, is truly possible. For me, personally and academically, the work of bell hooks in *Killing Rage: Ending Racism* and all her anti-oppressive works over the years serve as a powerful testament to the visionary agency of literary critique determined to end systematic oppression and to create a world in which we are all free to love one another.

Works Cited

Carlson, Bronwyn, et al. "Grindr is deleting its 'ethnicity filter'. But racism is still rife in online dating." *The Conversation*, June 7, 2020, https://theconversation.com/grindr-is-deleting-its-ethnicity-filter-but-racism-is-still-rife-in-online-dating-140077.

Funari, Vicky and Sergio De la Torre, directors. *Maquilapolis*. California Newsreel, 2006.

Goldman, Adam. "Gina Haspel, Trump's Choice for C.I.A., Played Role in Torture Program." *The New York Times*, March 13, 2018, https://www.nytimes.com/2018/03/13/us/politics/gina-haspel-cia-director-nominee-trump-torture-waterboarding.html.

Helal, Kathleen M. "Anger, Anxiety, Abstraction: Virginia Woolf's 'Submerged Truth.'" *South Central Review*, vol. 22, no. 2, 2005, pp. 78-94.

hooks, bell. *Ain't I a Woman: Black Women and Feminism*. London, Pluto Press, 1982.

---. *Killing Rage*. New York City, Holt Paperbacks, 1995.

---. *Teaching Community: A Pedagogy of Hope*. New York City, Routledge, 2003.

---. "Holding My Sister's Hand: Feminist Solidarity." *Teaching to Transgress: Education as the Practice of Freedom*, New York City, Routledge, 1994, pp. 93–110.

"New Analysis Shows Startling Levels of Discrimination Against Black Transgender People." *National LGBTQ Taskforce*, 2021, www.thetaskforce.org/new-analysis-shows-startling-levels-of-discrimination-against-black-transgender-people/.

Rockwell, Kate. "Sexy." Mean Girls (Original Broadway Recording), Atlantic Records, 2018, track 9. *Spotify*, https://open.spotify.com/track/4A1GfEVOELS3vo4tSa6bts?si=CILDFDFMRWKnNoP_kwBV9A.

Wilson, Harriet E. *Our Nig, or, Sketches from the Life of a Free Black*. Edited by P. Gabrielle Foreman and Reginald H. Pitts, London, Penguin Books, 2009.

14

Unseating My Complicity
Standing as an Ally for the Rights of the Marginalized
Ashley Richmond Kimmelman

Today I write not for others to exploit or appropriate the work of bell hooks or that of noted Black, Indigenous, People/Women of Color feminists, but I write to free myself from the pain of systemic oppression—unseating my complicity related to the perpetuation of racism. Having become critically conscious of the life-threatening impacts of it in BIPOC communities, I have determined to stand as an ally for the rights of the marginalized.

This essay will focus on personal experiences and observations related to my own coming to "critical consciousness" as both an individual and as a literary scholar. First, I will explore the valid critiques of white liberalism and white feminism centered on the critical perspective presented by bell hooks in *Killing Rage: Ending Racism*. I will also incorporate commentary on the subject from other creators of color working in a variety of media. Next, I will move into a reflection on my intentions as a student of literature, as well as the problems that may arise within my scholarly undertakings. I will interrogate the issues surrounding writing outside of one's identity—particularly those of white women studying works from Black Indigenous People of Color creators. Problematic elements focused on by hooks in *Killing Rage* will be touched upon including the following: scholars' trendy commodification of BIPOC voices as well as scholars using BIPOC writing and research in a way that upholds imperialist, white supremacist, capitalist, and/or heteronormative standards. Both of these items will be investigated here. Finally, I will synthesize each reflection together in a direct address to those whom I know and to myself. I will discuss my responsibilities as a straight, white feminist scholar, but more importantly my imperative duties as an individual who wishes to be an ally. To begin, I will look to the overarching ideologies informing my societal choices: liberalism and feminism.

Looking Back Over My Life

Growing up in a Southern white family where the majority of my extended family were both conservative and Catholic, or in some cases Jewish, I imagine there were little worse fates they could have imagined for me than being a liberal vegetarian who does not regularly attend religious services. I have often heard the horror stories of higher education turning nice girls into zealous misandrists who reject tradition with condescending disdain. I have seen the social media posts from Baby Boomers proclaiming that a college education does not grant one common sense. Now that I am a year into my doctoral program, I would not describe that feared end as being my fate. I did not fall from grace nor do I despise those who do not walk my path. That being said, there is still some truth to those fearful notions. My journey through life has allowed me to learn things beyond the limits of what I had experienced as a child from a small town. For that I am grateful. Still, I recognize that just because I do not identify as someone conservative or staunchly religious, I am not inherently better than those who are. There are some liberal-minded individuals who might differ with me on this score. Some feel that because they are not outwardly prejudiced—whether in terms of race, nationality, gender, sexual orientation or other aspects—they do not support oppression of marginalized groups. This assumption is disingenuous at best, and almost certainly dangerous to societal progress. bell hooks touches on such false notions in her work *Killing Rage: Ending Racism*. Within the latter essays included in her text, hooks repeatedly notes how liberal whites and people of all identities who benefit from class privilege can unwittingly contribute to systemic racism. In *Killing Rage* hooks puts it succinctly: "[G]oodwill can coexist with racism and white supremacist attitudes" (156). As a liberal white woman from a privileged background, I feel that assessing my own relationship to this dynamic is essential if I am to confront its more problematic elements in my life. I do not want to join the ranks of those whose good intentions pave the path to hell, as the old aphorism warns. Instead, I aim to begin a new narrative for myself. Self-reflection is of course important to everyone who wishes to become critically conscious, yet as I sit here reflecting on my own life, I find additional depth to this exploration in my pursuits as a literary scholar.

As a first-year doctoral student, one whose research interests are concerned with the ways writing intersects with contemporary notions of what it means to be socially just and politically active, I recognize the inherent power of words in "real life". Though I do not typically consider myself a writer in the creative sense, as someone whose work involves extensive critical writing, I understand that the gravity of words extends beyond the works I study to include my own. As scholars we should always be concerned with the impact our work has on our field of study and as well as on our readers. However, this is perhaps even more critical when writing about experiences that differ greatly from one's own—including the words I write here. I am a scholar who wants to include marginalized voices in the heart of my research; as a straight white woman from privilege this goal is riddled with opportunities for failure. hooks' words in *Killing Rage* remind me that even if my scholarly intentions seem ethical and rational in my own mind, intent is no guarantee of outcome. Reflection in regard to purpose has always been critical to my work and it within this thoughtful framework that I situate this essay. Therefore, today I write not for others, but for myself.

This essay will focus on personal experiences and observations related to my own coming to critical consciousness as both an individual and as a literary scholar. First, I will explore the valid critiques of white liberalism and white feminism centered on those presented by bell hooks in *Killing Rage*. I will also incorporate commentary on the subject from other creators of color working in a variety of media. Next, I will move into a reflection on my intentions as a student of literature, as well as they problems that may arise within my scholarly undertakings. I will interrogate the issues surrounding writing outside of one's identity—particularly those of white women studying works from BIPOC creators. Problematic elements focused on by hooks in *Killing Rage* will be touched upon including the following: scholars' trendy commodification of BIPOC voices and scholars as well as using BIPOC writing and research in a way that upholds imperialist, white supremacist, capitalist, and/or heteronormative standards. Both of these items will be investigated here. Finally, I will synthesize each reflection together in a direct address to myself and those whom I know. I will discuss my responsibilities as a straight, white feminist scholar, but more importantly as an individual who wishes to be an ally. To begin, I will look to the overarching ideologies informing my societal choices: liberalism and feminism.

Facing Issues within White Liberalism, Feminism, and Scholarship

One of the most prominent issues with the specific brand of white liberalism discussed by hooks in *Killing Rage*, is the tendency to hide within one's privilege when directly confronted by issues of racial and gender oppression. In one of my more recent graduate classes this issue reared its head when we were asked to discuss the place of race in literary studies. One of my classmates suggested race was only relevant to the conversation if the scholar's research was specialized in that area. For example, race was not relevant in their own work which dealt specifically with white authors of a bygone empire. Though admittedly not all scholarship deals directly with the subject of race, ignoring the impact of historical as well as contemporary inequality creates a void in one's work. By discounting the significance of imperialist white supremacist capitalist heteronormative structures on the works much is lost. This ability to distance oneself from "racial" conversations is one manifestation of the type of privilege discussed by hooks. It is a privilege to not grasp how the status quo has negatively shaped the world. This is a privilege which must be reckoned with if our work is to have real world value. This of course extends into realms outside of academia. Though individuals may be outspoken in their beliefs, it is not uncommon to see liberals or so called "white allies" retreat into the safety of their comfortable lives when threatened with uncomfortable truths. On this topic hooks writes the following of her white, liberal contemporaries:

> [M]any radical whites who had been allies in the black liberation struggle began to question whether the struggle to end racism was really that significant, or to suggest that the struggle was over ... Similarly, critiques of capitalism ... were also relegated to the back burner as people 'discovered' that it was important to have class privilege so that one could better help the exploited (190).

Though written in the mid-nineties the truth of this statement resonates still. Whether this phenomenon takes the form of legislature failing to make good on campaign promises or individuals refusing to stand up to family members to avoid causing a stir, with such retreats into privilege one becomes complicit in the system when words do not lead to action. As hooks explains: "When liberal whites fail to understand how they can/or do embody white supremacist values and beliefs ... they cannot recognize the ways their actions support and affirm the very structure of racist domination and oppression that they profess to wish to see eradicated (185). Although I would like to believe that this does not apply to me, I know that it certainly has been true at times. With just a brief moment of contemplation I can think of several incidents that demonstrate my failings, two of which I will detail here.

When I was in middle school, I ignored anonymous bullies who vandalized my school things while I was out of the room. Returning to the classroom one day, I discovered graffiti in the form of slurs and pejoratives specifically taking aim against my Jewish family members. I will not amplify such terms through repetition here. The unseen vandals did not care that I do not identify as Jewish myself; pride in my extended family's heritage seemed sufficient enough cause for taunting. At first, I did not know how to respond. I was embarrassed. Yet, I didn't see there being much option to deal with this. I wanted to avoid being *that girl*—the quiet nerd who only spoke up to tattle on her classmates. I drenched my books in white out (ironically including the Bible used for my religion class in Catholic school). I moved on quietly. I realize now I ignored those individuals, because I had the ability to do so. They had no real effect on my position in life beyond some small emotional repercussions. I decided to bury the experience and keep going. People were sometimes mean and that was just the way life was. Moving on seemed easier than confrontation. I realize now by hiding within other aspects of my privilege and not speaking out, I potentially allowed these individuals to continue their role in furthering the oppression on which our culture is built. I hope they have grown and evolved as adults in positive ways, but cannot say for sure. After all who can say for certain these youthful exploits did not continue to spread into new forms of hate, allowing them to harm others who do not share my privilege into their adult lives. I do not mean to shame those who do not stand up to bullies, nor do I rebuke my younger self in a vulnerable moment. Rather, I mean to point out the mindfulness that should accompany our choices of action or inaction. Though I myself have grown it is important to note that I still fail as an ally to those who find themselves under the boot of the imperialist white supremacist capitalist heteronormative sexist hegemony at times.

If I were to describe the white liberal reactions, I witnessed firsthand to the events surrounding the Black Lives Matter movement last summer in 2020, I would categorize the responses in two ways. The first group, of which I would consider myself a member, were those who were more reserved in their reactions. While those I am closest with were, thankfully, clear in their allyship, there were acquaintances from my youth whom I observed being decidedly antithetical to the goals of the movement. In their own words they were (of course) "not racist", yet their words and actions betrayed them as such. I had honest conversations with some of these individuals about their "beliefs" to marginal success; yet more often than I would like to admit I did not directly confront the racists in my midst. While at the time I felt that supporting my Black friends and being outspoken in my expressions of personal support were good ways to be an ally, my actions were simply not sufficient. My hesitation in the face of confrontation betrayed my intent. How can one determine what is enough when defending human rights? The answer: you can't. There is no quota to meet or boxes to check when fighting for human rights. Any attempt to quantify allyship is a failure to be an ally at all. Although not standing true as an ally in the face of confrontation is one overt way in which white liberals such as myself often fail, sometimes failures take more subtle forms. The other type of reaction my white liberal acquaintances expressed was not as obvious, but no less destructive.

Much has been said about the virulent racism that was exposed last year on social media during the summer of 2020, yet problems also stemmed from the opposing reactions. Opening my social media accounts last summer, I was often met with a flood of black squares and pictures of people reading *How to Be an Antiracist* (by Ibram X. Kendi). It was in vogue to be anti-racist. The squares and hashtags disappeared soon after their arrival. This rogue wave of allyship washing over social media streams and vanishing soon after, exposes a hidden facet of liberal support of white supremacy. Though less overt, it is one which is still vital to recognize if white liberals such as myself are to positively progress towards and elimination of systemic oppression of marginalized communities. White tourism of marginalized pain is something that is widely experienced, but not often discussed, particularly by those who perpetrate it. Vietnamese poet Ocean Vuong recalls such an experience in his piece "Not Even This" saying: "Once, at a party set on a rooftop in Brooklyn for an 'artsy vibe,' a young woman said, sipping her drink, *You're so lucky. You're gay plus you get to write about war and stuff. I'm just white.* [Pause.] *I got nothing.* [Laughter, glasses clinking]" (Vuong). Another poet, Hanif Willis-Abdurraqib more succinctly summarizes the issue: "violence begets / more photo opportunities" (Willis-Abdurraqib). When white liberalism treats human rights issues as fashionable causes to pick up and drop at will, they play into systems of oppression and the dynamics of domination. I don't mean to point fingers at my peers without recognizing that some culpability likely lies with me as well, I did after all join in on the aforementioned social media fury. However, I do wish to emphatically assert that white liberals and those of race, gender, or class privilege must acknowledge these types of harmful actions if we are to decenter ourselves in the conversation in order to be more thoughtful, impactful allies. These are only small examples experienced by myself and by those whom I observed; nonetheless, I think each clearly demonstrates the fact that even our smallest actions and inactions can further the grip of white supremacy on society if left unchecked. In addition to these hurdles felt by liberals in a general sense, feminists such as myself face special challenges in the path towards allyship.

The Failures of Modern Feminism

To say mainstream liberal feminism is built on a problematic history would be an understatement to say the least. In more precise terms, feminism as it exists in the popular imagination has been historically connected to white supremacists masquerading as feminists. Put simply, feminism often times exists only as "white feminism". In her first book, *Ain't I a Woman: Black Women and Feminism*, hooks asserts:

> American women irrespective of their education, economic status, or racial identification have undergone years of racist and sexist socialization to blindly trust our knowledge of history and its effect on present reality ... consequently the Sisterhood [college-educated middle and upper-class white women] talked about has not become reality (121).

As hooks continues, even the enlightened and "free" women of second wave feminism were still plagued by the evils of the past and a deep reliance on the very system they sought to dismantle. In seeking equality for themselves white feminists oftentimes placed obstacles in the path of others so that they could get ahead. Built on such a rotten foundation, I begin to wonder instead how feminism ever progressed at all. However, it is clear that some progress has been made. Later waves of feminism have become more inclusive and more concerned with equity rather than simply transforming the white patriarchy into the white matriarchy. With that said, as a white, cis woman, from a middle-class background, I know it remains vital to dissect my role in a movement that had been corrupted by its own adherents in its earliest days. Therefore, I must interrogate more deeply my responsibilities not only as a straight, white feminist scholar, but also as an individual who is allied with the marginalized.

As a young white girl raised by strong women, I always was instilled with the belief that I was capable and independent; labeling myself a feminist was the natural next step. As time has gone by I realize that, despite goodwill, I was playing into the hands of the ubiquitous "man"— a rotten system rooted in imperialism, white supremacy, capitalism, and gender bias. In this case the old adage about good intentions was correct: well-meaning words don't necessarily lead to good actions. Because of this disconnect between my beliefs and reality, I revisit my previous mentions of problematic feminism. In a TED Talk now famous for being sampled on Beyonce's "Flawless", Nigernian author Chimamanda Ngozi Adichie recounts an anecdote from her childhood. During an argument one of her oldest friends accusingly declared to Adiche, "'You know, you're a feminist.'" She notes that the moniker "feminist" was not intended to be complimentary. "I could tell from his tone," she recalls, "the same tone that you would use to say something like, 'You're a supporter of terrorism'" (Adiche). Like young Chimamanda found herself at the conclusion of her story, if I were to tell a younger version of myself that feminism was not a path to equity my youthful self would have been utterly confused. Everyone being treated the same wasn't bad, right? It turns out that I was wrong. Feminism may not be founded on a shared hatred of men and bras, yet an ironic resentment present nonetheless. Unexpectedly, the ugly parts of feminism have nothing to do with men; rather the hate plaguing the movement is the resentment feminists throw on each other. In her previous works bell hooks has discussed at length the pernicious effects of racism, classism, homophobia, and I would add transphobia, in various waves of the feminist movement. In bell hooks' *Teaching to Transgress: Education as the Practice of Freedom*, the essay "Holding My Sister's Hand" recounts hooks' dialogue with a group of white women whom she saw as positive allies. After some discussion with the women, she noted two commonalties she saw as being effective in their pursuit of allyship. Through "honest confrontation, and dialogue about race, and reciprocal interaction" it appeared that these women were able to earnestly address the flaws inherent in the system and move closer towards solidarity (*Teaching to Transgress* 106). I understand that two simple steps are not some panacea to cure the ills of an unjust world. That caveat aside, I find hooks' explication on these traits to be a good place to begin an earnest effort toward personal change, and as such would like to look at them more closely here.

Much like my intentions in my life and work, hooks writes that within the feminist movement itself "the call for sisterhood was often motivated by a sincere longing to transform the present" (*Teaching to Transgress* 102). Yet, this desire to change the present is marred by a common inability to acknowledge one's own complicity. hooks explains: "[w]hen black women responded ... by calling attention to both the past of racial domination and its present manifestations in the structure of the feminist movement, white women initially resisted the analysis. They assumed a posture of innocence and denial (*Teaching to Transgress* 102). Thinking back to my experiences interacting with other white people, I see this denial reiterated time and time again. At the risk of sounding hyperbolic, every single time I opened Facebook this summer during the rise of Black Lives Matter protests I was met with the outcry of white victimhood. Statements declaring "I have black friends" or "I didn't own slaves" reverberated across social media. Even in events surrounding the #MeToo Movement, incidentally founded by Black American activist Tarana Burke, one can see this denial takes many forms.

In "An Open Letter from Black Women to the Slutwalk" we see a recognition of the discrepancy faced by non-white non- cis gendered women at a supposedly feminist event. Slutwalks as described by the letter "emerged in 2011 after a police officer's comment to University of Toronto students which equated women 's 'slutty' dress with the probability of sexual assault. His comments inspired global protests against sexual profiling, slut shaming and sexual assault" (Black Women's Blueprint 9). A walk meant to empower women under the patriarchal gaze, it becomes clear that many deny more troubling aspects of such expressions of modern feminism. In the open letter the group declares:

> As Black women, we do not have the privilege or the space to call ourselves "slut" without validating the already historically entrenched ideology and recurring messages about what and who the Black woman is. We don't have the privilege to play on destructive representations burned in our collective minds, on our bodies and souls for generation…. The perception and wholesale acceptance of speculations about what the Black woman wants, what she needs, and what she deserves has truly, long crossed the boundaries of her mode of dress (10).

bell hooks notes that racism in post-Civil Rights waves of women was mostly an "unconscious, unacknowledged aspect of their thought, suppressed by their narcissism" these aspects remained all the same from early iterations of the movement (*Ain't I a Woman* 136). Even today to many individuals the term "women" is not all inclusive, but rather a reflection only of those who look like themselves. hooks describes such white women during Second Wave Feminism as being "insensitive", "unconcerned", and "patronizing" towards those perceived to be of lower classes and/or of other races (*Ain't I a Woman* 144). These women stated that their goal was to fight for Women's Rights, with the unstated caveat that they would not do so at the cost of their own privileged place in the American patriarchy. A description of these activists that I found particularly curious showed white women who saw themselves as generous for being welcoming, but who could not see that their "generosity" was self-serving— a fact clearly echoed in the words penned in "An Open Letter from Black Women to the Slutwalks" (*Ain't I a Woman* 144). I would like to think that third and fourth wave feminism have corrected some of the ills of the past, and I suppose the fact that we even use the phrases "white privilege" or "intersectionality" in mainstream conversations is a step in the right direction. Nonetheless, the eerie similarity of her description again makes me wonder: will we ever get to where we need to be? Forty years ago, hooks asserted that the failure of the earlier women's movements to address issues of race and class should be woefully acknowledged, but that this acknowledgement does not "free any of us from assuming responsibility for change" (193). This is something that I think still resonates today. Today individuals of all genders are becoming more aware of their privileges, myself included, but recognition does not equate with true change. In the concluding pages of *Ain't I a Woman* hooks writes of Black women who "fear feminism" while simultaneously "express[ing] a belief in feminism" in private. It is this exact denial and claims of innocence to which I speak here. A *New Yorker* article by the late Toni Morrison delves into this mentality further.

Morrison explains that "[t]he comfort of being 'naturally better than,' of not having to struggle or demand civil treatment, is hard to give up". She writes, "white people's conviction of their natural superiority is being lost ... The threat is frightening". As a white woman who would like to be a strong ally, the idea that this level of racism exists in me is horrifying. Nonetheless, as I am discovering it is this very acknowledgement that is needed for allyship. As Audre Lorde insists we must, "reach down into that deep place of knowledge inside ... touch that terror and loathing of any difference that lives there. See whose face it wears. Then the personal as the political can begin to illuminate all our choices" ("The Master's Tools Will Never Dismantle the Master's House" 113). Only after such "honest confrontation" of myself and an acknowledgment of my privileged place as a white middle-class woman in the imperialist white supremacist capitalist system can I make a change.

Decentering White Feminism

The second attribute that hooks notes as being essential in the path to allyship is that of dialogue and reciprocal interaction. hooks writes of armchair feminism as often being a means through which "one can partake of the 'good' that these movements produce without any commitment to transformative politics and practice" (*Teaching to Transgress* 71). To understand this lack of commitment one need only compare the outpouring of supportive hashtags that followed Ahmaud Arbery's murder almost exactly a year ago, to the virtual silence felt today, despite there being many victims still in need of justice. In a particularly unsettling passage in *Teaching to Transgress*, hooks describes Black people, and specifically Black women, as being like "a box of chocolates presented to individual white women for their eating pleasure, so that they can decide for themselves and others which pieces are most tasty (*Teaching to Transgress* 80). Treating others as objects for consumption and assuming an air of authority poisons the feminist movement by using—in the words of Audre Lorde—the very "master's tools to destroy the master's house" ("The Master's Tools" 112). How can we claim to seek freedom and equality, if that freedom is only bought through the subjugation of others in our place? It is clear that only through efforts of empathy, dialogue, and reciprocity with one another that we may dismantle the systemic oppression we seek to disrupt as feminists. I do not pretend that this is a necessarily peaceful or easy task. In fact, as hooks suggests, "[c]onfronting one another across differences, means that we must change ideas about how we learn; rather than fearing conflict we have to find ways to use it as a catalyst for new thinking, for growth" (113). Such change and confrontation is a momentous undertaking and, as Toni Morrison said, it can be a frightening thing for white women like me to consider; however, fear of change does not negate its necessity, but instead underscores its urgency. My own need for decentered feminist allyship deepens as a scholar working with non-cis male BIPOC creative works.

In the news this past year, white entertainer Jimmy Fallon and TikTok Influencer Addison Rae faced backlash for a seemingly innocent TV spot on "The Tonight Show". During this segment, Fallon holds up different cue cards listing TikTok dances for an ever-smiling Addison Rae to perform. Lighthearted in concept, many viewers were outraged by the glaring fact that "the show failed to credit the lesser-known TikTok users who created the choreography, many of whom are Black" (Wanshel). Using BIPOC voices and bodies because of their apparent trendiness is not a new phenomenon. As white rapper Eminem quips ironically in his Grammy nominated "Without Me": "I'm not the first king of controversy/I am the worst thing since Elvis Presley/To do black music so selfishly/And use it to get myself wealthy" (Eminem). bell hooks explains that "contemporary commodification of black culture by whites in no way challenges white supremacy when it takes the form of making blackness 'the spice that can liven up the dull dish that is mainstream white culture'" (*Killing Rage* 153). Even in the off chance that people that Jimmy Fallon, Addison Rae, or Eminem valued the foundational work laid out by BIPOC creators, their lack of recognition of their non-white forerunners in their own work only serves to reinforce whiteness as the norm and relegate BIPOC voices to the margins once more. hooks notes that "[w]hile it has become 'cool' for white folks to hang out with black people and express pleasure in black culture, most white people do not feel that this pleasure should be linked to unlearning racism" (*Killing Rage* 157). Herein lies the lesson that white creators and scholars alike should absorb. Using the "trendiness" of

BIPOC creative efforts and bodies as stepping stones to further one's own work is not anti-racist regardless of how positive the intent may be. As a white woman scholar, it is imperative that I question my own intentionality behind my work if I am to continue to unlearn racism and ground my work on anti-racist tenets. Nevertheless, even with this initial reflection I must continue to be critically conscious throughout the process, something that not all literary scholars and creators of privileged socio-economic status successfully do.

In a recent literary theory class I completed, one of my white peers asked whether or not it was possible for anti-racist white scholars to study BIPOC works without co-opting their voices or furthering imperialist white supremacist capitalist heteronormative mores. On this topic bell hooks writes that some of her own white feminist peers "appropriated the discourse of race to advance their career drawing from the scholarship and critical thinking of black women" (*Killing Rage* 99). She continues that "while white women can and must assume a major voice speaking to and about anti-racist struggle … it is equally important that they learn to speak with … women of color in ways that do not reinscribe and perpetuate white supremacy (*Killing Rage* 105). In response to my peer's question several of my classmates suggested similar ideas to hooks. They agreed that while overcoming one's learned Eurocentric values is difficult there were ways that their scholarly work could be respectfully framed. Two of my white peers noted that when working with BIPOC writing in their own feminist scholarship, they always back up their own thoughts with sources derived from credited BIPOC scholars. hooks concurs with this approach suggesting that "[w]ithout naming this input they can easily be seen as yet another group of radical white folks appropriating feminist critical discourse on race in ways that deny the vanguard activism of black women. By doing so they undermine the politics of solidarity" (*Killing Rage* 104). Beyond ensuring the discussion on the work of scholarship from the BIPOC community, it is important to recognize one's own place in the discourse. For example, in feminist scholarship such as what I and my peers undertake, hooks distinguishes between the positions of BIPOC scholars and white scholars. She delineates the differences in *Killing Rage* stating:

> It was individual black women and women of color who were and remain at the forefront of the struggle to maintain an antiracist revolutionary feminist agenda. It is a meaningful show of solidarity and sisterhood that individual radical white women are daring to challenge courageously the racism of their peers. (103)

The difference here between being the vanguard of a movement and being someone who stands in solidarity with those individuals should always be recognized within one's scholarly writing, particularly if one is white. One way to do this is by centering the conversation on BIPOC voices and identifying one's own positioning within the work. Though I am admittedly still unlearning my own imperialist, white supremacist, capitalist, and/or heteronormative ideals every day, making the effort to use BIPOC scholarship, centering the conversation on the BIPOC writers on which I write, and expressing my own positioning appear to be critical to producing scholarly work focused on the experiences of those who do not share my background of white, middle class, cis gendered privilege. I cannot say that I fully agree with my white classmate who suggested that white scholars and creators should not work with BIPOC pieces, but I recognize where this stance comes from. Many white creators and scholars appropriate BIPOC work to their advantage without regard to how their own derivative work tightens the grasp of racism, hatred, and white supremacy on society. From this reflection, however, one thing is clear that in order to be a scholar who writes from a place of love and respect for fellow human beings, I must show myself love by being critically aware of my own positioning and intent.

For all of this, I want to end on a note of positivity. I think that all of the problems I listed above can be addressed in a way that leads to a better future. However, optimism does not negate the necessity of accountability. As a white cis woman, I know that my fellow white liberals and those who come from race, gender, or class privilege, cultivate lives replete with unintentional, yet inexcusable support for the imperialist white supremacist capitalist nation as it stands. I know this to be true and do not excuse it. Though this fact cannot be ignored, my rebuke is not a permanent condemnation or becoming a social pariah through the "cancelation" feared by some, rather it is a wake-up call. It is a call to those who have caused harm as members who benefit and therefore reinforce oppression. These individuals, including myself, are called to take ownership of their actions, decenter themselves, and move forward in a spirit more committed to the ideas of social justice we vocalize. Particularly as a writer and a feminist this responsibility runs deep. If I am to continue on my path of feminist scholarship with an emphasis on writing by voices of color there are important questions, I need to ask myself first. What is my role in oppression and my intentions moving forward? How do I unlearn the harmful ideas instilled in me by the imperialist white supremacist capitalist patriarchy? How can I give space and a voice to those who most deserve it? These questions, among others, are just the beginning of steps that must be continually undertaken to ensure that I am on a path of anti-racist solidarity, not oppression or appropriation.

It is within this pensive attitude that I wish conclude my essay. Earlier I detailed my personal failures in letting my voice of dissent against systemic oppression be heard. I also described the reactions I witnessed from white people I knew in regard to the events surrounding the Black Lives Matter movement last summer in 2020. Though I cannot go back in time and alter my responses at those times, I would like to use what is left of my space here to address the subtleties of racism I left unchecked. As a white woman who would like to be a better ally to those unduly marginalized based on their race, nationality, gender, sexual orientation, etc. I feel it is my duty to speak up and speak out. Pairing bell hooks writing in *Killing Rage: Ending Racism*, with the work of several Black musicians, I will craft an open letter to myself and those white liberals with whom I am acquainted as a means to explain to them their role in upholding the imperialist white supremacist capitalist hold on the United States.

Where We Go from Here: From Critical Consciousness to the Future

To My Facebook Friends, Internet Acquaintances, and Me,

If I were a gambler, I would bet that many of us would not describe ourselves as racist. In fact, based on what I have seen of your online presence, most of you would be scandalized to learn that racist is precisely how outside eyes perceive you. You simply cannot be racist, you claim. Your knee-jerk reaction is to list off reasons why you are not. Your list includes: having Black friends, attending church, being "colorblind", or asserting that "all lives matter". While I do not share your claims, I do reject the moniker of racist in my own way. "I am not racist," I say, "How could I be?" With shared posts of activist knowledge, signed petitions, anti-racist book lists, and hashtags a plenty the descriptor of racist simply does not fit. We are not the same in our denial, but the consequence is shared. Our failure lies in our inability to see that a denial of the possibility of inadvertent racism in itself breeds white supremacist ideals. Moreover, my own failure to confront you until now makes me additionally culpable in the propping up this system. It is a dire state to find oneself in. Confrontation of one's transgressions is a painful experience leading to confusion, denial, regret, and fear. Yet I do not feel hopeless for our futures. Ignorance is not excusable, but it is also not a permanent state. Rather as author bell hooks posits, "self- recovery is ultimately about learning to see clearly … decolonization is also a way for us to learn to see clearly. It is the way to freedom for both colonized and colonizer" (*Killing Rage* 19). Therefore, it is not in the spirit of spite, but rather faith in the possibility of freedom gained through knowledge that I write this letter to both you and myself. I would like to share several examples to demonstrate our complicity in this system as well as divest you of ill-conceived misconceptions you may have about the impetus behind Black Lives Matter. To demonstrate the reach of our actions into our everyday lives, I will couple Black scholarship on racism from bell hooks with words from musicians with whom you may be familiar. I hope that by pairing the familiar with the unfamiliar understanding can be fostered with more ease.

One common thread I see on your Facebook rants is that Black people have no right to be mad. You always seem to claim: "These protesters weren't enslaved. I am not a captor." What is ironic is your own enslavement to the belief that racism ended in 1862. In the song "Mad," the artist Solange articulates the anger felt by the Black community as it persists through the present day. In this excerpt from the song, she is approached by an unnamed woman who asks about her anger: "'Why you always blaming?'/ 'Why you can't just face it?'/ 'Why you always gotta be so mad?'/ 'Why you always talking shit, always be complaining?' / 'Why you always gotta be, why you always gotta be so …'.'" She replies: "I got a lot to be mad about" (Solange 1:15-1:40). Just as Solange expressed, racism did not end with slavery; moreover, denial of that fact only deepens its hold. In turn, this ignites the righteous anger felt by the oppressed. bell hooks expands on this idea writing: "It is important that everyone in the United States understand that white supremacy promotes, encourages, and condones all manner of violence against black people. Institutionalized racism allows this violence to remain unseen and/or renders it insignificant" (*Killing Rage* 22). In other words, racism remains in the system even without its more obvious expressions of slavery or Jim Crow. Institutionalized racism is accepted as "the way things are", rather than something that can be changed. It is time that you understand that the white supremacist institution in place may benefit you, but this experience is not shared by all. To ignore the racist effects of the system on those who are different from you is to be racist.

Pretending that problems no longer exist is not the only way we support racist norms, standing still when called to action is also a manner in which we allow oppression to continue. In the essay "Killing Rage: Militant Resistance" in *Killing Rage: Ending Racism*, bell hooks recounts a story wherein her friend is forced to give up her seat to a white man who was assigned the same seat on a plane. While the man apologized he still took the seat from her friend. hooks argues that he had "an opportunity to not be complicit with the sexism and racism that is so-all pervasive in this society," but by choosing to accept the seat without speaking out he became complicit in the system—half-assed apologies aside (9). When we—you and I—reap the benefits of the capitalist patriarchal white supremacist system in place without stopping to listen to those who do not share in our experiences we are not unlike the man from hooks' story. Like that white man in hooks' story, it doesn't matter if we apologize, if we continue to use the system to our benefit in silence racism lives on. Many of you may argue that changes have been made. It's true that some things have changed for the better, but why would we want to settle for anything but the best? Much like your disavowal of slavery, you feel the changes brought about by the Civil Rights Act not even a century ago demonstrate that progress has been made. But racism didn't end in 1964, either. Singer Nina Simone in her song "Mississippi Goddam" demonstrates the frustration felt buy the Black community by this attitude. In the refrain she belts out, "But that's just the trouble/ 'Too slow'/ Desegregation/ 'Too slow'/ Mass participation/ 'Too slow'/ Reunification/ 'Too slow'/ Do things gradually/ 'Too slow'/ But bring more tragedy/ 'Too slow'/ Why don't you see it/ Why don't you feel it (Simone 3:54- 4:15). Simone reiterates hooks' complaint about the white man in her story. Complacency makes us complicit. Although you may not use racial slurs or commit hate crimes, doing nothing to promote change, much like denying that change is needed, only continues the cycle of abuse inherent in the institution.

I recognize that my words may come off as an attack. I'll admit it, to some degree it is. However, my words are an attack on ignorance—a state that you and I share. While you may complain that we are being attacked and "called out" by the writers, musicians, and poets I quote here, I feel that the term "called in" is more apt. I will be quick to state that this is not terminology original to me. "Calling in", as I have heard it used, comes from public academic, writer, lecturer, and Black woman Rachel Cargle. Cargle recently rose to new heights of fame for her anti-racist educational program "The Great Unlearn". She has a massive 1.8 million follower count on Instagram (as of the time I write this essay) where she uses her platform to discuss the myriad of ways individuals of all genders, ethnicities, and backgrounds are called to act as anti-racists and feminists. In a 2018 interview on the podcast *Call Your Girlfriend*, Cargle discusses the nuance that exists between calling someone out and calling them in. She states: "[holding] each other accountable is not calling out.

Holding each other accountable is not shaming … I think we all appreciate being held accountable in order to ensure we're really giving our best selves to the greater good" (Cargle, "White Fragility"). "Calling in", as described in the podcast, is that accountability played out. Cargle and the hosts of the podcast explain that when people are held accountable for their part, they aren't being labeled bad or incapable of change, rather they are called to participate in meaningful discourse, take ownership of their growth process, and help further anti-racism and feminism on a larger scale (Cargle, "White Fragility"). In another interview, this time speaking with activist and artist Willow Smith, Cargle expands this idea of accountability and responsibility in the anti-racist, feminist movement. She remarks on multiple experiences she has had with white women followers who have thanked her for doing anti-racist work for them—something she vehemently rejects. Cargle says, "I want to be like, 'Girl, I am not doing this work for you! I'm doing this work for all the black women who have been doing this forever. I'm doing it for the black descendants …'" (Cargle, "Willow Smith Explains"). Hearing this statement as one of her white women audience members is sobering. Reading of her thoughts and experiences leaves me with the following notable takeaway: as a white woman feminist the impetus for my anti-racist accountability is on me, not on others. This goes for you, too, however you identify. Though an important reminder this idea is not something new to me. I also felt this call to accountability reverberate throughout my life and work, I feeling I hope you now share.

As white people we possess a level of privilege that may not be initially obvious, but willful ignorance cannot be allowed to endure. Instead, we must both work on confronting our reality to recognize our complicity and complacency. I hope that we can both move towards a better existence for ourselves and serve as true allies to those who are oppressed by the imperialist white supremacist capitalist heteronormative nation as it stands. In reference to a white man she saw as an ally, bell hooks says that, "white people who shift locations … begin to see the word differently (*Killing Rage* 49). My hope is that this letter unsettles you and shakes the institutionalized racism upon which you have built your foundations of understanding the world around you. It is time we both unseat our complicity and stand together for the rights of the marginalized.

With Love,

Your friend

Works Cited

Adichie, Chimamanda Ngozi. "We Should All Be Feminists." *TED: Ideas Worth Spreading*, December, 2012. https://www.ted.com/talks/chimamanda_ngozi_adichie_we_should_all_be_feminists?language=en

Black Women's Blueprint. "An Open Letter from Black Women To The Slutwalk." *Gender and Society*, vol. 30, no. 1, 2016, pp. 9–13., www.jstor.org/stable/24756160.

Eminem. "Without Me". https://music.amazon.com/albums/B000VWSINI?marketplaceId=ATVPDKIKX0DER&musicTerritory=US&trackAsin=B000VWQFQ0

hooks, bell. *Ain't I a Woman: Black Women and Feminism*. New York: Routledge, 2015. Print.

---*Teaching to Transgress: Education as the Practice of Freedom*. New York: Routledge, 1994. Print.

--- *Killing Rage: Ending Racism*. New York: Henry Holt and Company, 1995. Print.

Lorde, Audre. "The Master's Tools Will Never Dismantle the Master's House." 1984. *Sister Outsider: Essays and Speeches*. Ed. Berkeley, CA: Crossing Press. 2007.

Morrison, Toni. "Making America White Again." *The New Yorker*, 21 Nov. 2016, www.newyorker.com/magazine/2016/11/21/making-america-white-again.

Vuong, Ocean. "Not Even This." Poetry Foundation, Poetry Foundation, Apr. 2020, www.poetryfoundation.org/poetrymagazine/poems/152940/not-even-this.

Wanshel, Elyse. "Jimmy Fallon Slammed for Snubbing ORIGINAL TikTok Dancers in Controversial Bit". *Huffpost*, 29 Mar. 2021. www.huffpost.com/entry/jimmy-fallon-slammed-tiktok-tonight-show_n_60622a6ac5b67ad387223ea7.

Willis-Abdurraqib, Hanif. "It's Just That I'm Not Really into Politics." BOAAT PRESS, Mar. 2017, www.boaatpress.com/its-just-that-im-not-really-into-politics.

15
Transforming Black Rage into Black Excellence
Alexander Rivera

The Essence of Black Rage

As humans, we often feel anger towards what we believe to be injustices. When we feel like we are wronged, or if someone close to us is wronged, we feel frustration or anger at those who are responsible for the wrongdoing. I've felt this type of anger throughout my life—seemingly more frequently as I grew older and began to understand how differently people think. There are so many people with different ideologies and beliefs that have been shaped by their own life experiences. Last year, after the death of George Floyd on May 25, 2020, I remember thinking "not again" as another Black man died at the hands of police. I grew weary of hearing these news stories, hoping for something to change. But then I saw the video. I saw the police officer, Derek Chauvin, kneel on Floyd's neck for 9 minutes and 29 seconds as bystanders begged Chauvin to get off Floyd while the other officers at the scene just stood by and watched as Floyd breathed his last breath. I remember wanting to cry when the video ended, but not just out of sadness for the tragic loss of another black man, but because I felt helpless. I felt angry. I believe this to be my first conscious experience of Black rage. Much like the rest of the nation, something had awoken within me that made me critically conscious of the way that Black people are mistreated here in the United States.

The day Derek Chauvin was found guilty in court, I remember feeling the exact same frustration and anger because later that evening, not because of the verdict, but rather a video surfaced of a white police officer taking the life of a young, Black girl named Ma'Khia Bryant. This time we saw the officer reaching for his gun, almost immediately, to try and deescalate the situation. Shots rang out in the video, and I could hear crying in the background. I held my hand over my mouth as the rest of the footage played out. Afterwards, I read countless comments online that said the shooting was justified. They painted her as a threat. They called her a wild animal that needed to be put down. They pulled out the typical racist slurs and negative stereotypes that have devalued Black people for years in an effort to justify her death. I wanted to scream into the void. It happened again, and I could do nothing to stop it.

I felt anger. I felt rage at the justification of another Black life lost to the hands of police brutality.

In bell hooks' book *Killing Rage: Ending Racism*, she discusses the topic known as black rage. She begins with an essay that tells the story about her Black girl friend, who hooks calls "K", and how she was forced to take a seat in coach when they had first class tickets. The stewardess verbally abused her because a white man had complained because he was supposed to sit in first class, and he indicated that "K" took his seat. "K" ultimately gave up her seat and sat in coach, and the white man took his seat next to hooks. This was not the only incident of racial prejudice that hooks and "K" endured on that day, but merely the catalyst that got hooks thinking about what she called a "killing rage." Black rage stems from witnessing or being victims of constant racial injustice.

In this essay, I analyze the concept of Black rage using hooks' work in *Killing Rage: Ending Racism* while incorporating my own life experiences as well as material from supplemental sources. In order to understand Black rage as a concept, I will delve into topics that fuel the emotion of Black rage such as the western beauty standards used to devalue Black men and women, as well as how forced assimilation feeds into the current white supremacist power structure intended to keep Black people oppressed and enraged. By the end of this essay, I will discuss ways in which we can overcome these hurdles as Black people, and how we can use black rage to help us dismantle the systems of oppression that keep us down.

In the chapter titled, "Beyond Black Rage: Ending Racism," hooks opens with the story of a Black gunman on a New York train who opened fire on people. After the incident, notes were found on his person detailing how much he hated racism. However, the media portrayed him as having a hatred towards white people which "set the stage for white folks to further demonize and dehumanize all Black folks while representing themselves as a group that is never carried away by killing rage" (22). What this did was shift the discourse away from the root of the problem: systemic and institutionalized racism. It furthered the idea of Black people being inherently violent and just dislike white people, even though his notes stated that he was angry at both white and Black people. He was angry at those who perpetuated the white supremacist system of oppression.

The stories of the Black gunman and hooks' friend, K, being forced to give up her seat, while being radically different in their outcome, both demonstrated how Black people must constantly deal with racism and microaggressions because of the color of their skin. These racial microaggressions are normalized by white supremacist society, and they are perpetuated because they are used to keep Black people and other people of color oppressed. In fact, they are often trivialized by white society to prevent Black people from potentially using their black rage. White supremacists try to not to take the movements seriously to ensure they never gain any traction. When I think of the way Black rage is trivialized or demonized, I think about the many protests that happened nationwide about police brutality. I cannot keep track of all the times I heard that Black Lives Matter (BLM) was a terrorist group intent on burning the country to the ground. In addition, I also think about moments that are more personal to me and led me to feel Black rage, and how they can sometimes be trivialized by others.

There are a few flashbulb memories—memories that I can recall quite vividly—that linger in my mind when I think of racial microaggressions of my past. One where I was told how "proper" I speak when I was a young boy, another moment in high school where I was accused of stealing a hat from a gift shop in Universal Studios, and lastly, a moment where I was forced to give up my seat on the monorail in Disneyworld because my presence seemed to make others uncomfortable. Out of all these memories, it was the last one that made me the most upset. The first two happened when I couldn't comprehend the gravity of the situations. I remember thinking the proper speech comment to be a compliment, and I was more confused than angry at the situation with the hat, but the monorail incident happened when I was much older and much more aware of racial microaggressions. I remember my friends and I were walking around Disney during one of their Food & Wine fests, and we had been walking, eating, and drinking all day. It was nighttime, and we were heading to Magic Kingdom to walk around a bit, and then to catch the fireworks show before we left for the day. On this monorail I had found a seat between my friend Rob and this couple. Two of my white friends told me I needed to stand up, while my other white friends, Rob, said that I had a right to sit since the seat was empty, but the other two insisted that I stand up so that the couple who were sitting were more comfortable. It took everything within me not to shout at them, but I didn't want to cause a scene as an angry black man, so I opted just to stand since the ride wasn't that long anyways. The rage boiled within me, but I did nothing about it.

I am far from the only person I know who has suffered from these types of microaggressions because of my race. Many of my other Black friends all went through similar circumstances where they felt rage in a situation, but in each case, they often decided to hold themselves back—to not cause a fight. One of my coworkers, who is a Black woman, was also a victim of this kind of mistreatment in the past. She has been yelled at and berated by her direct supervisor, who is a white man, and from white women who are in positions of power over her, and each time she held back her words when talking to them. I remember a particular moment where she had not completed a project by the time her boss, a white man, wanted the project done. One morning, he stormed into her office while I was present, and he began to shout and curse at her, which was completely uncalled for and unprofessional. She tried to explain the volume of work we were dealing with, and how she never got clear directions, but he proceeded to yell at her right in front of me. Looking back at it now, he was using his status as a white male in an effort to exert his authority over her as a Black woman, and so he proceeded to yell at her in a completely inappropriate manner. Even in this situation, she found herself not shouting back at him. Both of personal my examples show how Black people often hold back the anger they feel, but it also begs the question: why? Why didn't we speak out against these issues that hurt us so badly at the time, and led us to want to scream and shout, maybe even fight others? Why didn't we act on our rage?

It's because, as hooks says in *Killing Rage: Ending Racism*, "[w]hite rage is acceptable, can be both expressed and condoned, but black rage has no place and everyone knows it" (15). Going back to my coworker as an example, she has sat in meetings where her white supervisors would constantly yell at one another. After these meetings were done, she would ask a colleague why their white supervisor was so angry, and the response she got was, "That's just who they are. They weren't really mad." It astounds me how that level of white rage is acceptable, however, as a Black woman she is held to a higher standard with much more scrutiny. In one last example, we had an employee who was on the cusp of passing out because the air conditioning stopped working that day. My Black coworker decided that the other employee needed to go home out of concern for her safety, but members of our management team protested this by saying coverage needed to be found. My Black coworker told him that he needed to figure it out himself because this other employee needed to go home. He did not like her answer, and he complained to her direct supervisor who agreed with him that she was out of line for the way she spoke to him—conveniently forgetting all the ways in which he spoke out of line with her. But because she was a

Black woman, she was seen as being out of line and disrespectful while white rage remains unchecked.

My examples demonstrate what hooks said about Black rage in *Killing Rage: Ending Racism* is still true today. Black rage is not seen as legitimate because it is trivialized in many circles because many people believe that racism is over. That we, as Black people, are the ones who are dividing the country because we are always bringing up race. It leads to a sense of shame and feeling like our opinions don't matter whenever they are trivialized in such a manner.

As Black people, we are taught to hold back our rage in white supremacist society for a multitude of reasons. We are taught not to "cause trouble." In the example of the Black gunman that hooks talks about early on, she says, "this incident became the catalyst for a public discourse wherein Black rage could be mocked and trivialized, talked about as though there are no social conditions that should invoke such an extreme, potentially insane response" (24). When I looked further into the case, it appears that the defense contested that the defendant suffered from Black rage, which they classified as a mental illness like Post Traumatic Stress Disorder (PTSD). They said the "outburst on the L.I.R.R. reflected an underlying mental illness, namely an 'extreme racial stress' brought on by the destructive, racist treatment of blacks by whites" (Goldklang). However, much like the media dismissed the incident as a Black man angry at whites, critics of the legal defense, such as Professor Alan Dershowitz denounced "such 'abuse excuses' for their attempt to 'deflect responsibility from the person who committed the criminal act onto someone else who may have abused him or her or otherwise caused him or her to do it'" (Goldklang).

Critics of Black rage will look at the violent incident, such as the Black gunman on the train, and they will blame the individual while completely ignoring the problems present in the system, but it "is important that everyone in the United States understand that white supremacy promotes, encourages, and condones all manner of violence against black people" (hooks 22). Not only that, but white supremacy also condones violence against other marginalized groups as well by focusing on the individual and not the institutionalized issues that are present. For example, when we look at the white man who shot and killed 8 people in the Atlanta spas earlier this year, 6 of whom were Asian women, the police and officials attributed the problem on the individual having a "bad day" rather than a result of systemic racism. The fact that the sheriff who spoke at that press conference indicated the man was having a bad day demonstrates how society views white rage when compared to Black rage.

Because when Black people act on their rage, it can lead to a situation where we may lose our lives. In a white supremacist society, people do not want Black people to act on their rage, so in order to stop Black people from doing so, they will devalue the rage, or they will punish the Black person for acting on their rage in an effort to discourage other Black people from acting on it. However, these solutions are all reactionary. They do not target the root of the problem. Hate groups like the Ku Klux Klan can go unchecked and policies are repeatedly introduced that disadvantage Black people. Supporters of white supremacy along with those who are complicit in it would prefer to focus on getting the Black person to not feel rage rather than focusing on systemic racism, which is the root of the problem. When Black people recognize this problem, it becomes discouraging. It makes us ask why we should bother acting out our rage at all. And when we do act out our rage, it is often dismissed by some racial stereotype like the angry, Black woman stereotype which is seen as a joke by white supremacists.

In fact, the idea that Black people are always angry and animalistic is another reason black people may not act on their rage. For centuries, Black people have been devalued by white people, and our character has been reduced to attributes such as angry, violent, lazy, and lustful to name a few. These stereotypes have persisted throughout the years. When we look back at the incident with the Black gunman on the train, it was described as "another way to stereotype black males as irrational, angry predators" (23). This perception exists because white people feel threatened by Black rage, so they will use whatever methods they can to devalue black voices to discourage Black people from acting out on it.

In 1992 when rapper Ice-T released a song called "Cop Killer," which was a protest song speaking out against police brutality, white supremacists felt threatened at what he had to say as he critiqued the institutions that specifically targeted Black people. However, many conservatives "quoted lyrics out of context and charged author Ice-T with advocating social unrest" (Sieving). For about two months, public discourse surrounded the release of this song by Ice-T, ending with him "voluntarily" withdrawing the song on July 28. (Sieving). Ice-T had dedicated this sing to "every cop that has ever taken advantage of somebody, be 'em down or hurt 'em out of blind prejudice or race hatred" (Sieving). But what he ended up doing was enraging white conservatives because they felt this song would potentially upset the current white supremacist power structure if it were not removed. At the time this song released, many white people associated rap music with crime and violence, and Ice-T's song was the perfect catalyst to prove this point, so they felt like Ice-T's voice needed to be silenced, much like how white supremacists silenced Black voices in the past from great speakers like Malcolm X to all the black voices protesting police brutality in the Black Lives Matter movement today.

However, there are many Black people who are encouraged to approach situations with caution, because they feel if they speak out, then it could hinder progress to assimilate and succeed within the framework of white supremacy and make them visible. I know for myself, being invisible was a defense mechanism that I utilized, not realizing that this was another tool that kept me silenced. As hooks writes, "One mark of oppression was that black folks were compelled to assume the mantle of invisibility, to erase all traces of their subjectivity during slavery and the long years of racial apartheid, so that they could be better, less threatening servants" (*Killing Rage* 35). I've known Black women I worked with who also refused to question authority, even when they knew their supervisors were wrong, because they felt it was better just to sit back, be invisible, and do the work so that they can advance. I held this mentality as well for a long time, and the management team, which comprised of white men and women, fostered this environment where no one could talk back. If someone did, it made them a target and could jeopardize any upward mobility within the office structure. White supremacy encourages this invisibility from Black people, because without the talk-back that comes from Black rage, white people are not forced to face the pain and uncomfortableness associated with racism. White people are free to forget and deny racism while simultaneously encourages assimilation by Black people and other people of color, which in turn perpetuates white supremacy.

Passing as Invisible

I have written about this story before, but it bears repeating here considering what I intend to talk about in this next section. Growing up as a Black boy in a low-income household, I was always told that education was my top priority. Education was the ticket out of poverty, which would eventually lead to a better life. My parents would tell me ad nauseam that I needed to focus on my studies with the hope that education would put me on an even playing field with others and give me the same opportunities at success. This was because both of them didn't graduate from high school, and they felt as if the lack of education left them in a vicious cycle of poverty and debt, and they did not want to see that happen to me—they wanted me to have a shot at a better life where I could be judged on my successes and achievements. I strived to focus entirely on my studies while also being invisible. I thought if I kept my head down, then that would mean I would be able to move forward in life and escape the throughs of poverty my parents found themselves trapped in.

However, what I found was that despite how hard I worked, there were times where the color of my skin would lead people to diminish my own achievements. I remember a particular moment in high school where received my acceptance to the University of South Florida. My three other friends, who happened to be white males, had all applied to USF as well, but they didn't get in. When I told them the news that I had been accepted, they told me that it was because I was Black, and the school wanted to get more Black students admitted. They did not consider that it might have had to do with my own GPA or achievements in school, because while we all had similar test scores, my grades in school were marks above theirs. They would eventually congratulate me, but the fact that the first thing from their mouths was to diminish my own academic achievements had left an impression on me that I still feel a bit today. In what follows, I examine how supporters of white supremacy use assimilation to maintain our current structures of power while simultaneously continuing to devalue Black people because of their skin color, which in turn leads Black people not to act on the rage we feel. The consequence of assimilation is that it takes a vast amount of mental fortitude to bottle in feelings of rage.

bell hooks says in "Black Intellectuals: Choosing Sides," another essay in *Killing Rage: Ending Racism*, that "African Americans have been taught to value education—to believe that it is necessary for racial uplift, one of the means by which we can redress wrongs engendered by institutionalized racism" (226). This is what I believed growing up. Without really being aware of it, I believed that I needed to assimilate to move ahead, and that people would not judge me for my skin color, but rather they would focus on what I achieved as an individual. However, hooks also indicates that what we find is that instead of disrupting the white supremacist system that is intact, Black people end up assimilating into white supremacist society and becoming "gatekeepers" that end up upholding the current power structure in place, which unfortunately what I did for much of my life (226).

To begin, I feel we must first examine how bell hooks defines assimilation. Assimilation "is a strategy deeply rooted in the ideology of white supremacy and its advocates urge black people to negate blackness, to imitate racist white people so as to better absorb their values, their way of life" (*Killing Rage* 186). The way some Black people are taught to speak and carry themselves is one of the major factors here—especially if they grow up in a predominantly white neighborhood. I remember being told that I needed to dress and speak a certain way growing up. People like my white grandmother from my dad's side of the family would shame me if my hair got too long or nappy. Also, I would be told not to talk a certain way by one of my white babysitters who watched me while my parents worked. I heard talks from some of my white friends' parents about how I talked so properly and that was good, and all those times I took their words as compliments because I thought it was helping me get ahead in life. I did not realize how their comments helped me negate anything having to do with Black culture. However, now I see the detrimental effects this had on my perception of Black culture. Something I didn't start to embrace until later on in life when I started to become conscious of these different racist aspects that are designed to uphold white supremacy.

The problem arises because many of these supporters of white supremacy do not see these actions as inherently racist. They "insist that this is not a white supremacist society, that racism is not nearly the problem it used to be … that there has been change" (*Killing Rage* 187). The discourse I've seen online, typically from white males, has been that white supremacy is not a real thing. The typical argument centers around the idea of white supremacy being something the liberal media has falsified as an attempt to seize control away from white people. It's interesting because they are of the belief that the system is now inherently against them, that feminists and people of color have now flipped the structure of power to make white men the victims. I can't tell you how many times I've seen comments like "Why does everybody hate white men?" or that they are being unjustly targeted in greater numbers.

However, people of color have also jumped into these arguments to denounce the reality of white supremacy—Candace Owens being the first person that comes to mind. She and individuals like her believe that race should not be talked about—that every time someone else brings up the talking point of race, they are the ones who are being racist. This argument lines up with hooks' argument in the essay "Beloved Community: A World Without Racism" in *Killing Rage*. The idea behind the

"Beloved Community" is that we would transcend the idea of race. Race would be completely forgotten in favor of everyone looking at each other just as human beings. This ideal is nice in theory. However, I agree with hooks when she says that it is flawed reasoning to believe that we could achieve such a community "if we erased and forgot about racial difference" (263). To the supporters of white supremacy, this imagining of a post racial society doesn't mean that we just look at each other as humans, it really means that they want BIPOC individuals to assimilate into the existing white supremacist society. "[T]he notion that we should all forsake attachment to race and/or cultural identity and be "just humans" within the framework of white supremacy has usually meant that subordinate groups must surrender their identities, beliefs, values and assimilate by adopting the values and beliefs of the privileged whites" (266).

White supremacy's end goal is to create a society where everyone, regardless of race, follows one standard that maintains the current power structure. So, the strategy to do that while trying to keep racial harmony among different races and cultures is to get people of different races to forego their own cultures and beliefs and assimilate into the system designed to keep them oppressed. They encourage assimilation by saying that if BIPOC individuals are able to successfully assimilate, then they can progress further in life—just like how I was told it would help me growing up.

Another key strategy used to encourage assimilation is to insist that racism will continue to exist no matter what. Many supporters of white supremacy state that "this society [has] become so cynical about ending racism, so convinced that solidarity across racial differences can never be a reality, that they make no effort to build [a] community" that embraces racial differences (264). They want to weaponize racial differences to pit different races against one another. In the essay, "Beyond Black Only: Bonding Beyond Race," hooks points out that "To ensure that political bonding to challenge and change white supremacy will not be cultivated among diverse groups of people of color, white ruling groups pit us against one another in a no-win game of 'who will get the prize for model minority today'" (*Killing Rage* 199).

This tactic works on multiple levels to encourage assimilation. The first has to do with vilifying other races to people to prop up white supremacy. I think of discussions online revolving around the recent shooting in Atlanta, Georgia where eight people were killed, six of them being Asian. In an effort to shift the topic of the shootings being a crime of white supremacy, people online (again mostly white males from what

I could tell) would redirect the conversation by saying that Black people were responsible for the majority of Asian hate crimes within the past year. They would bring up statistics in an effort to prove their point and say that white supremacy was not a factor in the rise of Asian hate crimes, completely ignoring the rhetoric that was popularized by Trump and other conservatives that led to widespread Asian hate crimes. Another example is when white male conservatives would bring up illegal Hispanic immigrants entering the country through the Southern border. They would vilify them by saying they are responsible for crimes happening in America as well as stealing jobs from "hard working Americans" while simultaneously ignoring the corporations and businesses looking to hire cheap workers to maximize their profits. They capitalize on the circumstances of minorities entering the country to increase profits, but capitalism and white supremacy are never the ones in the spotlight in these scenarios—it's always the immigrant's fault. And this rhetoric has worked on not only white people, but on other people of color because they internalize the values of white supremacy.

By vilifying other races, they make it seem as if white supremacist society is the only culture that should be embraced. They discourage individuals from embracing their culture while simultaneously rewarding the minorities who have successfully assimilated. The second aspect of this tactic is that it simultaneously improves the image of white supremacist values by embracing "model minorities." It's why you see conservatives prop up groups like "Black People for Trump" or "Mexicans for Trump." They give them a platform and encourage them to follow the rules and values of white supremacist society so that they can successfully move up in our

social hierarchy. By elevating the model minorities, they are saying that the best way to achieve racial harmony is to discard your heritage, forget your cultures, and become a part of the white supremacist structure that permeates our society.

However, I resonate with what hooks says about building that "beloved community." She states, "What those of us who have not died now know, that generations before us did not grasp, was that beloved community is formed not by the eradication of difference but by its affirmation, by each of us claiming the identities and cultural legacies that shape who we are and how we live in the world" (*Killing Rage* 265). We need to embrace our racial identities, because there are years of culture and history tied to them. We cannot just forget about them because the conversations are difficult. This is one aspect that hooks has repeated in her other works as well: the idea that we need to talk about our differences to build understanding and reach a realm of racial harmony. Because by ignoring the issues of race, all we are doing is maintaining the structures of white supremacy that is designed to oppress people that fall outside the bell curve of white supremacist values and reward those who embrace those same values. By ignoring our racial identities and assimilating into white supremacist culture, we are reaffirming those racist ideologies against Black people (that they are dangerous, savages, lazy, etc.), as well as other xenophobic and racist ideas of other races while saying that the only values worth preserving are white supremacist ones. Instead, we need to have those uncomfortable conversations about race, and hold people accountable for the racist things, whether they be overt or subtle, to progress towards a society of racial harmony.

There are so many issues surrounding the topic of assimilation. While many may see it as the proper way to progress and transcend beyond racism, in reality it is inherently flawed because all it does is erase the different cultures that comprise our society and oppress the people who embrace those cultures. It does not create harmony between different races, but continues to sow discord between them, and perpetuating this false idea that talking about race is inherently bad. As hooks states in *Killing Rage: Ending Racism*, "… it is important for us to remember that the struggle to end white supremacy is a struggle to change a system, a structure" (195). Merging our ideologies into that structure not only keeps it in place but makes it increasingly difficult to dismantle it. But to begin to avoid any act of assimilation, we must also begin to value ourselves as Black people. I believe one of the best ways to fight back against white supremacy is by teaching young Black boys and girls to feel proud of their history and their people. But to do so, we need to begin by undoing the years of devaluation that has affected the Black psyche since the country's inception. To build confidence and pride, we need to look at the Western standard of beauty, because one of the dominant methods that white supremacy has devalued Black Americans is by creating a standard of beauty that does not include them.

Beauty in Blackness

For many years in America, white beauty was the standard that everyone was measured against. Only recently have people begun to embrace beauty that can be found in other races and cultures, but years of white supremacy propaganda have made it difficult for BIPOC individuals to embrace the beauty of their own skin. This subject of Black beauty is something that hooks touches on in *Killing Rage: Ending*

Racism, and I feel what she has to say about it is very profound. Her words resonated with me because I have seen how years of white beauty being the standard have made people resistant to the idea that any other type of beauty can measure up against it. Here, I will examine the history of Black representation, or the lack thereof, in mass media, which has led to a decline in promoting Black beauty and has led to Black people not loving Blackness and takes a toll on our mental health, as hooks would say. All these links have been used to perpetuate white supremacy and dominator culture, and even though there has been a paradigm shift in recent years, it makes it harder for Black people to get proper representation.

I begin here analyzing what hooks states in *Killing Rage: Ending Racism* about the history of mass media. As Black people continued to fight for equal rights, there came a time in the sixties when it seemed like white people were "ready to grant black folks social equality, that there were enough resources to go around" (110). hooks argues that at this point Black people let their guard down, and it was at this crucial point that they began to be more susceptible to the colonization of their minds. This is where the media comes into play. As television became more widespread and common, it was an easy way to marry the idea of success and white supremacy together. hooks says, "And white supremacist values were projected into our living rooms, into the most intimate spaces of our lives by mass media ... constantly reminding us of our marginalized status" (110). This is important because the idea of seeing Black representation on the screen diminished as more black people gained access to TVs: "The hunger to see black folks on the screen had been replaced by the desire to be close to the Hollywood image, to whiteness" (111).

Without proper representation from other races, you begin to associate success in Hollywood as being white, and success is oftentimes tied to monetary gain. Therefore, it is not a stretch to say to the young and impressionable Black boys and girls that you have to be white in order to be successful, or in other words, you have to assimilate to the same values that perpetuate white supremacy. The problem goes even further when you have Black people only occupying subservient roles in media like a servant or a sidekick, instead of them being in the leading roles. It gives off the impression that Black people can only strive to such a role—they can't aim for anything higher. Or even worse, they can only be a part of the main cast if they subscribe to white supremacist ideology.

The way Black people are portrayed in media is very important because, as hooks notes: "When black psyches are bombarded by mass media representations that encourage us to see white people as more caring, intelligent, liberal, etc., it makes sense that many of us begin to internalize racist thinking" (*Killing Rage* 117). As a young Black boy growing up, there were not many Black heroes on TV that I could idolize. There were some, but they were not as cool as some of my favorites like Batman or Spider-Man for example. These white heroes were the ones I looked up to, and I could see how I internalized wanting to assimilate into white dominator culture by idolizing these fictional characters. I did not realize it at the time, but they contributed to my feeling of wanting to assimilate into white culture. And if more of my white friends were exposed to Black heroes and characters growing up, maybe they could have become more critically conscious of anti-racist attitudes earlier in life. By having Black characters serve as comic relief, subservient roles, or just being absent, mass media has perpetuated white dominator culture.

The consequence for living in a society that makes whiteness the standard, is that it undermines Black beauty, which in turn has a negative impact on the mental health of Black people. In America, everyone was taught that the ideal features of beauty are white. This can be seen in the Black community as hooks points out when she says, "there existed in segregated black life color-caste systems wherein the lighter one's skin the greater one's individual social value (*Killing Rage* 120). This is because "racist white folks often treated lighter-skinned black folks better than their darker counterparts" (120). This ideal that lighter skinned Black people were more beautiful than darker skinned Black people is an ideal that is still mirrored today by some people. whiteness is still the standard of beauty in Western civilization. From my own personal experiences, I have had white women tell me that they do not date Black men because it's a "preference," or that some white friends just don't find Black women attractive. These white people always state that it is a "preference" to not date someone with darker skin, but really, it's white supremacist values that have been drilled into them while they were growing up. They were taught to only look at men or women who were white as the standard for beauty/attractiveness. Anyone who fell outside of those standards of beauty would be deemed as not their preference. It is problematic because that kind of thinking is racist and perpetuates white supremacy. It encourages men and women to mirror whiteness to be attractive.

When we look at the beauty standards that have dominated western cultures for decades, we find that:

Eurocentric aesthetic is prized in popular culture in the United States; value is placed on fair skin, light colored eyes, hair that is long, straight, and light in color, and smaller facial features and thinner bodies ... Conversely, features that are associated with an African-centered aesthetic (e.g., darker skin, larger/curvier bodies, short and kinky/curly hair, full lips, wider noses) are considered less attractive and less feminine. (Avery et al. 181)

When Black women internalize these beauty standards held up by Western society, they feel they must conform to these standards to be seen as attractive. They have all these external societal pressures which incentivizes them to conform as well: "For example, it has been found that Black women are judged more favorably when their appearance closely approximates Whiteness ... and aligns with hegemonic beauty ideals including being thin and more feminine in their gender expression" (Avery et al. 182). When women of color do not adhere to this Eurocentric aesthetic of beauty, it often leads to low self-esteem and feelings of shame because they feel as if they are being pressured to fit to a standard that is very difficult to achieve or maintain, instead of being valued for who they are. But you also find that when they do conform to the western standards of beauty, then they are sometimes looked down on by other members of their own community, or sometimes by members outside of their community.

I have seen this a lot in the cosplay community (people who dress up as their favorite movie, game, anime character). Whenever a Black person cosplays as their favorite fictional character, they are oftentimes bombarded with messages of harassment and criticism, saying that the character they are dressing up as is not Black, so they should pick a Black character to dress up as. This is problematic on multiple levels because they are saying that Black people cannot live up to the white character they are dressing up as, and in addition, there may not be a Black character in the show, movie, comic book, anime, or other piece of media that they can dress up as. It is a lose-lose situation for Black creatives because according to white people, they do not meet the standard to cosplay as a character that is white, or they do not have someone to dress up as because the show/movie/game may lack proper representation or diversity. Both of these issues perpetuate the notion that Blackness is not beautiful.

Of course, the effects of these white supremacist values of beauty extends further than media and cosplaying, but it does affect the way that Black people are able to move up the social ladder. As hooks states, "Being seen as desirable does not simply affect one's ability to attract partners, it enhances class mobility in public arenas—in educational systems and in the workforce" (*Killing Rage* 129). Unfortunately, I have been privy to how this played out in the workplace. At my job, a Black woman was applying for a position to move up in the office. She applied to be a Financial Advisor, and when she was going for the job, there were comments made about the way she fixes her hair by some of the older white women. She was put under more scrutiny because they did not understand why she wore a head wrap on some days. They knew nothing about Black women's hair and questioned whether her look was "professional" enough. However, I know that if she straightened her hair to mimic the white standard of long, straight hair, then they would not have said anything to her about the way she kept her hair. By not exposing white people to different standards of beauty, you wind up with situations where someone is placed under more scrutiny for not subscribing to that standard, and it is not fair. All it does is bring feelings of shame to Black people when they are criticized for not meeting the white standards of beauty.

This can lead Black people into a state of "black self-hatred" where they will try and attain a level of whiteness "and access the privileges it affords ... irrespective of the consequences" (Akinro & Bunyuza-Memani 310). We see this in Jamaica where "studies have indicated an aggressive desire for whiteness by skin bleachers (310). And it's not just with skin color, Black people will try to attain whiteness in many ways: from the way they may talk, carry themselves, dress, or even who they may hang out with. All of this contributes to the perpetuation of white supremacy because, as hooks states: "Most folks in this society do not want to openly admit that 'blackness' as [a] sign primarily evokes in the public imagination of whites ... hatred and fear" (*Killing Rage* 147). By not embracing Blackness, we continue to feed this idea that blackness is something to fear which leads to Black people assimilating into white culture. This is a major problem because it continues to reinforce white dominator culture.

However, I will say that nowadays we are seeing far more representation in the mainstream media. More films about the Black experience, more shows, books, and video games that star black characters are being made. We are seeing more and more Black artists pop into the mainstream consciousness. This is not to say that everything is good now. Far from it. With the advent of more diversity, you also find more resistance and criticism. My biggest example is with the film *Black Panther*. It was such a huge success, and even went on to be the second highest grossing Marvel movie, only behind *Avengers Endgame*. This movie gave so many Black people a superhero in the mainstream to look up to. However, so many white people have gone out to bash the movie because they feel like it only made money because it starred Chadwick Boseman, a Black man, and that the movie wasn't any good. They will say the same thing about any major media that contains a starring female lead or a BIPOC star. They feel like the corporations, publishers, artists are all just catering to a specific market to make money, and they completely ignore that some people, especially under-represented minorities, just want to see more characters in the mainstream who are not white.

But this is the right path to take. It will take decades of new media, but I believe it is possible to tear down the white standard of beauty in media through diversity, which can lead to BIPOC men and women to feel more confident in who they are. We need much more representation in mainstream media to break the collective consciousness of white supremacy. We need to expose white people to more Black stories, because as hooks states, White people are affected by racism too, just in a different way. By exposing white people to more diverse stories, we may begin to tear down the centuries of white supremacy propaganda that has pervaded our society. We need to teach children about anti-racist attitudes and give them heroes and heroines who are not just white. We need to teach everyone that there is more than one standard of beauty. We need to teach everyone to love Blackness.

Transforming Black Rage

As I reach the final section of this essay, we are still left with a dilemma when it comes to black rage. bell hooks says, "Denying that rage is at times a useful and constructive response to exploitation, oppression, and continued injustice, but it creates a cultural climate where the psychological impact of racism can be ignored, and where race and racism become topics that are depoliticized" (*Killing Rage* 26). By staying silent and assimilating, we may avoid a situation where we feed into the racist stereotypes associated with Black people. By acting on our rage, we open ourselves up to scrutiny and criticism from white people about how we conduct ourselves, which in turn devalues our status as Black individuals and does nothing to further the cause of liberation from Black supremacy. If Black rage is not acted upon or spoken about, we end up becoming complicit in white supremacy. Racism will be ignored by white people if it is ignored by Black people. So, the question becomes: what do we do with Black rage? How can we utilize it?

Looking back to the beginning of this essay where I discussed the story of bell hooks' friend, K, being kicked out of first class as well as the story of the Black gunman on the New York train, we can see that they are both instances of Black rage. Both hooks and this gunman felt such a powerful hatred towards those who perpetuated white supremacy that they wanted to kill. However, only one of them did. In her personal story, hooks explained that she felt like she wanted to kill this man, but instead she decided to talk to him, and she wrote down her hatred. She transformed her rage into something that can be used to engage with the discourse around white supremacy.

What we are seeing today is how rage has become a part of the Black political discourse of today: "It circulates in social media spaces and finds expression at meetings and rallies. The embrace of rage is part of a revaluation of values central to the new black activism" (Lloyd). To feel Black rage is important, but we must not let it consume us. In today's discourse, we must redirect rage in order to facilitate change and to challenge white supremacy. Black men and women run into problems when they feel like they cannot express their rage. White supremacist society condemns, trivializes, and shames Black people from feeling rage as I mentioned previously. But when this happens, and Black people do not act on it, the anger "can turn inward, focus[ing] on the self, and so [it] become[s] self-hatred, perhaps resulting in depression" (Lloyd).

I know when I felt like I withheld my anger last summer after the death of George Floyd, it felt as if I was helpless. I fell into my own depression which put a strain on many of my relationships as I tried to climb back out of it. I didn't climb out of my well of depression until I sought a therapist where I could properly explore the anger and frustration I felt during that time. Afterwards, I refocused my efforts to spread awareness of the injustice plaguing Black people at the hands of the police. I donated to charities and participated in protests. I felt like I had started making a difference.

In addition, we must be mindful of the way that others interpret our rage. Each situation involving black rage needs to be assessed and approached differently because as hooks says, sometimes Black rage "is an appropriate response to injustice" (*Killing Rage* 26). A lot of Black rage is felt because people are often ignorant to racism. In *Killing Rage: Ending Racism* when hooks mentions talking to one of her friends, who is a Black woman married to a white man, she points out something I feel is an important element on how and when to utilize Black rage. She writes, "After we finish our laughter, we talk about the way white people who shift locations, as her companion has done, begin to see the world differently. Understanding how racism works, he can see the way in which whiteness acts to terrorize without seeing himself as bas, or all white people as bad" (49). We need to create open dialogues with white people, letting them know why we feel black rage, because talking about our rage will help them understand the injustices we experience, which can eventually lead to change.

Black rage is not just a tool to be utilized as a vehicle of change. It is how we feel. We must not be afraid of expressing our rage. White supremacy has taught us to repress our rage—to remain invisible. Because the goal of white supremacy is to uphold the current power structure, and to do that, BIPOC individuals must remain oppressed. To do so, they tell us that we are not beautiful. The tell us to look up to the white men and women who are heroes in this country, so that we may ascribe to be like them. They devalue our natural features and call us ugly, and most importantly they try to tell us how to feel. All of this should make us angry as Black men and women, but we must not turn our anger inwards. We must not fall into the pit of despair, wallowing in our own rage and sadness. We must redirect this anger to change the discourse. Once we initiate the conversation, we can begin to dismantle the oppressive structures that make us angry in the first place and shift the paradigm towards an anti-racist society. In her closing remarks in "Beyond Black Rage: Ending Racism," hooks talks about the fact that "[w]hite supremacy is frightening. It promotes mental illness and various dysfunctional behaviors on the part of whites and non-whites. It is the real present danger—not black rage" (*Killing Rage* 30).

Works Cited

Akinro, Ngozi, and Lindani Mbunyuza-Memani. "Black Is Not Beautiful: Persistent Messages and the Globalization of 'White' Beauty in African Women's Magazines." *Journal of International and Intercultural Communication*, vol. 12, no. 4, Routledge, 2019, pp. 308–24, doi:10.1080/17513057.2019.1580380.

Avery, Lanice R., et al. "'Pretty Hurts': Acceptance of Hegemonic Feminine Beauty Ideals and Reduced Sexual Well-Being Among Black Women." *Body Image*, vol. 38, Elsevier Ltd, 2021, pp. 181–90, doi:10.1016/j.bodyim.2021.04.004.

Goldklang, Deborah L. "Post-Traumatic Stress Disorder and Black Rage: Clinical Validity, Criminal Responsibility." *Virginia Journal of Social Policy & the Law*, vol. 5, no. 1, Oct. 1997, pp. 213–243. *EBSCOhost*, search.ebscohost.com.ezproxy.lib.usf.edu/login.aspx?direct=true&db=ofm&AN=502452939&site=ehost-live.

hooks, bell. *killing rage: ending racism*. Henry Holt and Company, New York. 1995.

Lloyd, Vincent. "The Ambivalence of Black Rage." CLCWeb: Comparative Literature and Culture, vol. 21, no. 3, Purdue University Press, 2019, doi:10.7771/1481-4374.3550.

Sieving, Christopher. "Cop Out? The Media, 'Cop Killer,' and the Deracialization of Black Rage." *The Journal of Communication Inquiry*, vol. 22, no. 4, SAGE Publications, Inc, 1998, pp. 334–53, doi:10.1177/0196859998022004001.

Part IV
Mission Accomplished: Hope for a "Beloved Community"

To fully embrace the transformative power of love, we would need to have the revolution of values Martin Luther King called for before his untimely demise.

bell hooks, *Writing Beyond Race: Living Theory and Practice* (2013)

In community one can feel that we are moving forward, that struggle can be sustained … That sense of home that we are talking about and searching for is a place where we can find compassion, recognition of difference, of the importance of diversity, of our individual uniqueness.

Cornel West, *Breaking Bread: Insurgent Black Intellectual Life* (1991)

… deep in my heart I believe that our moral and spiritual passions can lead to a better day for our nation. I know that when we get out of our own way and let the spirit of love and hope shine through we are a better people.

Michael Eric Dyson, *Tears We Cannot Stop: A Sermon to White America* (2017)

16

Remaining Critically Aware of the Struggle Against Racism
A Woke Student-Teacher Dialogue
Alexander Rivera and Gary L. Lemons

AR ("Alex" Rivera): I wrote down a few questions to go over with you, but I'll treat this more like a conversation—to kind of get things started. You know, a lot of people—people of color, white people—are not really critically conscious of racism, which is something that you kind of reinforced in the African American literature classes I've taken with you. It's that people aren't really aware of the racism that's happening around us. And not like the overt racism, what I mean is like the more subtle things like systemic racism, which is being talked about more today. So, my first question to you Dr. Lemons is when did you first realize, or rather, when can you recall that you first became critically conscious of racism, and was there a particular moment that caused you to become critically conscious of it?

GLL (Gary L. Lemons): Well Alex, this is a critically important question because we have to get to the root of our path to critical consciousness supporting anti-racism, and it is about the self. It begins with "remembering" as bell hooks would say in many of her writings. And she is using remembering to not only go back in time and recall one's experiences, but to put the pieces together again of one's life over the course of time. And going back—it's a really interesting question from the standpoint experiential recall. I'm thinking back to the first time ... Ah, alright here we go! I don't know, Alex, if I mentioned this before in any of the classes you've had with me.

Remembering the Trauma of Racism

When I was an undergraduate student in a small PWI (Predominately White Institution), I was the first editor of that university's yearbook, and I don't know if you did this when you were in high school or in college, but most of these institutions will have something like a yearbook where it's going back over the course of the year and documenting events, class members, and all of that. This was a standard at this particular college. Well anyway, I was the co-editor with a white female student. It was my sophomore year there. And by the way, it was not only a title, but it was also within the context of financial aid. So, we got aid to co-edit this yearbook. And one of the things that was so inspiring to me was that I got to bring my artistic training to the table because as an undergraduate, I was a double major in Studio Art and English. So, I was able to incorporate my artistic concepts into the book. I did the cover design for the book, but anyway, long story short: one of the things that my co-editor and I wanted to do was really show how diverse the college student population really was in terms of different racial identities. And so, we wanted to make sure that in almost every picture we had of people of varying races at various events—particularly with BIPOC in the pictures interacting with white people.

Because we really wanted to make these pictures look "diverse" in terms of multi-racial identity, so we were just excited get our work done. Alex, we finished the project at the end of the spring semester during April. We had to then send the draft to the edited version of the yearbook to the publisher, and the publisher said, "Oh, everything looks so beautiful." But before we did that, we had to get approval from our white male faculty advisor. The co-editor and I were also students in his journalism course. So, he was our professor and also the advisor for the yearbook.

Well, when we got the proofs back and everything, the co-editor and I were so excited and we brought them to him and he said, "Wait, wait just a moment. There's a problem here." And we said, "What's the problem?" He said, "There's not that many people of color students at this college" And we were like, "What do you mean?" And he continued, "Well almost every picture here you got students of color in almost every picture. And we were like, "Um, we weren't concerned about the actual statistics about how many people of color were at the college. We just wanted to make sure that we showed racial diversity and inclusion." And he said, "Well this isn't going to work. I do not approve this." And we were shocked, and you know what he also did, Alex? Because you know we did 20 hours per week on the yearbook. That was the way that our funding was given to us as financial aid to produce this work. So then he said, "So since you all are going against what I told you, then you're fired … both of you. You will not be editors of this yearbook. You're fired."

We left his office walking out into the street basically in tears because we thought for sure he would think that showing racial diversity in the yearbook would be a great idea, especially related to the way we conceptualized the book. But anyways, as we were walking, my white female co-editor, who was very radical in her ideas of racial inclusion said, "Gary, you know what we need to do? Let's stage a protest." And I said that before we do that, we need to go to the vice president of the university to say what we think the problem is. So, we scheduled a meeting, and he met with us, this white guy, and we said that this was not something we wanted to hold against the college, but it was something to promote diversity and inclusion. So, he was actually for us and said, "Let's have a public meeting about this." So, he organized a public meeting in the student center where professors and many students came together. At the meeting the vice president said, "These two students have produced a version of the yearbook that is inclusive, and we really think this is important, but they have been fired." Then we saw all the students shout out that we shouldn't have been fired, and the professors were all for us, and so we staged this major protest. In the next week we had students out there with all these signs for racial diversity, inclusion, and everything. It was a big deal! But ultimately, you know what Alex. In spite of the protest, that white professor appointed another white female student to take our place as co-editors of the yearbook. It was published, but guess what? The new student editor had not changed anything we had produced in the yearbook.

Actually, for her to have changed stuff in it and taken out pictures would've cost the college more money—so nothing got changed! The only thing added in to yearbook was this student's name as the editor who replaced us. However, our names as co-editors were still listed as under her name. But guess what? Did he [the professor] return that next academic year? No. No we were not told why he didn't return? Now I don't know Alex if the university may have fired him, or he just decided to leave. We didn't know any of the details, but he left, and yet the book still was published. And every time I look at it now, I remember this occurrence as significant symbol of the liberating difference a protest for racial justice can make. So, me and my co-editor did our work, and the work we accomplished supporting racial diversity and inclusion is a legacy for "CHAT" I will always remember. You've got to stand up for anti-racist activism, and you've got to speak out against it, and you've heard me say this many times before classes you taken with me. So, that's my response to your first question, and since that time Alex, this was back in the 1970s (the mid-70s), and ever since that time, I've been on a journey toward my calling for anti-racist justice. This is where I've been led in this evolution of teaching, particularly related to Alice Walker's womanist standpoint as stated in *In Search of Our Mothers Gardens.* As I have quoted her words so many times in my writings, she focuses it on being "committed to survival and wholeness of entire people ..."[1] So that's one of the things that I've continued to write and teach about. This is really where we are today in the need to speak out and to stand up for justice for all the oppressed.

AR: Wow, that was amazing. Yeah, just the fact that that journalism professor and advisor for the yearbook saw that, and his first reaction was just to say "No" to the commitment that you and your co-editor had made to demonstrating the importance of racial diversity at the college you both attended—even as you two decided to go against the statistical standard of "minority" representation in PWIs. You know, I really commend you and your radical white co-editor back then who was there with you standing up against that because a lot of people would not do that—would not stand up against that way of thinking. And I do wonder what happened to that professor. Did he leave on his own terms, or did the school really think he caused way too many problems? You never told that story in any of the classes I took with you before, so I'm glad I was able to hear about it in this conversation. So, kind of shifting a little bit and talking about white people acting as allies or not, one of the things that I've seen a lot lately—like one of the more common things some white people who consider themselves anti-racist say—is that they believe racism no longer exists. One of the big things that they say is they don't see color, and therefore we should as a society move past "seeing" racism. When you hear those types of comments, how does that make you feel?

Reciting the Need for Critical Race Consciousness and the Myth of the "American Dream"

GLL: Well, you know, one of the things I think—and I'm going back to the phrases that you used that bell hooks continuously uses—is this phrase, "critical consciousness." One of the things I think that is so difficult to engage is the topic of race with white people in particular. Because for BIPOC communities, we're always having to deal with issues of racism even to the extent that many of us have internalized white supremacy and work against each other within a classist framework. This whole idea that, well, as BIPOC folks we know that in the idea of the "American Dream", we have to pull ourselves up by our bootstraps and work harder to get into these PWIs academically and professionally.

Well, what many white people don't know is that working harder means that we have to work twice as hard as they do to succeed. Because there is this systemic and institutionalized ideology that BIPOC who are not educated, who are lower class, who really have no idea of what the "American Dream" is should not be allowed to conceptualize for themselves what it should be. The idea that "We live in a post racial-society," in light of the civil rights movement, is rooted in the idea that we're historically in a better place now, so why should we talk about race? Well Alex, as you know, and I'm sure as BIPOC and many white people all over this United States visually witnessed via cell phone recording and news media reports about the murder of George Floyd, that we must talk about racial injustice.

In this context, technology is working in ways that acts of racism against BIPOC can clearly be documented, especially in the historical reality of the way that Blacks have had to deal with issues of white supremacy. When those six Asian women, who were killed in Georgia, it was reported in the news that the young white man shot them basically said he just was having a bad day, so that's why he shot them. My response: "Hey let's stop for a moment. Where's the critical consciousness around the ways that racism and white supremacy are being perpetrated?"

The truth of the matter is over the course of 400 years, the normalization and perpetuation of white supremacy and racism has never ended. You might ask, "Dr. Lemons, we got to educate white people around the implications of race related to racism and white supremacy?" And I say, "Yes." Because some good white people might say, "Oh why do we have to talk about that? We're all just human beings?" But did you see the video? Have you watched the news? Have you been on the internet? They might say, "Oh, now I'm starting to get the difference that the color of your skin makes in the way that you are treated." Or we should say, "mistreated?" So, do I get tired of educating white people about the implications and the perpetuation of racism and white supremacy? "Yes." However, in the college classroom, I know that teaching African American literature for critical antiracist consciousness is my calling.

AR: Yeah, I definitely agree with that. It is very vital that we contribute towards that education, particularly to our white allies. One thing that I find when I'm interacting with, typically white males, is ... say about the topic of George Floyd's dying caused by Derek Chauvin, as well as what happened to Daunte Wright recently where he was shot in his car where the white officer claims she had her taser in her hand, but many of the white males that I've seen online, kind of like talking about the situation, say that it wouldn't have been a problem if he just complied. Or he had a warrant out for his arrest, so he should've been more cooperative with the police and that wouldn't have happened. And whenever I read those types of comments, I feel a type of frustration or rage, and I don't know how to really approach those people without like blowing up. So, how would you say would you approach a situation like that, or how would you communicate with those types of individuals?

GLL: Well Alex, I think this is critically important from an emotional standpoint from how we relate our racial trauma, particularly to white males. Now of course gender becomes a big issue, because in the context of the Daunte Wright situation the officer was white and female. But your question has to do with these white males generalizing the racial and gender context of the situation. More specifically had they said if this "*black* male had complied," the exchange between you and them might have become more racially charged, but at the same time thoughtfully insightful.

Getting right to the point of your question, and you know immediately I thought of bell hooks' *Killing Rage: Ending Racism*. One of the things she says is that folks in BIPOC communities have to deal with our rage, especially related to personal experiences of racism. How do we express our rage?" Do we express our rage by saying, "Okay you pull that gun on me, I'll pull one on you? Or you hate me I'mma hate you too?" Ummm, no. One of the things that bell hooks does in *Killing Rage* is to consistently quote Martin Luther King, Jr. and his whole premise of how to deal with racism—particularly in the Civil Rights movement. He promoted the idea that Black folks should stand up, speak, and march in protest to racism, but that we should not act out hate or violence against white people. He did not condemn anger against the enactment of racism, but he insisted that we should not respond with violence toward white supremacists. As we know, not only in Minneapolis, Minnesota but across the U.S. (and here in Florida), there are anti-racist white allies for BIPOC. As activist allies in the struggle, many of them acted in demonstrations that caused the police to respond against them by shooting rubber bullets, pepper spraying, curfews, and arrests to shut down the protests. In the face of this, folks involved in activist protests against racism must openly express our feelings of the traumatic emotional experience of it. Talking openly with each other about this pain and hurt is the path to inner-healing and wellbeing.

As you know, and I've said so many times over and over again, the more we repress our rage, the more this "dis-ease" leads to disease. Because as you know, BIPOC folks have the highest stats of disease, mentally, emotionally, and physically, and that has often to do with emotional repression of pain. So, you say, "Well can you get right to the point about your rage?" Okay, when you read comments particularly about white males who say, "Why are you making such a big deal out of this? If *he* had simply adhered and stopped?" But what we know is that human beings are complicated—you never know. This must be contextualized within differences race, gender, sexuality, generation, ability, and cultural differences. How a police officer is going to react to a "suspect" is related to having been or not been trained to be aware of these differences. I would want to say, the "individual" should have listened to the police officer, but we can't really reduce everyone to this particular way of reacting. But I think for me to release my rage, is to do exactly what we're doing—to talk about it. Am I angry with the way that BIPOC communities are being treated and have been treated over the course of time? Absolutely.

One of the things I do, Alex, in terms of therapeutic inner-healing is to move into a spiritual realm, and bell hooks has two chapters in her book, *Remember Rapture: The Writer at Work* about how spirituality becomes a place where we create a self-empowering space to engage our inner pain to say that "I'm just not over this. I'm just hurt by this. I'm so angry about this." Whatever the "this" is in this spiritual space of self-liberation, here we can get in touch with our inner-being. I want to say that our Creator (and that's with a capital C) has provided us with a heart-filled Spirit for inner-healing. As Alice Walker openly expresses in her book *In Search of Our Mothers' Gardens*, it begins with loving oneself.[2] I believe if the Spirit of love doesn't help me through trauma, then I can't make it through this by myself. This is what I call "soul work", having an inner heartfelt conversation with oneself soulfully. This allows me to converse with the Spirit in ways that I can express my rage longing for creative power to release it. I say to the Spirit, "You gotta help me move through this rage and let go of it." This communicative foundation is the source of my inner wellbeing to release my rage. And I think that's exactly what bell hooks is saying, because if you remember that's the way she opens her book *Killing Rage: Ending Racism* in the chapter titled "Killing Rage: Militant Resistance." She opens it talking about both her and her Black female friend's experience of racism during and after their flight on the plane when they arrived in New York City. She states:

> … I feel that the vast majority of black folks who are subject daily to forms of racial harassment have accepted this as one of the social conditions of our life in white supremacist patriarchy that we cannot change. This acceptance is a form of complicity…. Confronting my rage, witnessing the way it moved me to grow and change, I understood intimately that it had the potential not only to destroy but also to construct. Then and now I understand rage to be a necessary aspect of

resistance struggle. Rage can act as a catalyst inspiring courageous action" (10-11; 16).

I agree with hooks; it's how you demonstrate your rage in struggle against racism. Channeling it through activist resistance is critically important. This is where I believe "CHAT" begins. To play on hooks' words, it can act as "a necessary aspect of resistance struggle" and can "act as a catalyst inspiring courageous action." There has to be a place where we can actively express our demonstration for anti-racism. There must be a place where we can speak and stand against racism, not to perpetuate hate. As anti-racists, we want promote the need end racial injustice that demands that BIPOC are to be treated with human dignity and respect. So, I'll sum it up like this, Alex—rage is not to be suppressed or repressed, but it's how we deal with it that helps us to release it. And it's not by silence, it's about demonstrating it in a therapeutic process for wellbeing, and that it is for me a love for the Spirit of creative power for liberation of the oppressed grounded in a meditative practice.

Healing Rage through Meditative Practice

AR: That makes a lot of sense trying to like find that type of spirituality because that's something that Ruth King talks about as well in her book *Mindful of Race: Transforming Racism from the Inside Out.* And as you mentioned, what we read about in bell hooks' work, she does talk about finding that type of spirituality as well. So, you mentioned that you are able to sort of do that on your own. In her book, Ruth King goes over different types of mindfulness practices that helps with different types of trauma or all these uncomfortable feelings. She defines being mindful as being present or aware of all of our feelings and thoughts, and it's like the first step that she shows or demonstrates towards racial healing because it really helps us investigate our feelings. Some of the things she said is doing a sitting meditation, a walking meditation—you know, going out and observing all the things around you and then looking inward to do some self-reflection as well. What are some things that you do to get you to that place of spirituality? Do you do some type of prayer? Maybe some meditation or some yoga, walking, any creative outlets? How do you handle reaching that level of spirituality?

GLL: Yes, this is a really good question and thank you for posing it. I wake up every morning engaging in a meditative process. I focus on reading varying spiritual writings that provoke to enable me to self-reflect beyond the realm of the rational. And actually, Alex, I have created a journal of spiritual writings. I wrote an article based on my meditative, contemplative practice. I titled the piece "Black Contemplative Art: Practice in the Spirit of Womanist Love." In it, I talk about the creative power of sacrificial, activist love for humane justice for the oppressed. In this meditative context, I continually ask myself, "Are you willing to give your life for the oppressed." Contemplating my commitment to anti-racist struggle, this question remains personally, politically, and spiritually compelling.

No matter what white supremacists think about me, I now love being Black rooted in the liberating, creative power of *Blackness*. Loving myself for being Black enables me to love others freely across differences of identity that are not dehumanizing. As I and others in *Liberation for the Oppressed* have referenced Dr. Martin Luther King, Jr.'s vision of a "beloved community," I believe that love for the oppressed must be demonstrated in action. As you and I know, bell hooks continues to reference his love-filled vision of activism for anti-racist justice. At the end of *Killing Rage: Ending Racism* in the chapter "Beloved Community: A World without Racism." Envisioning a "world without racism" centers much of my meditative practice. Alex, this is where I release my rage because I know I can't make it without the Creator's liberating presence in my daily life struggle against racism.

Coming to Terms with the Need for Anti-Racist Love: In Spite of …

GLL: I read a lot of works by radical Black theologians: James H. Cone, Howard Therman (bell hooks actually often quotes Howard Thurman), Kelly Brown Douglas, and Cornel West, among others. As you know, having been a student in "The Bible as Literature" I teach, I am an ordained minister trained in Christian theology. One of the things that I always underscore in teaching this course is that healing from the trauma of racism and white supremacy begins in the self. Becoming self-aware of one's internalization of racist ideology—particularly connected to the history of 500 years of African enslavement in the U.S.—begins the process of loving oneself free from the shackles of white supremacy. Loving oneself in spite of the systemic and institutionalized perpetuation of it becomes a liberatory power enabling one to survive the trauma of racism. Moreover, in this self-healing process, self-love acts to break ground to plant the seed of love for all humanity—in spite of racial hatred perpetuated by white supremacists. Now, one of the "commandments" in the book of Leviticus in the Bible states: "… love your neighbor as yourself" (19:18 NLT). Now this is an ongoing personal challenge for me, Alex. My feeling of rage against racism and white supremacy—especially in this day and time—is formidable. Am I supposed to love somebody who hates me and would murder me because of white supremacist myths and stereotypes based on the color of my skin? I'm supposed to love you when you're killing me with your knee on my neck? These racially charged scenes remain in my mind—"Oh, I thought I just had my taser...." Well, your taser is very clearly yellow and right on your side, and your gun is black. Now you've been working for 26 years, and when you pulled out [your gun], you thought you were pulling out your taser, and you didn't look to see what color your taser was. But you saw the color of the one you shot, right? Even though he was acting out. Now I'm also thinking about that Black military veteran, who had his uniform on and everything, but he purposefully pulled over into a gas station where the lights were clearly on. And he was like, "Yes what's going on? Why are you stopping me?" Then immediately it was like, "You, give me your driver's license." "Yeah, okay. Is everything alright?" "Get out. I told you to get out." But I don't understand." So, we find out, Alex, that it was said that this Black male did not have a plate on the back of the vehicle.

So, I know without meditation grounded in spiritual journaling and resources for Black wellbeing interconnected self-love, I would not possess the liberating power to enact love in the face of anti-Black racism. For self-liberation against the trauma of racist injustice, I must put my life on the line demonstrating activist love for the oppressed. As our ancestors did against their dehumanization in the centuries of legalized enslavement on this land, so I have come to understand that I must prepared to give my life in love to save lives of the oppressed. This I surmised and accepted as the sacrificial service that defines *soul work*.

Soul Work and the ART of Racial Mindfulness

AR: Wow, that was very powerful, and I really like how you underscored and emphasized being kind to others, because I believe that's something Ruth King also talks about in her book *Mindful of Race*. In the second part of it, she provides strategies for how we find that sort of spiritual state for being mindful of race. We then have to channel that into compassion or kindness in order for us to effectively communicate compassion for other oppressed people. She even says at one point that compassion takes effort. It takes a lot of willpower and effort because like you said, it's kind of looking at a situation where someone doesn't like you because of the color of your skin or they think that you're beneath them, so you have to comply to what they are saying—or doing against you. And it's like, being angry is easy because you can just explode and express what you're really feeling to them. But taking that sort of rage and just being mindful and present about it, and then transforming that into compassion is a lot of work. That's something that we in a BIPOC communities have to do, I wanna say on a consistent/frequent basis, especially given everything that's going on now. It is difficult to reach that level.

Another one of the things Ruth King talks about is creating a community with other BIPOC individuals. Ah! She calls it a *Racial Affinity Group.* She says,

> However given the unintended harm caused by unawareness and cumulative impact when we gather across races, we need a different way, or perhaps an alternative way, to explore the ignorance and innocence of our racial conditioning and racial character with those of our same race. I recommend racial affinity groups (RAGs) as an ongoing forum for investigating and transforming our individual and collective habits of harm. (165)

Is this something that you have kind of experimented with, or gotten together with other Black people, men and women, to discuss your own racial trauma and pain as a way of healing? King lists different things of doing meditations and asking people to share stories within the group as a way of healing to empower one's voice. So yeah, is that anything you have done before, or is that something you feel that you would like to do with others?

GLL: I wrote down this phrasing because I'm gonna get Ruth King's book! As referenced in the Introduction and Part I of *Liberation for the Oppressed,* I began a community-based project funded by a University of South Florida "Understanding and Addressing Blackness and Anti-Black Racism" research grant I received in 2020. The contents of the project—"Black men for CHAT on the Emotional Freedom Train(ing), Get on Board!"—are detailed in Part I of the book. It focuses on EFT therapy as conceptualized by Risasi Milima, a Black Therapeutic Clinician here in Tampa. Based on his therapeutic practice. He and I conceptualized a 12-track, six-month program for Black male emotional, physical, and spiritual wellbeing. From October 2020 through March 2021, we met with participants twice a month in online sessions. As Milima bases his therapy in Africentric Resilience Therapy (ART), he founded our sessions upon the seven principles of Kwanzaa. Do you know those?

AR: I don't. I'm not familiar with them.

GLL: In the introduction to Part I of *Liberation for the Oppressed* "Black Men Breathing Together on the Emotional Freedom Train(ing)," it documents that the seven principles of Kwanzaa were created by Maulana Karenga in 1966 when he was professor and Chair Africana Studies at California State University. He conceptualized the principles in Swahili, and in the U.S. they are celebrated from December 26 to January 1. The principles are (1) "Umoja" (unity), (2) "Kujichagulia" (self-determination), (3) "Ujima" (collective work and responsibility), (4) "Ujamaa" (cooperative economics), (5) "Nia" (purpose), (6) "Kuumba" (creativity), and (7) "Imani" (faith). I believe Ruth King's idea of compassion for our cultural heritage really embodies Karenga's concept of Kwanzaa. As you point out, our ancestors our no longer physically with us. They're gone, but their spirit of survival still lives in us. And what do we do with our lives? Once again, I think it's about sacrificing time, energy, and commitment to critical consciousness for compassion and love for those have been oppressed. We can make it through the trauma of racism, even though as Audre Lorde says in her "Litany for Survival," "We were never meant to survive." Some of us haven't. We need to speak and act out healing. Speak love. Speak compassion. Create communities of solidarity and alliances. That's what the brothers dialogued about on the Emotional Freedom Train(ing), as conceptualized by Risasi Milima (a Black male Clinical Therapist). Over the course of the EFT program, we created a self-liberating environment where "brothers" could openly share our thoughts and feelings with each other—especially being Black and male in the U.S.

AR: This is basically what Ruth King is talking about as well, as far as creating a space for Black individuals to share their feelings during these trying times. We do need to speak out against the injustice of racism and white supremacy. One of the ways I've kind of been doing that is a through these racial mindfulness practices as a way to become conscious of the situations and conscious of our own problems so we can begin talking about them with other people—even as racism is an uncomfortable topic to talk about for a lot of people. Black people, white people, everybody. It's something people don't want to talk about, or they steer away from it because it's painful or uncomfortable, but it is important for us to talk about it. It is important to be mindful of it.

So yeah, I really do think it's amazing that you all put that anti-racist project together, Dr. Lemons. We're kind of coming to the end of our conversation here. There is basically one more thing that I want to ask you, and then I want to actually share a poem with you by a Black author. His name is Tamaz Young. *Unrequited Expressions* is the name of his book. It's a collection of poetry that deals with a lot of different issues such as racism, mental health, love, family, and loss. And I feel like you'd really enjoy it. And so, one of the ways that I've sort of begun to practice mindfulness is through sitting meditations, doing daily journals of what I've seen throughout the day, what I've heard—just focusing on the things around me, and then just take that mindset and focus on things inward, kind of like reflecting on my own experiences. I will share with you one of the things that I've found that's really helped me is reading poetry throughout the course on poetry I took taught by Dr. Heather Sellers[2] (in spring semester 2020) in the USF English department. I began looking for more poetry outside of this course even as it really helped ground myself in the present, and it really helped me focus on mindful types of experiences I've had. So, my question to you is have you had any experience with poetry or writing, if so, have you written any or have you just focused on reading poetry?

GLL: This question is so critically engaging for me because I have, over the course of my academic publishing career, most of my writings are framed in a traditional, academic format—where you write based on scholarly research, a conceptual thesis, substantial secondary support, so on and so forth. However, in the last couple of years, I've started a path to creating writing via "spoken word".

AR: Yeah! I believed you mentioned that early on in one of the classes I recently took with you. So, do you feel like it's helped empower your voice in any way?

GLL: Well, you know, having historically been trained within the traditional, Eurocentric standpoint about what research and scholarship are supposed to be about, I started to get a clear sense that I needed to step outside of that tradition. Embracing my Africentric heritage, I have become culturally connected to who I am as a person of Nigerian descent. As a result, I have begun creatively to articulate that and express my love for *Blackness*. Creatively, choosing to explore the liberating power of spoken word has given me the freedom to express my inner-feelings. bell hooks, says in *Remembered Rapture: The Writer at Work* that she always believed she would become a writer, even as a young girl, and it started with poetry. And so, in looking back over the course of my academic training in PWI's, I say to myself: "Wow, it took me all these years to finally own my Black-self." The joy of having begun to express it in spoken word is life-saving.

As illustrated in my writings in *Liberation for the Oppressed,* I have purposely included spoken word in my "academic" discourse. Alex, even now in my scholarly framework. I ask, "What is it that you want me to say?" And this is why over time autocritography became the methodological framework for much of my scholarship.

Intersecting the personal and the professional with the political, pedagogical, and the spiritual is about my journey toward freedom. In sum, as I declare in the "Preface" to *Liberation for the Oppressed*, this is my calling for *soul work*.

AR: Beautiful, I really like that "soul work." Because it really is coming from the soul so that makes a lot of sense. I too, am not really formally trained in writing poetry, and what I've really liked about the class I took with Dr. Sellers was her encouraging students in it to write what we see and be mindful of everything, and not really focus so much on the form like a sonnet or anything like that. She compelled us to write out on the page what we see or really find through mindfulness practices. I feel like that's helped empower my voice in a lot of ways. And that's what I've noticed about studying poetry from other Black authors, and kind of like what you were saying about writing poetry in the way that you speak is kind of exemplified in the poems I've read.

Creating Africentric Alliances across Racial Differences

GLL: By the way, let me share why I admire and consider Dr. Sellers as an ally for "CHAT". I recall several years ago having a chat with her at a small Black owned art shop in St. Petersburg, Florida. The art shop was located in the 'hood, and all the artwork showcased by the Black sister who own the shop featured African designs. And here was Heather with this little Black girl shopping through all this African stuff. She and this little Black girl were holding hands. I asked Heather, "Hey, who is this child?" She told me her name and said she was this little Black girl's mentor. I will always remember that moment saying to myself, "Look at this!" It was clear to me that Heather was enabling this little Black girl to love herself bringing her to shop through this African artistry collection. Listen, for you to have taken that poetry class with Dr. Sellers was not by happenstance. It was about bringing you to a deeper level of self-mindfulness. Remember everything in the lives of those who believe in the liberating, transformational power of the Creator is meant to be for our greater good. I believe this poetry class and the BIPOC literature courses you have taken with me were actually to enable you to begin envisioning your life-calling for self-liberation as a Black man committed to creative "CHAT" to free the oppressed.

AR: You know, I've been struggling with trying to figure that out for a while, but I know now that I just want to get my voice out there in order to help and potentially inspire others to kind of speak out against the kinds of oppression and injustices, we as BIPOC people experience every day because it is wrong. And it's something for most of my life, it's not something I really focused on because it really didn't affect me I felt. But as I've started studying all this, and becoming more aware of all the injustices that are happening as I've grown older, I feel like it is something I really want to do, even if it's through creative writing or publishing essays, or teaching. That's something I want to pass on to other people, so that we can work towards breaking down or dismantling this system that's used to oppress others. So, that's where I say I am right now. So, to close our dialogue, which has been fantastic, by the way, I just want to share with you excerpts I will cite from a poem by Tamaz Young. Its title is "I'm a Black Man"—

I'm actually a Black man
There's a difference of which we can't lose sight
That results in the difference of plight
I wish that every Black man was always treated right
Like talking to a cop without fight or flight
Or just owning a gun simply because it's his guaranteed right
Sometimes I can't have these things, I'm not white

              …
I'm a Black man
If assumed to commit crime, I might be beaten
But if the white man kills thirty in a school, no force in arrest is given
My mental health would never be the reason
But the white man might get time off for his thinking
You need to see that I'm Black, this is the reason
If you don't see color, at least the struggle is worth believing

I'm a Black man
I love the color of my skin
I hate the stereotypical boxes that society puts me in
I love the fact that I'm not living under enslavement
I hate that institutionalized racism is the substitution
I don't want to be white; I love who I am
I ask that you value me like any other man

GLL: Wow! … So, inspirational and obviously radically liberating for Black male movement from an object to subject positionality—loving the worth of himself for "who" he is.

AR: Thank you so much, Dr. Lemons. Thank you for doing this interview as part of my writing assignment in Dr. Sellers' poetry class. I really appreciate this insightful dialogue.

Notes

[1] A womanist—"Loves music. Loves dance. Loves the moon. *Loves* the Spirit. Loves love and food and roundness. Loves struggle. *Loves* the Folk. Loves herself. *Regardless*" (xii).

[2] Dr. Sellers is a professor of creative writing in the Department of English at the University of South Florida (Tampa campus).

Works Cited

hooks, bell. *Killing Rage: Ending Racism.* Henry Holt and Co., 1995.

---. *Remembered Rapture: The Writer at Work.* Henry Holt and Co., 1999.

King, Ruth. *Mindful of Race: Transforming Racism from the Inside Out.* Barnes and Nobles, 2018.

Young, Tamaz. *Unrequited Expressions.* FriesenPress, 2021.

17

Oppression, Resistance, and Empowerment
The Power Dynamics of
Naming and *Un*-naming in African American Culture
Maggie Romigh

My "Introduction" and "Conclusion"

In what follows, I offer readers insight into writings taken from the dissertation I wrote while pursuing a Ph.D. in the Department of English at the University of South Florida. The Editor of *Liberation for the Oppressed*, Dr. Gary L. Lemons, was my major professor when I was working on the dissertation. Related to the concept of his book project, at his request. I agreed to include the "Introduction" and the "Conclusion" of my dissertation in this anthology. In the Introduction to my dissertation (which I titled "Swimming in a Sea of Racism"), I identify myself as a "white" woman scholar, communicating how I approach and discuss certain writings in the field of African American literature. In this interpretive framework, I acknowledge particular events occurring in my personal life that influenced my scholarly focus. As my dissertation centered on naming and un-naming in African American literature, in what follows there are many references both to the dissertation itself and to African American literature more broadly. Like all cultural artifacts, African American literature both reflects and reinforces the culture from which it springs, in essence, the reality of Black existence and survival in the U.S. The ubiquitous trope of naming in African American literature, therefore, indicates that the power dynamics of naming and un-naming are a critically important part of Black communal relationships and Black culture. While the body of my dissertation focused mostly on the way African American authors use individual names to indicate the balance of power in relationships within their work, in my Conclusion (titled "The Power of Naming in History and Culture"), I also discuss the many names white people have used to describe Black people in the U.S. and the way Black people have resisted white supremacy through self-naming, claiming empowering names for themselves as individuals and as a distinctively defined *Black* collective for survival in the U.S.

Introduction: Swimming in a Sea of Racism

> darling,
> you feel heavy
> because you are
> too full of truth
>
> open your mouth more.
> let the truth exist
> somewhere other than
> inside your body.
> della hicks-wilson

First and foremost, in this Introduction, I include autobiographic information related to myself and to the focus of this dissertation in order to address any possible misunderstandings about misappropriation of cultural material. In a 2019 keynote address at Loyola Marymount University's Center for Service and Action, Dr. Stefan Bradley titled his talk, "I need an accomplice, not an ally" (qtd. in Yamamoto 5). According to Yamamoto, Bradley pointed out the distinction between an "ally," one who sympathizes with the struggles of Black people and will help when it is convenient, and an "accomplice," one who will "risk everything" to stand with Black people in their struggles for equality and equity (qtd. in Yamamoto 5). I include autobiographical information in this introduction to position myself as ally who is working toward becoming an accomplice, as I write about African American literature and African American lives. I also include autobiographical information in this introduction because own experiences have shaped my ideas about naming, about African American literature in general, and about the focus of my work specifically. My "Introduction," therefore, takes an autocritographical approach as conceptualized by self-proclaimed feminist and African American writer Michael Awkward. Awkward, who employs "autocritography" as a methodological approach in his text *Scenes of Instruction, A Memoir,* says,

> [autocritography is] a self-reflexive, self-consciously academic act that foregrounds aspects of the genre typically dissolved into authors' always strategic self-portraits. Autocritography, in other words, is an account of individual, social, and institutional conditions that help to produce a scholar and, hence, his or her professional concerns. Although the intensity of

investigation of any of these conditions may vary widely, their self-consciously interactive presence distinguishes autocritography from other forms of autobiographical recall (24).

What follows is an account of the individual and social constructs that helped to shape me as a scholar and sparked the curiosity that led me to discover the area of scholarly interest explored in this dissertation.

A Witness to Racial Injustice: My Path to Critical Consciousness

I write about African American literature because, as an older Southern white lesbian of working-class roots, I have a been a witness to racial injustice, and I feel heavy with the truth of what I have witnessed during my lifetime. This is why I must "open [my] mouth" as della hicks-wilson exhorts her readers to do.

I was born in the tiny farming town of Omega, Georgia, and grew up in Brunswick, Georgia, a town that gained national attention in 2020 when two white men were caught on video, as they chased down and murdered a Black man, Ahmaud Arbery, who was jogging. For two months those white men were not arrested, and they were only arrested after the video went viral and people began to express outrage at this injustice. Brunswick was my home from the time I was a toddler until I was seventeen years old.

My father was a peanut sharecropper in Omega when I was born, but he moved our family to Brunswick when I was six months old, to take a job as a laborer in a chemical factory. Before my birth, my father had achieved a ninth-grade education, my mother an eighth-grade education. In Brunswick, my family was labeled by upper-class Southern whites as "poor white trash" because of my family members' lack of education and because of our low-income status. In my family, casual racism and bigotry were passed on to me before I was taught my ABCs. My parents' racism was not spiked with hatred but with pity for and fear of Black people. My father and my stepmother truly believed that Black people were inferior to white people, both mentally and ethically.

Two experiences, early in my life, "woke" me and made me begin to question the ingrained racism of my family and my community. I want to talk about the second event first, which was listening, in my classroom at my segregated school, to a speech by Dr. Martin Luther King Jr., when I was nine years old. My parents had taught me that Black people were not as smart and capable as white people, but, listening to Dr.

King, it was immediately clear to me that he was smarter than any adult I knew, far smarter than my white parents, smarter than my white teachers, even smarter than our white preacher. For me, that knowledge knocked down the last shaky foundations of racism and prejudice. But the first moment of my awakening was even more powerful, and I have carried it like a stone in my heart, with horror, with shame, with sadness, and with anger, for almost sixty years.

When I was seven years old, I was on a rare excursion downtown with my dad, walking along a sidewalk. An old Black man approached my dad with his hand extended, but, when he opened his mouth, only a horrible jumble of guttural noises came out. My dad ignored the man and kept walking. I looked up at my dad and said, "Daddy, what's wrong with that old colored man?" Without breaking stride, my dad said, "He doesn't have a tongue." Puzzled, I asked, "What happened to his tongue?" In the same tone he would have used to say the man fell and skinned his knee, my dad said, "The Ku Klux Klan caught him talking to a white woman, so they cut out his tongue."

My dad kept walking, while I stood stunned, eyes wide and mouth agape, in the middle of the sidewalk, unable to express the roiling emotions that overwhelmed my small body and heart in that moment. I was shocked; I was horrified; I was ashamed; I was angry. I wanted to go back and save that old Black man; I wanted to hammer my white father with my small white fists for the nonchalant tone in which he delivered this inconceivable story. It was in that moment that I was awakened to the ugly sea of white supremacy that I swam in, that we all swim in, every day, but that I had never noticed before.

After that awakening experience, I saw my community with open eyes; I paid attention to interactions between white people and Black people. I saw the discrimination and humiliation and even violence Black people faced every day, and I was ashamed of my family and my white community. I made a decision to speak out about racism whenever I could, and, though I received quite a few beatings from my dad and my stepmother when I tried to tell them how wrong they were to disrespect Black people, I continued to speak up. I knew I had to speak up, to voice the horrors of racism that the old Black man could no longer articulate. In my own small way, I have always worked to overcome racism and injustice, and today I still feel the need to raise my voice, as an ally to that tongue-less old Black man who could not even say his own name.

My Journey and Naming

I first became interested in the link between power and naming in African American literature when I was a junior at Eckerd College taking a Southern Literature class and reading Maya Angelou's autobiographical fiction, *I Know Why the Caged Bird Sings*. In that text, Angelou specifically discusses the significance of naming for African Americans when she writes: "Every person I knew had a hellish horror of being 'called out of his name.' It was a dangerous practice to call a Negro anything that could be loosely construed as insulting because of the centuries of their having been called niggers, jigs, dinges, blackbirds, crows, boots and spooks" (91). But Angelou also subtly illustrates a link between power and naming in that text, as every person in her story calls her childhood self by a different name.

Looking back, it seems now that I didn't simply choose the topic of naming; I feel like the topic chose me. I am sensitive to issues of naming because of my own experiences being named and renamed. In fact, I did not know my own legal name until I was five years old. As a toddler, I was called "Lisa." On the first day of kindergarten, the teacher asked each student to raise his or her hand when she called our names. When she said "Lisa," I raised my hand. But the teacher said to me, "No, sweetie. Your name isn't Lisa. Your name is Melissa." I had never heard that name, but I thought it was pretty, so I shyly said, "Okay." All day I answered to the name "Melissa," enjoying it more every time I heard it. That afternoon, I went home and told my dad and my stepmother than my name was "Melissa." They explained, "Yes, that's your real name, but we don't pronounce it "Melissa," we pronounce it "Me-lisa," so we shortened it to "Lisa." I thought "Melissa" was much prettier, so, with all the dignity of a five-year-old, I insisted that my name was not "Me-lisa" or "Lisa" anymore. I wanted to be called "Melissa." My parents ignored my request and continued to call me "Lisa." However, at school I was "Melissa."

My little sister began to talk when I was about nine years old, and she could not say "Melissa" or "Lisa." She called me Lee-Lee, and the entire family soon picked up that nickname. So by the time I was ten, I had been called "Lisa," "Me-lisa," "Melissa," and "Lee-Lee." Over the years, friends gave me other nicknames, including Missy, Mel, Melli, and Candy (because my initials were M. M.) Additionally, when I was seventeen years old and a first-year college student, I published a few sexually explicit poems in the community college literary magazine. Since I knew my parents would read the magazine because I was the editor, I used the ironic pen name "Virginia" for the sexual poems and my own name for my other poems. In my childhood and early adulthood, my identity seemed as flexible as my name; I performed one identity for my parents, another for my teachers, still another with my friends, another as a writer of poetry, each identity having its own name.

When I was thirty and had finally settled into my own skin and my own sense of self, a friend said to me, "Your name doesn't suit you." Puzzled, I asked, "What do you mean?" She said, "Melissa is such a prissy name, and you're such a down-to-earth person." I laughed, and responded somewhat sarcastically, "Okay. What do you think my name should be?" She cocked her head to the side, peered at me quizzically, and then replied, "Maggie." When I heard the name, it felt like slipping my hand into a custom-fitted glove. I said, "I love that! You can call me Maggie if you want to." Over the years, every time another friend heard someone call me "Maggie," that friend would say something about how the name suited me, and then he or she would begin to call me "Maggie" as well. The snowball effective soon lead to most of my friends calling me "Maggie," and, when I went to work in a library where another employee was named "Melissa," "Maggie" became the name I was called at work as well. Ultimately, "Maggie" is the name I chose for myself. It is the name I use when I publish, when I teach, when I meet new people. Even my mother, who chose the name "Melissa" from a book, not knowing its correct pronunciation until many years later, now calls me "Maggie." I use my legal name only when it is required. And when people refuse to use the name "Maggie," I feel that they are slighting me, ignoring something that is important to me. My very identity is tied up with the name "Maggie."

"The Significance of Naming"—My Study of African American Literature

All this personal history makes me sensitive to issues of both racism and naming, so when I first read Angelou's *I Know Why the Caged Bird Sings*, when I was a forty-year-old junior at Eckerd College in St. Petersburg, Florida, I recognized immediately that the author was making a point about naming in her text. For a class assignment, I wrote an essay called, "The Significance of Naming in Maya Angelou's *I Know Why the Caged Bird Sings*," which focused on the importance of naming in the text, both as Angelou directly discusses it in the text and as it applies to her more subtle references to those people who named and un-named her throughout her life. On my essay, Dr. Jan Adkins wrote, "This is graduate level work!" Reading that, I found myself considering, for the first time, the possibility of going beyond a B.A. taking my studies further. Without the writing of that paper, I would never have dreamed that I, as the daughter of an uneducated sharecropper/factory worker father, as the daughter of an uneducated mother who abandoned me when I was only three years old, could achieve such a thing as a graduate degree. Much later, as a sixty-year-old college instructor with an M.A. degree, I came back to the topic of naming in African American literature when I was teaching a composition class and searching for a topic to use to model for my students, so I could show them how to conduct research and how to write a literature research paper.

Quickly, I discovered that the topic of naming in African American literature was deep and wide and rich and infinitely intriguing, so I kept researching and writing about the topic long after that semester ended. The more instances of naming as a trope in African American literature that I found, the more fascinated I became. After I had written thirty-eight pages of text and presented a paper at a conference on the subject, I realized, first, that the link between power and naming is almost ubiquitous in African American literature and, second, that not many scholars have written about naming in African American literature.

In my research, I have found only seven scholars who directly discuss the significance of naming in African American literature. Debra Walker King is the only African American I have found who has written about the topic. King wrote *Deep Talk: Reading African-American Literary Names,* and she has explored this topic the most deeply of all scholars who have addressed the subject. Kimberly W. Benston discusses naming in the poetry of four African American writers and in the classic novels *Black Boy* and *Invisible Man* in two published articles. Ruth Rosenburg, Sima Farshid, Elizabeth T. Hayes, Sigrid King, and Jim Neighbors all have written a single article each on the topic, and they discuss naming in relation to either one or two specific texts in those articles. It dawned on me one day that if I kept researching naming in African American literature, I was going to end up writing a book, and that was when I knew I needed help. This series of discoveries led me to the decision to return to graduate school to pursue naming in African American literature as the topic of my doctoral research and dissertation.

When I took my first class in African American Literature at the University of South Florida, with Dr. Lemons, I knew I had found my mentor. I also discovered in his class the methodology called "autocritography." It has given me ways to ground my research in my experience and has allowed me to find my voice in writing about

African American authors who use naming to illustrate how they and their characters rebel against un-naming, find empowerment in self-naming, and use naming to undermine white cultural hegemony and systematic racism.

During the past three years, mostly years of the Trump administration, as I've been working on my dissertation, the power of naming has been reinforced for me as I've witnessed and supported the Black Lives Matter movement. After every death of a Black person at the hands of the police, protestors carry signs "Say Her Name," or "Say His Name." In memes on social media, the call echoes, "Say Their Names." In speech after speech during the Commitment March on Washington, on August 28, 2020, grieving Black families, mothers and fathers, sisters and brothers, spoke into the microphone, "Say his name," or "Say her name." Al Sharpton introduced each speaker by exhorting the crowd to "Say their names," or "Call their names." And the crowd roared the names of the dead, those people who were killed by police who had no reason to act with such violence, such brutality. The repetition of those names continues to empower the Black Lives Matter protestors, reminding them of the hundreds of Black people who have been senselessly killed. The repetition of those powerful names reminds me that white people have, throughout history, tried to reduce Black people to namelessness. To claim their humanity, Black people must claim their own names and endow those names with power. Since African American literature so powerfully reflects the lives of Black people, both real and imagined, I continue to discover the powerful significance of names and naming in literature written by African American authors.

Conclusion: The Power of Naming in History and Culture

In "Cultural Hierarchy and the Renaming of African People, "Obiagle Lake asserts, "Before the enslavement and diasporization of Africans into the western hemisphere, Africans referred to themselves by hundreds of different names" (261). In the Americas, however, Caucasian (white) people of European ancestry ignored the hundreds of tribal names and lumped together all people of African descent, calling them "negroes" and "blacks," terms which, as Lake says "stripped the slaves of their cultural identity and family ties" (261). The more respectable names assigned to people of African descent include: "negros," "colored," "blacks," "Moors," "Ethiopians," "Afros," and "Africans"; while some of the more derogatory terms include "niggers, jigs, dinges, blackbirds, crows, boots and spooks" as noted in the previous quote from Angelou's memoir (91). The names imposed upon Africans and their descendants have shifted over time. The terms Caucasian people have used to name people of color have often underscored efforts to demean and subjugate African Americans. What people of African descent have decided to call themselves has shifted over time as well. As times change, each generation has argued about what name they determine to use for themselves: "Colored, Negro, Afro-American, African-American, or Black," and there has never been a complete consensus. Henry Louis Gates, Jr. wrote in his 1969 Yale application, "My grandfather was colored, my father was a negro, and I am black" (qtd. in Kaplan and Bernays 70), which underscores the shifting ideas Black people have had about how to name themselves as a people.

The Power of Self-Naming

In 1988, when Jesse Jackson and the leaders of seventy-five groups representing Black people in America met at Chicago's Hyatt Regency and called a press conference to announce that the members of their race preferred to be called "African-Americans," they were recognizing the loss of tribal identities and expressing that the Black people living in the U.S. (as represented by these seventy-five African American leaders) wanted to be connected by ethnic identity instead of by racial identity. This choice of names was significant, and it underscored the idea that names are more than just labels; they are strongly tied to identity. These Black leaders were not only claiming a name for themselves as a group, they were rejecting those names that had been assigned to them by white people throughout history.

Ben L. Martin argues that names "are more than just tags; they can convey powerful imagery. So naming—proposing, imposing, and accepting names can be a political exercise" (Martin 83). By choosing a name for themselves, that group of African American leaders was exercising political muscles, claiming the right to identify themselves. The most important part of the announcement was the recognition of *choice* because most names historically assigned to African Americans were not names they chose. They were names imposed on people of African descent by the white people who had kidnapped and enslaved their ancestors. Over and over again, European imperialists fought against giving Black people civil rights equal to those of white people and struggled to keep Black people separated and subjugated in a white supremacist hierarchal society. As Debra Walker King says in *Deep Talk: Reading African-American Literary Names*, each of the names used to define Black people "represents attempts to define the being or essential nature of a people from within a structure of meaning and deep-level communication that is itself shaped by the systematic exclusion of that people" (47). By choosing a name for themselves, the group of Black leaders who came together in 1988 was reclaiming power that had been taken from their ancestors by white supremacist captors and oppressors. They were claiming their cultural and political right to self-identify as a people.

Un-Naming and Re-Naming as Tools of Oppression

Juri Lotman says, "No language can exist unless it is steeped in the context of culture; and no culture can exist which does not have at its center, the structure of natural language" (qtd. in Mphande 105). Historically, when slave owners ignored the given names of new captured slaves and insisted on renaming those captives they considered to be their property, they were using language to take possession of Black men, women, children. Thus, un-naming and renaming were active acts of subjugation. As Elizabeth T. Hayes argues, "To name is also to claim dominion: naming children, slaves, domestic animals, or real estate is an announcement of figurative, if not literal ownership of the named" (669). Like most people choose to give a name to a domestic or working animal, white slave owners felt they had the right to name the African and African American people they had enslaved.

Language is powerful. It is shaped by the way people look at the world, and the way people look at the world shapes their language. Nowhere is this more evident than in the naming process, whether it being the naming of a place, a people, or a single individual. When white people of European descent were enslaving the people of African descent, language and naming were used to subjugate Black people and to erase their human identity. In her thesis, "African Names and Naming Practices: The Impact Slavery and European Domination had on the African Psyche, Identity and Protest," Liseli A. Fitzpatrick points out the various ways Europeans used language to "suppress and erase African identity" in enslaved people (ii). The language used by slave traders and slave owners reflected the extreme contempt in which those white people held Black people. That contempt was evident in the way slaveowners treated the names of the people they claimed as property, erasing the names of both tribal groups and individuals, effectively un-naming them, then arrogantly renaming those groups and individuals without thought or care for the erasure of their identity.

Lupenga Mphande argues that there was a "widely held belief among whites that slaves had neither history nor culture, and that they could have legal right to a name" (107). Mphande says that white supremacist attitudes "reduced slaves to

278

namelessness, and thus made them available for name re-assignment by their owners" (107). Throughout the history of slavery, slave owners not only un-named captured African people, they renamed those enslaved people, often using cruel, derogatory, and demeaning names as tools to break down the dignity and identity of those enslaved peoples. As Fitzpatrick argues, "slaveowners assigned new names to the Africans or even left them nameless, as a way of subjugating and committing them to perpetual servitude" (ii). Slave owners sometimes relished the irony of giving the Black people they had enslaved names that were taken from mythological gods and heroes, like "Zeus" or "Hercules," to further emphasize the lack of agency of the Black slaves bearing such regal names while serving their white masters. Not only were slaves deprived of their own names and assigned new names by their masters, those names were often changed several times throughout the slaves' lives, on the whim of a white owner or a white child, or after slaves were sold to new owners (Fitzpatrick 46). Sometimes slaves were called simply "wench" or "buck" or "boy" or "girl" or "gal," reducing those enslaved people to namelessness. Without names, those enslaved people were stripped of their humanity, their individuality, and their dignity, treated as little more than animals.

The denigration of Black people as a whole and the destruction of the individual through the un-naming and the branding of that person as a slave through renaming was a subjugating reality for most slaves. It is therefore not surprising that the Africans and African Americans who experienced being claimed like domestic animals would continue to be negatively impacted by that experience throughout their lives and throughout the lives of future generations. Unfortunately, such acts of un-naming did not end with legal emancipation. They continued up to and beyond the Civil Rights protests of the 1960s, especially in the Deep South, which I witnessed myself while growing up in Georgia. Because of this historical reality, the psychic scar of generations of un-naming continues to affect the self-liberating consciousness of African Americans.

Resisting White Supremacy Through Self-Naming

Sigrid King argues, "Naming has always been an important issue" for African Americans "because of its link to the exercise of power. From their earliest experiences in America, [African Americans] have been made aware that those who name also control, and those who are named are subjugated" (King, Sigrid 683). Slave owners' acts of un-naming, naming, and re-naming were acts of dominance, acts that exerted power over the un-named. Given the history of slavery and the powerlessness of those slaves whose very names were stolen from them, it becomes evident why names and naming are important in African American culture and are sometimes still linked to a sense of power or powerlessness. Debra Walker King argues, "Black naming practices are acts of resistance against ancestral loss and spiritual death. This is one reason why names and naming are so important to African Americans. It is why many blacks give their children unique names, African names, or create names using their historical memories and hopes as sources that call forth the untainted cosmic forces of resistance" (41). By resisting the racist naming of African Americans rooted in the history of white hegemonic culture, Black people are actively pushing back against the history of un-naming and the loss of African identity. They are empowering themselves and their children through naming they creatively conceptualize.

Names and naming are a significant trope in African American literature, whether the author is writing about the historical reality of slavery or writing about a character who is trying to claim power by renaming himself or herself. As Debra Walker King says, "In the literature of black writers, we read the story of people who struggle against a legacy of unnaming and learn of their victory over its effects" (41). King's point is that in African American literature, when characters claim their own names or rename themselves, they are reclaiming their lives, reclaiming their own identities in a political way that can only be fully understood in the historical and sociological context of slavery.

Say Their Names

My exploration and explication of the power of naming in African American literature in this dissertation is rooted in my personal experience with the various names that have been used to define me in my childhood and beyond; in my childhood (and adult) experiences witnessing the un-naming and humiliation of Black people by white supremacists; in my on-going awakening to Black subjugation in the U.S.; and in my growing understanding of the link between power and naming in African American literature as it is discussed by other scholars, particularly Debra Walker King; and in my own deep reading of the texts I have explored and explicated in this dissertation. Because of my deeper understanding of the significance of naming in African American literature and culture, I want to echo and amplify the ubiquitous call of the Black Lives Matter movement: "Say their names." Like Toni Morrison's character Milkman mused on the names of the people in his community after he had become awakened to the power of names (329-330), I muse upon the names of hundreds of Black people whose lives have been cut short by police violence.

The article, "Say Their Name," published on a Gonzaga University's website gives what they say is an *incomplete* list of the African Americans who, between January, 2010 and June 12, 2020, were killed by police or who died while in police custody because of neglect or lack of response to requests for medical help. Say their names:

Aaron Campbell, Steven Eugene Washington, Danroy "DJ" Henry Jr., Derrick Jones, Reginald Doucet, Raheim Brown, Jr., Derek Williams, Kenneth Harding Jr., Alonzo Ashley Jr., Kenneth Chamberlain Sr., Ramarley Graham, Manual Levi Loggins Jr., Raymond Luther Allen Jr., Dante' Lamar Price, Nehemiah Lazar Dillard, Wendell James Allen, Jersey K. Green, Shereese Francis, Rekia Boyd, Kendrec McDade, Ervin Lee Jefferson, III, Tamon Robinson, Sharmel T. Edwards, Shantel Davis, Alesia Thomas, Chavis Carter, Reynaldo Cuevas, Noel Palanco, Malissa Williams, Timothy Russell, Darnisha Diana Harris, Shelly Marie Frey, Johnnie Kamahi Warren, Jamaal Moore Sr., Kayla Moore, Kimani "KiKi" Gray, Clinton R. Allen, Kyam Livingston, Larry Eugene Jackson Jr., Carlos Alcis, Jonathan Ferrell, Barrington "BJ" Williams, Miriam Iris Carey, Andy Lopez, Jordan Baker, McKenzie J. Cochran, Yvette Smith, Gabriella Monique Nevarez, Victor White III, Tyree Woodson, Dontre Hamilton, Eric Garner, John Crawford III, Michael Brown Jr., Ezell Ford, Dante Parker, Tanisha N. Anderson, Akai Kareem Gurley, Tamir Rice, Rumain Brisbon, Jerame C. Reid, Natasha McKenna, Janisha Fonville, Tony Terrell Robinson, Jr., Meagan Hockaday, Mya Shawatza Hall, Phillip Gregory White, Eric Courtney Harris, Walter Lamar Scott, Freddie Carlos Gray Jr., Brendon K. Glenn, Sandra Bland, Samuel Vincent DuBose, India Kager, Jeremy "Bam Bam" McDole, Jamar O'Neal Clark, Quintonio LeGrier, Bettie "Betty Boo" Jones, Alton Sterling, Philando Castile, Joseph Curtis Mann, Korryn Gaines, Terrence LeDell Sterling, Terence Crutcher, Alfred Olango, Deborah Danner, Chad Robertson, Jordan Edwards, Charleena Chavon Lyles, Aaron Bailey, Stephon Alonzo Clark, Saheed Vassell, Antwon Rose Jr., Botham Shem Jean, Chinedu Okobi, Charles "Chop" Roundtree Jr., Emantic "EJ" Fitzgerald Bradford Jr., Atatiana Koquice Jefferson, Manuel "Mannie" Elijah Ellis, Breonna Taylor, Michael Brent Charles Ramos, Dreasjon "Sean" Reed, George Perry Floyd, Aaron Bailey, Javier Ambler,

Sterling Lapree Higgins, Elijah McClain, John Elliot Neville, Aiyana Mo'Nay Stanley-Jones, Tony McDade, Carlos Carson. ("Say Their Name")

Additionally, according to Khaleda Rahaman, 229 Black people have been killed by police in the U.S. since George Floyd was asphyxiated by a white police office on May 25. 2020, while bystanders filmed his death. Rahaman's list includes five people whose names were withheld by police, but the recorded names of those Black people are:

Tony McDade aka Natosha McDade, Modesto "Marrero Desto" Reyes, Momodou Lamin Sisay, Derrick Thompson, David McAtee, Tyquarn Graves, Kamal Flowers, Lewis Ruffin Jr., Phillip Jackson, Michael Blu Thomas, Rayshard Brooks, Cane Van Pelt, Donald Ward, Brandon Gardner, Terron Jammal Boone, Derrick Canada, Skyleur Toung, Robert D'Lon Harris, Rasheed Mathew Moorman, Aloysius Larue Keaton, Kevin O. Ruffin, Ky Johnson, William Wade Burgess III, Joseph W. Denton, Paul Williams, Malik Canty, Erroll Johnson, Richard Lewis Price, Hakim Littleton, Vincent Demario Truitt, Aaron Anthony Hudson, Darius Washington, Vincent Harris, Jeremy Southern, Chester Jenkins, David Earl Brooks Jr., Darrien Walker, Ashton Broussard, Amir Johnson, Julian Edward Roosevelt Lewis, Salaythis Melvin, Jonathan Jefferson, Rafael Jevon Minniefield, Kendrell Antron Watkins, Anthony McClain, Adrian Jason Roberts, Trayford Pellerin, Damian Lamar Daniels, Julius Paye Kehyei, Michael Anthony Harris, Robert Earl Jackson, Dijon Kizzee, Deon Kay, Steven D. Smith, Major Carvel Baldwin, Steve Gilbert, Jonathan Darsaw, Robert Coleman, Darrell Wayne Zemault Sr., Charles Eric Moses Jr., Dearian Bell, Patches Vojon Holmes Jr., Kurt Andras Reinhold, Willie Shropshire Jr., DeMarco Riley, Jonathan Price, Stanley Cochran, Tyran Dent, Anthony Jones, Kevin Carr, Dana Mitchell Young Jr., Fred Williams III, Akbar Muhammad Eaddy, Dominique Mulkey, Marcellis Stinnette, Rodney Arnez Barnes, Gregory Jackson, Mark Matthew Bender, Ennice "Lil Rocc" Ross Jr., Jakerion Shmond Jackson, Walter Wallace Jr., Maurice Parker, Kevin Peterson Jr., Justin Reed, Michael Wright, Reginald Alexander Jr., Frederick Cox Jr., Rodney Eubanks, Vusumuzi Kunene, Brandon Milburn, Tracey Leon McKinney, Angelo "AJ" Crooms, Sincere Peirce, Arthur Keith, Shane K. Jones, Shawn Lequin Braddy, Jason Brice, Kenneth Jones, Rodney Applewhite, Terrell Smith, Rondell Goppy, Ellis Frye Jr., Cory Donell Truxillo, Mickee McArthur, Udofia Ekom-Abasi, James David Hawley, Kevin Fox, Dominique Harris, Maurice Jackson, Andre K. Sterling, Casey Christopher

Goodson Jr., Kwamaine O'Neal, Mark Brewer, Donald Edwin Saunders, Thomas Reeder III, Joseph R. Crawford, Joshua Feast, Charles E. Jones, Bennie Edwards, Jeremy Daniels, Johnny Bolton, Larry Taylor, Andre Maurice Hill, Isaac Frazier, Sheikh Mustafa Davis, Shamar Ogman, Marquavious Rashod Parks, Larry Hamm, Helen Jones, Jason Cooper, Jaquan Haynes, Shyheed Robert Boyd, Dolal Idd, Carl Dorsey III, La Garion Smith, Tre-Kedrian Tyquan White, Vincent Belmonte, Shawn McCoy, Robert "Lil Rob" Howard, Jason Nightengale, Matthew Oxendine, Patrick Warren Sr., Lymond Maurice Moses, Kershawn Geiger, Reginald Johnson, Zonterious Johnson, Christopher Harris, Eusi Malik Kater Jr., Tyree Kajawn Rogers, Randy Miller, Roger D. Hipskind, Karl Walker, Marvon Payton Jr., Jenoah Donald, Dontae Green, Treyh Webster, Christopher Hagans, Andrew Hogan, Dustin Demaurean Powell, Gregory Taylor, Jordan Walton, Brandon Wimberly, Daverion Kinard, Arnell States, Benjamin Tyson, Donald Francis Hairston, Chandra Moore, Andrew Teague, Howayne Gale, Tyshon Jones, Tyrell Wilson, Nika Nicole Holbert, Christopher Ruffin, Daryl Lenard Jordan, Kevin L. Duncan, Frankie Jennings, Travon Chadwell, Malcolm D. Johnson, Donovan W. Lynch, Matthew Blaylock, Michael Leon Hughes, Willie Roy Allen, DeShawn Latiwon Tatum, Noah R. Green, Diwone Wallace, Gabriel Casso, Desmon Montez Ray, Dominique Williams, James Lionel Johnson, James Alexander, Raheem Reeder, DeShund Tanner, Faustin Guetigo, Daunte Wright, Miles Jackson, Mathew Zadok Williams, Anthony Thompson Jr., Pier Alexander Shelton, Lindani Myeni, Innes Lee Jr., Roderick Inge, Larry Jenkins, Dequan Cortez Glenn, Doward Sylleen Baker, Ma'Khia Bryant, Andrew Brown, Michael Lee McClure, Marvin Veiga, Hanad Abidaziz, Terrance Maurice Parker, Eric Derrell Smith, La'Mello Parker, Latoya Denis James, Ashton Pinkee, Adonis Traughber, Kalon Horton, Lance Lowe, Tyrone Penny, Darion M. Lafayette, and Kortnee Lashon Warren. (Rahaman)

Unfortunately, the list of names will not end here. Daily, in the U.S., African Americans face the threat of escalating violence from police officers who should be trying to deescalate any potentially violent situation. These hundreds of names represent thousands of Black people killed since police organizations were first formed as a force to return escaped slaves, and they will be joined by hundreds more in the future, until white supremacy has been rooted out of police departments across the nation. This is why the Black Lives Matter movement uses the hashtag #SayTheirNames. Because my research has led me to understand the empowerment of self-naming aligned with anti-racism and because I want to honor the African Americans who have lost their lives because of racial prejudice in the ranks of police across the U.S., I say their names

As a dedicated scholar in the field of African American literature, I maintain my status also as an anti-racist ally for Black people since my first awakening to the dehumanizing effects of white supremacy when I was a child. My study of naming in African American literature has awakened in me an even deeper understanding of the depths of racism and a need to acknowledge the ongoing struggle that African Americans continue to face. In each of the chapters that compose this dissertation, I researched and analyzed the historical struggle Black writers confronted to reclaim their African ancestry. In doing so, I join them as they use their writing to resist the damaging effects of naming and un-naming in the history of racism and white supremacy in the U.S.

Works Cited

Angelou, Maya. *I Know Why the Caged Bird Sings*. New York: Random House, 1971.

Awkward, Michael. *Scenes of Instruction: A Memoir.* Durham, NC: Duke U.P., 1999. *Nookbook*.

Benston, Kimberly W. "I Yam what I Am: Naming and Unnaming in Afro-American Literature." *Black American Literature Forum*, vol. 16, no.1, Spring 1982, pp. 3-11. http://www.jstor.org.ezproxy.lib.usf.edu/stable/2904266?

---. "I Yam what I Am: Topos of (Un)naming in Afro-American Literature." *Black Literature and Literary Theory.* Ed. Henry Louis Gates, Jr. London: Methuen, 1984. pp. 151-172.

Farshid, Sima. "The Crucial Role of Naming in Toni Morrison's Song of Solomon." *Journal of African American Studies*, vol. 19, no. 3, Sept. 2015, pp. 329-338. *EBSCOhost*, doi:10.1007/s12111-015-9301-5.

Fitzpatrick, Liseli A. "African Names and Naming Practices: The Impact Slavery and European Domination had on the African Psyche, Identity and Protest." Thesis. Ohio State University, 2012. https://etd.ohiolink.edu/!etd.send_file?accession=osu1338404929&disposition=inline

Hayes, Elizabeth T. "The Named and the Nameless: Morrison's 124 and Naylor's 'the Other Place' as Semiotic Chorae." *African American Review*, vol. 38, no. 4, 2004, pp. 669–681. *JSTOR*. www.jstor.org/stable/4134424.

hicks-wilson, della. "darlin' you feel heavy." *Facebook* meme. https://www.facebook.com/photo.php?fbid=10102178990063504 Accessed 6 Nov. 2018.

Kaplan, Justin, and Anne Bernays. *The Language of Names*. New York, NY: Simon & Schuster, 1997.

King, Debra Walker. *Deep Talk: Reading African-American Literary Names*. Charlottesville, VA: UP of Virginia, 1998.

King, Sigrid. "Naming and Power in Zora Neale Hurston's *Their Eyes Were Watching God."*

Black American Literature Forum vol. 24, no. 4, 1990, pp. 683-696. http://www.jstor.org.ezproxy.lib.usf.edu/stable/3041796?

Lake, Obiagele. "Cultural Hierarchy and the Renaming of African People." *The Western Journal of Black Studies.* vol. 21, no. 4, 1997, pp. 261-267. http://eds.b.ebscohost.com.ezproxy.lib.usf.edu/eds/pdfviewer/pdfviewer?vid=7&sid=aa4af00a-a247-4fd2-945c-0915b7eaa617%40pdc-v-sessmgr06

Martin, Ben L. "From Negro to Black to African American: The Power of Names and Naming."

Political Science Quarterly 106 (1 Nov. 1991): 83-91. *JSTOR.* http://www.jstor.org.ezproxy.lib.usf.edu/stable/2152175?

Morrison, Toni. *Song of Solomon.* Plume / Penguin, 1977.

Mphande, Lupenga. "Naming and Linguistic Africanisms in African American Culture." *Selected Proceedings of the 35th Annual Conference on African Linguistics.* John Mugane et al. eds. Cascadilla Proceedings Project. Somerville, MA: 2006. http://citeseerx.ist.psu.edu/viewdoc/download doi=10.1.1.575.9611&rep=rep1&type=pdf

Neighbors, Jim. "Plunging (outside of) History: Naming and Self-Possession in *Invisible Man.*" *African American Review*, vol. 36, no. 2, 2002, pp. 227-242. *JSTOR.* http://www.jstor.org.ezproxy.lib.usf.edu/stable/1512257?

Rahman, Khaleda. "Full List of 229 Black People Killed by Police Since George Floyd's Murder." 25 May 2021 https://www.newsweek.com/full-list-229-black-people-killed-police-since-george-floyds-murder-1594477

Romigh, Maggie. "The Significance of Naming in Maya Angelou's *I Know Why the Caged Bird Sings.* Unpublished.

"Say Their Name." Gonzaga University. *Gonzaga University.* 6 Aug. 2020. http://www.gonzaga.edu/about/offices-services/diversity-inclusion-community-equity/say-their-name

18

For the Love of the Serving: A White Man Finding Soul Communion with Black Domestic and Service Workers
Scott Neumeister

The aim of soul work ... is a richly elaborated life, connected to society and nature, woven into the culture of family, nation, and globe. The idea is not to be superficially adjusted, but to be profoundly connected in the heart to ancestors and to living brothers and sisters and the many communities that claim our hearts.

Thomas Moore, *The Care of the Soul*

The communion of love our soul seeks is the most heroic and divine quest any human can take.

bell hooks, *Communion: The Female Search for Love*

I have worked with the style of writing known as autocritography for over eleven years now, progressing through my graduate literary studies at the University of South Florida and beyond. This genre merges literary criticism with memoir in a way that brings the scholar into intimate dialogue with the work(s) studied. I continue to be amazed at the moments when autocritographically reflecting on a particular piece of either literature or theory opens critically conscious insights on some aspect of my life. Occasionally, writing that I encounter will impel me to recall some unexamined biographical juncture in my life for the first time; or perhaps the text calls me to re-member some pattern of my life with an even clearer and more insightful gaze. I would call autocritography "soul work" in alignment with this book's theme and Thomas Moore's epigraphic words, because fostering critical consciousness is a work of "connecting the heart" to others in "many communities," especially marginalized ones.

The book that inspired an entire semester's worth of inquiries and deeper soul-reflection was bell hooks' *Ain't I a Woman: Black Women and Feminism*. I read it within the first week of a fall 2015 graduate English class focused solely on her work, with Gary L. Lemons as my professor. While I have previously written on many topics related to my ongoing exploration of hooks' work (including a piece in *Hooked on the Art of Love: bell hooks and My Calling for Soul-Work*, edited by Lemons), the subject matter that most often guided my autocritographical writings during that particular semester of hooks immersion was that of Black domestic and service workers. This essay is based primarily on that four months of intensive *hooksean* explorations and realizations. In past writings, specifically one published with Lemons in 2013 ("Brothers of the Soul: Men Learning about and Teaching in the Spirit of Feminist Solidarity") and others I created in his classes, I have briefly touched on three periods in my life when I experienced extended contact with these workers of color. My semester-long dive into hooks' work, as well as insights I gained from other Black feminist critics in my graduate school career, provided a clearer critical lens for me to examine more profoundly the influence of these folks: a black domestic worker in my house as a child, as well as Black Duke University service workers in the food services and housekeeping departments during my undergraduate years in the 1980s.

I wish to critique via a primarily hooksean perspective these three autobiographical experiences in order to trace an arc of early cross-difference solidarity building in my life. I will also contend that, despite the possible ambiguities of these workers' overt devotion to serving, I maintain that their openness to dialogue, be real, and—as hooks titles her book—be *all about love* helped avoid reinscribing my position as simply another white, patriarchal oppressor. On the contrary, they provided me the beginning steps that eventually led me, as Moore states, to "be profoundly connected in the heart ... to living brothers and sisters," even across multiple areas of difference.

Mixed Messages: Domestic Service and Seed-Sowing

Unknowingly she implanted in our psyches a seed of the racial imperialism that would keep us forever in bondage.

bell hooks, speaking about her sixth-grade teacher, in *Ain't I a Woman*

As a child, my most impactful exposure to the idea of Black domestic work came via the character of Mammy (Hattie McDaniel) in the film *Gone with the Wind*. While others have perceptively analyzed that particular character (from John D. Stevens' "The Black Reaction to *Gone with the Wind*" to Phil Patton's "Mammy: Her Life and Times"), in this case my internalization of the stereotype matched closely what Patton summarizes: "Nurturing and protective, self-sacrificing, long-suffering, wise, often world weary but never bitter, Mammy mixed kindness with sternness and wreathed her own identity inside the weight of heartiness, her own sexuality inside her role as surrogate mother, teacher and cook." Her presence in the film serves only the white privilege of the main characters; it has no self-actualizing aspect whatsoever. She is not so passive as to be worthless in times when action is required, nor so overbearing as to stand in the way of the ultimately superior white authority. She merely serves as a strong ally without truly requiring anything. Patricia Hill Collins' insightful work on controlling images of Black women forefronts the mammy as "the normative yardstick used to evaluate all Black women's behavior" in that it "symbolizes the dominant group's perception of the ideal Black female relationship to elite white male power" (71). Of course, to my very young mind, none of these factors operated consciously. Receiving Mammy's image primarily on an emotional level, I derived from my multiple viewings of the film perhaps the most basic element about Black domestic workers—before encountering an actual one—could be summarized in a single word: "safe." hooks concurs with this potential reaction, explaining in *Ain't I a Woman*, "The mammy as portrayed by whites *poses no threat* to the existing white patriarchal social order for she totally submits to the white racist regime" (85; emphasis added). And while I agree with hooks' call for all people to re-view films such as this with "The Oppositional Gaze," as she terms it in her essay of that title, that critically interrogates "the negation of black female representation in cinema" (97), *Gone with the Wind* did plant a single, positive seed within me alongside all of the negative ones: a seed of openness toward the Black domestic worker.

Clear as a Bell: hooks Illuminates My Past

Besides my ignorance of the origins and pitfalls of the mammy image I knew, I was woefully unaware growing up of any details about the history of slavery, again having *Gone with the Wind* as a primary teacher. Both Hill Collins and hooks ground their discussions of the mammy image in evolution of slave life in the South. In *Ain't I a Woman* particularly, hooks provides a detailed look at the commodification of Black work by white slave owners, and in particular the masculinizing of Black women, alongside of their being granted permission into white households. She emphasizes how "it was crucial that [the Black female domestic worker] be so thoroughly terrorized that she would submit passively to the will of white master, mistress, and their children" (20). Moreover, whereas Black male slaves were only considered as labor producers in the fields, black women could either be "a laborer in the fields, a worker in the domestic household, a breeder, [or] as an object of white male sexual assault" (22). The female slave consequently encountered multiple possibilities for oppressive and dehumanizing roles within the slave owners' control.

hooks also details how, while white women still firmly sat under the dominion of the male patriarch, the domestic sphere lay within the control of the female. The Black female house slave was therefore under two layers of oppression—the more distant, but still threatening, patriarch, and the closer and ominous matriarch. Indeed, much of the expectation of the Black female included reproducing the white female's tasks, manners, and so on, and as a consequence hooks asserts that female domestic slaves "were merely imitating the behavior of white mistresses" (46).

In reading hooks' insights into slavery and domestic work, my mind immediately raced back to memories of Lucille, the Black domestic worker who was in my home weekly for almost five years. Raised in a white, middle-class home and neighborhood, I was about eight years old when I began to notice some tension between my mother and father regarding household chores. My mother, who did not work outside the home, nevertheless had many external activities and interests such as the Garden Club and her sorority, for which she remained an active sponsor well past her college days. Her outside endeavors were apparently impinging on her ability to maintain what my father thought was a suitable house, and thus the "need" for some domestic help arose. I do not know the process by which Lucille became employed by my family, but there were many firsts with her. She was the first Black woman, first partially disabled person, first underclass person to enter into my house (that I knew of). She was the first adult I knew that did not have her own vehicle (my mother had to drive her to and from the closest bus stop). She was the first person I had ever encountered with fewer than half of her teeth. And finally—and very pertinent to the analysis—she was the first person with all of these traits to interact with and have extended contact with my mother and me in the domestic space of my house.

To my uncritical or uninformed mind, our hiring Lucille to do housework simply represented a job that needed to get done. And since this was really all I perceived in my youth, I had never delved into the politics of the scenario ... until hooks' *Ain't I a Woman* inspired me to do so. Learning from hooks the incisive herstory of African women coming to the United States as slaves, I became overwhelmed with thoughts of how fraught my domestic scenario really was—the oppressive, white supremacist background that shadows such an arrangement as this. For a Black woman entering into service in a white family's home, herstorical baggage comes through the door as well, even in a supposedly free and capitalistic market for all. There is no "fresh start" for a Black woman working in a house; the weight of hundreds of years of domination and abuse lurks like a shadow on the situation. hooks' brief but insightful recounting of the narrative of African women's labor tore the veil from my eyes, revealing the subtext of the *real* situation in my house all those years ago.

Subtly Superior: A House of Condescension

I want to continue my autocritigraphical reflection by saying that neither of my parents were *overtly* racist, i.e. they neither said things or acted in ways that directly disparaged people of color. But as I delve into my memories, their particular attitudes surrounding Lucille, given that she was Black, underclass, and not fully-abled, betrayed not only racist undertones but intersectional implications oppression based on gender, class, and ability. This present-moment revelation stuns me, for now another veil is lifting from part of the mechanism by which I internalized white patriarchal hegemonic ideals at home—by way of instilled values I heretofore had minimalized. I got the impression from my mother, via conversation and action, that both giving Lucille the work that we did and even shuttling her to and from the bus stop constituted a sort of *favor* we were doing her. The scenario aligned with this sentiment: Lucille is obviously in need of this money, because she can't even afford her own transportation. How lucky she is that we pay her *and* provide her the means of getting here! This subtle attitude somehow converted the "free marketplace" I mentioned above to a kind of charity performed by my parents, so that giving her a job doubled as altruism. This patronizing attitude, in retrospect, seems to me the first sign of a partially sublimated bias.

Besides giving self-aggrandizing and unwarranted pity, my mom also criticized some of Lucille's actually cleaning actions that were ineffective or even damaging. I recall two items in particular—one being the parquet floor, the other, the sterling silverware—that Lucille did not clean to Mom's standards. In retrospect, I now comprehend that Lucille did not have the bodily strength, either though age or infirmity, to rub these surfaces hard enough to produce the expected results. I remember *very* clearly, when my mother pointed out the less-than-perfect condition of the floor to Lucille, Lucille, in desperation, tried some harsher chemical on a spot, ruining the appearance of an area before stopping the process. While Mom did not get conspicuously angry, she did later disparage to my father both Lucille's "laziness" in not using more "elbow grease" and her attempt to substitute chemicals for hard work. Combined with this attitude, she resigned the chemical incident to Lucille's ignorance, a supposed lack of education on such vital domestic information. Both Lucille's inadequate strength and knowledge, compared to the white, middle class, matriarch without disabilities, reinforced the rule of the domestic sphere by such a woman. Again, without my critical eye, I witnessed, passively and absorptively, the lack of Lucille "imitating the behavior of [her] white mistres[s]."

Work as Witness: Love Leads to Dialogue

My contrasting memories of Lucille center on my experiences of her as a person. Appearance-wise, she somewhat fit into the image of the mammy—slightly overweight and often wearing a handkerchief over her head. Moreover, I recall that she always applied herself conscientiously to her work, but that work never encompassed the full list of mammy tasks that might have included caring for me, cooking, or the like. She simply cleaned and seemed focused in her tasks. I now realize (primarily via both hooks and Hill Collins) that my admiration for the duties performed touches on a reinforcement of oppressive hegemony. Her main distinction from the mammy that I noted was in her engagement with my mother and me. She did not have an expansive personality, nor a servile one. She did not speak too often or too little. She was never overly cheerful or blatantly morose. Her nature defied the controlling image personality just enough to disallow her easy subordination to an oppressed positionality.

More so than her work ethic, however, Lucille was a woman who embodied one of hooks' most pervasive ethics: love, emanating from a spiritual faith. I am well aware that, on the surface, this fact rounds out the quartet of what Hill Collins sarcastically dubs the four cardinal virtues of "true womanhood": "piety, purity, submissiveness, and domesticity" (71). I certainly hope that Hill Collins would not propose that a Black, or any color, woman would *need* to show all the opposing qualities of faithlessness, degeneracy, disobedience, and worldliness to somehow become "real" or "unobjectified." To discount Lucille's grounded spirituality—neither a pious, holier-than-thou stance, nor a detached other-worldliness—would be to minimize how it pervaded her being and presented her as a person open to the spirit of life, open to the world, and open to dialogue. She always spoke positively to my mother and me, always sang hymns and spirituals while she worked, and always exuded a joy that was catching. I also acknowledge that her "piety [and] purity" could have been performative, but there were times when I was alone with her in the house and Lucille did not know I was nearby, and she *still* sang joyful in her tasks. She often told me of her plans for church (she came on Wednesdays and had church in the evenings on that day) and how much she enjoyed her times of fellowship and worship.

But she never proselytized; she truly embodied what I think the quote—attributed to St. Francis, but more likely just embodying a Franciscan ideal—means: "Preach the gospel at all times. Use words if necessary." I think Lucille's love demonstrated what hooks describes in *Salvation: Black People and Love*: "Only love can give us the strength to go forward in the midst of heartbreak and misery ... The transformative power of love is the foundation of all meaningful social change" (17). And change it did perform: the door to my future dialogue with people of color opened because of her transformative love toward me and her work.

I now realize, via my self-reflective, hooks-inspired examination of my family's time with Lucille, that two seeds were being planted in my young mind. On the one hand, I witnessed in my own household the scenario that hooks describes: "Where the black female domestic worked as an employee of the white family ... black women workers were exploited to enhance the social standing of white families. In the white community, employing domestic help was a sign of material privilege and the person who directly benefited from a servant's work was the white woman" (155). My parents' attitudes towards Lucille, while not overtly hostile, nevertheless displayed condescension and *pointing out* of difference that made our areas of privilege seem superior to me. However, while I do not know Lucille's internal feelings about her time of service to my family, hooks' observation that such domestic workers "bitterly resented" their position does not entirely ring true from my experience because, on the other hand, her overtly loving attitude served as an inspiration to me. She made me unafraid to speak to her *across* difference and surely planted a positive seed in me that eventually trumped the negative ones and brought me to feminism/womanism, a liberatory path, and a dedication to helping others do the same.

Durham Demographics: Living in a Racially Different Space

Future feminist movement will be sustained only if the needs of masses of women are addressed. By working to rethink the nature of work, feminist activists will be shaping the direction of the movement so that it will be relevant to all women and lead them to participate.

bell hooks, *Feminist Theory: From Margin to Center*

When in 1984 I arrived as a freshman at Duke University in Durham, North Carolina, I had little knowledge of the city's racial makeup: around 45% of the city's population was black, compared to my Florida home county of Hillsborough's roughly 8% (U.S Census Bureau). Nor did I realize how, right next to the "Gothic Wonderland," as the campus is sometimes called, existed swaths of low-income housing. My freshman dormitory complex stood on the edge of Duke. Every day, as I would walk to eat or to attend class on campus, I would see scores of university service employees, dressed in what would become familiar blue outfits, walking to and from their local houses—or carpooling or utilizing city buses—as they arrived at and left their various Duke jobs. The large majority of these workers were Black, with a slight majority of these being female. The women tended to work in the food service areas, while the men worked as crews for the physical plant, including domestic workers for the dormitories. In fact, North Carolina in the 1980s lagged in the advancement of Black women in jobs. Rose Brewer points out that in the state, "there had not been major penetration into white-collar work for these women. They were nearly all in the lower reaches of the occupational structure" (39), a fact for which she blames, "a special kind of racial order in North Carolina ... White male domination and control of key political and economic institutions." Just as with the case of Lucille, unaware of the sociopolitical scenario into which I was stepping, I blithely accepted the racial dynamic of my new surroundings.

I often ate during my freshman year at the cafeteria situated in Trent, the dormitory just next door to my own. Behind the main cafeteria counter, a consistent group of black women would ask the student diners what items they wanted, and these women would then serve the food from large, heated trays and hand it to the students. This process ensured that speaking to these women of color—whom my friends and I eventually dubbed "The Dining Hall Ladies" or "The Trent Lunchroom Ladies" because of their dependable presence—became a multiple-times-a-day necessity for any student who wanted a hot entrée. Now, I had occasionally dined at similar Morrison's or Picadilly's cafeterias in Tampa, and I even remember seeing and occasionally interacting with black servers and wait staff there. But the regularity of my speaking to these women was unlike any other previous contact with Black folks except Lucille, whom I only talked to weekly during summers.

Food and Fellowship: Speaking Love

As I elucidated above, the memory of my relationship with Lucille across difference and in a similar service mode reverberated with me as I began to recall dialogue with these women of color in exchanges beyond simply what I wanted to eat. There was one particular woman who seemed to be the eldest and most respected of the crew whom I always anticipated engaging. Even more than Lucille, she embodied the mammy image, especially being more round-faced, wearing an apron, and always being seen within the dining context. She reminded me of Lucille in age, but also particularly in temperament, for she also seemed smilingly to radiate an inner joy and love of her work. Because of the nature of the always-moving cafeteria line, I could not speak at any length or in depth to any of the Lunchroom Ladies, but I clearly remember the change in their voices, body language ... in their *spirits* when I spoke to them and showed interest in them as humans, not as servers.

I mentioned above that my friends and I dubbed our servers the Lunchroom Ladies, and this social dining aspect brings up another topic I wish to address—my unwitting influence on others into fostering our more-than-diners relationship. This small group of companions was very homogenous: all white, male, upper-middle class, heterosexual, non-disabled. When I first began to naturally evolve into these conversations with the Lunchroom Ladies, any friends who were with me could not help but notice my doing so, since we were flowing through the cafeteria line as a group. I would either block their progress or hold them up from proceeding too far ahead. Over time, I noticed a change: my friends also began to engage conversationally with the Ladies, no doubt influenced by my own doing so. I had unwittingly inclined their hearts into dialogic alliance-building.

In an interesting and unexpected feedback loop, both my friends and I started noticing larger amounts of food put onto our plates as we would talk, a further sign of the Ladies' recognition of the simple yet heartfelt solidarity across difference in which we were participating. Although hooks speaks of this notion of solidarity mostly from the female act of "Sisterhood" in *From Margin to Center*, her theories about its powerful potential applies to any kind of unification:

> [We] do not need to eradicate difference to feel solidarity. We do not need to share common oppression to fight equally to end oppression. We do not need [common oppositional] sentiments to bond us together, so great is the wealth of experience, culture, and ideas we have to share with one another. We can be [people] united by shared interests and beliefs, united in our appreciation for diversity, united in our struggle to end sexist oppression, united in political solidarity. (67)

I felt, at an unconscious level, a kinship with these women in many aspects beyond simple humanity: from being Durham residents and operating under the dominance, as Brewer posits, of the same white male-dominated institution, to a shared belief that a dialogue that represents love can take place even over a cafeteria counter.

Moreover, all of *our* interactions were taking place with a backdrop of the other majority white, upper-middle class, abled Duke students in the cafeteria; *their* communications with the Ladies often ranged from robotically aloof and impersonal ("I'll have the meatloaf"), to completely self-absorbed in group conversations which the Ladies had to "interrupt," and sometimes to being rude with comments that subtly or overtly demeaned, flaunted privilege, or were even alcohol-fueled. As hooks remarks about prevailing attitudes towards positions like those the Ladies occupied, "Service work is particularly devalued in capitalist patriarchy ... In paid service jobs, workers are compensated economically, but these compensations do not lessen the extent to which they are psychologically exploited" (104). The general devaluation and exploitation of service work, particularly work performed by women of color, seemed amplified within the demographics of that private, majority white institution. I know that, for me, I genuinely and deeply appreciated the work of the Lunchroom Ladies. How else would I have gotten that food so easily if they hadn't served it to me? The respect reflected in my group's interactions stood in contrast to much of the indifference or disrespect the Ladies received. Compared to most of our peers, my friends and I might have appeared even more different than we actually were.

Performative Patriarchy: Expressing Internalized White Supremacy

Unfortunately, the word *appearance* has an even stronger connection to these events, because underlying what were genuine and heartfelt steps toward solidarity, other, darker aspects crept into our interactions with and feelings about the Ladies: one fed by the performative demands of whiteness under whose influence we all were at the time, the other fed by hegemonic masculinity. At one point, my group's conversation while dining turned toward a particular manner of speaking that the Ladies had, influenced by what I would identify as a Southern black accent. We polite white boys would always end our conversations with a "Thank you" to the Ladies, and they would reply in their accented way of saying "You're welcome," which to our privileged, white ears sounded like "You whackem." So, despite feeling a sincere connection to these women of color, we still submitted to the strong undercurrent of enhancing our whiteness by performing racism—patronization and mockery of the Ladies for the way in which they spoke. Joseph Boskin pinpoints how mammies are "distinctly Southern in their spoken words" (qtd. in Patton 80), and on this account perhaps I was manifesting evidence of the racism planted via *Gone with the Wind*'s controlling image. While no other racial bigotry surfaced in the times with my friends, the fact remains that we still undercut our mini-solidarity evolution with manifestations of the white supremacy we had internalized. Racist patriarchy is a demon quite challenging to exorcise.

In addition, another interaction shaded the purity of what was happening. There was a particular young lady—an attractive, white female student—who would often work the cash register at the end of the cafeteria line. Both my companions and I *also* attempted friendliness with this woman, but of course for subtly sexually-motivated reasons. Despite our efforts, this young woman never smiled, barely looked up from her duties, and never conversed beyond asking for payment. My friends and I decided to ironically dub her "Miss Warmth" for her icy reception of our juvenile attempts at ingratiation and flirting. But then we conflated and compared our bridge-building with the Lunchroom Ladies with and to that of the baser-agenda philandering with Miss Warmth. We wondered to each other: why didn't *she* open up, as the Ladies had? How could people of color be friendlier to us than another white person? Despite the sexual undertones of the interaction, the fact that we actually compared this white woman to these Black women to somehow justify our indignation highlights more disturbing manifestations of the intricate layering of intersectional oppression in the minds of the oppressors.

Comrades in the Struggle: Links Toward Liberation

I highlight these two acts of oppression to emphasize that my friends and I were not saints, highly enlightened and liberated vanguards of feminist/womanist movement. Indeed, I hope that nothing I have written positions me as a magnanimous but inwardly-contemptuous do-gooder—a self-righteous Pharisee, thanking Heaven that I am so wonderful and not-like-those-others. I offer this reflection on a self that was older than the one that connected with Lucille to continue tracing the events and relationships that constructed and shaped my identity and led me to a place of active "conscientization," my ongoing commitment to personal and political change to end sexist oppression in all its intersecting forms. And although I have no way of knowing, perhaps the moments of proto-feminist/womanist love shared with those Lunchroom Ladies served as a link in a chain of interactions in their lives, interactions that empowered, instilled a sense of worth, and made them feel that feminism/womanism is "relevant to *all* women and lead *them* to participate" (hooks, *Feminist Theory* 107; emphasis added).

Loving is First Seeing: Finding the Invisible (Black) Man

I am invisible, understand, simply because people refuse to see me. Like the bodiless heads you see sometimes in circus sideshows, it is as though I have been surrounded by mirrors of hard, distorting glass. When they approach me they see only my surroundings, themselves or figments of their imagination, indeed, everything and anything except me.

Ralph Ellison. *The Invisible Man*

Many an object is not seen, though it falls within the range of our visual ray, because... we are not looking for it. So, in the largest sense, we only find the world we look for.

Henry David Thoreau, Journal entry for July 2, 1857

I turn now from my experiences with Black female to Black male service work at Duke. In 1986, starting my junior year, I moved into an all-male dormitory ominously called Stonehenge. It was my first time staying in a completely sex-segregated living environment, my two previous dorms having been coed by floor or wing. Immediately within the first weeks of school, I perceived the character of this dorm as different from the previous two. There were far fewer people of color—I only knew one personally, an Asian-American—and the atmosphere was much more drinking- and party-oriented than I had experienced before. As the semester progressed, I witnessed weekend parties extend from the dorm's commons room into the halls. The students participating in them always left trash such as empty beer bottles, cans, and pizza boxes scattered about, despite the ample presence of large plastic trash cans in both the commons area and the stairwells. Moreover, much of the partying brought about vomiting, as well as urination, that missed toilets and urinals inside the bathrooms ... and sometimes not even making it inside them. Going through my Monday morning routine of showering in filthy bathrooms and walking through the trashed, beer- and body fluid-smelling halls to go to class often disgusted me to the point of nausea.

Into this scene of unsanitary mayhem courageously came a group of black male housekeepers, dressed in blue. Without a word, they would go to work picking up, mopping, sanitizing, and polishing the dorm to return it to some semblance of decency. By the time of my return back to my room on Monday afternoons, the halls were again passable, the bathrooms sparkling and even scented pleasantly, and the commons room fit for human habitation. These folks were, to my mind, miracle workers. Perhaps because of my experience with Lucille, having witnessed the relatively minor transformations within my home living space she performed, I stood in amazement at what these gentlemen did on Monday mornings. And while not every weekend had F5-level tornadic destruction or pervasive bodily excretions, the requirements of cleanup needed usually far exceeded anything at my house growing up. It was a job none would envy and few would want, but these men did it, despite the Sisyphean knowledge that it would be there to do all over again week after week.

There was one particular Black gentleman who seemed primarily responsible for my floor, which contained the commons room and thus the bulk of the work. I came to know that his name was Dwayne through his name tag. Many mornings as I did my morning routine, I witnessed Dwayne silently performing his tasks without any acknowledgement from my fellow students. To most, he was an Ellisonian "Invisible Man," both in physical presence and in being the agent behind what my privileged peers probably thought of as the *expected* cleanup of the living spaces they unmindfully had trashed. Initially, my interaction with Dwayne was a simple nodding of the head with eye contact, a straightforward action that, in retrospect, probably carried gravity for such an erased individual. I tried to ensure that any time I saw Dwayne I could take my path near enough to him that we could exchange a wordless acknowledgment of each other. Even silence can convey love if it also contains real *seeing*, real affirmation of living presence and the right *to be*. My disgust at what my peers did to our living space and my gratitude for Dwayne's intervention to correct it led me to my Thoreauvian looking for him and making him part of my "world."

One day, I came up outside the dorm mid-morning, after the majority of the cleanup had been performed, to find Dwayne outside smoking a cigarette. In this moment, I decided against the usual silent greeting and went up to speak to him. I started with a simple, "Hey," and he replied, "How's it going?" In the ensuing conversation, I told him how much I appreciated his work in the dorm, and that I recognized how doing hard work is even harder when the very people who create it have no awareness about the impact they make. I thanked him for the picking up, the trash emptying, and the mopping and cleaning of the bathrooms. A smile cracked his face, and a twinkle came to his eye, but he did not gush with words or show deep emotion. He just played it "real cool," as hooks titled her 2004 book *We Real Cool:*

Black Men and Masculinity. From then on, our interactions were always begun with his cool "How's it going?" query.

Negotiating the Culture: Embodiment as Resistance

As I noted above about Lucille and her positionality as a Black, female domestic worker, until reading the historical/critical framework that hooks provides in her theory, I had no idea about the baggage carried and social standpoint occupied by these black, male university workers as they did their daily tasks and lived their lives in Durham. The contemporary timeframe of the mid-eighties was producing cultural icons for Black men from the exploding market of music, particularly hip-hop and rap. The focus was on stylishness, money-making, and misogyny. As hooks states about the culture's ongoing influence over Black men, "This was the masculinity the pimp embodied; it was represented in the movies as glamorous and powerful" (hooks, *Salvation* 139). In the shadow of this overarching, impactful "playboy image," here were Dwayne and his cohorts dressed exactly the same, each in a blue Duke University Facilities Management uniform, performing the most unglamorous, disempowering, and un-playboyish job of cleaning up after spoiled, majority white, upper-class college men. I can barely imagine one of these black men ever confessing what they did for a living to a woman who had internalized the above-mentioned ideal of Black masculinity.

My moment of making Dwayne "visible" was probably not without complications, as I look at it retrospectively. hooks reminds us in *We Real Cool* that "the price of visibility in the contemporary world of white supremacy is that Black identity be defined in relation to the stereotype whether by embodying it or seeking to be other than it" (xii). I wonder: was Dwayne at all angered by not fitting with that pimp image, especially to a white man? Or was he proud to embody the hard-working Black image, who never complains and serves the white man faithfully? Or perhaps a combination of both of these? Or neither? While I cannot go back in time to ask him, I know that after that brief conversation, many more followed which, just as with the Dining Hall Ladies, were short in themselves, but nevertheless contained a form of love across difference that I have already indicated. If I had been the kind of person I am now, i.e. in the process of conscientizing and made more aware and confident of the powers of conversation, I would have said and maybe done more with Dwayne. I still feel that my conversations rooted in a genuine state of seeing—recognizing and appreciating each other as human—exerted a positive influence on both of our lives.

Decolonizing Those Who Serve and Love: Getting the House in Order

Perhaps in each of these progressive instances of dialogue across difference, but particularly with Dwayne, I was performing a work of decolonization, what hooks defines in *Salvation* as "the recognition of equality among humans, coupled with the understanding that racial categories which negatively stigmatize blackness were created as a political tool of imperialist white domination" (73). And perhaps I was acknowledging in Lucille, the Dining Hall Ladies, and Dwayne what Duke Chapel custodian Oscar Dantzler, a two-decade housekeeper, asserts: "Lots of people downgrade other people for what they do. Every night, I go and get in my bed, and *I tell myself that Duke can't run* if they didn't have us housekeepers." Dantzler was part of Patrick Shen's 2009 documentary *The Philosopher Kings*, a decolonizing work itself that highlights the stories of college workers who keep the "houses" running. Each of the people in my life that I have described kept or fed me in my houses, either permanent or temporary. Those houses could not have functioned as they did, nor I in them, without those workers' love of serving. Dantzler's words embody hooks' ultimate goal of decolonization: "learning to be positive, to affirm ourselves ... to cultivate self-love, to intervene on shaming that is racialized" (73-4). I realize I have much to thank them for, not just for the logistics and aesthetics of my life, but for the roots of my desire to resist hegemonic oppression. I hope that, in my interactions with these domestic and service workers, my verbal and non-verbal recognition, appreciation, and affirmation in some way conveyed the hooksean keystone of love for them, an evolving ethic that still pervades my ongoing journey into critical consciousness, feminist/womanist movement, and soul work for social justice for our "living brothers and sisters and the many communities that claim our hearts."

Works Cited

Beyer, Adam. "The Chapel's Caretaker: a conversation with Oscar Dantzler." *The Chronicle*, 21 Oct. 2014, www.dukechronicle.com/article/2014/10/chapels-caretaker-conversation-oscar-dantzler.

Brewer, Rose M. "Theorizing Race, Class and Gender: The New Scholarship of Black Feminist Intellectuals and Black Women's Labor." *Race, Gender & Class*, vol. 6, no. 2, 1999, pp. 29-47.

Collins, Patricia Hill. *Black Feminist Thought*. Routledge, 1990.

Gone with the Wind. Directed by Victor Fleming, Metro-Goldwyn Mayer, 1939.

hooks, bell. *Ain't I a Woman: Black Women and Feminism*. Taylor and Francis, 2015.

---. *Communion: The Female Search for Love*. HarperCollins, 2002.

---. *Feminist Theory: From Margin to Center*. South End Press, 2000.

---. *Salvation: Black People and Love*. William Morrow, 2001.

---. "The Oppositional Gaze." *The Feminism and Visual Culture Reader,* edited by Amelia Jones, Routledge, 2003, pp. 94-104.

---. *We Real Cool: Black Men and Masculinity*. Routledge, 2004.

Moore, Thomas. *The Care of the Soul: A Guide for Cultivating Depth and Sacredness in Everyday Life*. HarperCollins, 1992.

Patton, Phil. "Mammy, Her Life and Time." *American Heritage*, vol. 44, iss. 5, 1993, www.americanheritage.com/mammy-her-life-and-times.

Stevens, John D. "The Black Reaction to *Gone with the Wind*." *Journal of Popular Film*, vol. 2, no. 4, 1973, pp. 366-71.

The Philosopher Kings. Directed by Patrick Shen, Transcendental Media, 2009.

Thoreau, Henry David. *Summer: From the Journal of Henry D. Thoreau*, edited by H. G. O. Blake, Houghton, Mifflin and Company, 1893.

United States Census Bureau. *1990 Census of Population: General Population Characteristics North Carolina.* United States Census Bureau, www2.census.gov/library/publications/decennial/1990/cp-1/cp-1-35.pdf.

---. *1990 Census of Population: General Population Characteristics Florida.* United States Census Bureau, https://www2.census.gov/library/publications/decennial/1990/cp-1/cp-1-11-1.pdf?#.

19

Staging Justice: *American Son*
Director Fanni Green and Producer Karla Hartley

In March 2021, Stageworks Theatre (Tampa, Florida) produced the play *American Son*,[1] by Christopher Demos-Brown. What follows is a compelling conversation with Fanni Green, the Director of the play. I (Gary L. Lemons) preface the dialogue by asking Karla Hartley, the Producing Artistic Director of Stageworks Theatre why she chose to stage it (as stated in "A Note from Karla"[2]).

Karla: Every once in a while I run across a play that intrigues to the extent that it hovers in the back of my mind for months and maybe years. These are plays that I know I want to produce. It's just a matter of when. I first saw *American Son* in its premier public reading at the National New Play Network's annual convening in Miami. I selected the play for the 2020-2021 season in the fall of 2019, well before the murder of George Floyd sparked protests around the world, but, unfortunately, a play about policing and the Black community has always been relevant and will likely continue to be until substantive, systematic change can be made within the justice system.

Gary: While you clearly address your decision to produce the play at Stageworks, as it represents the critical need for "substantive, systemic change … within the [United States'] justice system," in what ways does the play's focus on the complexities of racial identity affect you personally?

Karla: What I find most intriguing about *American Son* is the balanced storytelling of the different perspectives of the four characters. Each character sees the situation that unfolds in the play differently and each of those viewpoints are explored. Most deeply I connected to the work as a mother of a child in a marginalized community. I connected to the deep worry that one's child may be hurt or killed because of who they are.

Any healthy society engages in conversations about relevant issues even if those conversations may be difficult. Art is meant to shine a light on issues that need discussion. The link between art and social justice is inexorable. Stageworks has a long history of doing work that explores the racial divide and makes positive social change. We will continue to fulfill this part of our mission. We want to be a part of making our society the best it can be.

I also connected to the acute helplessness and desperation of a parent who wants nothing more than to see her child walk into a room healthy and safe. Moreover, I connected to the idea that there may come a time that I will have to live with and accept the potential devastation of unintended consequences. For me as its producer at Stageworks, this play is personal and profound. It needs to be seen and heard by every community in the nation and around the world. I knew I wanted to produce it, and I knew I wanted Fanni Green to direct it and Andresia Moseley to play the lead role as the African American mother.

Gary: Considering Karla Hartley's desire for you, Fanni, to direct *American Son*, what prompted your decision to take it on?

Fanni: The story of the play is a caption of what is happening right now in the United States, I believe. The truths and the alliances that populate the play first drew me to it. The seduction of the rhythms, the silences and the continuous sound of rain (throughout the play) are all challenges I embraced.

Gary: What are your thoughts about the racial issues that arise in the progression of the plot—particularly related to interracial marriage? The Black female character (Kendra) and the white male character (Scott) are married (but even before the play begins no longer live together). Do you think their marital separation has anything to do with race and gender identities rooted in the history racism and sexual stereotypes in America?

Fanni: I think it is important to see the interracial couple as a fractured family. I do not think issues of race and gender are greater than longstanding, inner feelings of betrayal and bitterness as demonstrated by both Kendra and Scott.

Gary: What are your thoughts about the representation in the play about Kendra's concerns as Black mother as to whether her voice is being heard by the white police officer or her "ex"-white husband?

Fanni: I actually do think as a Black mother, Kendra, is being heard by the white police officer. He follows police protocol. We see him assess, assist, assuage her feelings of pain—even as he operates inside of a system that self-protects itself.

Kendra's frustration with the officer grows in response to his representation of the system.

The script indicates Scott and Kendra are yet married but separated-estranged. The husband (Scott) tries to listen to his wife but he cannot hear the depth of her concerns. It appears the foundational history of their interracial marriage and parenting, the husband's profession, his desertion, and what Kendra might call his ignorant arrogance—all deafen Scott. It seems Kendra's fear and her revelation drive her ultimately to assert herself.

Gary: Can you relate to Kendra's feelings of Black motherhood—especially connected to yourself as a Black mother of Black sons?

Fanni: Yes, I can relate to Kendra's feelings of what it means to be a Black mother. My experience of being a mom to two sons growing up as Black teenagers and becoming young adults—as well as the mother of a Black daughter (now a young adult, too)—allows me to connect to what I feel is Kendra's desperation, fear, and regret. I too have longed for no danger to befall my sons or daughter. Especially when they would be out as teens late at night, I pray they never be stopped by the police— ever. It is unfair perhaps, distrustful, even. Yet I am thankful they are alive.

Having shared my personal experiences, I know an actress playing Kendra need not be a mother in reality. Rather she must at the least be able to imagine, locate, and allow Kendra to share with the actor the gift of what I call, Kendra's, "quaking...."

Gary: What are your thoughts about Jamal (the "biracial" son of Kendra and Scott) having racially aligned himself with preference for his Black identity rather than with the white identity of his father?

Fanni: Since we are given the story of Jamal's pursuit of racial identity via his Black mother, it might be fair to consider her motives and the implications of her report to the police officer related to her son's "racial" description.

Gary: In relationship to this question, why do you think the author of the play chose to title it—*American Son*? Clearly, there is no reference to "race" in the title of the play, although it is critically important in the plot.

Fanni: The title of the play itself is evocative, don't you think? For our production at Stageworks, *American Son* means the son, Jamal, is as American as he is Black. Jamal was born of his parents, is treasured by them, and resides in their love. Jamal was born in the United States and is, therefore, an American. He should be loved and treasured as an American offspring—not only him, but his two Black friends also.

Gary: How do you address the white police officer's responses to Kendra's concerns about her son in contrast to the Black officer's attitude in his report of the details related to what happened that ultimately causes the killing of Jamal?

Fanni: The playwright sets up a progression of police representation and male authority in the play. First, Officer Larkin, the white cop at the police station downplays the mother's concern about where her son is. Secondly, Scott, her husband (who is by profession an FBI officer) tries to handle the situation and the painful feelings of Kendra, his estranged wife. Then, the Black police Lieutenant tells the mother that her son, Jamal, is unprepared to live in the world as a Black man. Each man/officer—Black and white—in the play insists Kendra calm down. Finally, toward the end of the play, the Black lieutenant—who reports the facts of the investigation as to Jamal's whereabouts—offers the opportunity to retreat into racial neutrality or allows himself to specifically follow police protocol and policy.

Gary: Does it make a difference that it is a Black policeman who shoots the son, rather a white officer? Do you think the playwright desire is to downplay the documentation and currency of racism in ways white police officers deal with/(mis)treat Black males and females?

Fanni: It does make a difference that it is a Black police officer who shoots the son. The playwright in doing so, perhaps, reminds us to consider human error and panic. The play was first produced in 2016. It doesn't appear to be the playwright's intention to downplay the current documentation of police brutality of Black boys and men (particularly) by white police officers. It is important to remember the son does not appear an actual cast member in the play. The play explores the themes of family, community, and identity.

Gary: In the play, it seems clear that Scott (the white father) has issues with Kendra (the Black mother) calling into question his denial of the son's choice to identify more with his African American identity that his white side—even though he is "bi"-racial. Do you think his mother has played a role in this as having supported her son identifying more with being and "acting" Black than white?

Fanni: No, I do not think the mother has played a role in Jamal's identification with his African-American side. Rather, I think she's served as solace and connection. I think the script leads us to believe that society has identified the son as Black—based on racial stereotypes. I would say the son's melanin in his skin renders him African-American more than "bi"-racial. Might the white father in the play be pressing for a militaristic future for his son, be his way to promote the legacy of the family line? Might this be the father's fight to remain an influence in his son's life although he's not in the house, nor with the son's Black mother?

Gary: What were the most challenging issues for you in directing this play related to ways popular media—TV shows, movies, and advertising—are now promoting interracial relationships? In light of this, even though this play does not give the impression that interracial relationships—especially between Blacks and whites—is not still a major issue in Black and white communities.

Fanni: My challenge as the play's Director was to ground each character's truth in a dramatic presence that would stand with and against another character's truth. Current media representation of interracial relationships was not a place of challenge for me.

Gary: Do you think that this white male playwright challenges the audience to think more seriously about the fact that racism continues to be a major issue in this nation?

Fanni: Yes. I also think this white male playwright gives the audience a specific glimpse into police protocol training, racial, and psychologically (un)conscious biases.

Gary: Finally, what is your hope that the audience will take away from viewing the play?

Fanni: It is my hope that the audience members will commit to dismantling racist practices of presumption and identification executed by police. It is my hope that audience members will talk to one another's heart and walk in one another's shoes.

Gary: As we close this conversation, in the "Director's Note,"[3] you make a compelling statement that underscores your call for an empathetic standpoint related to the audience's take-away—especially considering the play's tragic ending with the shooting of the interracial couple's son, Jamal. Please share your comments once again.

Fanni: The lines repeated at the end of the play [spoken by Scott, Jamal's white father] for me metaphorically articulate the present moment of our American history. The father says: "I can't breathe. I … I … can't breathe. I can't breathe—"[4]

What do I mean? The lines reveal constriction, fear and loss. They are the conclusion of choices and responses.

I mean, what are the issues that identify this present moment in our American History for you? The lines make me wonder, for instance, if my own choices and responses to disease, racism, and poverty, for instance, are the legacy I want to leave for history to interpret.

I ask you [audience members], after the bows have been take and you depart this simulated realism, do you think the lines at the end of the play are a final report about our American condition? Or might they serve as a moment of assessment, before we … Do what?

Notes

[1] As indicated in the printed copy of the program for audience members attending the Stageworks' production of *American Son*, the playwright Christopher Demos-Brown notes that the play was staged in 2019 at the Booth Theatre on Broadway in New York City. It was directed by Kenny Leon, who would also direct the film adapted version of the play. It appeared on Netflix in summer 2021—staring Kerry Washington, Steven Pasquale, Jeremy Jordan, and Eugene Lee.

[2] Most of Karla Hartley's comments originally appear in the printed copy of the play's program for audience members attending the production of *American Son* at Stageworks (March 12-28, 2021).

[3] Fanni Green's "Director's Note" originally appear in the printed copy of the play's program for the audience members attending the production of *American Son* at Stageworks (March 12-28, 2021).

[4] As spoken by the father, these words appear on page 74 in the script of *American Son*.

Work Cited

Demos-Brown, Christopher. *American Son.* Samuel French. 2019.

20

On a *Black* Course to Liberation: For a "World without Racism", Gary L. Lemons with Toyosi Adigun, Jennifer Eubanks, Clifton Ford, Farha Kader, Diana Kovalenko, Chada Riley, Blythe Sanschagrin, Nicholas Sicignano, Jose Soto Diaz, Maleah Tinl, Estrella Uy, and Tatiana Walker

Killing Rage: Ending Racism—Where Teacher and Students Unite in the Struggle

I have taught undergraduate and graduate courses in African American literature at the University of South Florida (on the Tampa campus) for over a decade. Considering the uprising of local, national, and international anti-racist demonstrations protesting the murder of George Floyd on May 25, 2020—in the spring 2021 semester, I chose to teach bell hooks' book *Killing Rage: Ending Racism.* Having previously taught many of her books, it would be the first time that I would choose to teach it in both my undergrad and graduate Black literature courses that semester. More than ever, during that time of teaching online due to the pandemic of COVID-19 and the traumatic experience of Floyd's murder—as discussed in "chat" and writings by students in both courses—I would comprehend the critical relevance of hooks' visionary activism as a Black feminist, scholar, and professor. Even though I have remained committed to students becoming critically aware of issues related to anti-Black racism and white supremacy, I must admit that engaging them in discussions of *Killing Rage: Ending Racism* was, indeed, a deeply emotional challenge for me personally. However, hooks continually writing about her experiences in this book as a Black woman surviving the trauma of racism in her life set me on a *Black* course for self-recovery. In truth, it enabled me to be more boldly committed to teaching freedom for the racially oppressed—at the intersection of gender, class, sexuality, and ability.

With this in mind, as a Black male teaching anti-Black racism, I will always remember some years ago when I first read James Baldwin's motivational essay "A Talk to Teachers." [1] Though in it he clearly says, "I am not a teacher myself," he expresses what "[he thinks] to be the entire purpose of education in the first place." Moreover, he states:

The paradox of education is precisely this—that as [students begin] to become conscious [they begin] to examine the society in which [they are] being educated. The purpose of education, finally, is to create in [them] the ability to look at the world for [themselves], to make [their] own decision.... To ask questions of the universe, and them to live with those questions, is the way [they achieve their] own identity.... The obligation of anyone who thinks of [themselves] as responsible is to examine society and try to change it and to fight it—at no matter what risk. This is the only hope society has. This is the only way societies change. (1)

While Baldwin did not formally identify as a teacher, according to David Ikard in *Lovable Racists, Magical Negroes, and White Messiahs* (2017), Baldwin had much to teach about what he believed should be the primary goal education. Thinking about it related to questioning one's identity based on anti-Black racist, social conditioning and being personally accountable for changing it for the better of all people globally, I am drawn to Ikard's commentary on Baldwin's standpoint with regard to the ideology of race:

An often-overlooked trailblazer in whiteness studies, Baldwin treats race in general as a pathological discourse with the dire ideological, social, and psychological consequences for even the whites who invented and policed. Baldwin argued that whites could only enjoy their privilege fully on an emotional level if they convinced themselves that blacks were somehow less human than whites and deserving of domination. (12)

As Ikard engages Baldwin's critique of white supremacy in the passage above, I further discuss it as revealed in "A Talk to Teachers." Writing about Black dehumanization in the face of white supremacy, Baldwin contemplates the possible psychological trauma of its internalization in a Black child's experience of it—

... by the time the Negro child has had, effectively, almost all the doors of opportunity slammed in his [or her], and there are very few things he [or she] can do about it. *He [She] can more or less accept it with an absolutely inarticulate and dangerous rage inside—all the more dangerous because it is never expressed. It is precisely those silent people whom white people see very day of their lives...* (my emphasis 2)

Baldwin's words, like those of hooks, clearly address the imploding danger of silence, internalized "rage." Throughout *Killing Rage: Ending Racism,* hooks' imperative call to eradicate racism must begin with critical discussion/dialogue about the psychological damage of the inner *dis*-ease of rage. Enabling BIPOC students and white students in my African American literature classes to confront it openly is about being a risk-taking professor in the college classroom. Baldwin and hooks willfully put their thoughts on the line about their own struggle against anti-Black racism. Particularly related to the life-saving purpose of anti-racist teachers for "CHAT"—I must do the same.

In my mind, I hear both of Baldwin and hooks challenging me to hold myself and my students accountable toward "ending racism." Not only must we contemplate ways to approach it conceptually, we must strategically create an analytical platform on which we can actively stand together in alliance against its deadly effects— especially interconnected to issues of sexism, classism, homophobia, ableism, as well as other forms of systemic and institutionalized oppression. In *Teaching to Transgress: Education as the Practice of Freedom* (1995), hooks states:

> In my classrooms, I do not expect students to take any risks that I would not take, to share in any say that I would not share. When professors bring narratives of their experiences into classrooms discussions it eliminates the possibility that we can function as all-knowing, silent interrogators. It is often productive if professors take the first risk, linking confessional narratives to academic discussions so as to show how experience can illuminate and enhance our understanding of academic material. But most professors must practice being vulnerable in the classroom, being wholly present in mind, body, and spirit. (21)

In teaching *Killing Rage: Ending Racism,* I not only challenged myself to be openly vulnerable about its personal implications in my life stories, but I also felt led to compel my students to take on the responsibility of interrogating the traumatic effects of white supremacy in their own lives. During the spring semester of 2021, considering the fact that both my African American literature courses had to be conducted online, I experienced with my students a life-transformative wholeness "in mind, body, and spirit." Ultimately, I comprehended the risk-taking power of "practice being vulnerable in the classroom." With deep humility and gratitude, I joined my students in building liberatory communal alliances while we read and analyzed the writings in *Killing Rage: Ending Racism.*

A Course-Template for Black Survival and Self-Determination

As I discuss in the "Introduction" to *Liberation for the Oppressed,* months before the spring 2021 semester began, during my community-based work on the 2020 University of South Florida anti-Black racism grant I received, I had already begun to contemplate student research related to my aim for it. In truth, my thoughts about the power of love for racial justice—linked to the history of Black survival and self-determination in the U.S.—has always been integrally interconnected to my teaching practice. During that semester, it would become clear to me that students reading and writing about *Killing Rage: Ending Racism* could profoundly impact their racial consciousness, especially related to renewed hope for racial equality.

In truth, the more students openly discussed their differences related to the multi-dimensionality of African American life and the culture, the closer they came to becoming critically conscious of what it means to be "Black" as personified in the writings of Black authors, particularly related to issues of racial injustice. During the semester, I witnessed the emergence of a "beloved community" in our computer-generated classroom centered on ethical principles of social justice—especially connected to the survival of African Americans facing the history of white supremacy. Our weekly class discussions of *Killing Rage: Ending Racism* would come to embody hooks' longstanding commitment to anti-racism based on her belief in an—

> ethic of love as the platform on which to renew progressive anti-racist struggle, and offering a blue-print for black survival and self-determination, this work courageously takes us to the heart of the matter. To give ourselves love, to love blackness, is to restore the true meaning of freedom, hope, and possibility in all our lives" (*Salvation: Black People and Love* xxiv).

During the semester, rather than configuring the course-work in a traditional lecture mode, I situated each class session around a student team panel composed of four students. Each assigned panel would verbally present to the class what I called a "Discussion Starter Paper." The paper contained a critical, textual analysis and a personal response to each text assigned. Initially, my intention was that the students' discussion starter papers would foster necessary groundwork for building a committed allyship to support social justice initiatives organized in beyond our virtual classroom environment.

In addition to assigning students to read *Killing Rage: Ending Racism*, in the undergraduate African American literature course, I also challenged them to think about it in thematic relationship to the fictional texts they studied by other Black writers assigned during the semester. At the end of the term, I was personally drawn to the students' responses to the last chapter of the book "Beloved Community: A World Without Racism." When I read their responses, it became clear to me that my students had been significantly influenced by hooks' hope for community solidarity grounded in anti-racist alliance. One statement hooks makes in the chapter particularly drew my students' attention during our final, online class meeting. Invested in Dr. Martin Luther King, Jr.'s vision of anti-racism, hooks states:

> In the late sixties, Martin Luther King posed the question 'Where do we go from here.' To live in anti-racist society, we must collectively renew our commitment to a democratic vision of racial justice and equality. Pursuing that vision, we create a culture where *beloved community* flourishes and is sustained. Those of us who know the joy of being with folks from all walks of life, all races, who are fundamentally anti-racist in their habits of being, need to give public testimony. We need to share not only what we have experienced but the conditions of change that make such an experience possible (271).

What follows is an extended excerpt of the dialogue between my undergraduate students, as they address hooks' vision of a "Beloved Community: A World Without Racism." It represents the aim of the course as a life-transforming blue-print for building student allyship for social justice. The "chat" openly reveals the complex variances of the students' identities, rather than hiding or suppressing them. Collectively, these students boldly discuss their differing interpretations of the book's final chapter. As hooks points out, "… [a] *beloved community* is formed not by the eradication of difference but by its affirmation…" (265).

A Life-Changing Student Dialogue: "The Passage that Impacted Me the Most"

In response to "Beloved Community: A World Without Racism" in what follows, I include personal reflections written by 12 students in the course who gave me permission to reprint their discussion in *Liberation for the Oppressed*. Together their voices—across differences of race, gender, ethnicity, culture, sexuality, and ability—actualize the transformative power of critical anti-racist consciousness.

Farha Kader—After reading "Beloved Community: A World Without Racism," the passage that I found most important is:

> Whites, people of color, and Black folks are reluctant to commit themselves fully and deeply to an anti-racist struggle that is ongoing because there is such a pervasive feeling of hopelessness—a conviction that nothing will ever change. How any of us can continue to hold those feelings when we study the history of racism in this society and see how much has changed makes no logical sense. Clearly, we have not gone far enough. In the late sixties, Martin Luther King posed the question 'Where do we go from here.' To live in anti-racist society we must collectively renew our commitment to a democratic vision of racial justice and equality. Pursuing that vision, we create a culture where *beloved community* flourishes and is sustained. (271)

Dr. King posed the question "Where do we go from here?" hooks goes on to say, "To live in anti-racist society we must collectively renew our commitment to a democratic vision of racial justice and equality" (271). hooks calls to attention the significant rise of Black leaders who call for Black separatism. Many people who support this idea generally also believe that it is necessary because white supremacist ideology will continue to persist in our society no matter what is done to prevent it. While this idea is grounded in alleviating racial tension amongst Blacks and whites, the idea that creating harmony via separation is not an effective strategy to end racism. hooks urges all folks who strive for an end to racism also to strive to form a beloved community in which differences among people are celebrated and welcomed. To add to this, hooks states that while the struggle to end systematic racism has come a long way, there is still much that still needs to be done. hooks calls out white folks who claim that they support the Black liberation struggle but will not and choose not to engage with Black folks in any way. By having a mentality like this, white supremacist values will only continue to persist. As a result, hooks urges colonized white folks and people of color to question why they feel scared when in the presence of a Black person and teach themselves to love others despite their physical differences. hooks points out that "[a]s long as white folks are taught to accept racism as 'natural' then they do not have to see themselves as consciously creating a racist society by their actions" (270).

I recently saw a video on social media of a little Black girl about four years old crying because she thinks she is ugly. Her mother consoled her by reminding her that she is beautiful and that Black is beautiful. It truly broke my heart to see that a child so young would believe such a thing about herself. This shows how pervasive white supremacist ideals really are in our society and how easily they can influence young people's thoughts and perceptions. It only further solidifies the things that bell hooks urges us all to become more aware of. The more aware we are of how racism affects those around us, the more easily we will be able to one day overcome white supremacy and live in a world without racism.

Toyosi Adigun—I believe the reason why today in our society it is so hard for me as a Black woman to trust a white person who has apologized for committing a racist act is related to whether or not they are really sincere in their apology. It is because there are those among them who have utilized Black life and Black trauma to gain popularity and fame. It has become a trend for liberal white people to be actively anti-racist. But, still with my hesitance, I find myself offering chances to forgive because, like hooks underscores, hope is the major reason why we have been able to survive as Black people and American society is not in the same state that it was in the 16th century institutionalization of slavery. In "Beloved Community: A World Without Racism," bell hooks says:

> Unfortunately, so many white people are eager to believe racism cannot be changed because internalizing that assumption downplays the issue of accountability. No responsibility need be taken for not changing something if it is perceived as immutable. To accept racism as a system of domination that can be changed would demand that everyone who sees him- or herself as embracing a vision of racial social equality would be required to assert anti-racist habits of being. We know from histories both present and past that white people (and everyone else) who commit themselves to living in anti-racist ways need to make sacrifices, to courageously endure the uncomfortable to challenge and change. White, people of color, and black folks are reluctant to commit themselves fully and deeply to an anti-racist struggle that is ongoing because there is such a pervasive feeling of hopelessness—a conviction that nothing will ever change. (270-271)

In criticizing apologies and political statements made by certain white celebrities and global industries, I admit that I fail to acknowledge that there were white people who never even felt the need to do this fifty years ago. The loss of Black lives and racial injustice was not a matter of importance in our society just mere decades ago.

Just the fact that we are able to view racial and social equality as a possibility in the future is incredible and must be acknowledged. I find symbolism in the way hooks chose to structure the title *Killing Rage: Ending Racism*. For me, it was not necessary that she placed a colon between *Killing Rage* and *Ending Racism* which meant that the latter was a part of the former, but rather that they were an extension of each other. hooks began her book by retelling a racist moment that she and her friend had experienced while on an airplane plight, a moment that brought her to tears and that produced a "killing rage" within her. Now, this moment could be seen as any reason to write-off white people all together, because as Black people we've had our share of "killing rage" moments.

However, when you reflect upon the fact that hooks utilized that as a catalyst to actively discuss and enact ways in which we need to end racism, you would think that she was some Jesus-like figure, the way she is able to overlook the trauma that she and other Black people have faced and be so forgivable. But, if you look past that, you can realize that hooks is trying to say that this beloved community is not only something that she has envisioned, but something that we can all hold onto, until it is a reality. The saying, "Rome was not built in a day" should be changed to "Racism did not end in one day." This can be proven with just the fact that hooks wrote this book over twenty years ago, and look at how far we have come. What hooks reiterates throughout this chapter is an idea of appreciating each other and our differences rather than living in a world where all our differences are erased. That would be like living in *The Giver* and we all saw how that turned out. I believe that in the same way the fight for racial equality has opened the eyes of millions of white people who have been blinded and protected through white supremacy, it has also opened my eyes as well. For example, through hooks' writing I was able to further my knowledge of how historically connected Jewish and Black people actually are facing the deadening effects of white supremacy. Similarly, in the same way that through the active fight to end systemic oppression of Asian-Americans and Pacific Islanders, I have learned an array of information about their cultures that I would not likely sought out had it not been for the rage that lives in all of us. This "killing rage" is not an end all-be-all, but rather a catalyst for societal progression, change, and love.

Jennifer Eubanks—bell hooks writes in the final chapter of *Killing Rage: Ending Racism*:

> What those of us who have not died now know, that generations before us did not grasp, was that beloved community is formed not by the eradication of difference but by its affirmation, by each of us claiming the identities and cultural legacies that shape who we are and how we live in the world. To form a beloved community, we do not surrender ties to precious origins. We deepen those bondings by connecting them with an anti-racist struggle which is at heart always a movement to disrupt that clinging to cultural legacies that demands investment in notions of racial purity, authenticity, nationalist fundamentalism. The notion that differences of skin color, class background, and cultural heritage must be erased for justice and equality to prevail is a brand of popular false consciousness that helps keep racist thinking and action intact. Most folks are threatened by the notion that they must give up allegiances to specific cultural legacies in order to have harmony. Such suspicion is unhealthy. Unfortunately, as long as our society holds up a vision of democracy that requires the surrender of bonds and ties to legacies folks hold dear, challenging racism and white supremacy will seem like an action that diminishes and destabilizes. (265)

This passage spoke to me as hooks was so profound in saying that differences should be validated rather than eliminated. This concept in a clearer way is an extension of a point that I was trying to make last week in class when I said: "Looking for connections to bind and further, celebrating differences rather than seeking division, is the key to relationship building, across potential dividing lines of race and beyond. The openness in exchanging thoughts, doubts, fears, reservations, confusion, and more will only help individuals to stop being blinded by what may be differences and start seeing what is the inherent sameness in us all." Further, I loved that bell hooks called out the fact that many intolerant or close-minded people feel threatened by thinking that they have to give up their history or personal connections and are being forced to embrace new ones. This in a way speaks to the misconceptions of so-called "cancel culture," with so many white supremacists feeling that the small bubble of a world that they knew would be taken away if a person from a culture unknown to them is honored. We have seen this with white supremacists defending the right to ostentatiously display massive monuments dedicated to slave owners and Confederate War generals at government building and schools, even naming the building after them. They claim to want to honor their "heritage" which they can do in their own lawn, but not on the public properties of our nation's people ... schools, libraries, parks, and more. How dare someone defend maintaining the naming of a high school after Robert E Lee when you are forcing and perpetuating shame, hatred, and bigotry on citizens that have been subjugated from the time of our nation's birth and defend such hate to preserve your memory of attending high school there 50 years ago?

Accepting that racism is wrong and that hateful connotations are associated with hateful people and experiences. I am proud to have been born in Atlanta, Georgia. I love Southern food, Southern accents, Southern architecture, and I only drink Coca-Cola. I also want every Confederate monument, flag, or any other symbol of hate removed immediately from any public space and hopefully one day from every private one without force or debate. I know that by helping to celebrate, honor, and grant respect to our rainbow citizenry that has made us who we are today does not take anything away from my memories and what I love. I feel it is our duty to atone for the sins of the past by not continuing them today. It is time to consider who we want to be as a nation, a community, and a citizen of humanity.

Clifton Ford—In "Beloved Community: A World Without Racism," here is the passage that impacted me the most:

> Of course, many white people are comfortable with a rhetoric of race that suggests racism cannot be changed, that all white people are 'inherently racist' simply because they are born and raised in this society. Such misguided thinking socializes white people both to remain ignorant of the way in which white supremacist attitudes are learned and to assume a posture of learned helplessness as though they have no agency—no capacity to resist this thinking. Luckily, we have many autobiographies by white folks committed to anti-racist struggle that provide documentary testimony that many of these individuals repudiated racism when they were children. Far from passively accepting it as inherent, they instinctively felt it was wrong. Many of them witnessed bizarre acts of white racist aggression towards black folks in everyday life and responded to the injustice of the situation. Sadly, in our times so many white folks are easily convinced by racist whites and black folks who have internalized racism that they can never be really free from racism. (270)

Racism is a learned trait, not inherited. Individuals are not genetically predisposed to being racist. We are all born with pure hearts, acquiring thoughts, ideas, and stereotypes from our environment. We are a product of our surroundings, the individuals that we meet, and dialogues we choose to engage in. Being that racism is learned, it can also be unlearned. Individuals with racist views can become non-racist, embracing individuals of all colors and ethnicities. During this difficult time in American history, the murder of George Floyd and other innocent African Americans, white Americans are now put in the spotlight. Like Black Americans, we cannot judge a race by one "bad apple". Just as stereotypes of Black Americans must be abolished, the stereotype that every white American is racist must also be broken. During the Black Lives Matters movement, there were (and still are) many white Americans on the front lines along with their Black counterparts. Together, they fight for racial justice and a stop to police brutality. For America to succeed as a nation, we must stop the stereotyping of all races. All races must come together as one and fight for a central cause. This is not to negate the pride of one's race. However, there should not be a superior race, only one human race.

Diana Kovalenko—The passage that impacted me the most in the last chapter of *Killing Rage: Ending Racism* is: "What those of us who have not died now know, that generations before us did not grasp, was that beloved community is formed not by the eradication of difference but by its affirmation, by each of us claiming the identities and cultural legacies that shape who we are and how we live in the world" (265). In this chapter, bell hooks ends her book with a message not of hatred and division but of love and acceptance. Throughout each essay and chapter within *Killing Rage*, hooks asserts that through decolonization, "unlearning white supremacy by divesting of white privilege if we were white or vestiges of internalized racism if we were black," people do not "surrender ties to [their] origins," but create a beloved community that is guided in anti-racist principals of acceptance and love for one another (265). hooks underscores the differences in identity between those who are Black, white, and other ethnicities. While she also talks about the issues and tensions between these communities, it is not the differences between them that causes conflict but the beliefs derived from white capitalist patriarchal supremacy that frames and controls society systematically through institutions and the minds of people in this society.

I often hear from people and anti-racist discourse how they wish "color didn't exist" or people would see each other the same, and before reading *Killing Rage*, I thought that divesting of color could be an appropriate response to racism. However, hooks shows how deeper racism runs than skin color (extending to mindsets, media, institutions such as schools and workplace, religion, between ethnicities, and so on) and how it also is an indicator of our identity. People should not have to let go of their skin color to be treated fairly or change anything about their culture and ethnicity. The problem does not lie in color but in the mind. The process of decolonization that hooks teaches us about provides us with a guide to identifying ingrained racism, bias, and prejudice. It teaches us to identify our own white privilege (especially in ways I hadn't considered before) and the structures that causes oppression to those who were not born with white privilege. The African American literature we've read in this class in correspondence with *Killing Rage* puts hooks words into practice, demonstrating societal issues in multiple settings and from multiple perspectives. While many factors contribute to formed beliefs (setting, upbringing, economic status, etc.), hooks shares that these things are not points that should hold us back from taking on the fight against racism or understanding society from different perspectives. I may not be a Black woman or have faced the problems one may have faced, but I can empathize and stand by her, not allowing my differences to blind me to someone else's experiences. The only way to stand against white supremacist capitalist patriarchy is to stand alongside one another, embracing our identities and differences, making a difference in shaping the world we want to live in through the decolonization of our minds.

Chada Riley—In the final chapter of *Killing Rage: Ending Racism* bell hooks discusses how much of an impact white supremacy and racism have on American life. Relating their history to the movement for Civil Rights, she states: "Martin Luther King imagined a beloved community where race would be transcended, forgotten, where no one would see skin color. This dream has not been realized. From its inception it was flawed vision. The flaw, however, was not the imagining of a beloved community; it was the insistence that such a community could exist only if we erased and forgot racial difference" (263). I agree with hooks in the fact that the concept of skin-color blindness is a ridiculously flawed concept. Racism is an embedded concept in this society that should be directly addressed. And on the positive side, our racial differences should not be ignored.

The watering down of Blackness and other marginalized communities has been a form of an indoctrination tactic of white supremacy for many generations. Assimilation into the norm of white culture in America silences the cultural voices of Black Indigenous People of Color (BIPOC). A skin-color blind America will still run under the cover of white supremacy. You must honor who you are and where you come from. It is ridiculous to imagine a society that does not recognize skin-color as a part of who a person is, but it does not define them. However, as hooks points out, "The loving ties of care and knowing bind us together in our differences" (264). The recognition of the differences of people allows for understanding and acceptance of those differences. Ignoring them perpetuates internal biases and assumptions born from indoctrinated ideologies of white supremacy. Disbanding allegiance to one's culture for BIPOC community alliance and family ties only furthers the perpetuation of white supremacist notions. They further cultural disbandment for the sake of racist indoctrination against community unity. Community unity emerges from the coming together of like-minded individuals that act to accomplish social justice for the oppressed.

These like-minded individuals for social justice need to be grounded in self-determination for survival. They cannot allow themselves to be watered-down until they become assimilated into the privileged image of white culture. They must represent their pro-justice point of view fully and unapologetically in order to speak in a righteous voice in whatever societal situation they are in professionally or personally. It must be okay to be yourself whether you come from the ghetto, or the suburbs, whether you are light, dark, or pale, no matter your religious beliefs, sexual orientation, or lifestyle choices. People should respect other people regardless. The issue of racism cannot be ignored because when I walk into a room the only fact that a person immediately knows about me is that I am a Black woman. Whatever assumptions, bias thoughts, and ignorant stereotypes the people in the room have follow that, and that is the issue. We must disband the ideologies of white supremacy and the false perception that being white is better than every other race. In order to move forward to a realistic form of the beloved community that Martin Luther King spoke of, we must all join the struggle for anti-racism.

Blythe Sanschagrin—The passage that impacted me the most in the closing chapter of *Killing Rage: Ending Racism* is:

> The fear whites direct at blacks is rooted in the racist assumption that the darker race is inherently deprived, dangerous, and willing to obtain what they desire by any means necessary. Since it is assumed that whenever fear is present one is less powerful, cultivating in whites fear of blacks is a useful neo-colonial strategy as it obscures the reality that whites do much more harm to blacks daily than vice versa. (268)

While there were several passages in the chapter I thought would be excellent to talk about, I chose this one because it made me have a few flashbacks to my childhood, one being the time that I took candy from a Black employee of a Publix my grandmother was shopping at. I got a beating like never before, and I will never forget it. At the time I did not understand that the reason for the beating was that my grandmother was fearful of the Black man. But in retrospect, I had taken candy from other employees at that Publix, and it seems obvious that it was because he was Black that she was so fearful. Another white family member once thought that a Black girl was following her which resulted in her physically assaulting the Black girl before running away in fear. These assumptions are obviously racist, and I believe this fear of Black individuals is heavily promoted through the media to this day. More than just being racist, this issue is dangerous (e.g., because police officers also have these racist biases; Black individuals may be harmed by fearful white individuals, etc.). I'm glad to have read this chapter because I am looking at this issue with new eyes and in terms of how fear is used as a tool to maintain white supremacy by promoting a sense of being "less powerful."

Nicholas ("Ziggy") Sicignano—The passage that impacted me the most in "Beloved Community: A World Without Racism" is: "Many white people who see themselves as non-racist are comfortable with lives where they have no contact with Black people..." (267). These words remind me of many of the exchanges I have had with many white neighbors, peers, friends, acquaintances and family about the election and presidency since Donald Trump. The more I tried to discuss "white privilege," the more combative even the most moderate of my friends would get. It became maddening trying to point out something so obvious to them only to be met with defensiveness and combativeness. The worst of these conversations is the repeated injunction: "I am NOT racist" or "Are you calling me racists?" or "What slaves have I owned?" I have a sense of hopelessness with these encounters, but understand my duty to stay engaged. My hope is to be able to make the distinctions that hooks makes in Killing Rage: Ending Racism when dealing with different forms of racism. hooks seldom talks about general racism; she differentiates the racism of our ancestors from the racism of Jim Crow and even further from today's world of "neo-colonial racism" where white power is characterized by "historical amnesia." I think armed with these distinctions, I can stay engaged and hopefully do my part in helping build a beloved community.

Jose Soto Diaz—The passage that impacted me the most in the chapter is:

Clearly we have not gone far enough. In the late sixties, Martin Luther King posed the question 'Where do we go from here.' To live in anti-racist society, we must collectively renew our commitment to a democratic vision of racial justice and equality. Pursuing that vision, we create a culture where beloved community flourishes and is sustained. Those of us who know the joy of being with folks from all walks of life, all races, who are fundamentally anti-racist in their habits of being, need to give public testimony. We need to share not only what we have experienced but the conditions of change that make such an experience possible. The interracial circle of love that I know can happen because each individual present in it has made his or her own commitment to living an antiracist life and to furthering the struggle to end white supremacy will become a reality for everyone only if those of us who have created these communities share how they emerge in our lives and the strategies we use to sustain them. Our devout commitment to building diverse communities is central. These commitments to anti-racist living are just one expression of who we are and what we share with one another, but they form the foundation of that sharing. Like all beloved communities we affirm our differences. It is this generous spirit of affirmation that gives us the courage to challenge one another, to work through misunderstandings, especially those that have to do with race and racism. In a beloved community solidarity and trust are grounded in profound commitment to a shared vision. Those of us who are always anti-racist long for a world in which everyone can form a beloved community where borders can be crossed, and cultural hybridity celebrated. Anyone can begin to make such a community by truly seeking to live in an anti-racist world. If that longing guides our vision and our actions, the new culture will be born and anti-racist communities of resistance will emerge everywhere. That is where we must go from here. (271-272)

It is true that we have not gone far enough in trying to finally attain true gender, racial, and/or ethnic equality in this country or globally. However, I do believe that it is eventually possible. I believe this because of my experiences growing up as an Army brat, a child of a career Soldier, especially one who has lived in various places because they received orders to transfer to a different duty station. The diversity of cultures within these varying places tends to be dismissed related to the idea that people are culturally different from one another. Most military brats I grew up with felt as if they were not from one specific place. In my experience, I witnessed that in these subcultural places one was and is more likely to see race as just being another idea rather than seeing culture as being racially or ethnically differently connected. However, the bond between the brats I experienced was unbreakable. Even though many of us often felt as if we were not from one specific place, personally, I always cherished my Puerto Rican heritage. Not being white is not a justification for racism. In 2016, Diane Maye, a former Air Force officer, defense industry professional, and Political Science Ph.D. Graduate from the George Mason University published an article, titled "How Can Tolerance for Diversity Be Customary in The Most Conservative of Institutions?" In the article she shared how her experience helped shape her views of what a possible "'post-racial' and 'non-discriminatory' world could look."

To support that possibility, she shared her insights by writing that the "most recent generations of Military-Americans have been exposed to many people and many cultures." Anecdotally, I found in my experience as a military brat that children of military personnel made friends with the other children based not on race but on shared interests. Even more telling, quite a few mixed-race families lived on bases where family was stationed. According to several studies, military personnel are much more likely to marry outside of their primary race than their civilian counterparts. And, before Angelina Jolie and Madonna made it vogue, there were also many military children who had been adopted into families not in the same racial category. A contributing factor that opened my mind and made me welcome the cultural differences in the varying base communities was by simply experiencing the complex structure of my own culture which is composed of indigenous (Taino), African, and Spanish nationalities. Other contributing factors to my consciousness for the significance of cultural diversity while growing up was tied to building friendships with children of Korean, Hawaiian, Philippino, African Americans, Whites, and Latinos—as well as experiencing European cultures, such as French, Italian, and German. Although American society in general has shown progress in various ways related to movements against racism, we still yet have far to go—particularly in regard to differences such as skin color. Differences in skin color and/or heritage should be celebrated and shared since we all have something we can learn from each other. However, like Martin Luther King, Jr. said: "unarmed truth and unconditional love will have the final word in reality." I feel optimistic in the thought that true gender, ethnic, and social equality will eventually prevail.

Estrella ("Elly") Uy—(The passage that impacted her the most is the same one quoted by Jose on pages 271-272 in "Beloved Community: A World Without Racism." Only included here are its last two sentences here: "Anyone can begin to make such a community by truly seeking to live in an anti-racist world. If that longing guides our vision and our actions, the new culture will be born and anti-racist communities of resistance will emerge everywhere. That is where we must go from here.")

Based on this last passage, I believe that this class parallels what hooks considers a beloved community. Throughout the semester, we have been honest with each other and ourselves; we have supported each other no matter our race, gender, religion, socioeconomic class, gender identity, or sexuality; we acknowledged our privilege and lack thereof; we identified and affirmed our differences; and among so many other things, we all did it out of love. While we may not have been able to fully end racism and overall dismantle white supremacy in the U.S.—this semester, we proved that love is infectious. Last semester, my significant other had told me about a conversation he had with his Black roommate. They were on the topic of racism. My partner, who easily gets frustrated with bigotry, discrimination, and unwarranted hatred asked his Black roommate if he hated people that acted upon those ignorant beliefs. His roommate responded by saying: "No." He doesn't inherently hate those people because those are the people that need the most help. To me, that was the most profound and loving thing that I have ever heard from a person of color regarding racist and bigoted people. The fact that there are people like that in my generation, and people with that kind of love in this class, gives me hope that hooks so called beloved community is nowhere near a far stretch.

Maleah Tinl—The passage that impacted me the most in the last chapter of *Killing Rage: Ending Racism* is: "It is this generous spirit of affirmation that gives us the courage to challenge one another, to work through misunderstandings, especially those that have to do with race and racism" (272). I chose to quote this passage because it also seems to be the perfect encapsulating wording to reserve for one of our last class meetings this semester. In these class meetings, we have all actively been learning and unlearning—learning how to be loving and accepting and unlearning ingrained or internalized racism and white supremacist values. As we have learned from reading bell hooks, racism cannot end if people do not first acknowledge their own internalized racism and/or white supremacist ways of thinking and challenge them. I believe we have created a constructive, safe place for our peers and ourselves to call each other out on our mistakes and to be able to address and acknowledge our awareness of certain racist ways of thinking and acting we may have committed in the past or even now. Understanding how we are all living in a system of white supremacy and racial oppression is a crucial step in the unlearning process, and creating an atmosphere where we know that our confessions and active change will be met with unconditional forgiveness and grace as we become more loving and accepting of all people—all races, colors, ethnicities, genders, sexuality, and classes—is an important step in the direction of forming what hooks aspires to be a "beloved community."

Tatiana Walker—The passage that impacted me the most in the final chapter of *Killing Rage: Ending Racism* is bell hooks' statement: "Most folks in this society have become so cynical about ending racism, so convinced that solidarity across racial differences can never be a reality, that they make no effort to build community" (264). In part, I do not wholly agree with bell hooks here. Her words in this passage are too generalized when she says, "[m]ost folks in this society have so cynical about ending racism." I don't think "most" people, especially those in BIPOC communities believe that unity is unachievable, so they put no effort to turn hopelessness into a reality of possibility for change. I think the problem is that sometimes we give racists too much negative credit.

There are so many historical and contemporary examples where BIPOC try to educate our white counterparts on the internalized trauma we must live with daily, and the generational racist curses first established by their ancestors. Instead of listening to us and acknowledging our pain, we are often given the message that we should leave the trauma of racism in the past. We should act as if it's not happening anymore because white folks today are not their ancestors who enslaved Africans, colonized, and abused so many groups of people including their own underclass, poor whites. We BIPOC in this day and time are not our ancestors who had to endure such pain and misery so why take on the emotional and mental baggage they had to suffer. Historically and even today, I think that so many Black leaders have tried so hard to create change that they're disappointed with the fact that we still haven't finished the jobs our ancestors and inspirational leaders have left us to do. Many of them lost their lives fighting for our rights and unity, and we still are living in the invisible shackles of slavery and Jim Crow days.

It's upsetting and discouraging to keep preaching the same message to a group of people who play deaf. Ever had a conversation with a wall? Personally, I haven't encountered one person whether Black, white or any other person of color who doesn't want world peace and equality. The problem is that our definitions of world peace often differs in relationship to dynamics of institutional power. This globalized system creates an uncomfortable space to have open and honest discussions about who owns what or should be in charge of this or that. We all need to be simply honest with ourselves about human obsession with the need for power—especially when it is about strategies of oppression of the "other" or those "less" than. Like I expressed before in our class to my white counterparts, it is not revenge BIPOC communities should be seeking as a outcome to racial injustice. If we all wanted insight revenge, we would've been successful hundreds of years ago when the first colonizers entered our land.

The oppressed should not seek to achieve world domination in competition for the ruling power of domination. We should seek peace. BIPOC need to be seen us equals, to be treated as equals, and respected as equals. We don't need enemies. We want acknowledgement, understanding, and an opportunity just as human beings. We want control over our lives and to know that we can take a walk down a street and not be killed simply because the color of our skin or ethnicity. Recent events have shown that not all people are bad but the ones who go against the message of what a "beloved community" represents are the ones who cannot and will not have charge of our lives—even as we continue our struggle to survive.

Hope for a Life-Saving Community

Of the 31 students who originally enrolled in the course, as represented, only 12 gave me permission at the end of the semester to include their personal responses to *passages that impacted them the most* in the final chapter of *Killing Rage*. Did I expect more students in the class to decide to share publicly their personal reflections related to taking a stand against racism? Considering that the majority of the students enrolled in the class were white, which has been consistently the case for me teaching African American literature in a PWI, I must admit that this was not surprising—considering the possible "hit-back" one might possibly encounter for speaking out against racism. In truth, there were BIPOC students in the course also who chose not to permit me to share publicly their perspectives.

Reflecting on my students' commentary, I continually hear the voices of these 12 students boldly addressing the critical need for community allyship in the ongoing struggle to end racism. I am fully grateful to each them for their willingness to speak out—beyond the online environment of the classroom we engagingly sustained. Beyond it, they determined to be heard in the reality of a world filled with *dis-ease*. Even so, in the face of the life-threatening efficacy of racism and the COVID-19 pandemic, they held on to the hope we came to envision in a *Black* course on a path to freedom. As Ibram X. Kendi shares with readers of his book *How to Be an Antiracist* (2019), "Racist ideas make people of color think less of themselves, which makes them more vulnerable to racist ideas. Racist ideas make White people think more of themselves, which further attracts them to racist ideas" (6). Having realized the internalized trauma of racist ideas as a young Black male before graduating from high school, he states: "A racist culture had handed me the ammunition to shoot Black people, to shoot myself, and I took and used it. Internalized racism is the real Black on Black crime" (8). In his journey toward critical *anti*-racist consciousness, Kendi closes "My Racist Introduction" recognizing that "[all of us] know how to be racist. We know how to pretend to be not racist. Now let's know how to be antiracist" (11). More than ever, as my 12 students have expressed, now is the time for us to talk back / "chat" and act in resistance to the life-threatening perpetuation of racism rooted in ideas of white supremacy.

Where Do We Go from Here? On a Path to "Restorative Justice"

In my study of hooks' writings over the years, I found that she consistently references and openly discusses with people Dr. King's impact upon her spiritual idea of love as the strategic agent for racial healing and community building across differences. In "The Beloved Community: A Conversation Between bell hooks and George Brosi" (2012), bell reiterates the impact of Dr. King's vision of community committed to social justice. George Brosi (a noted Appalachian white male author and editor) opens the dialogue emphasizing hooks' focus on love "as a huge dimension of [her] work and also liberation." He states:

> I thought it might be constructive for us to talk about the concept of the beloved community. In our last conversation it seemed like we were lightly dancing around that concept because we talked about the topics that you have dealt with in your writing. Love has been a huge dimension of your work and also liberation. It seems that, in a lot of ways, the beloved community is a concept that has come

out of struggles for liberation in an attempt to express how the process of liberation can be infused with love. This concept assumes a group effort to change social institutions and an effort to make the means of that struggle consistent with the ends. The beloved community defines the relationships among those working for change and also the desired result of these efforts. In other words, those of us working for institutional change endeavor to become a beloved community among ourselves as we are striving for all of society to exemplify the beloved community. (76)

hooks' response:

Martin Luther King was my teacher for understanding the importance of beloved community. He had a profound awareness that the people involved in oppressive institutions will not change from the logic and practices of domination without engagement with those who are striving for a better way. (76)

Brosi underscores King's idea of the importance bringing people together to enact institutional and social change. He remarks: "The whole concept of inclusion is so key to notions of the beloved community." He later comments that "[t]he whole concept of the beloved community assumes engagement in efforts for institutional change, and the kind of personal and interpersonal changes we [he and hooks] are speaking of make our efforts for social change that much more compelling" (77; 78). bell closes the conversation with the following:

Absolutely. Which takes us back to integrity, when there is congruence between what we think, say and do. *That's a big cultural crisis right now, and one of the things that can solve that crisis is the practice of community because no one is healed in isolation, and as we begin to work with other, we have to engage all of these things we are talking about: compassion, forgiveness, a willingness to listen, to hear difference, a willingness to be inclusive and all of those ingredients come together to make it possible for us to experience the joy of community."* (my emphasis 86)

In the all-inclusive spirit of this world without racism that hooks envisions, inspired by Dr. King, she asserts that "[this] new culture will be born and anti-racist communities of resistance will emerge everywhere. *That is where we must go from here*" (my emphasis). From the beginning of his visionary leadership to dismantle racial injustice in the U.S. to the end of his life on April 4, 1968, the concept of a "beloved community" would be the guiding light for Dr. King's "dream" of freedom for the oppressed.

Moreover, in hooks' conversation with Brosi, she maintains that community alliance for ending institutionalized oppression is not about creating strategies to avoid conflict. Rather than devoting so much attention to its negativity for her, it is a matter to be dealt with focusing on the liberatory implications of a beloved community. hooks openly admits that—

One of the things that has always made me sad is the extent to which civil rights struggles, black power movements, and feminist movements, have, at times, collapsed at the point where there was conflict, and how conflict between people in the groups was often seen as a negative. The truth is that you cannot build community without conflict. The issue is not to be without conflict, but to be able to resolve conflict, and the commitment to community is what gives us the inspiration to come up with ways to resolve conflict. The most contemporary way that people are thinking about as a measure of resolving conflict and rebuilding community is restorative justice. (76)

Note

[1]http://richgibson.com/talktoteachers.htm 2014. "A Talk to Teachers" was first published in 1963 in *The Saturday Review* (December 21). The article was titled "The Negro Child—His Self-Image." It would later be included in Baldwin book *The Price of the Ticket, Collected Non-Fiction 1948-1985* by Saint Martins, 1985.

Works Cited

Brosi, George and bell hooks. "The Beloved Community: A Conversation between bell hooks and George Brosi." *Appalachian Heritage,* The University of North Carolina Press, vol.40, no. 4, Fall 2012, pp. 76-87. https://doi.org/10.1353/aph.0109

hooks, bell. "Beloved Community: A World Without Racism." *Killing Rage: Ending Racism,*

Henry Holt and Company, 1995, pp. 263-272.

Ikard, David. *Lovable Racists, Magical Negroes, and White Messiahs*, The University of Chicago Press, 2017.

Kendi, Ibram X. *How to Be an Antiracist*. Random House. 2019.

Conclusion
"CHAT" Continues—Beyond 8 mins., 46 secs.

Our goal is to create a beloved community and this will require a qualitative change in our souls as well as a qualitative change in our lives.

Dr. Martin Luther King, Jr., "Birth of a New Nation" (speech delivered, 1957)

In this contemporary moment, considering the violent and deadly acts of racism in the U.S., there remains a critical need for demonstrative dialogue supporting anti-racist justice. Progressive anti-racist allies—across differences of race, gender, class, sexuality, generation, and ability—must continue to join together to conceptualize liberating strategies devoted to the eradication of racism. Ultimately, ways to advocate life-survival for Black Indigenous People of Color in the U.S. must be actively engaged. Critically aware of the emotional and physical trauma BIPOC communities are experiencing in this day and time, there must be a renewed call for MLK's life-saving, soulful vision of a "beloved community."

Thus, overall, the mission for *Liberation for the Oppressed* has been accomplished. The writers' works that compose this book have actualized *Community Healing through Activist Transformation*. In *A Call to "CHAT"*, their collective demonstration of a "beloved community" embodies the emancipatory power of actively engaged dialogue for building anti-racist alliances. United in mind, body, and soul the writers in this book openly reveal the critical need for community healing addressing the real, deadly effects of "imperialist white supremacist capitalist patriarchy" as called out by bell hooks. Embracing the legacy of liberatory love as envisioned by bell, join me as I create yet another self-transformative chat with her—

"Begin(ing) the Practice of Loving" for Self-Recovery

Gary: bell, in your book *Outlaw Culture: Resisting Representations,* you speak about preeminent importance of critical consciousness.

bell: "Folks want to know how to begin the practice of loving. For me that is where education for critical consciousness has to enter. When I look at my life, searching it for a blueprint that aided me in the process of decolonization, of personal and political self-recovery, I know that it was learning to look both inward and outward with a critical eye. Awareness is central to the process of life as the practice of freedom." (248)

Gary: Aware of the intersectionality of systemic oppression—across differences of race, gender, class, sexuality, ability, culture, and generation—as I learned from you that the classroom can be a critical location for the demonstration of teacher/student activism: "… bearing witness to education as the practice of freedom." As I share the evolution of my personal, political, and professional career in writings I have published—I continue to practice writing and teaching for anti-racist justice. In your book *Teaching to Transgress*: *Education as the Practice of Freedom*, you really promote the idea that the classroom can act as s strategic space to teach against racism.

bell: "as a catalyst … that calls everyone to become more and more engaged … active participants in learning" (11).

Gary: Strategically, as I and many of the writers in *Liberation for the Oppressed* maintain, it can also "perform" as a critical site to build alliances against oppression and domination for the vision of a "beloved community." In *Teaching Community: A Pedagogy of Hope,* you clearly underscore this related to your vision of the transformative power of love related to community healing.

Love as the Community "Bridge" of Connection for the *Other*

bell: "It is the love that I can generate within myself, as a light and send out, beam out, that can touch people. Love can bridge the sense of otherness. It takes practice to be vigilant, to beam that love out. *It takes work* (emphasis added).… To be guided by love is to live in community with all life. However, a culture of domination, like ours, does not strive to live in community. As a consequence, learning to live in community must be a core practice for all of us who desire spirituality in education." (162—63)

Gary: In another one of your books titled *Writing Beyond Race: Living Theory and Practice*, you write in the chapter "Moving Past Blame: Embracing Diversity," you address the term "diversity" as it applies to how we relate to each other on a daily basis.

bell: "Diversity is the reality of all our lives. It is the very essence of our planetary survival. Organically, human survival as a species relies on interdependence of all life. Fundamentalist thinking, supporting dominator culture, denies this truth, socializing citizens to believe that safety resides in upholding the tyranny of the same, in protecting homogeneity." (26)

Calling Out "Imperialist White Supremacist Capitalist Patriarchy"

Gary: In teaching your writings, I continually reference the phrase "imperialist white supremacist capitalist patriarchy" you employ in them to illustrate your intersectional approach to systemic oppression. How have people responded to your use of this terminology?

bell: "When I first began to use the phrase *imperialist white supremacist capitalist patriarchy* to characterize the interlocking systems that shape the dominator culture we live within, individuals would often tell me that they thought it was just too harsh a phrase. In the past ten years, when I've used the phrase at lectures, more often than not audiences respond with laughter. Initially, I thought this laughter was an expression of discomfort, that the true nature of our nation's politics were being exposed. But as the laughter followed me from talk to talk I began to see it as a way to deflect attention away from the seriousness of this naming. Time and time again critical theory has taught us the power of naming accurately that which we are challenging and to transform. But one way to silene accurate naming is to make it appear ridiculous, to strident, too harsh." (*Writing Beyond Race*, 36-37)

Gary: I completely understand how your giving name to oppression and domination through an intersectional standpoint would cause folks to laugh it off, not take it seriously, and/or find it too critical. In teaching African American literature through the lens of intersectionality, I have experienced negative feedback from students—especially when I have insisted that analyzing writings by Black authors must be grounded in a viewpoint that strategically interlinks issues of racism to sexism, classism, homophobia, and ableism. Clearly, we must confront a socially constructed environment rooted in "interlocking systems that shape the dominator culture we live within" every day. Devon W. Carbado in the Introduction to *Black Men on Race, Gender, and Sexuality* (1999), clearly underscores this point if racism is not critiqued through the lens of intersectionality. Carbado states,

> The gender critique of antiracist discourse opened the door for the sexuality critique. And here, too, Black feminists—heterosexuals and lesbians—have led the charge. The argument they advance is that antiracist proponents often ignore or deny the relationship between racism and homophobia. This, they maintain, entrenches the notion that racism and homophobia are separate, distinct, and oppositional social phenomena. The ideological entrenchment of this idea facilitates the antiracist marginalization of Black gay and lesbian experiences.

For, if racism and homophobia are understood to be un related, Black gay and lesbian discriminatory experiences that are not overtly or obviously race based can be attributed *solely* to their sexual orientation. (2)

As many of the writers in *Liberation for the Oppressed* and I address, the struggle against racism must be interlinked to the deconstruction of a*ll* "other" forms of internalized systemic domination. bell, I mention here that many of the scholarly, pedagogical, and spoken word writings I include in this book illustrate the transformative impact Dr. Martin Luther King, Jr.'s activism for freedom of the oppressed has had upon your life as an activist Black feminist theorist, cultural critic, and professor. Like my students who have written about the impact of your book *Killing Rage: Ending Racism* (1994)—I, too, am particularly drawn to its final chapter "Beloved Community: A World without Racism." Yet, even after the publication of this book, in *Writing Beyond Race: Living Theory and Practice* (2013) you continue to write about Dr. King's vision of love as the "hope" for community healing and liberation.

Hope for the "Strength to Love" on a "nonconformist" Path to a "Beloved Community"

bell: "Like many Americans I read King's slim volume of sermons *Strength to Love,* first published in 1963, to give me hope. By then it was evidence that King's vision that love was the most constructive way to create positive social change benefiting everyone was changing our culture. Motivated by our belief in a love ethic, masses of Americans worked in the late sixties and early seventies to unlearn the logic of domination and dominator culture…. King's insistence on love had provided folk an enduring message of hope. Tragically, he did not live long enough to be an enlightened voice for self-love among [B]lack people…. However, in *Strength to Love* he spoke directly to those advocates of patriarchal imperialist violence, be they white or [B]lack, when he stated,

The hardhearted person never truly loves…. The hardhearted person lacks the capacity for genuine compassion…. The hardhearted individual never sees people as people, but rather as mere objects or as impersonal cogs in an ever-turning wheel… He depersonalizes life.

… King's vision of redemptive love held the promise that both oppressor and oppressed could recover from the wounds of dehumanization." (96)

Gary: I, too, having recently read the original version of *Strength to Love* (1963) find King's vision of love as key to community healing from the life-threatening effects of racism and white supremacy, not only for BIPOC but for whites as well—especially for underclass poor white folks. During his time of imprisonment in jail in Birmingham, Alabama, King addresses this point (as written in *A Gift of Love: Sermons from Strength to Love and Other Preachings*, 2012). He recalls his conversation with some of the white jail wardens coming to the cell where he and other Black males involved in the demonstrations had been placed:

> … the white wardens and all enjoyed coming around the cell to talk about the race problem. And they were showing us where we were so wrong demonstrating. And they were showing us where segregation was so right. And they were showing us where intermarriage was so wrong. So I would get to preaching, and we would get to talking—calmly because they wanted to talk about it. And then we got down to the point … to talk about where they lived, and how much they were earning. And when those [white] brothers told what they were earning, I said, 'Now, you know what? *You ought to be marching with us. You're just as poor as Negroes.' And I said, 'You are put in the position of supporting your oppressor, because through prejudice and blindness, you fail to see that the same forces that oppress Negroes in American society oppress poor white people. And all you are living on is the satisfaction of your skin being white, and the drum major instinct of thinking that you are somebody big because you are white* (my emphasis). And you're so poor you can't send your children to school. You ought to be out here marching with every one of us every time we have a march.' (170-171)

In this dialogue with the (poor) white wardens, King calls out their racist ignorance at the intersection of their economic oppression in the system of white supremacist capitalist domination—even at the expense of white poverty. King references this as a form of racist "blindness" as he states: "… [T]he poor white has been put into this position, where through blindness and prejudice, he is forced to support his oppressors. And the only thing he has going for him is the false feeling that he's superior because his skin is white—and can't hardly eat and make his ends meet week in and week out" 171). It is clear in his conversation with the white wardens that King knew that the ideology of white supremacy was not only dehumanizing for Black Americans but also for white folk whose skin color did not save them from economic disparity. This is precisely why King said to the white wardens they "ought to be … marching with every one of us every time we have a march." While Dr. King certainly called out their anti-Black racism, he did not dismiss strategic ways to form anti-oppressive alliances. It is through his vision of love for liberating *all* the oppressed that you emphasize in your writings. You certainly communicate this in *Writing Beyond Race: Living Theory and Practice*—especially in the chapter "A Path Away from Race: On Spiritual Conversion."

bell: "When I traveled the nation asking folk what enabled them to be courageous in struggling for freedom—whether working to end domination of race, gender, sexuality, class, or religion—the response was love.

All over the world people working for peace and justice evoke King's vision of a beloved community where peopled committed to nonviolence would create a new social order based on justice and love. This was King's prophetic vision.... King's vision of living our lives based on a love ethic is the philosophy of being and becoming that could heal our world today. A prophetic witness for peace, an apostle of love, Martin Luther King has given us the map. His spirit lights the way, leading to the truth that love in action is the spiritual path that liberates." (97)

"Love in Action"

Gary: Thinking about Dr. King's life-sacrifice for justice—I, too, envision him prophetically. He stood for peace in the face of anti-Black racism rooted in white supremacy. I, too, believe him to have been "an apostle of love." At the end of chapter two—"Transformed nonconformist" in *Strength to Love*, Dr. King closes with a radically symbolic message about the choice to "march" He says,

> We must make a choice. Will we continue to march to the drumbeat of conformity and respectability, or will we, listening to the beat of a more distant drum, move to its echoing sounds? Will we march only to the music of time, or will we, risking criticism and abuse, march to the soul-saving music of eternity? More than ever before we are today challenged by the words of yesterday, 'Be not conformed to this world; but be ye transformed by the renewing of your mind.' (20)

Dr. King personified his vision of "love in action." Ultimately, as an unwavering advocate for Black racial equality, he sacrificed his life for the cause. Yet, even in the life-threatening face of white supremacy, Dr. King gave "us the map" to hope for "love in action [as the] spiritual path that liberates." Mapping the course of the writings in *Liberation for the Oppressed*, I believe that "CHAT" is the life-saving path to *soul work*.

Toward the publication of this book in the editorial process, I tirelessly read the individuals' soulful writings in the manuscript over and over again. This process deepened and enriched my personal, professional, and spiritual calling. Truthfully, the writers in *Liberation for the Oppressed,* both in and beyond academia, created a well-grounded path toward "Understanding and Addressing Blackness and Anti-Black Racism in Our Local, National, and International Communities." Moreover, in solidarity with each other, their writings not only demonstrate the healing power of *soul work*, they also lead readers on a route to revolutionary wholistic change.

Michael Eric Dyson, noted Black male academic scholar and minister, reinforces the inspirited agency for hope required to address the historical *and* contemporary dehumanizing effects of racism—not only for Blacks but for white folks as well. In his book *Tears We Cannot Stop: A Sermon to White America*, he openly shares his feelings of hope for anti-racist alliance:

> … deep in my heart I that our moral and spiritual passions can lead to a better day for our nation. I know that when we get out of our own way and let the spirit of love and hope shine through we are a better people.
>
> But such love and hope can only come about if we first confront the poisonous history that has almost unmade our nation and undone our social compact. We must face up to what we as a country have made of the black people who have been the linchpin of democracy, the folk who saved America from itself, who redeemed it from the hypocrisy of proclaiming liberty and justice for all while denying all that liberty and justice should be to us. (4-5)

Like Dyson, as I shared in the Preface to *Liberation for the Oppressed,* I am also a professor and an ordained minister committed to anti-racist activism. Thus, I fully affirm his work in *Tears We Cannot Stop*. I believe Dyson's "sermon to white America" is precisely what should be the wellspring for pedagogical practice committed to the struggle to end racism—*and* all forms of systemic and institutionalized oppression.

The Will to Serve the Oppressed: My Justification

As a Black male professor and an ordained minister for nearly three decades, first and foremost, I have dedicated my life to justifying my will to teach for social justice—particularly related to the survival of Black Indigenous People of Color in and beyond the borders of the U.S. Considering this, I have continuously represented the power of empathetic imagination in my scholarship and theological journey. *Black Male Outsider, a Memoir: Teaching as a Pro-Feminist Man* laid the groundwork for my autocritographical confession at the intersection of my academic profession and ministerial vocation. While it is based on my professional course-work on the struggle for Black male self-survival, over time, I have sync'd my practice of empathetic compassion with that confessed by radical, Black theologian James H. Cone. In the "Introduction" to the 50th Anniversary Edition of his book *Black Theology and Black Power*, Cornel West interprets Cone's journey for self-survival as an "existential crisis." West maintains that it is one rooted in "self-examination, self-interrogation, self-clarification and, most importantly, self-justification" (xiv). This explains precisely what my journey for self-validation committed to *liberation for the oppressed* is "rooted in." In truth, it has been a long time coming. In 2019, I co-authored *Let Love Lead on a Course to Freedom* with Scott Neumeister and Susie Hoeller. This work is based on my pedagogical approach to "The Bible as Literature," a course I often teach in the English department at the University of South Florida. In the book's Preface, I begin quoting an excerpt from Audre Lorde's poem "A Litany for Survival"—

> For those of us
> who were imprinted with fear
> like a faint line in the center of our foreheads …
>
> this instant and this triumph
> We were never meant to survive.

In response to these words, I write:

> … [I]t has been my testament to having survived what I never thought I would—as a student and teacher of 'English' in majority white colleges and universities. For all intents and purposes, though [feeling I was] never meant to survive," I have. While it has taken most of my life as a teacher in the college classroom to comprehend what this has meant, in this present moment, I have a clear sense that it has never been about my academic training in relation to what I have been *called* to do. (vii)

In ongoing activist-oriented dialogue with BIPOC and white anti-racist allies, I have realized my professional and spiritual calling for "CHAT". Supporting my commitment to community-based, *higher* education for critical anti-racist consciousness, also in 2019 I had two of my edited books published. Together, they illustrate my professional and inspirited love for bell hooks' soulful idea of "engaged pedagogy" (*Teaching to Transgress: Education as the Practice of Freedom*, 15), Alice Walker's universal concept of womanist liberation, and Maulana Karenga's Africana principles of Kwanzaa.

The first book, *Hooked on the Art of Love: bell hooks and My Calling for Soul-Work*, includes written and visual pieces of art. I open the book with these words, "I represent bell hooks' longstanding love for personal, political, pedagogical, *and* artistic liberation" (7). In the second book *Building Womanist Coalitions: Writing and Teaching in the Spirit of Love*, I begin stating that it "includes works by teachers/professors, students, and creative artists (poets as well as actors/directors). They embody an unwavering defense of human rights and social justice" (4). Collectively, the writers in *Building Womanist Coalitions* employ the personal, political, and the pedagogical to navigate ways to interrogate the complexities of racial identities—in and outside BIPOC communities. Together the writers in this book strategically exercise language that advances the womanist call for inspirited love of freedom for the marginalized.

I contend that the writings in *Liberation for the Oppressed* boldly represent a compelling complement to *Hooked on the Art of Love* and *Building Womanist Coalitions*. Together these three works showcase the critical need for community building across differences of identity for anti-oppressive alliance. Together they constitute a wholistic testimony for an inspirited awakening of folks "[c]omitted to survival and wholeness of entire people ..." as Alice Walker asserts *In Search of Our Mothers Gardens* (xi). Yet, in the closing chapter of *Killing Rage: Ending Racism*, bell hooks maintains:

> Clearly we have not gone far enough. In the late sixties, Martin Luther King posed the question 'Where do we go from here[?]' To live in anti-racist society we must collectively renew our commitment to a democratic vision of racial justice and equality.... We need to share not only what we have experienced but the conditions of change that make such an experience possible. (271)

In hindsight, I believe bell's motivational response to Dr. King's question profoundly articulates the fact that "we have not gone far enough." In more words and action, "entire people" ... "[need to reveal] the conditions of change that make such an experience [of racial justice] possible." In continued support for "CHAT" to free the oppressed, bell's revolutionary legacy of radical self-liberation is reborn in *Liberation for the Oppressed*—like the mystical rise of the phoenix *re*-living love for life forever.

"Phoenix"

danyealah green-lemons[1]

Dead awake—

embers churning in my soul

A cold cauldron

flaming hot …

somebody snipped my wings

somebody walked off with alla my stuff

some

body

waged

war

with me—an embodied ember.

You didn't know I was burning—

I could smell the heat

She didn't know

I was an embryo

writhing with rage

They didn't know I was crying
flames into the dirt
birthing brilliance
bearing boldness
bodying them all—

all them worries
all them woes
all them wounds
all them weighted sighs
all them buried cries
all them
all them
all them

all them falling
at an altar of alchemy
anchoring a strength
anchoring a force
anchoring a scared little girl
free.

Note

[1] bell hooks was a spiritual mother for me. In the Black church, "mothers" are elder women held in high regard. *Mother bell* is how I referred to her, personally. I felt her tenderness through her words—a soft, yet bold "getting together"—as Black folks would say, "a calling out." She was a Black woman gifted in truth-telling. I carry her truths, her "getting-togethers" with me as I have embarked on my own spiritual journey of liberation. Thank you, Mother bell for sharing your gifts.

Works Cited

Carbado, Devon W. "Introduction: Where and When Black Men Enter." *Black Men on Race, Gender, and Sexuality*. Edited by Devon W. Carbado. New York University Press, 1999, pp. 1-17.

Dyson, Michael Eric. *Tears We Cannot Stop: A Sermon to White America.* St. Martin's Press. 2017.

hooks, bell. *Outlaw Culture: Resisting Representations.* Routledge, 1994.

--- *Teaching to Transgress: Education as the Practice of Freedom.* Routledge, 1994.

--- *Teaching Community: A Pedagogy of Hope.* Routledge, 2003.

--- *Writing Beyond Race: Living Theory and Practice.* Routledge, 2013.

King, Jr., Martin Luther. *Strength to Love*. William Collins Sons & Co., 1963.

--- *A Gift of Love: Sermons from Strength to Love and Other Preachings*. Beacon Press. 1963, 1981, 2012.

Lemons, Gary L., Scott Neumeister, and Susie Hoeller. *Let Love Lead on a Course to Freedom. *BookLocker.com, Inc., 2019.

Lemons, Gary L., *Hooked on the Art of Love: bell hooks and My Calling for Soul Work.* BookLocker.com, Inc., 2019.

--- *Building Womanist Coalitions: Writing and Teaching in the Spirit of Love.* University of Illinois Press, 2019.

CPSIA information can be obtained
at www.ICGtesting.com
Printed in the USA
BVHW010757310322
632853BV00028B/828

9 781647 199944